MW00582177

Mary Livermore Library
UNC Pembroke
Pembroke, NC 28372-1510

Ref
ML
156.7
.B66
N67
2008

Boston Symphony Orchestra

An Augmented Discography

James H. North

The Scarecrow Press, Inc.
Lanham, Maryland • Toronto • Plymouth, UK
2008

SCARECROW PRESS, INC.

Published in the United States of America
by Scarecrow Press, Inc.
A wholly owned subsidary of
The Rowman & Littlefield Publishing Group, Inc.
4501 Forbes Boulevard, Suite 200, Lanham, Maryland 20706
www.scarecrowpress.com

Estover Road
Plymouth PL6 7PY
United Kingdom

Copyright © 2008 by James H. North

All rights reserved. No part of this publication may be reproduced,
stored in a retrieval system, or transmitted in any form or by any
means, electronic, mechanical, photocopying, recording, or otherwise,
without the prior permission of the publisher.

British Library Cataloguing in Publication Information Available

Library of Congress Cataloging-in-Publication Data
North, James H.
  Boston Symphony Orchestra : an augmented discography / James H. North.
    p. cm.
  Includes bibliographical references, discography and index.
  ISBN-13: 978-0-8108-6209-8 (cloth : alk. paper)
  ISBN-10: 0-8108-6209-3 (cloth : alk. paper)
  eISBN-13: 978-0-8108-6239-5
  eISBN-10: 0-8108-6239-5
  1. Boston Symphony Orchestra–Discography. 2. Boston Symphony Chamber
Players–Discography. I. Title.
  ML156.7.B66N67 2008
  016.78026'6-dc22   2008024253

⊖™ The paper used in this publication meets the minimum requirements of
American National Standard for Information Sciences—Permanence of
Paper for Printed Library Materials, ANSI/NISO Z39.48-1992.
Manufactured in the United States of America.

Contents

Foreword

The term "discography" sounds rather dry, perhaps; but somehow, when you see what James North has achieved with his discography of the Boston Symphony Orchestra, what's on the page takes on a life of its own that's both unexpected and uniquely exciting. Some of my earliest and most vivid memories of the Boston Symphony Orchestra are of recordings that I heard on RCA Victor; and the era of compact discs has more recently provided an access to past recordings that we could never have imagined. Since becoming the BSO's music director four years ago, my connection to the quality of music-making that the Boston Symphony Orchestra has stood for throughout its more than 125-year history has of course been magnified enormously; and the notion that a BSO performance led by me has already been added to this amazing list represents not just a special thrill, but an extraordinary privilege.

Represented in the main listings of this book are 133 composers, 36 conductors, 267 soloists (including some of the orchestra's great principal players), and more than 90 years of recorded history starting with the BSO's very first recordings made with Karl Muck in 1917 (Tchaikovsky, Wolf-Ferrari, Wagner, Berlioz, and Beethoven—so much to be grateful for even in those very first sessions). Then there's the astonishing history of recordings made during the 25-year-tenure of the legendary Serge Koussevitzky, whose championing not only of the well-known classical repertoire, but also of composers like Prokofiev, Stravinsky, Ravel, and Sibelius (all of whom he knew personally!) and such major American composers as Aaron Copland, William Schuman, and Roy Harris, is represented here.

Charles Munch's recordings remind us how much more music he conducted—and conducted so excitingly—than just the Berlioz and other French repertoire for which he's rightly famed, not to mention works commissioned for the BSO's 75th anniversary that he also recorded during that time. And it was during Munch's time that his great predecessor Pierre Monteux, the BSO's music director from 1919 to 1924, returned to Symphony Hall not only as a guest conductor, but to lead an important series of recordings including, among other things, music of Debussy, Tchaikovsky, and two seminal works by Stravinsky—*Petrushka* and *Le Sacre du printemps*—that had received their world premieres under his baton decades earlier.

The recordings led by Erich Leinsdorf, William Steinberg, and certainly Seiji Ozawa still seem close enough to our own time that further comment on them is not needed here. But it's interesting to note that during Steinberg's relatively brief tenure, guest conductors like Claudio Abbado, Rafael Kubelik (who made one of his great recordings of Smetana's *Má Vlast* with the BSO), and Eugen Jochum show up, as well as the young Michael Tilson Thomas, who served as Steinberg's assistant conductor.

Though the earliest of these recordings were made in RCA's studios in Camden, New Jersey, most of them were of course made in Symphony Hall in Boston, one of the world's great concert and recording venues; and there were also a number made at Tanglewood, the BSO's summer home.

It's also fascinating to think about the different companies who recorded the orchestra over the years. The presence of Abbado, Kubelik, and Jochum reflects to some degree the fact that during Steinberg's time at Symphony Hall, the BSO moved from RCA to Deutsche Grammophon. And then, with the arrival of Philips during Seiji Ozawa's tenure, came the opportunities for Colin Davis (now Sir Colin), who was then the BSO's principal guest conductor, to make a number of significant recordings with the orchestra, including an essential, complete Sibelius symphony cycle. Also during Ozawa's era, exclusive contracts became less the norm, so that, besides Deutsche Grammophon and Philips, companies like CBS, Telarc, EMI, and Erato collaborated with the orchestra on an occasional basis.

The thoroughness of James North's achievement goes far beyond the "official" recordings of the BSO itself, covering also recordings issued by the U.S. government during World War II, recordings of the Boston Symphony Chamber Players, and—to the limited extent it's possible to document such things—so-called "pirate recordings" of live concert performances.

The history of the Boston Symphony Orchestra comes to life here in a way I could not possibly have anticipated when I first started flipping through these pages. I'm exceedingly grateful to have this book, and I know it will provide hours and hours of pleasure not only to those who love the BSO, but to all music-lovers whose interests extend to the past, present, and future of the orchestra's recorded legacy.

James Levine, Music Director, Boston Symphony Orchestra

Acknowledgments

This discography should have at least a dozen authors, but if I started at the top and ran down this list I would not know where to stop. Without these people, there would be no book; without any one of them, it would be less complete, less interesting.

Bridget P. Carr, Boston Symphony Senior Archivist, insisted for years that I should compile a BSO discography—over my constant objection that there were others more qualified than I—and then provided more assistance than I could have dreamed of, often supplying fresh information which sent me off in entirely new directions. In addition to suffering ceaseless questions at her Archives with unfailing courtesy, charm, and efficiency, Bridget put up with an almost continuous flow of email. Assistant Archivist Barbara Perkel filled in with equal courtesy, charm, and efficiency whenever Bridget was unavailable.

Edward D. Young has been a constantly informative source, not only for his superb Koussevitzky discography, but for his unpublished summation of Boston Symphony broadcasts during the Koussevitzky era and his report of BSO material held by the Library of Congress..

Lawrence H. Jones is the proprietor of Polyphony, a leading source of rare classical recordings on LP and open-reel tape. Larry, whom I had not known personally, began helping me through sheer human kindness, making it clear that, although he found discographic matters of interest, he just didn't have the patience for them. He supplied at least half the information in the appendix on two-track tapes, and, as a fan of Charles Munch, he provided me with much information about 45-rpm sets of that conductor's recordings. I asked Larry for so much help—which he continued to provide in generous measure, even emailing lovely scans of record labels—that I believe I finally got him hooked on the beauties of discography. Don Tait was the radio host of Chicago Symphony concerts and for 35 years a well-loved classical-music voice of station WFMT Chicago. An enthusiastic collector of Serge Koussevitzky recordings, Don connected me with that maestro much as Larry Jones did with Munch, supplying many discographic details and stories—including the wonderful one about his conversation with Arthur Fiedler that caps an early entry in this discography.

Thomas Tierney, Manager of Sony BMG Archives and Library, and Michael Panico, Sony BMG Archives Manager, guided me through their voluminous collections. It was Tom who—among many other courtesies—handed me the folder in which I stumbled upon the session log of a previously unknown pair of BSO recordings. Thomas C. Christie and other staff members of the Rodgers and Hammerstein Archives of Recorded Sound at the New York Public Library for the Performing Arts enabled me to see and hear BSO-related recordings that even the BSO did not possess. Bryan Cornell of the Library of Congress pursued intra-library listings of Armed Forces Radio and Voice of America recordings that do not appear in publicly accessible catalogues. Leah Weisse, WGBH Archives, Boston, researched the sessions for Leonard Bernstein's video recordings for the 1973 Charles Eliot Norton Lectures.

Douglas Yeo, Boston Symphony bass trombonist, supplied fascinating inside stories of BSO performances and recording sessions. Harry Shapiro, long time (1937-1975) BSO second horn, kept me enthralled for two hours with delightful reminiscences of the BSO and its conductors.

Richard A. Kaplan, Associate Professor (Retired) at the Louisiana State University School of Music, proprietor of K & S Records, clarinetist, and *Fanfare* critic, gave continuing advice and criticism on musical and discographic matters. Leslie Gerber of Parnassus Records shared the BSO portions of his immense database of LPs and CDs; Leslie also located rare, out-of-print records for the Boston Symphony Archives. Michael H. Gray, the star discographer who loves to pass on his efforts to others for their glory rather than his own, gave me his discographic data on the BSO.

My thanks for specific contributions go to Mark Obert-Thorn, for his exacting discographic notes in Naxos and Biddulph CD booklets; to John Newton of Soundmirror, Inc., for remembering his microphone setups for a recording session decades past; and to Robert L. Miller, of Audio Radiance Recordings, whose conversations have enriched my understanding of BSO performances and recordings. Lawrence F. Holdridge showed me the labels of two records by "Members of the Boston Symphony Orchestra" published ca. 1912.

The whole team at Scarecrow Press, led by acquisitions editor Renée Camus and production editor Jayme Bartles, has been a pleasure to work with, as always. Deborah Justice did a superb job of proofreading.

My brother-in-law Reinout Hunningher and my son Benjamin J. North served as my computer gurus; Ben also subbed for me at the BSO Archives once when I couldn't come to Boston, taking dozens of photos of exotic labels on 16-inch transcription discs that had not been previously available. My deepest gratitude goes to my wife, Louise V. North, who never dreamed that she was promising to edit and proofread as well as to love and cherish.

Introduction

With the blossoming of the Internet, in particular its explosion of music stores, the word *discography* has become almost a household term. At the same time, it has been seriously debased: one site offered a Leon Fleisher discography consisting of a single compact disc. Discography does not mean "what we have to sell at this moment." It may be easier to explain what it is not than what it is. Members of ARSC (the Association for Recorded Sound Collections) have been debating the matter for years, attempting to set standards for such works. It is a very personal issue: One individual wants certain types of information, another something else. Our view is that it should be a useful blend of musical and technical information, providing knowledge to a variety of readers. The key word is useful; why else go to all the trouble? A knowledgeable critic was disappointed by our previous discography's limited scope, whereas a transfer engineer was delighted to see performance timings—a small example of being useful. One thing we can agree on is completeness: whatever information you choose to present, get all of it.

This introduction is primarily a user's manual. Some of it may seem eerily familiar, as structure, phrases, and even a few sentences have been purloined from that earlier work.

There are really two discographies here: first, the authorized—mostly commercial—recordings of the Boston Symphony Orchestra, and second (in Appendix H) the recordings of the Boston Symphony Chamber Players. The Boston Pops, which once consisted of BSO musicians, has no place here; it has made even more recordings than the BSO and demands its own discography. Arthur Fiedler does make an appearance as conductor of the BSO and, in Appendix G, of Arthur Fiedler's Sinfonietta.

The basic question for any discography is which recordings to include and which not. Suppose a recording is labeled "Members of the Boston Symphony." Some such are by privately contracted ensembles which may employ musicians from the BSO and may or may not include other musicians; e.g., Boston Records 205: Britten *Serenade for Tenor, Horn, and Strings*, with "Members of Boston Symphony String Section." Other similarly labeled records are official BSO recordings which use a reduced ensemble. If the Boston Symphony Orchestra, Inc. was paid for the recording, it is included, otherwise not. If so, paper records called payment sheets have been kept, listing every participating musician. Payment sheets are extremely reliable sources of information; whenever there was an inaccuracy or an omission, a later correction was made and has been preserved with the payment sheet. No BSO treasurer would overpay, and no musician, no union, would accept an underpayment. Payment sheets and recording logs kept by record companies represent the two sides of a contract, plus—after 1942, when the BSO finally joined the American Federation of Musicians—union data as well. No rule escapes exceptions, however. Occasionally, the BSO and its musicians donated their services for a recording. Two cases spring to mind: the Mozart Requiem at the memorial service for John F. Kennedy, and the national anthem for the American Heritage Society. Leonard Bernstein's audio/visual recordings for his Norton Lectures at Harvard are also excepted, as they are important BSO recordings despite being privately contracted by Amberson, Inc. (Bernstein's company). Some recordings are included despite being "end runs" around the recording log/payment sheet pairings, most of them historical live performances issued by the BSO, either on its own or in conjunction with other organizations. The latter include most of the Boston Symphony's video recordings. Note that video recordings made for television which were not preserved in a commercial form are not included. An example is the January 30 and 31, 1966, Leinsdorf/BSO sessions with pianist Claude Frank for the American Broadcasting Company's TV documentary *Saga of Western Man: Beethoven, Ordeal and Triumph*, broadcast on March 23, 1966.

In the BSO and Boston Symphony Chamber Players discographies, recordings are listed chronologically by session dates; when a single recording took more than one day, it is ordered by the date of the initial session, so that the sequence will correspond to that of assigned matrix numbers in the 78-rpm era. Matrix numbers were assigned before or at the beginning of a session, however, and the works were not always recorded in the order planned. When we know the actual order during a session, we follow it; otherwise we go by the matrix progression. The entry for a single recording includes as much of the following information as is pertinent and is known to us:

COMPOSER
Work (Timing)
Orchestra and conductor
Soloists and other assisting artists
Session date(s). Recording venue
Record company, producer
Matrix numbers and takes used
Issue numbers on 78-rpm discs, 45s, LPs, CDs, SACDs, 2-track tapes, and DVDs
Comments appropriate to each recording may be added in italics.

BRAHMS, JOHANNES
Concerto for Violin and Orchestra in D, op. 77 (37:57)
BSO, conductor Serge Koussevitzky
Jascha Heifetz, violin
April 11, 1939. Symphony Hall
RCA Victor, producer Charles O'Connell
Matrix: CS-035424/32: 2,2,3,2,1,2,3,2,1
78s: M-581 (15526/30). AM-581 (15531/35). DM-581 (16053/57). **45s:** WCT-71 (17-0419/23). **LPs:** LCT-1043. ARM4-0945 (4). **CDs:** 09026-61735-2 (2). Pearl 9167. Biddulph LAB-041. Naxos 8.110936. *WCT-71 and post-war (1946 onwards) issues of M-581 and DM-581 have the Air from Bach's Suite No. 3 (August 13, 1945) as a tenth-side filler.*

In several cases, including most of the videos, a group of recordings has been gathered into a single "Collection" entry. The structures of these entries vary slightly from that described above and from each other; we hope that each will be clear without further explanation.

Musical compositions are given formal titles in the main listing but may be abbreviated in the appendixes. Titles, which often follow neither rules nor logic, are given in the form and languages most commonly encountered in America. This leads to some apparent inconsistencies: *The Pines* and *The Fountains of Rome*, but *Feste romane*; *Wiener Blut* yet *The Voices of Spring*. We use the French title for Debussy's *La Mer*, yet we call each movement by its English translation: *From Dawn to Noon on the Sea*. An attempt has been made to follow D. Kern Holoman's *Writing about Music*: "Generic titles . . . are given in roman type. . . . True titles, i.e., those assigned by the composer, are given in italics." We follow Holoman in using roman type within quotation marks for opera arias. When a composer chooses an unconventional form for a title, it takes precedence over any rule.

Timings are given in minutes and seconds; they are nevertheless approximations, as timings vary from one issue to another due to the pitches of different transfers or the length of pauses between movements. Timings listed in early Victor recording logs are merely approximations; starting in 1944 they became more accurate, and are often the source for these listings; for each musical break—such as between movements—five seconds have been added. Timings listed in CD booklets are often in error, so they have been checked on one consistent CD player. With 78s and LPs, listed timings have been checked by playing the record on a carefully calibrated turntable. The author's intention is that no recording should still be playing when the allotted time span has elapsed; thus, when multiple sources disagree, the largest number is used. However, compact disc releases on some English labels (Pearl and Andante) tend to run longer than other transfers and may exceed the listed timings. One suspects that their transfer engineers adjusted turntable speed to produce the conventional A = 440 Hz, not recognizing that the BSO in Koussevitzky's era tuned to a higher pitch (most people today recognize that this was so, but no one—even within the BSO—seems to know exactly what that pitch was). "World premiere" following the timing indicates that this live performance was given in the week of the first performance or that this studio recording was made immediately following such a premiere. First recordings of a piece are not noted, as there are several measures at hand: Koussevitzky's Prokofiev Fifth was recorded before Rodzinski's, but the latter was issued first.

To conserve space and avoid needless repetition, the Boston Symphony Orchestra is abbreviated BSO in most entries. There have been several official BSO recordings of chamber music (Stravinsky's Octet and *L'Histoire du soldat*, Hanson's Serenade, etc.); for them, credit is given to "Members of the BSO." That phrase is also used when a reduced ensemble is employed (Delibes's Suites from *Coppélia* and *Sylvia*). In such cases, we simply follow the record label's identification.

Vocal soloists are listed with either their voice range or, in the case of operatic performances, the roles they sing; instrumentalists are listed with their instruments. No distinction is made between leading soloists and those who have a minor role or a single solo turn. Among the many choral groups that have recorded with the Boston Symphony, two predominate: The New England Conservatory Chorus, directed by Lorna Cooke DeVaron, appears twenty times, from 1956 to 1979; that chorus is abbreviated NECC, although its noted director is accorded her full name. Similarly, the Tanglewood Festival Chorus under John Oliver (which is active in Boston as well as in Lenox) appears on 30 BSO recordings, from 1973 to 2003; it is abbreviated TFC. Other choruses, such as the Harvard Glee Club and the Radcliffe Choral Society, are given their full titles. Neither choruses nor their directors are listed in the Soloists appendix.

For Boston Symphony commercial recordings, there is seldom a question as to the date or the site of a recording, as both record company logs and orchestral payment sheets survive. Live performance recordings, both those released at the time and those issued later in historical compilations, have been checked against printed concert programs in the Boston Symphony Archives. Note the gap in RCA sessions from March 20, 1940, to November 22, 1944. The American Federation of Musicians had been battling the BSO trustees for decades, and was finally able to prevent them from recording; by the time that dispute was settled and the orchestra unionized (1942), the AFM was on strike against all recording activities in America. Concerts were still allowed, however, and the gap is now partially filled by recently issued live performances. Union rules for symphonic recording allowed no more than forty-five minutes of music from each three-hour session to appear on the finished record, and many recording dates consisted of both morning and afternoon sessions. Any number of recordings gestated over two or more days, in some cases months. While each such date is noted, this discography orders recordings by the date of the initial session, and cross-references in the appendixes refer to that date.

The vast majority of BSO recordings were made in Symphony Hall; a handful were made in Tanglewood, both in the Theatre Concert Hall and in the Koussevitzky Music Shed, and a few in New York's Carnegie Hall and elsewhere. The dates shown here indicate when the BSO recorded at each site:

New Office Building, Victor Talking Machine Co., Camden, New Jersey
   (October 2–5, 1917)
Symphony Hall, 301 Massachusetts Avenue, Boston
   (November 13, 1928, to October 6, 2007)
Carnegie Hall, 154 West 57th Street, New York
   (February 2, 1934, to October 26, 1991)
Hunter College Auditorium, 695 Park Avenue, New York
   (April 1, 1944)
Theatre Concert Hall, Tanglewood, Lenox, Massachusetts
   (August 13, 1946, to July 9, 1956)
Koussevitzky Music Shed, Tanglewood, Lenox, Massachusetts
   (August 6, 1947, to August 7, 2007)
Manhattan Center, 311 West 34th Street, New York
   (December 2, 1953, to January 10, 1963)
United Nations General Assembly, New York
   (December 12, 1954)
Sanders Theater, 45 Quincy Street, Cambridge, Massachusetts
   (January 20, 1959, to April 17, 1962)
NHK Hall, Uchisaiwai-cho, Tokyo
   (May 4, 1960)
Cathedral of the Holy Cross, 75 Union Park, Boston
   (January 19, 1964)
WGBH TV Studios, 125 Western Avenue, Boston
   (November 27 to December 12, 1972)
Houghton Chapel, Wellesley College, Wellesley, Massachusetts
   (October 10, 1981)
Festival Hall, 2–3 Nakanoshima, Kita-ku, Osaka, Japan
   (March 1, 1986)
Alte Oper, Opernplatz 1, Frankfurt am Main
   (December 13, 1988)
Smetana Hall, Municipal House, Namesti Republiky 5, Prague
   (December 16, 1993)

Many recordings were edited from live performances, with the addition of patch sessions under studio conditions. In such cases, it is impossible to say just how much of the issued recording is a live performance. Nevertheless, we write "Symphony Hall (live)" for them, with the understanding of those conditions.

Over the course of innumerable technological developments—from acoustic 78s to digital CDs—the steps proceeding from recording session to the marketplace have maintained a surprising consistency. In the vast majority of cases, then and now, the final product becomes available 6 to 18 months after the sessions. We do not list the date of first issue unless it is an exception; in such cases, we may note it in italicized comments at the end of the entry and may explain why we think it was delayed.

An article in *Phonograph Monthly Review*, July 1929, (supplied by Don Tait) reports: "This was in the old days of the Boston Talking Machine Company, formed originally to record the Boston Symphony. But Mr. Higginson could not be won to the idea; perhaps it was just as well, for eighteen years ago [1911] the phonograph can hardly have done his orchestra due justice." Yet "Members of the Boston Symphony Orchestra" appear on the ca. 1912 label of The Phono-Cut Record Co. 5048-A: Unrath: *King Carl*, March for Orchestra (courtesy of Lawrence F. Holdridge). The BSO began recording for the Victor Talking Machine Company in 1917, at that company's manufacturing plant in Camden, New Jersey. The BSO's first electrical recordings were made for Victor by the Western Electric Company in Symphony Hall on November 13, 1928. On January 4, 1929, Victor merged with the Radio Corporation of America, becoming its RCA Victor Division, and soon began to make its own recordings in Symphony Hall. The economic depression of the early 1930s almost wiped out the record industry; after an October 30, 1930, recording, RCA Victor did not renew its contract with the BSO. In an effort to recruit the orchestra, Columbia recorded a live performance in Carnegie Hall on February 2, 1934, but the recorded sound was unsatisfactory, so the BSO did not sign with that company. RCA soon re-signed the orchestra, and recording resumed on January 22, 1935. The BSO remained with RCA until the end of the Leinsdorf era in 1969, making a few more records under William Steinberg in 1970. Deutsche Grammophon began recording with Michael Tilson Thomas on January 26, 1970; ironically, that initial session with a non-American company was devoted to the BSO's first recording of music by Charles Ives. By that time, recording contracts were generally made with individual conductors and soloists rather than with an orchestra; Colin Davis brought Philips to Symphony Hall on January 4, 1975. Thereafter, recordings were often contracted one at a time or for a projected series, and the floodgates opened to admit New World Records, CBS (later Sony), Telarc, Hyperion, Nonesuch, EMI, Erato, English Decca, and—for film scores—Dreamworks and Warner Brothers. The BSO's own issues were made in affiliation with WCRB Productions, the Boston Symphony Transcription Trust, WGBH Boston, and IMG Artists; it also issued historical CDs, produced by Brian Bell, on its own label, BSO Classics.

The term *producer* refers to the on-site manager in charge of a session, rather than the European meaning of an executive back at headquarters. In the 78-rpm era, he was usually the Director of Artists and Repertory and was often listed on the recording log of a session by a statement such as "Mr. O'Connell present." The producer may be credited on a record cover or a CD booklet, but various issues of a given recording do not always agree as to who was in charge; we attempt to solve such conundrums by returning to original documents.

Matrix numbers are given for recordings made through November 29, 1950, the final BSO recordings to be published on 78-rpm discs. At first, matrix numbers used a generic prefix CVE, the E standing for electrical recording. Take numbers used for initial releases are shown where known. If the take used for the issued record had to be dubbed, the take number is prefaced by an R (for "Re-recording"). For more detailed information about record manufacturing, see Edward D. Young's pioneering Koussevitzky discography in *ARSC Journal*, Volume 21, Nos. 1 and 2. It cannot be stated too often that Young's work has been a primary source (along with session logs, payment sheets, and the discs themselves) for information about the Koussevitzky 78s listed in this volume.

Only American issues are listed, plus those of international provenance that have been generally available in the United States. We also make exceptions to our American-only rule when we can find no American edition in a given medium (often CD); in such cases we list foreign (primarily English and Japanese) issues when known. We include all the American issues we could discover, with no claim to completeness. Reissues of piecemeal excerpts from a recording are not listed unless they form an accepted concert work by themselves, such as the Suite No. 2 from *Daphnis et Chloé*. In this connection, one LP needs special mention: RCA Victor SRL-12-11, "Hearing is Believing," is primarily a narration, with snippets from a dozen BSO recordings. Among other items, it has a composite performance of Berlioz's *Rákóczy March* that segues from Muck to Koussevitzky to Munch.

Record companies have been inconsistent in their use of the hyphen: is it V-567 or V 567? For general legibility among the many forms of record numbers, we use a hyphen to separate prefix and number: set M-529, LM-1700, AGL1-1266, 09026-60686-2. The -2 suffix denotes a compact disc; a -1 represents an LP. A -4 suffix is for cassette tapes, which are not included here. Two-track reel-to-reel tapes are, as they were the first issue of many stereo recordings.

For 78-rpm albums and 45-rpm box sets, we list both the album number and individual record numbers. Koussevitzky's December 29, 1936, recording of Sibelius' Fifth Symphony illustrates several points:

M-474 (15019/23). AM-174 (15024/28). DM-474 (16308/12)

M- sets are in manual sequence, in which the work proceeds from side A to side B of each record, and then on to the next record's side A. In this case, the work takes only seven sides, so the eighth side is a filler (*Pohjola's Daughter*, from May 6, 1936). AM- sets are in so-called slide sequence, for an early form of automatic record changer. The work proceeds through all the A-sides, and then the B-sides in the same record order (thus: 15024-A through 15028-A, followed by 15024-B through 15028-B). DM- sets are for the more familiar drop changer, for which the listener turned over the entire stack to play the B-sides in reverse order (16308-A through 16312-A, and then 16312-B through 16308-B). Note that the record numbers for the M- set and the AM- set are usually sequential (15019/23, followed by 15024/28); DM- sets were issued later, which accounts for the larger record numbers (16308/12).

In the final years of 78s, Victor (following the lead of wartime V-Discs) issued a few 78-rpm records on "RED SEAL *DE LUXE* NON-BREAKABLE" red vinyl material, at nearly double the price of corresponding shellac issues. Koussevitzky's 1945 "Eroica" was issued first on shellac sets: M-1161 (11-9796/801) and DM-1161 (11-9802/07), and then on vinyl: V-8 (18-0060/65) and DV-8 (18-066/71). Critics of the day (*American Record Guide*: October 1945 to July 1949) praised the beautiful sound and quiet surfaces of these discs, but their high price kept sales low. The soft material was easily scratched and generated much static electricity, attracting dust and grit which were then ground into the grooves by the heavy pickups of the era. Few clean copies survive today.

RCA Victor began issuing 45-rpm records in 1949 and LPs in 1950. At first, each 45 simply mimicked its original 78; thus the WDM- sets contained the same music on each disc as their DM- equivalents (and, above record number 12-3000, matching numbers; e.g. 49-3000). Soon an extended-play 45 was developed, allowing up to eight minutes per side; a single record was now prefaced ERA-, the "E" for "extended", and the A for "one record." Multi-record sets were thus ERB- (for 2), ERC- (for 3), etc.; the prefix 549- replaced 49- for extended play 45s in sets. This led to some recordings being reissued on fewer sides: Munch's 1940 *Béatrice et Bénédict* Overture, running 7:19, was issued twice on 45s, first on two sides (49-3078) and later on one (ERA-68). When RCA began issuing stereo LPs in 1958, it dropped 45s of classical music from its catalogue.

For multiple-LP and CD sets, we generally list only the set number, not those of individual discs within the set. When the component discs are also available as single discs, however, we also list individual disc numbers. The "Pierre Monteux Edition" is a 15-CD box. Five of those discs include BSO recordings, for which we list both the set number, 09026-61893-2 (15), and the number of the single CD. The same is true with Seiji Ozawa's 14-CD set of the Mahler Symphonies. When there have been multiple issues of a given recording, we list them in numerical order; unfortunately, this cannot be relied upon to indicate chronological sequence, as record companies have been inconsistent in their assignments of numbers. We do try to put the original issue at the head of the list.

Many of Koussevitzky's BSO recordings were reissued on LP on RCA's Camden label (one of the earliest "cheap" LP series, on noisy pressings having poor sound quality) with CAL prefixes. The "A" stood for single records; the BSO also appears on a six-record set, CFL-100. For these LPs, RCA chose a *nom de plume* for each orchestra, the BSO becoming the Centennial Symphony Orchestra. Everyone soon caught on, so we make no reference to the "Centennial." By 1956, the cat was out of the bag, and Camden issues abandoned the pseudonyms—and also improved the quality of the pressings.

RCA Victor (later RCA, then BMG, then Sony BMG Music) kept many of its BSO recordings available by reissuing them every decade or so, using a new series of letter/number designations each time. Beginning with the LP era, roughly 1949, the prefix LM- designated long-playing records of classical music. When stereo arrived in 1958, records were issued both in monaural, with LM- prefixes, and in stereo, as LSC-. We list such dual issues as LM/LSC-1984. Note, however, that stereo recording began in 1954 but stereo LPs were not issued until 1958, so the monaural LM issue may have preceded its LSC equivalent by several years, the stereo appearing only on two-track tape. The final LP to include a monaural version was LM/LSC-3006 (Beethoven Symphony No. 4 and *Leonore Overture No. 2*, recorded in December, 1966). When a set has more than one unit (LP or CD), we add a parenthetical postscript to indicate the number of discs in the set: LM-6001 (2).

In 1963, a series of lower-priced reissues appeared on the Victrola label, beginning with RCA's "second-best" sellers such as Munch's Franck Symphony (second to Monteux's). A few recordings by less popular stars, such as Jaime Laredo's Mendelssohn and Bach Concertos, originated on the Victrola label. The series soon expanded to encompass lower priced reissues of most Munch recordings, excepting the best sellers, such as Saint-Saëns' Third Symphony, which remained on the full-price LSC series. Mono/stereo pairs were labeled VIC/VICS-1032; for reissues of mono-only recordings, there was no VICS- record, and after reissues appeared only in stereo, no VIC-. Many Leinsdorf recordings eventually joined the VICS catalogue. In 1976 a third series began: AGL1-5236. For some early stereo recordings (1954-1956), the initial issue included only monaural (LM-) records, and the VICS- series was the first stereo version. In a few cases, the third series saw the first issue of the stereo version (AGL1-2702, Brahms's Second Symphony and *Tragic Overture*). In the 1980s, many Leinsdorf recordings joined the AGL1- series as well. Each of the AGL1- prefix's four symbols carried a specific meaning: AGL2- indicated a two-record set, AGM-1 a monaural record, etc. That basic three-issue sequence is complicated by many special cases: In the LM/LSC- era, many RCA recordings— mostly operas, but also a few BSO recordings—appeared in the higher-priced Soria series, which featured deluxe packaging; for these, the mono/stereo prefixes were LD/LDS.

While this compilation does not offer aesthetic judgments on the quality of performances or of recorded sound, it seems appropriate to note that the pressing quality of RCA stereo LPs ran a generally downward course from the original LSC- issues, through the VICS- series, and into the AGL1- reissues; this followed a descending price curve as well. In addition, the LSC- series itself had several variants: initial issues were generally on "shaded-dog" pressings, which were often followed in turn by "white-dog" and 'no-dog' pressings, again in a (generally) declining quality of pressing. Further variants occur even within each such category: pressing numbers stamped into the vinyl surface indicate chronological order of production. Audiophiles will fully understand such distinctions; others will need no definitions.

Our intention is to list records from other countries only when there is no American issue in a given medium, but the VIC/VICS- series of LPs causes great confusion. It appeared both in the United States and in England, often with identical numbers but sometimes with different ones, so a single recording may have appeared on two different VIC/VICS pairs, and a single VIC/VICS- number may represent two entirely different sets of music: The English VICS-1620 contains BSO recordings of Beethoven and Schubert symphonies, the American VICS-1620 has a program of Bartók music played by the Chicago Symphony. In a few cases the contents of English and American issues vary only slightly: The English VICS-1323 includes four pieces; the American one makes a single substitution: Debussy for Dukas. In an attempt to verify national provenances, we have filtered the contents of a decade's worth of Schwann and Gramophone catalogues, as well as examining the labels and covers of every VIC/VICS LP we could locate.

In the compact disc era, RCA's identifying numbers evolved slowly from the form 5673-2-R to 09026-65678-2; along the way, some issues were given five-digit numbers (61234-2-R), but also included the 09026 prefix elsewhere in their documentation; we list them as 09026-61234-2. After BMG merged with Sony in 2004, the prefix became 82876, for both CDs and Super Audio CDs. Note that all BSO SACDs (on Pentatone as well as RCA) are hybrid, multichannel issues. A series of supposedly audiophile CD reissses of 1950s and 1960s RCA recordings was issued in the 2000s by JVC, but these are Japanese discs which duplicate American CDs, so none of them are listed here. A recent series of Japanese RCA releases of Charles Munch BSO material is included where there has been no American CD issue of a recording.

The online retailer ArkivMusic.com now offers on-demand CD-R reissues of out-of-print CDs, licensed from the copyright holders. At this time (April 2008), they include 63 CD issues of 118 Boston Symphony recordings, from Koussevitzky to Haitink. These are especially valuable for recordings which had a very short shelf life on the American market, such as Haitink's Brahms Symphonies on Philips. ArkivMusic CDs come with copies of the original booklet covers but no program notes, and their identifying numbers mimic the original CD issue: 09026-61657-2 becomes ArkivCD 61657.

As suggested above, a BSO recording may have been issued and reissued on several different labels. When the sequence refers to various labels of the same company (Victor, RCA Victor, RCA, Camden, Victrola, BMG, Sony BMG), these labels are implied by their prefixes (such as DM-, LM-, LSC-, CAL-, VICS-, 09026-, 82876-). When a reissue comes from a different company (such as an ArkivCD or a Pentatone SACD), that name is printed.

Charles Munch led multiple BSO recordings of several works in the early stereo era: Berlioz's *Symphonie fantastique* in 1954 and 1962; Ravel's *Daphnis et Chloé* in 1955 and 1961; *Boléro* in 1956 and 1962; *La Valse* in 1955, 1958, and 1962; and Debussy's *Prélude à l'après-midi d'un faune* in 1956 and 1962. Many reissues of these works fail to identify which recording is used. We have attempted to identify each case based on label copy information at the Sony BMG Archives and, when no such information was available, on various characteristics of each performance. We doubt that we have always succeeded.

The labels which merged to become Universal (Decca-London, Deutsche Grammophon, and Philips) began using a scheme of six-digit numbers separated by a space (414 567-1) late in the LP era and often carried that number over to the first CD issue: (414 567-2). Most reissues used the same scheme. We list multiple such label numbers in numerical order, but that does not imply chronological release dates; in fact, we can discover no consistent scheme for their application.

The first three appendixes offer alphabetical listings of composers, conductors, and soloists; each entry uses an abbreviated form of most titles and contains the minimum information needed to reference the main listing (by date). Appendixes D and E excerpt information about two-track tapes and video recordings, respectively, drawn from the main section, where they would otherwise be difficult to locate.

Several appendixes are devoted to related recordings of interest, while not living up to discographic standards: Appendix F discusses and samples BSO recordings issued by branches of the United States government. Appendix G offers catalogues of recordings made by ensembles of BSO musicians under other names, either pseudonyms for recording purposes (New Orchestral Society of Boston, Columbia Symphony Orchestra) or true performing ensembles (Zimbler Sinfonietta, Arthur Fiedler's Sinfonietta). Appendix H, a discography of the Boston Symphony Chamber Players, is an entirely independent entity containing its own performer listing and composer index.

Because Serge Koussevitzky had the opportunity to record only part of his large repertoire, we also include, in Appendix I, a list of unauthorized "pirate" recordings, live performances led by Koussevitzky and by other conductors. There can be a fine line between a legitimate recording and a pirate: In 1956, the BSO made a grand European tour, giving 28 concerts in 19 cities; the trip was part of joint Soviet and American efforts to expand cultural relations. In September, they played three concerts in Moscow and one in Prague, all of which were recorded by local radio stations. Performances from two of the Moscow concerts were issued on three Melodiya LPs, and two from Prague on a Multisonic CD. These recordings were not authorized by the BSO, so they appear in Appendix I. Some of the Moscow tapes became available to the BSO in America, and plans to issue an LP commemorating the visit were well advanced, but the project did not come to fruition. There were some quality problems with sections of the tapes, and the delicate, ever-shifting balance of relations between the two countries during the Cold War period took a sudden turn for the worse when the USSR brutally suppressed the 1956 Hungarian uprising.

Several intriguing recordings never materialized. Those recorded but not released are listed in this discography, as they may still exist in recording company archives and may yet be issued—at least one RCA Victor Koussevitzky /BSO recording (Cowell: *Hymn and Fuguing Tune No. 2,* April 27, 1949) was not issued until the compact-disc era. Many scheduled recordings were cancelled for one reason or another. A Leinsdorf session (October 16, 1967) to record Schumann's Second Symphony was cancelled at the last moment by Roger Hall, manager of RCA's Red Seal Division, because "It won't sell." (Leinsdorf: *Cadenza,* and much agitated correspondence between RCA and the BSO).

Discographies, by their very nature, are fallible. The demand of completeness raises an impossible standard. But each discography should extend knowledge. Edward D. Young's 1990 Koussevitzky discography is the most admired one of the Boston Symphony; yet the passage of time, pure hindsight, and the luck of a detective on a given day has generated further information, both corrections (noted in comments to individual entries) and previously unknown recordings (see March 20, 1940). That does not invalidate Young's work, which will never be matched for its depth of understanding, both about the conductor and about the recording process. Each discography represents a different, independent point of view. Discographers are that rare breed that loves to be corrected; I urge readers to discover errors, inconsistencies, and omissions herein, asking only that they supply me with all such information.

BSO Discography

TCHAIKOVSKY, PETER ILYICH
Symphony No. 4 in F Minor, op. 36: IV: Finale: Allegro con fuoco (8:10)
BSO, conductor Karl Muck
October 2, 1917. Camden, NJ
The Victor Talking Machine Company. BSO Classics producer Brian Bell
Matrix: C-20815/16: 2,2
78s: 74553/54. 6050. **LPs:** SRL 12-11 (portion). **CDs:** BSO Classics 171002.
Columbia had used a small group from the New York Philharmonic to record in
*January, 1917, but the BSO was "100 strong" (*Boston Herald, *September 28,*
1917). Victor then recorded 90 players of the Philadelphia Orchestra on Octo-
ber 22 (Oliver Daniel: Stokowski: A Counter Point of View. *New York: Dodd,*
Mead & Co., 1982, 304-305).

WOLF-FERRARI, ERMANNO
The Secret of Suzanne: **Overture (2:31)**
BSO, conductor Karl Muck
October 3, 1917. Camden, NJ
The Victor Talking Machine Company. BSO Classics producer Brian Bell
Matrix: B-20817: 2
78s: 64745 (unissued test pressing). **CDs:** BSO Classics 171002

WAGNER, RICHARD
Lohengrin: **Act III Prelude (3:12)**
BSO, conductor Karl Muck
October 3, 1917. Camden, NJ
The Victor Talking Machine Company. BSO Classics producer Brian Bell
Matrix: B-20818: 2
78s: 64774. 547. **LPs:** SP-33-181 (LM-2651). BSO 0118.237. **CDs:** BSO Clas-
sics 171002

BERLIOZ, HECTOR
La Damnation de Faust, op. 24: *Rákóczy March* (4:14)
BSO, conductor Karl Muck
October 3, 1917. Camden, NJ
The Victor Talking Machine Company. BSO Classics producer Brian Bell
Matrix: C-20819: 2
78s: 74555 (unissued). **CDs:** BSO Classics 171002

BEETHOVEN, LUDWIG VAN
Symphony No. 7 in A, op. 92: Finale (beginning) **(3:24)**
BSO, conductor Karl Muck
October 4, 1917; October 5, 1917. Camden, NJ
The Victor Talking Machine Company. BSO Classics producer Brian Bell
Matrix: B-20820/21: 2,2
78s: No number assigned (unissued). **CDs:** BSO Classics 171002. *The second side of the finale has not survived in any form.*

TCHAIKOVSKY, PETER ILYICH
The Nutcracker, op. 71: **Waltz of the Flowers** (4:12)
BSO, conductor Karl Muck
October 4, 1917; October 5, 1917. Camden, NJ
The Victor Talking Machine Company. BSO Classics producer Brian Bell
Matrix: C-20822: 2
78s: 74561 (unissued). **CDs:** BSO Classics 171002

BERLIOZ, HECTOR
La Damnation de Faust, op. 24: *Ballet des Sylphes* (2:22)
BSO, conductor Karl Muck
October 5, 1917. Camden, NJ
The Victor Talking Machine Company. BSO Classics producer Brian Bell
Matrix: B-20823: 2
78s: 64746 (unissued). **CDs:** BSO Classics 171002

TCHAIKOVSKY, PETER ILYICH
Suite No. 1 in D, op. 43: Marche Miniature (1:58)
BSO, conductor Karl Muck
October 5, 1917. Camden, NJ
The Victor Talking Machine Company. BSO Classics producer Brian Bell
Matrix: B-20824: 2
78s: 64766. 547. **CDs:** 09026-63861-2 (2). BSO Classics 171002. *In early 1961, Arthur Fiedler came to Discount Records in Chicago to sign records, escorted by an RCA Victor type. Not many people showed up, embarrassingly, and there sat Fiedler at a card table, alone. I got him to autograph his Liszt LP for me and then—I don't know why—asked him if he had played in the 1917 Muck/BSO Victors. In his usual preemptory way, Fiedler said "yes, I did. It was hot! Muck was BITCHY." (Don Tait, email, December 20, 2007)*

STRAVINSKY, IGOR
Pétrouchka: **Suite (16:49)**
BSO, conductor Serge Koussevitzky
November 13, 1928; November 14, 1928. Symphony Hall
Made for the Victor Talking Machine Company by Western Electric.
 BSO Classics producer Brian Bell
Matrix: CVE-47910/14: 3,3,1,1,1
78s: M-49 (6998-7000). AM-49 (6882-84). **LPs:** L-1001 (10-inch 1930s LP).
 CDs: BSO Classics 171002 (includes an alternate take, Matrix: CVE-47911: 2, of Tableau Two: In Petrouchka's Room) **(3:50)**. Pearl GEMM-9020

STRAVINSKY, IGOR
Apollon musagète: **Pas de Deux (3:58)**
BSO, conductor Serge Koussevitzky
November 14, 1928. Symphony Hall
Made for the Victor Talking Machine Company by Western Electric.
 BSO Classics producer Brian Bell
Matrix: CVE-47915: 2
78s: M-49 (7000). AM-49 (6884). **CDs:** BSO Classics 171002. Pearl GEMM-9020

RAVEL, MAURICE
Daphnis et Chloé: **Suite No. 2 (15:41)**
BSO, conductor Serge Koussevitzky
November 15, 1928; December 20, 1928. Symphony Hall
Made for the Victor Talking Machine Company by Western Electric.
 BSO Classics producer Brian Bell
Matrix: CVE-47916/19: 2,5,5,4
78s: 7143/44. **CDs:** BSO Classics 171002 (includes an alternate take, Matrix: CVE-47918: 4, from Pantomime to Danse Générale) **(3:25)**. Pearl GEMM-9090

STRAUSS, JOHANN JR
Voices of Spring, **op. 410 (4:31)**
BSO, conductor Serge Koussevitzky
December 18, 1928. Symphony Hall
Made for the Victor Talking Machine Company by Western Electric
Matrix: CVE-47937: 2
78s: 6903; backed by *Wiener Blut* (December 20, 1928). **CDs:** Biddulph WHL-019. Preiser 90090. *Re-recorded on a 33⅓-rpm disk in 1933 (matrix LCS-75660) but not so issued.*

BEETHOVEN, LUDWIG VAN
Symphony No. 6 in F, op. 68 "Pastoral" (37:52)
BSO, conductor Serge Koussevitzky
December 18, 1928; December 19, 1928. Symphony Hall
Made for the Victor Talking Machine Company by Western Electric
Matrix: CVE-47938/42, 49883, 47943/46: 2,3,2,2,3,1R,2,1,1,1
78s: M-50 (6939-43). AM-50 (6944-48). **CDs:** Biddulph WHL-019. *The Bee-*
thoven "Pastoral" was originally recorded on nine sides, with the third
movement repeat not observed. After the matrices were recorded, Victor
engineers synthesized the repeat by transferring the first 2'32" from the
third movement (up to where the repeat would start) to form a new side.
(Alert listeners to the original 78s might notice the same burbled French
Horn note at 1'33" into each side.) The transfer technology of the 1920s
produced rather crude results; so, for this reissue, more modern equipment
was used to achieve the same effect from the original undubbed matrix.
(Mark Obert-Thorn, program notes to the Biddulph CD).

STRAUSS, JOHANN JR
Wiener Blut, op. 354 (4:24)
BSO, conductor Serge Koussevitzky
December 20, 1928. Symphony Hall
Made for the Victor Talking Machine Company by Western Electric
Matrix: CVE-47947: 3
78s: 6903; backed by *Voices of Spring* (December 18, 1928). **CDs:** Biddulph
WHL-019. Preiser 90090. *Re-recorded on a 33⅓-rpm disk in 1933 (matrix*
LCS-75660) but not so issued.

PROKOFIEV, SERGEI
Symphony No. 1 in D, op. 25 "Classical" (11:38)
BSO, conductor Serge Koussevitzky
April 22, 1929. Symphony Hall
RCA Victor
Matrix: CVE-48979/81: 1R,4,2. *"R" (for "Re-recorded") matrices are dubbings.*
78s: 7196/97. **CDs:** Pearl GEMM-9487. *On January 4, 1929, the Victor Talking*
Machine Company merged with the Radio Corporation of America, becom-
ing its RCA Victor Division. RCA Victor soon began making its own re-
cordings at Symphony Hall, replacing Western Electric.

PROKOFIEV, SERGEI
The Love for Three Oranges: **March (1:42). Scherzo (1:30)** (3:17)
BSO, conductor Serge Koussevitzky
April 22, 1929. Symphony Hall
RCA Victor
Matrix: CVE-48982: 1
78s: 7197. **CDs:** Pearl GEMM-9487. *The Pearl CD also includes the December*
10, 1936, recording of the March and Scherzo.

HAYDN, FRANZ JOSEPH
Symphony No. 94 in G "Surprise" (21:14)
BSO, conductor Serge Koussevitzky
April 22, 1929; April 24, 1929. Symphony Hall
RCA Victor
Matrix: CVE-48983, 48986, 48984/85, 48987/88: 2,2,1,1,1,2
78s: M-55 (7058/60). AM-55 (7061/63). DM-55 (16766/68). **LPs:** CAL-146.
  CDs: Pearl GEMM-CDS 9185 (2). *The Pearl set includes an alternate take (CVE-48988: 1) of the finale.*

RAVEL, MAURICE
Boléro **(13:23)**
BSO, conductor Serge Koussevitzky
April 14, 1930. Symphony Hall
RCA Victor, producer Mr. Davis
Matrix: CVE-56820/22: 1A,2,2
78s: M-352 (7251/52). DM-352 (18434/35). **LPs:** CAL-161. **CDs:** 09026-61392-2. 09026-63670-2. *Originally released as a pair of single records, 7251 and 7253. The album M-352 appeared several years later.*

SATIE, ERIK
Gymnopédie No. 1 (orchestrated and renumbered by Debussy) **(4:23)**
BSO, conductor Serge Koussevitzky
April 14, 1930. Symphony Hall
RCA Victor, producer Mr. Davis
Matrix: CVE-56823: 1
78s: M-352 (7252). DM-352 (18434). **CDs:** Pearl GEMM-9090. *See above.*

TCHAIKOVSKY, PETER ILYICH
Symphony No. 6 in B Minor, op. 74 "Pathétique" (43:21)
BSO, conductor Serge Koussevitzky
April 14, 1930; April 15, 1930; April 16, 1930. Symphony Hall
RCA Victor, producer Mr. Davis
Matrix: CVE-56824/25, 56832/33, 56826/31: 1A,1A,2,1A,2,2,1,1,1A,2
78s: M-85 (7294/98). AM-85 (7299/303). DM-85 (16565/69). **LPs:** LM-85 (L-11640/2) LAM-85 (L-11713/15). *One of Victor's short-lived 1931 long playing issues.* **CDs:** 09026-60920-2. ArkivCD 60920. Biddulph WHL-034/35 (2)

RAVEL, MAURICE
Ma Mère l'oye: **Suite (18:28)**
BSO, conductor Serge Koussevitzky
October 27, 1930; October 29, 1930. Symphony Hall
RCA Victor, producer Mr. Rob. Smith
Matrix: CVE-56865/67, 56975: 1,2,2,1
78s: 7370/71. **LPs:** CAL-161. **CDs:** Pearl GEMM-9090

MUSSORGSKY, MODEST
Pictures at an Exhibition (orch. Ravel) **(29:58)**
BSO, conductor Serge Koussevitzky
October 28, 1930; October 30, 1930. Symphony Hall
RCA Victor, producer Mr. Rob. Smith
Matrix: CVE-56868/74: 1,1,1,3,2,2,2
78s: M-102 (7372-75). **AM**-102 (7376-79). **DM**-102 (17204/07). **LPs:** CAL-111. VICS-1514e (U.K.). **CDs:** 09026-61392-2. Naxos 8.110154. Pearl GEMM-9020. Andante 1978 (3). *This was the first recording of Ravel's 1922 orchestration, which was commissioned by Koussevitzky and published by his Paris firm Editions Russe. He maintained exclusive performing rights to the score for seven years.*

RAVEL, MAURICE
La Valse **(11:54)**
BSO, conductor Serge Koussevitzky
October 29, 1930; October 30, 1930. Symphony Hall
RCA Victor, producer Mr. Rob. Smith
Matrix: CVE-56876/78: 1,2,2
78s: 7413/14. **CDs:** 09026-61392-2. *Also recorded on 33⅓-rpm discs in 1933 (matrix LCS-76783/84) but not so issued.*

DEBUSSY, CLAUDE
Tarantelle Styrienne, **"Danse"** (orch. Ravel) **(4:43)**
BSO, conductor Serge Koussevitzky
October 30, 1930. Symphony Hall
RCA Victor, producer Mr. Rob. Smith
Matrix: CVE-56879: 2
78s: 7414. **CDs:** Pearl GEMM-9090. Andante 1978 (3)

DEBUSSY, CLAUDE
Suite No. 2 for Piano: "Sarabande" (orch. Ravel) **(4:38)**
BSO, conductor Serge Koussevitzky
October 30, 1930. Symphony Hall
RCA Victor, producer Mr. Rob. Smith
Matrix: CVE-56880: 2
78s: M-102 (7375). AM-102(7379). DM-102 (17204); final side of *Pictures at an Exhibition* (October 28, 1930). **CDs:** 09026-61392-2. Andante 1978 (3)

HARRIS, ROY
Symphony No. 1 "1933" **(26:15)** *A BSO commission, premiered January 26, 1933.*
BSO, conductor Serge Koussevitzky
February 2, 1934. Carnegie Hall (live)
Columbia Records
Matrix: 230624/30
78s: M-191 (68183-D/86-D). **LPs:** ML-5095. AML-5095. CML-5095. **CDs:** Pearl GEMM-9492. *The early-1930s economic depression nearly wiped out*

the record industry. Unhappy with RCA Victor for not renewing its contract, the BSO wanted to sign with Columbia Records, but that company was in even worse financial straits than Victor. Columbia recorded this live performance of the Harris Symphony in Carnegie Hall, but the sound on the records was unsatisfactory, so the BSO did not sign with Columbia.

HARRIS, ROY
4 Minutes — 20 Seconds, for flute and string quartet **(4:20)**
Georges Laurent, flute; Burgin String Quartet (Richard Burgin, Robert Gundersen, Jean Lefranc, Jean Bedetti)
February 2, 1934. Carnegie Hall
Columbia Records
Matrix: 230631
78s: M-191 (68186-D). *Side 8 filler to Harris Symphony, above. In the notes to the album, the composer writes: "This short piece was written expressly for Columbia Records, to fill a time-space of less than four minutes and thirty seconds—more than four minutes." This is not strictly a BSO recording.*

STRAUSS, RICHARD
Also sprach Zarathustra, **op. 30 (31:45)**
BSO, conductor Serge Koussevitzky
January 22, 1935. Symphony Hall
RCA Victor, producer Charles O'Connell
Matrix: CVE-88903/11: 3,1,2,1,1,2,2,1,1
78s: M-257 (8619-23). AM-257 (8624-28). DM-257 (16653-57). **LPs:** CAL-173. Neiman-Marcus First Edition DMM4-0260 (4) (a product of RCA Special Products). **CDs:** 09026-60929-2 (2). Biddulph WHL-054. ArkivCD 60929 (2). *Five years had passed since the BSO had recorded for RCA Victor, and recording techniques had been much improved. This recording was marketed as a sound spectacular and was generally greeted as such by critics and public alike.*

MENDELSSOHN, FELIX
Symphony No. 4 in A, op. 90 "Italian" (23:14)
BSO, conductor Serge Koussevitzky
January 23, 1935. Symphony Hall
RCA Victor, producer Charles O'Connell
Matrix: CVE-88912/17: 1,1,2,2,3,4
78s: M-294 (8889-91). AM-294 (8892-94). DM-294 (16703-05). **LPs:** CFL-104 (6). CAL-146. **CDs:** Pearl GEMM-9037

This announcement appeared in a BSO concert program in January 1935:

An
UNUSUAL
BROADCAST

2-3 P.M. (STA. WBZ) WEDNESDAY, JANUARY 23

NEXT week the BOSTON SYMPHONY OR-
CHESTRA, DR. SERGE KOUSSEVITZKY, *Conductor*, will make records for the RCA Victor Company, at Symphony Hall.

ONE hour of one recording session will be
broadcast. It will thus be possible to hear the
orchestra playing while the records are actu-
ally being made. The studio procedure will
also be explained. Extracts will be played
from Strauss' "Thus Spake Zarathustra," Sibelius' Second Symphony, and Mendelssohn's "Italian" Symphony.

RCA Victor recorded some of this broadcast, on matrix CVE-1919-1 and -2
(Edward D. Young. *Serge Koussevitzky: A Complete Discography, Part II.*
ARSC Journal 21, 2 (1990)), but the masters no longer appear in Sony BMG's
inventory (Thomas Tierney, email February 13, 2008).

BEETHOVEN, LUDWIG VAN
Symphony No. 8 in F, op. 93
BSO, conductor Serge Koussevitzky
January 23, 1935; January 24, 1935. Symphony Hall
RCA Victor, producer Charles O'Connell
Matrix: CVE-88918/23: (takes made: 1,1,2,2,1,1)
Unreleased. Re-recorded December 30, 1936.

SIBELIUS, JEAN
Symphony No. 2 in D, op. 43 (41:17)
BSO, conductor Serge Koussevitzky
January 24, 1935. Symphony Hall
RCA Victor, producer Charles O'Connell
Matrix: CVE-88924/34: 1,1,1,1,1,1,1,1,1,1,1
78s: M-272 (8721-26). AM-272 (8727-32). DM-272 (16678-83). **LPs:** CAL-
108. **CDs:** Naxos 8.110170, Pearl GEMM CDS-9408 (2)

TCHAIKOVSKY, PETER ILYICH
Symphony No. 4 in F Minor, op. 36 (39:08)
BSO, conductor Serge Koussevitzky
May 4, 1936; May 6, 1936. Symphony Hall
RCA Victor, producer Charles O'Connell
Matrix: CS-101220/28: 2,1,1,1,1,1,2,1,1
78s: M-327 (14185-89). AM-327 (14190-94). DM-327 (16740-44). **LPs:** CAL-
109. CFL-106 (6). **CDs:** Biddulph WHL-034/35 (2)

IV. Finale: Allegro con fuoco (8:31). **LPs:** CAL-336

SCHUBERT, FRANZ
Symphony No. 8 in B Minor "Unfinished" (20:50)
BSO, conductor Serge Koussevitzky
May 6, 1936. Symphony Hall
RCA Victor, producer Charles O'Connell
Matrix: CS-101229/33: 1,1,1,2,1,
78s: M-319 (14117/19). AM-319 (14120/22). DM-319 (16737/39). **LPs:** CFL-
104 (6). CAL-106. **CDs:** Pearl GEMM-9037

SIBELIUS, JEAN
Pohjola's Daughter, op. 49 (12:10)
BSO, conductor Serge Koussevitzky
May 6, 1936. Symphony Hall
RCA Victor, producer Charles O'Connell
Matrix: CS-101234/36: 1,1A,2
78s: M-474 (15019/23). AM-474 (15024/28). DM-474 (16308/12). Coupled
with Sibelius Symphony No. 5 (December 29 1935). **LPs:** LCT-1152. VIC-
1047 (U.K.). **CDs:** Naxos 8.110168. Pearl GEMM CDS-9408 (2)

LIADOV, ANATOLY
The Enchanted Lake, op. 62 (7:21)
BSO, conductor Serge Koussevitzky
May 6, 1936. Symphony Hall
RCA Victor, producer Charles O'Connell
Matrix: CS-101237/38: 1,1A
78s: 14078. **45s:** CAE-157 (side 1). **LPs:** CAL-155. **CDs:** Biddulph WHL-044.
*CAE was the Camden label's prefix for extended-play 45s. This is coupled
with Mussorgsky's* Khovanshchina *Prelude, December 28, 1936.*

SCHUBERT, FRANZ
Rosamunde: **Ballet Music No. 2 in G (4:05)**
BSO, conductor Serge Koussevitzky
May 8, 1936. Symphony Hall
RCA Victor, producer Charles O'Connell
Matrix: CS-101239: 1
78s: M-319 (14119). AM-319 (14122). DM-319 (16737); final side filler of
Schubert Symphony No. 8 (May 6, 1936). **Vdiscs:** 153. **CDs:** Pearl
GEMM-9179

LISZT, FRANZ
Two Episodes from Lenau's "Faust:" No. 2, Mephisto Waltz (11:23)
BSO, conductor Serge Koussevitzky
May 8, 1936. Symphony Hall
RCA Victor, producer Charles O'Connell
Matrix: CS-101240/242: 1,1,1
78s: M-870 (18409/10). DM-870 (18411/12). **LPs:** CAL-159. CFL-103 (6).
   CDs: EMI 5 75118 2 (2). Pearl GEMM-9179. ArkivCD 75118. United Art-
   ists UAR022 (4)

BERLIOZ, HECTOR
La Damnation de Faust, op. 24: *Minuet of the Will-o'-the-Wisps* (5:35).
   Dance of the Sylphs (2:02). *Rákóczy March* (4:07). Total (11:44)
BSO, conductor Serge Koussevitzky
May 8, 1936. Symphony Hall
RCA Victor, producer Charles O'Connell
Matrix: CS-101243/45: 1,1,1
78s: 14230/31. **LPs:** LCT-1146. LVT-1013. VIC-1222 (U.K.). **CDs:** Biddulph
   WHL-028. United Artists UAR022 (4)

Rákóczy March (Presto only) and *Dance of the Sylphs*: M-1063 (11-9232).
   Part of a four-record set: Children's Treasury of Music, Volume 2.

VIVALDI, ANTONIO
Concerto Grosso in D Minor, op. 3, no. 11, RV. 565 "L'estro armonio"
   (orch. Siloti) (12:26)
BSO, conductor Serge Koussevitzky
May 8, 1936. Symphony Hall
RCA Victor, producer Charles O'Connell
/48: CS-101246/48: 1,1,1
78s: M-886 (18527/58). DM-886 (18529/30). **LPs:** Turnabout TV-34784. **CDs:**
   Pearl GEMM-9179

TCHAIKOVSKY, PETER ILYICH
Serenade in C for String Orchestra, op. 48: Waltz (3:20)
BSO, conductor Serge Koussevitzky
May 8, 1936. Symphony Hall
RCA Victor, producer Charles O'Connell
Matrix: CS-101249: 1
78s: 11-8727; backed by Grieg's *The Last Spring* (March 20, 1940). M-327
   (14189). AM-327 (14194). DM-327 (16740); last-side filler for Tchai-
   kovsky's Symphony No. 4 (May 4, 1936). 11-8727. **LPs:** CAL-155. CAL-
   282. CAL-336. **CDs:** Biddulph WHL-034/35 (2)

HANDEL, GEORGE FRIDERIC
Concerto Grosso in B Minor, op. 6, no. 12: Larghetto (4:23)
BSO, conductor Serge Koussevitzky
May 8, 1936. Symphony Hall
RCA Victor, producer Charles O'Connell
Matrix: CS-101250: 1
78s: 14231. M-795 (18063/67). DM-795 (18073/77). **CDs:** Pearl GEMM-9179.
Issued first as a single record, backed by Berlioz's Minuet of the Will-o'-the-Wisps (above), this recording was added to post-war editions of M/DM-795, with Mozart Symphonies Nos. 29 and 34. It was not included in the AM-795 set.

TCHAIKOVSKY, PETER ILYICH
Romeo and Juliet **(fantasy-overture) (19:51)**
BSO, conductor Serge Koussevitzky
December 28, 1936. Symphony Hall
RCA Victor, producer Charles O'Connell
Matrix: CS-03159/63: 1,1,1,1,1
78s: M-347 (14353/55). AM-347 (14356/58). DM-347 (16753/55). **LPs:** LCT-1145. LVM2-7510 (2). **CDs:** 09026-60920-2. ArkivCD 60920. Biddulph WHL-034/35 (2). United Artists UAR022 (4). *Victor session logs begin listing side timings at this point, but they remain approximations (within five seconds per side) until 1944.*

MUSSORGSKY, MODEST
Khovanshchina: **Prelude "Dawn on the Moskva River"** (orch. Rimsky-Korsakov) **(6:35)**
BSO, conductor Serge Koussevitzky
December 28, 1936. Symphony Hall
RCA Victor, producer Charles O'Connell
Matrix: CS-03164/65: 1,1
78s: 14415. **45s:** CAE-157 (side 2). **LPs:** CAL-155. **CDs:** Biddulph WHL-044.
CAE was the Camden label's prefix for extended-play 45s. This is coupled with Liadov's The Enchanted Lake, May 6, 1936.

FAURÉ, GABRIEL
Elégie, **op. 24 (7:40)**
BSO, conductor Serge Koussevitzky
Jean Bedetti, cello
December 28, 1936. Symphony Hall
RCA Victor, producer Charles O'Connell
Matrix: CS-03166/67: 1,1
78s: 14577. **CDs:** Pearl GEMM-9090

SIBELIUS, JEAN
Symphony No. 5 in E♭, op. 82 (30:08)
BSO, conductor Serge Koussevitzky
December 29, 1936. Symphony Hall
RCA Victor, producer Charles O'Connell
Matrix: CS-03168/74: 2,1,1,2,1,1,1
78s: M-474 (15019/23). AM-474 (15024/28). DM-474 (16308/12). Coupled with *Pohjola's Daughter* (May 6, 1936). **LPs:** LCT-1151. LVT-1015. VIC-1047 (U.K.). **CDs:** Naxos 8.110170. Pearl GEMM CDS-9408 (2). *The jacket of LCT-1151 credits the BSO for performances of both the Fifth and Seventh Symphonies, but—as the label corroborates—the latter is Koussevitzky's May 15, 1933, recording with the BBC Symphony Orchestra.*

SIBELIUS, JEAN
Swanwhite, **Incidental Music, op. 54: *The Maiden with Roses* (3:05)**
BSO, conductor Serge Koussevitzky
December 29, 1936. Symphony Hall
RCA Victor, producer Charles O'Connell
Matrix: CS-03175: 1
78s: M-347 (14355). AM-347 (14358). DM-347 (16753); final side to Tchaikovsky's *Romeo and Juliet* (December 28, 1936). M-272 (8726). DM-272 (16678); final side to post-war sets of Sibelius Symphony No. 2 (January 24, 1935). M-1170 (11-9879). DM-1170 (11-9880); final side of Hanson Symphony No. 3 (March 20, 1940). **CDs:** Naxos 8.110168. Pearl GEMM CDS-9408 (2). *The first issue, M-347, mislabeled the music as* The Maiden with THE Roses *(Don Tait, email March 2, 2008); a Library of Congress catalogue entry still does.*

HAYDN, FRANZ JOSEPH
Symphony No. 102 in B♭ (22:20)
BSO, conductor Serge Koussevitzky
December 29, 1936. Symphony Hall
RCA Victor, producer Charles O'Connell
Matrix: CS-03176/78, 03180/81, 03179: 1,1,1,1,1,2
78s: M-529 (15304/06). AM-529 (15307/09). DM-529 (16173/75). **CDs:** Pearl GEMM-CDS 9185 (2). Andante AN-1180

BEETHOVEN, LUDWIG VAN
Symphony No. 8 in F, op. 93 (24:15)
BSO, conductor Serge Koussevitzky
December 30, 1936. Symphony Hall
RCA Victor, producer Charles O'Connell
Matrix: CS-03182/87: 1,1,2,1,1,1
78s: M-336 (14257/59). AM-336 (14260/62). DM-336 (16745/47). **LPs:** CAL-157. CFL-104 (6). **CDs:** Pearl GEMM-CDS 9185 (2). Dante LYS-173

PROKOFIEV, SERGEI
The Love for Three Oranges: **March (1:38), Scherzo (1:31) (3:14)**
BSO, conductor Serge Koussevitzky
December 30, 1936. Symphony Hall
RCA Victor, producer Charles O'Connell
Matrix: CS-03188:2
78s: M-459 (14950). AM-459 (14953). DM-459 (16362). **LPs:** LCT-1144.
LVT-1012. **CDs:** Pearl GEMM-9487. *The Pearl CD also includes the April
22, 1929, recording of the March and Scherzo.*

TRADITIONAL
Fair Harvard (arr. Koussevitzky) **(6:30)**
BSO, conductor Serge Koussevitzky
Harvard Glee Club and Radcliffe Choral Society, G. Wallace Woodward, dir.
March 23, 1937. Symphony Hall
RCA Victor, producer Charles O'Connell
Matrix: BS-07485/86: 1,2
78s: 4333 (10-inch disc). **CDs:** Pearl GEMM-9179. *The chorus had 350 voices.*

BACH, JOHANN SEBASTIAN
The Passion According to Saint Matthew, **BWV 244** (sung in English)
(193:14)
BSO, conductor Serge Koussevitzky
Jeanette Vreeland, soprano; Kathryn Meisle, contralto; John Friebe, tenor; Keith
Falkner, baritone; Fritz Lechner, bass; Ernest Victor Wolff, harpsichord;
Carl Weinrich, organ; Harvard Glee Club and Radcliffe Choral Society, G.
Wallace Woodward, dir.
March 26, 1937. Symphony Hall (live pension fund concert)
RCA Victor, producer Charles O'Connell
Matrix: CS-013267, 07488/508, 07510/11, 07513/23, 07550, 07525/31,
013268/69, 07534, 013270/71, 07537/41
78s: Volume I: M-411 (14635/44). AM-411 (14663/72). DM-411 (16477/86).
Volume II: M-412 (14645/52). AM-412 (14673/80). DM-412 (16487/94).
Volume III: M-413 (14653/61). AM-413 (14681/89). DM-413 (16495/503).
CDs: Rockport RR-5012/14 (3)

PROKOFIEV, SERGEI
Concerto for Violin and Orchestra No. 2 in Minor, op. 63 (23:57)
BSO, conductor Serge Koussevitzky
Jascha Heifetz, violin
December 20, 1937. Symphony Hall
RCA Victor, producer Charles O'Connell
Matrix: CS-014400/05: 2,2,1,2,2,2
78s: M-450 (14907/09). AM-450 (14910/12). DM-450 (16377/79). **45s:** WCT-
28 (17-0113/15). **LPs:** LCT-6. ARM4-0945 (4). Time-Life Records STL-
P02. **CDs:** 09026-61735-2 (2). Pearl 9167. Biddulph LAB-018. Naxos
8.110942. *This recording was made at 80.6 rpm and the pitch was never
corrected, so all issues display a concomitant loss of energy and brilliance.*

BRAHMS, JOHANNES
Concerto for Violin and Orchestra in D, op. 77 (37:57)
BSO, conductor Serge Koussevitzky
Jascha Heifetz, violin
December 21, 1937. Symphony Hall
RCA Victor, producer Charles O'Connell
Matrix: CS-014406/15: one take made of each side.
Unreleased. *Two recordings were made on this day, with different side breaks.*

BRAHMS, JOHANNES
Concerto for Violin and Orchestra in D, op. 77 (37:05)
BSO, conductor Serge Koussevitzky
Jascha Heifetz, violin
December 21, 1937. Symphony Hall
RCA Victor, producer Charles O'Connell
Matrix: CS-014416/24: one take made of each side
Unreleased. *The first movement is on five sides instead of six. The concerto was re-recorded on April 11, 1939.*

PROKOFIEV, SERGEI
Lieutenant Kijé Suite, **op. 60 (21:55/20:47)**
BSO, conductor Serge Koussevitzky
December 22, 1937. Symphony Hall
RCA Victor, producer Charles O'Connell
Matrix: CS-014425/29: 1,1,1,1,1
78s: M-459 (14948/50). AM-459 (14951/53). DM-459 (16362/64). **LPs:** LCT-1144. LVT-1012. **CDs:** Pearl GEMM-9487. *The 78s include a spoken introduction by Koussevitzky, "Let us begin," that is not on any other issue.*

CASADESUS, HENRI GUSTAVE
Concerto in D major (arr. Maximilian Steinberg). Formerly attributed to C.P.E. Bach **(16:05)**
BSO, conductor Serge Koussevitzky
December 22, 1937. Symphony Hall
RCA Victor, producer Charles O'Connell
Matrix: CS-014430/33: 1,1,1,1
78s: M-559 (15418/19). **LPs:** CAL-174. Turnabout TV-34784. **CDs:** Pearl GEMM-9179

MOZART, WOLFGANG AMADEUS
Symphony No. 29 in A, K. 201 (17:05)
BSO, conductor Serge Koussevitzky
December 22, 1937. Symphony Hall
RCA Victor, producer Charles O'Connell
Matrix: CS-014434/37: 1,1,1,1
78s: M-795 (18063/67). AM-795 (18068/72). DM-795 (18073/77). **LPs:** CFL-105 (6). CAL-160. **CDs:** Pearl GEMM-CDS 9185 (2). *See comments under Mozart's Symphony No. 34 (March 18, 1940).*

BEETHOVEN, LUDWIG VAN
Mass in D, op. 123 "Missa Solemnis"
BSO, conductor Serge Koussevitzky
Jeanette Vreeland, soprano; Kathryn Meisle, contralto; John Priebe, tenor; Mack Harrell, bass; E. Power Biggs, organ; Harvard Glee Club and Radcliffe Choral Society, G. Wallace Woodward, dir.
April 26, 1938. Symphony Hall (live)
RCA Victor, producer Charles O'Connell
Matrix: CS-022334/58 (one take of each side).
Unreleased. Re-recorded December 2 and 3, 1938. *This is thought to be Leonard Bernstein's first recording; a Harvard undergraduate, he sang in the chorus.*

BRAHMS, JOHANNES
Symphony No. 4 in E Minor, op. 98 (38:42)
BSO, conductor Serge Koussevitzky
November 30, 1938; December 1, 1938; December 3, 1938; November 8, 1939. Symphony Hall2
RCA Victor, producer Charles O'Connell
Matrix: CS-028855/63: 3,2,2A,2,1,1,3,2,3
78s: M-730 (17514/18). AM-730 (17519/23). DM-730 (17524/28). **LPs:** LM-2902. VCM-6174 (3). **CDs:** Pearl GEMM-9237. Dante LYS-289. United Artists UAR022 (4). *A note in the Victor log for November 30, 1938, reads: "First Regular Date using Complete Wide Range System."*

COPLAND, AARON
El salón México **(11:00)**
BSO, conductor Serge Koussevitzky
Rosario Mazzeo, clarinet
December 1, 1938. Symphony Hall
RCA Victor, producer Charles O'Connell
Matrix: CS-02864/66: 1,1,1
78s: M-546 (15363/64). DM-546 (18448/49). **Vdiscs:** CL-13/14. **45s:** 7ERL-1040 (Spanish HMV). **LPs:** LCT-1134. AVM1-1739. VIC-1211 (U.K.).
CDs: Biddulph WHL-050. Pearl GEMM-9492

DEBUSSY, CLAUDE
La Mer **(23:21)**
BSO, conductor Serge Koussevitzky
December 1, 1938; November 7, 1939. Symphony Hall
RCA Victor, producer Charles O'Connell
Matrix: CS-028867/72: 6,4,3A,2,4,4
78s: M-643. (15851/53). AM-643 (15854/56). DM-643 (15957/59). **LPs:** CAL-376. VICS-1514e (U.K.). **CDs:** Pearl GEMM-9090

BEETHOVEN, LUDWIG VAN
Mass in D, op. 123 "Missa Solemnis" (80:56)
BSO, conductor Serge Koussevitzky
Jeanette Vreeland, soprano; Anna Kaskas, contralto; John Priebe, tenor; Norman Cordon, bass; E. Power Biggs, organ; Harvard Glee Club and Radcliffe Choral Society, G. Wallace Woodworth, dir.
December 2, 1938; December 3, 1938. Symphony Hall (live)
RCA Victor, producer Charles O'Connell
Volume I: Matrix: CS-028873/84: 2,2,1R,1R,2,1R,2R,1R,2,2,2,2. Volume II: Matrix: CS-208885/96: 1R,1R,1R,2,1R,1R,2,1R,2R,2,1R,2A
78s: Volume I: M-758 (17816/21). AM-758 (17828/33). DM-758 (17840/45). Volume II: M-759 (17822/27). AM-759 (17834/39). DM-759 (17846/51). **CDs:** Pearl 9282 (2). *Two live performances were recorded, using the identical matrix numbers. Take numbers are confusing, because a recut side 1R may have come from either take. Edward D. Young believes that only the December 3rd takes were used for the issued records.*

RUSSIAN FOLK SONG
The Song of the Volga Boatman (arr. for wind instruments by Stravinsky) **(2:40)**
BSO, conductor Serge Koussevitzky
December 3, 1938. Symphony Hall
RCA Victor, producer Charles O'Connell
Matrix: CS-030404: 2
78s: M-546 (15364). DM-546 (18448). Final side filler of Copland's *El salón México* (December 1, 1938). **CDs:** Pearl GEMM-9020

BEETHOVEN, LUDWIG VAN
Symphony No. 2 in D, op. 36 (29:41)
BSO, conductor Serge Koussevitzky
December 3, 1938; April 12, 1939. Symphony Hall
RCA Victor, producer Charles O'Connell
Matrix: CS-028897/403: 1,1A,2,2,1,1,2
78s: M-625 (15771/74). AM-625 (15775/78). DM-625 (15779/82). **LPs:** CAL-157. **CDs:** Pearl GEMM-CDS 9185 (2). Dante LYS-383

BRAHMS, JOHANNES
Concerto for Violin and Orchestra in D, op. 77 (37:57)
BSO, conductor Serge Koussevitzky
April 11, 1939. Symphony Hall
RCA Victor, producer Charles O'Connell
Matrix: CS-035424/32: 2,2,3,2,1,2,3,2,1
78s: M-581 (15526/30). AM-581 (15531/35). DM-581 (16053/57). **45s:** WCT-71 (17-0419/23). **LPs:** LCT-1043. ARM4-0945 (4). **CDs:** 09026-61735-2 (2). Pearl 9167. Biddulph LAB-041. Naxos 8.110936. *WCT-71 and postwar (1946 onwards) issues of M-581 and DM-581 have the Air from Bach's Suite No. 3 (August 13, 1945) as a tenth-side filler.*

PROKOFIEV, SERGEI
Peter and the Wolf, op. 67 (24:45)
BSO, conductor Serge Koussevitzky
Richard Hale, narrator
April 12, 1939. Symphony Hall
RCA Victor, producer Charles O'Connell
Matrix: CS-035433/38: 3,3,3,2,2,2
78s: M-566 (15442/44). AM-566 (15445/47). DM-566 (16122/24). **LPs:** CAL-101. **CDs:** Pearl GEMM-9487. *Richard Hale enjoyed a long career as both an operatic baritone and as a stage actor. Both contributed to the success of this early recording, which was not matched until that by Leonard Bernstein 21 years later. Hale was also the narrator for the U.S. premiere, on March 25, 1938, with Prokofiev conducting the BSO.*

SCHUMANN, ROBERT
Symphony No. 1 in B♭, op. 38 "Spring" (32:59)
BSO, conductor Serge Koussevitzky
November 6, 1939; November 7, 1939; November 8, 1939. Symphony Hall
RCA Victor, producer Charles O'Connell
Matrix: CS-043562/69: 1,1,3,2,2,2,3,1
78s: M-655 (15895/98). AM-655 (15899/902). DM-655 (15903/06). **CDs:** Pearl GEMM-9037. *When Dr. Koussevitzky was asked, during a recent interview in New York, to name some of his favorite recordings, he selected Robert Schumann's First Symphony ("Spring"), Tchaikovsky's Sixth Symphony ("Pathetique"), "La Mer" by Debussy, and the "Mephisto Waltz" of Franz Liszt. (An uncredited paragraph, page 724 of the 1944/1945 season programs)*

HANDEL, GEORGE FRIDERIC
Semele: **"Oh sleep! Why dost thou leave me?" (4:02)**
BSO, conductor Serge Koussevitzky
Dorothy Maynor, soprano
November 6, 1939. Symphony Hall
RCA Victor, producer Charles O'Connell
Matrix: CS-043570: 3
78s: 15826. **45s:** WCT-1115 (449-0145/48). **LPs:** LCT-1115. LM-3086. F2OL-6919/20 (1). **CDs:** Pearl GEMM-9179. *The set WCT-1115 and the LP LM-1115 are titled "Critic's Choice Chosen by Irving Kolodin." Maynor's aria is on side one, band one. (Don Tait: email, November 6, 2007)*

MOZART, WOLFGANG AMADEUS
Die Zauberflöte, K. 620: **"Ach, ich fühl's" (4:25)**
BSO, conductor Serge Koussevitzky
Dorothy Maynor, soprano
November 6, 1939. Symphony Hall
RCA Victor, producer Charles O'Connell
Matrix: CS-043571: 1A
78s: 15826. **LPs:** LM-3086. **CDs:** Pearl GEMM-9179

RUSSIAN FOLK SONG
Dubinushka (orch. Rimsky-Korsakov), **op. 49 (4:00)**
BSO, conductor Serge Koussevitzky
November 7, 1939. Symphony Hall
RCA Victor, producer Charles O'Connell
Matrix: CS-043572: 2A
78s: M-941 (11-8346). DM-941 (11-8347). **CDs:** Biddulph WHL-044

RIMSKY-KORSAKOV, NIKOLAI
The Legend of the Invisible City of Kitezh and The Maiden Fevronia: **Act 2**
    Entr-Acte "The Battle of Kershenetz" (4:20)
BSO, conductor Serge Koussevitzky
November 7, 1939. Symphony Hall
RCA Victor, producer Charles O'Connell
Matrix: CS-043573: 2
78s: M-870 (18410). DM-870 (18411). **LPs:** LM-2901. VCM-6174 (3). VIC-
    1283 (U.K.). **CDs:** Biddulph WHL-044

SIBELIUS, JEAN
Tapiola, **op. 112 (17:10)**
BSO, conductor Serge Koussevitzky
November 7, 1939. Symphony Hall
RCA Victor, producer Charles O'Connell
Matrix: CS-043574/77: 1,2,2,1
78s: M-848 (18310/11). DM-848 (18312/13). **LPs:** CAL-159. **CDs:** Pearl
    GEMMCDS-9408 (2)

HARRIS, ROY
Symphony No. 3 (16:28) *World premiere of a BSO commission.*
BSO, conductor Serge Koussevitzky
November 8, 1939. Symphony Hall
RCA Victor, producer Charles O'Connell
Matrix: CS-043578/81: 2,2,1,1
78s: M-651 (15885/86). DM-651 (18454/55). **LPs:** LCT-1153. LVT-1016. VIC-
    1047 (U.K.). **CDs:** EMI 5 75118 2 (2). Pearl GEMM-9492. ArkivCD 75118

MCDONALD, HARL
San Juan Capistrano: **Two Evening Pictures:** *The Mission* **(4:44);** *Fiesta*
    (4:26)
BSO, conductor Serge Koussevitzky
November 8, 1939. Symphony Hall
RCA Victor, producer Charles O'Connell
Matrix: CS-043582/83: 2A,2A
78s: 17229. **CDs:** Pearl GEMM-9492

FAURÉ, GABRIEL
Pelléas et Mélisande: Suite from the incidental music to Maeterlinck's drama, op. 80: *Prélude, Fileuse, Sicilienne* (12:35)
BSO, conductor Serge Koussevitzky
March 18, 1940. Symphony Hall
RCA Victor, producer Charles O'Connell
Matrix: CS-047100/02: 2,3,2
78s: M-941 (11-8345/46). DM-941 (11-8347/48). **LPs:** LCT-1152. **CDs:** Biddulph WHL-044.

MOZART, WOLFGANG AMADEUS
Symphony No. 34 in C, K. 338 (19:09)
BSO, conductor Serge Koussevitzky
March 18, 1940; March 19, 1940. Symphony Hall
RCA Victor, producer Charles O'Connell
Matrix: CS-047103/07: 2,2,2,2,2
78s: M-795 (18063/67). AM-795 (18068/72). DM-795 (18073/77). **LPs:** CAL-160. CFL-105 (6). **CDs:** Pearl GEMM-CDS 9185 (2). Dante LYS 133. United Artists UAR022 (4). *The 78-rpm albums include Symphony No. 29 (December 22, 1937). The final side was originally blank, but post-war editions of the M- and DM- sets added Handel's Larghetto (May 8, 1936).*

FOOTE, ARTHUR
Suite for Strings in E, op. 63 (15:05)
BSO, conductor Serge Koussevitzky
March 19, 1940. Symphony Hall
RCA Victor, producer Charles O'Connell
Matrix: CS-047108/11: 2,1,2,1
78s: M-962 (11-8571/72). DM-962 (11-8573/74). **LPs:** LM-2900. VCM-6174 (3). BSO PRM-234 (promotional). Turnabout TV-34784. **CDs:** Pearl GEMM 9492.

Matrix numbers CS-047112/114, although sequentially among those of this session, were assigned to Arthur Fiedler's Sinfonietta, which recorded in Symphony Hall on March 21, 1940. Those recordings appear in Appendix G.

STRAVINSKY, IGOR
Capriccio (17:33)
BSO, conductor Serge Koussevitzky
Jesús Maria Sanromá, piano
March 19, 1940. Symphony Hall
RCA Victor, producer Charles O'Connell
Matrix: CS-047115/18: 2,2,2,1
78s: M-685 (16883/84). DM-685 (18460/61). **LPs:** LCT-1152. **CDs:** Pearl GEMM-90206. *Koussevitzky's heavy Russian accent amused many listeners and was often parodied. When Charles O'Connell made a suggestion to him at a recording session, the conductor is said to have replied: "You vill take care of de apparat, I vill take care de music." (http://www.classical. net/music/guide/society/krs/excerpt4.htm. March 9, 2008)*

HANSON, HOWARD
Symphony No. 3 in A Minor, op, 63 (34:38) *A BSO commission.*
BSO, conductor Serge Koussevitzky
March 20, 1940. Symphony Hall. *The world premiere was November 3, 1939.*
RCA Victor, producer Charles O'Connell
Matrix: CS-047119/27: 1,1,1,1,1,1,1,1,1
78s: M-1170 (11-9875/79). **DM-**1170 (11-9880/84). **LPs:** LCT-1153. LVT-1016. **CDs:** Biddulph WHL-044. Dutton CDEA-5021

GRIEG, EDVARD
Elegiac Melody, op. 34, no. 2 "The Last Spring" (4:38)
BSO, conductor Serge Koussevitzky
March 20, 1940. Symphony Hall
RCA Victor, producer Charles O'Connell
Matrix: CS-047128: 1
78s: 11-8727; backed byTchaikovsky's Waltz (May 8, 1936). M-886 (185228). DM-886 (18529); final side filler of Vivaldi's Concerto Grosso (May 8, 1936). LE-3 (99-2103). **45s:** CAE-161. **LPs:** CAL-155. Turnabout TV-34784. **CDs:** Naxos 8.110168. Pearl GEMM-9179

BIZET, GEORGES
Carmen: **"Je dis que rien ne m'épouvante"** (Micaëla's aria) **(5:15)**
BSO, conductor Serge Koussevitzky
Dorothy Maynor, soprano
March 20, 1940. Symphony Hall
RCA Victor, producer Charles O'Connell
Matrix: CS-047129 (2 takes)
Unreleased. *These two recordings have not previously been recognized in discographies of the BSO. Their RCA Victor recording log is in the Dorothy Maynor folder at Sony BMG Archives, as is that for her November 6, 1939, recordings. Excessive length—both run well over the maximum length of a 78-rpm disc at that time—prevented the pressing and release of these arias.*

CHARPENTIER, GUSTAVE
Louise: **"Depuis le jour"** **(5:15)**
BSO, conductor Serge Koussevitzky
Dorothy Maynor, soprano
March 20, 1940. Symphony Hall
RCA Victor, producer Charles O'Connell
Matrix: CS-047130 (2 takes)
Unreleased. *Maynor was "discovered" by Koussevitzky at Tanglewood in 1939, where she sang this, her signature aria. She re-recorded "Depuis le jour" with Eugene Ormandy and the Philadelphia Orchestra on October 20, 1940; issued on RCA Victor 17698, that version runs 4:36. It may be heard at http://www.bassocantate.com/opera/maynor.html (February 6, 2008). An African-American excluded from opera houses by the bigotry of the era, Maynor nevertheless had a successful career in concerts and on recordings. She founded the Harlem School of the Arts in 1963.*

LIADOV, ANATOLY
From the Apocalypse, **Symphonic Picture, op. 66** (broadcast) **(8:35)**
BSO, conductor Serge Koussevitzky
May 1, 1943. Broadcast from Symphony Hall
BSO/IMG Artists
CDs: CB-100 (12)

GLINKA, MIKHAIL
Russlan and Ludmilla: **Overture** (broadcast) **(5:31)**
BSO, conductor Serge Koussevitzky
April 1, 1944. Broadcast from Hunter College, New York City
BSO/IMG Artists
CDs: CB-100 (12)

TCHAIKOVSKY, PETER ILYICH
Symphony No. 5 in E Minor, op. 64 (47:18)
BSO, conductor Serge Koussevitzky
November 22, 1944. Symphony Hall
RCA Victor, producer Macklin Marrow
Matrix: D4-RC-616/27: 2,1E,1,1A,1A,1A,1,1,1,1,1,1
78s: M-1057 (11-9192/97). DM-1057 (11-9198/203). **45s:** WDM-1057 (49-0112/17). **LPs:** LM-1047. LM-2901. VCM-6174 (3). VIC-1283 (U.K.). **CDs:** BSO Classics 441122. EMI 5 75118 2 (2). Biddulph WHL-034/35 (2). ArkivCD 75118

BERLIOZ, HECTOR
Roman Carnival Overture, **op. 9 (8:41)**
BSO, conductor Serge Koussevitzky
November 22, 1944. Symphony Hall
RCA Victor, producer Macklin Marrow
Matrix: D4-RC-628/29: 2,2
78s: 11-9008. **45s:** 49-1178. **CDs:** BSO Classics 441122. Biddulph WHL-028

DEBUSSY, CLAUDE
Prélude à l'après-midi d'un faune **(9:35)**
BSO, conductor Serge Koussevitzky
November 22, 1944; November 28, 1944. Symphony Hall
RCA Victor, producer Macklin Marrow
Matrix: D4-RC-630/31: 1,(unknown)
78s: 11-9128 (this number was assigned, but no shellac record was released). 18-0042 (red vinylite disc). **CDs:** BSO Classics 441122

CORELLI, ARCANGELO
Suite for Strings (arr. Pinelli) **(7:52)**
BSO, conductor Serge Koussevitzky
November 22, 1944. Symphony Hall
RCA Victor, producer Macklin Marrow
Matrix: D4-RC-632/33: 1,1
78s: 12-0768 (unreleased). **CDs:** BSO Classics 441122. Pearl GEMM-9179

RAVEL, MAURICE
Daphnis et Chloé: Suite No. 2 (14:58)
BSO, conductor Serge Koussevitzky
November 23, 1944; November 27, 1944; January 2, 1945; January 3, 1945.
   Symphony Hall
RCA Victor, producer Macklin Marrow
Matrix: D4-RC-634/37: 5,1A,1,2
78s: M-1108 (11-9596/97). **DM**-1108 (11-9498/99). **LPs:** CAL-156. CFL-102
   (6). **CDs:** 09026-61392-2

BEETHOVEN, LUDWIG VAN
Symphony No. 5 in C Minor, op. 67 (33:11)
BSO, conductor Serge Koussevitzky
November 23, 1944; November 27, 1944; November 23, 1945. Symphony Hall
RCA Victor, producer Macklin Marrow
Matrix: D4-RC-638/45: 1AR,1,2,1,2,1A,2,2A
78s: DM-1313 (12-0959/62). V-5 (18-0030/33). DV-5 (18-0034/37). **45s:**
   WDM-1313 (49-0425/28). ERB-15 (549-5025/26). **LPs:** LM-1021. CAL-
   405. **CDs:** Dante LYS-383. Dutton CDBP-9706. United Artists UAR022
   (4). *Because two sides ran well over five minutes, this set was not released
   until 1949, when RCA was able to accomodate the longer timings; after
   dubbing several sides in an attempt to remove excess noise, the symphony
   was issued on 78s and on 45s. The recording log shows hand-written entries, presumably made in 1949, for red vinyl records 18-0030/33 (in such
   cases, alternate versions in automatic sequence are seldom written in). Sets
   V-5 and DV-5 appear on recording cards ("blue cards") in the Sony BMG
   Archives, with label copy pasted on the back, but those red vinylite "Red
   Seal De Luxe" 78s were apparently withdrawn at the last moment, as exten-
   sive searches have failed to turn up any report of such an album. We ask
   any reader who can document a vinyl set to notify us through the publisher.*

BERLIOZ, HECTOR
Harold in Italy, op. 16 (41:55)
BSO, conductor Serge Koussevitzky
Wiliam Primrose, viola
November 28, 1944. Symphony Hall
RCA Victor, producer Macklin Marrow
Matrix: D4-RC-646/55: 1,1,1,1,1,1,1,1,1,1
78s: M-989 (11-8751/55). DM-989 (11-8756/60). **LPs:** LCT-1146. LVT-1013.
   VIC-1222 (U.K.). **CDs:** Biddulph WHL-028. Dutton CDEA-5013. United
   Artists UAR022 (4)

GOULD, MORTON
Spirituals for Orchestra (18:39)
BSO, conductor Dimitri Mitropoulos
December 16, 1944. Broadcast from Symphony Hall
BSO/IMG Artists
CDs: CB-100 (12)

BARTÓK, BELA

Concerto for Orchestra (with the original ending) **(36:47)** *Written for the Koussevitzky Music Foundation in memory of Mrs. Natalie Koussevitzky. Broadcast premiere.*
BSO, conductor Serge Koussevitzky
December 30, 1944. Broadcast from Symphony Hall
BSO/IMG Artists
CDs: CB-100 (12). Naxos 8.110105. *Koussevitzky and the BSO gave the world premiere on December 1, 1944, in Carnegie Hall. BSO bass trombonist Douglas Yeo related (1990) a story preserved by his colleagues about the dress rehearsal for the first performance: Bartók sat in the balcony, furiously writing on a pad all the things he wanted to tell Koussevitzky at the break. The two men sat in the conductor's room, and after the break Koussevitzky mounted the podium and, looking up at Bartók in the balcony, announced to the orchestra that "Gentlemen, Mr. Bartók is very pleased." (North: "Excursions with a Trombone"). This broadcast appeared on a pirate LP, Baton 1008, before the BSO issued its 12-CD historical set.*

KHACHATURIAN, ARAM

Concerto for Piano and Orchestra in D♭ (33:36)
BSO, conductor Serge Koussevitzky
William Kapell, piano
January 1, 1945. Symphony Hall
RCA Victor, producer Macklin Marrow
Matrix: D5-RC-600/07 (takes made: 2,2,2,2,1,1,2,1)
Unreleased. Re-recorded April 19, 1946.

BRAHMS, JOHANNES

Symphony No. 3 in F, op. 90 (35:53)
BSO, conductor Serge Koussevitzky
January 2, 1945. Symphony Hall
RCA Victor, producer Macklin Marrow
Matrix: D5-RC-614/21: 2,2A,2,1A,2,2,1,2
78s: M-1007 (11-8832/35). DM-1007 (11-8836/39). **45s:** WDM-1007 (49-0635/38). **LPs:** LM-1025. LVM2-7510 (2). **CDs:** Dante LYS-257. Pearl GEMM-9237 **(36:16).** *English CDs of Koussevitzky's BSO are consistently slow, the transfer engineers seldom understanding that it played at an elevated pitch.*

MOZART, WOLFGANG AMADEUS

Symphony No. 39 in E♭, K. 543 (25:33)
BSO, conductor Serge Koussevitzky
January 3, 1945. Symphony Hall
RCA Victor, producer Macklin Marrow
Matrix: D5-RC-622/27: 1,1,1,1,1,2A
78s: DM-1379 (12-1173/75). **45s:** WDM-1379 (49-1126/28). **LPs:** LM-1141

SCHUBERT, FRANZ
Symphony No. 8 in B Minor "Unfinished" (24:01)
BSO, conductor Serge Koussevitzky
January 3, 1945. Symphony Hall
RCA Victor, producer Macklin Marrow
Matrix: D5-RC-628/33: 2,1,1,1,2,1A
78s: M-1039 (11-9082/84). DM-1039 (11-9085/87). **45s:** WDM-1039 (49-0154/56). ERB-11 (549-5017/18). **LPs:** LM-7. LM-9032. VIC-1018 (U.K.). **CDs:** United Artists UAR022 (4)

RACHMANINOFF, SERGEI
The Isle of the Dead, op. 29 (18:44)
BSO, conductor Serge Koussevitzky
April 23, 1945; April 24, 1945. Symphony Hall
RCA Victor, producer Macklin Marrow
Matrix: D5-RC-918/22: 2,2,1,2,2
78s: M-1024 (11-8957/59). DM-1024 (11-8960/62). **45s:** WDM-1024 (49-1230/32). **LPs:** LM-1215. LM-9032. **CDs:** EMI 5 75118 2 (2). Biddulph WHL-045. ArkivCD 75118. United Artists UAR022 (4)

RAVEL, MAURICE
Rapsodie espagnole (16:18)
BSO, conductor Serge Koussevitzky
April 23, 1945; April 24, 1945; April 25, 1945. Symphony Hall
RCA Victor, producer Macklin Marrow
Matrix: D5-RC-923/26: 3P,1,2P,2P
78s: M-1200 (12-0163/64). DM-1200 (12-0165/66). **LPs:** CAL-376. LRM-1016. **CDs:** Naxos 8.110154. Andante 1978 (3)

RACHMANINOFF, SERGEI
Vocalise, op. 34, no. 14 (5:03)
BSO, conductor Serge Koussevitzky
April 24, 1945. Symphony Hall
RCA Victor, producer Macklin Marrow
Matrix: D5-RC-927: 2P
78s: M-1024 (11-8959). DM-1024 (11-8960). **45s:** WDM-1024 (49-1230); *last side filler for both the 78-rpm and 45-rpm sets of* The Isle of the Dead (above). **LPs:** LM-2901. VCM-6174 (3). VIC-1283 (U.K.). **CDs:** Biddulph WHL-045. United Artists UAR022 (4). *Edward D. Young's exemplary Koussevitzky discography, as published in* ARSC Journal *21:1, appears to have a typo in this matrix number.*

STRAUSS, RICHARD
Till Eulenspiegels lustige Streiche, op. 28 (15:00)
BSO, conductor Serge Koussevitzky
April 24, 1945. Symphony Hall
RCA Victor, producer Macklin Marrow
Matrix: D5-RC-928/31: 2P,3P,2P,2P
78s: M-1029 (11-8991/92). DM-1029 (11-8993/94). V-1 (18-0000/01). DV-1 (18-0002/03). **LPs:** CAL-101. CFL-102 (6). **CDs:** Biddulph WHL-054. Dutton CDEA-5013. Preiser 90337. ArkivCD 90337. United Artists UAR022 (4). *Issued in October 1945, Set V-1 was the first release of RCA's series of "Red Seal De Luxe" red vinylite discs, which ran through 1949, when RCA announced the 45-rpm speed.*

THOMPSON, RANDALL
Testament of Freedom (24:13)
BSO, conductor Serge Koussevitzky
Harvard Glee Club, G. Wallace Woodworth, dir. *Sixty male voices.*
April 24, 1945. Symphony Hall. *The world premiere was on April 6, 1945.*
RCA Victor, producer Macklin Marrow
Matrix: D5-RC-932/37: 2P,2P,2P,2P,2P,2P
78s: M-1054 (11-9176/78). DM-1054 (11-9179/81). **CDs:** Biddulph WHL-050.
A setting of four passages from the writings of Thomas Jefferson.

PISTON, WALTER
Prelude and Allegro for Organ and Strings (8:13)
BSO, conductor Serge Koussevitzky
E. Power Biggs, organ
April 24, 1945; February 7, 1946. Symphony Hall
RCA Victor, producer Macklin Marrow
Matrix: D5-RC-938/39: 1,4A
78s: 11-9262. **LPs:** Columbia M4X-35180. *Biggs plays the Symphony Hall organ by George S. Hutchings.*

SHOSTAKOVICH, DMITRI
Symphony No. 8 in C Minor, op. 65: I. Adagio (26:01)
BSO, conductor Serge Koussevitzky
April 25, 1945. Symphony Hall
RCA Victor, producer Macklin Marrow
Matrix: D5-RC-940/945: 2,2,2,3,2,2. *Matrix numbers are from test pressings.*
CDs: BSO-CD2 (RCA 60148-2-RC) (promotional). Biddulph WHL-045. *Shostakovich heard Koussevitzky's April 22, 1944, broadcast in Russia. The composer wrote the conductor from Moscow on February 10, 1945, criticizing the interpretation and performance in great detail. In the final days of Word War II, with no international air mail, the letter may have taken ten weeks to arrive in Boston, so the composer's criticisms may have been a factor in the discontinuation of this recording. The letter is in the Library of Congress; an English translation was published by Richard Pleak in the* Journal of the Dimitri Shostakovich Society, *August 1, 1989.*

BACH, JOHANN SEBASTIAN
Suite No. 3 in D, BWV 1068 (20: 24)
BSO, conductor Serge Koussevitzky
August 13, 1945. Theatre Concert Hall, Tanglewood
RCA Victor, producer Richard Gilbert
Matrix: D5-RC-1200/04: 2A,1P,2P,2A,2A
78s: M-1123 (11-9583/87). DM-1123 (11-9588/92). Coupled with Suite No. 2
(below). **LPs:** CAL-158. **CDs:** Pearl GEMS-0103 (3). *The Air from this*
suite appears as final side filler in post-war issues of the Brahms Violin
Concerto (April 11, 1939): 78-pm albums M-581 (15530-B) and DM-581
(16053-B), and in the 45-rpm set WCT-71 (17-0419-B).

BACH, JOHANN SEBASTIAN
Brandenburg Concerto No. 4 in G, BWV 1049 (16:31)
BSO, conductor Serge Koussevitzky
Richard Burgin, violin; Georges Laurent and George Madsen, flutes
August 13, 1945; August 14, 1945. Theatre Concert Hall, Tanglewood
RCA Victor, producer Richard Gilbert
Matrix: D5-RC-1205/08: 2A,2P,2P,1A
78s: M-1050 (11-9156/59). DM-1050 (11-9260/63). Coupled with Brandenburg
Concerto No. 3 (below). **LPs:** CAL-174. **CDs:** Pearl GEMS-0103 (3)

BACH, JOHANN SEBASTIAN
Brandenburg Concerto No. 3 in G, BWV 1048 (12:39)
BSO, conductor Serge Koussevitzky
August 14, 1945. Theatre Concert Hall, Tanglewood
RCA Victor, producer Richard Gilbert
Matrix: D5-RC-1209/11: 1,1A,1A
78s: M-1050 (11-9156/59). DM-1050 (11-9160/63). Coupled with Brandenburg
Concerto No. 4 (above). **LPs:** CAL-174. **CDs:** Pearl GEMS-0103 (3)

BACH, JOHANN SEBASTIAN
Suite No. 2 for Flute and Strings in B Minor, BWV 1067 (20:25)
BSO, conductor Serge Koussevitzky
Georges Laurent, flute
August 14, 1945. Theatre Concert Hall, Tanglewood
RCA Victor, producer Richard Gilbert
Matrix: D5-RC-1212/16: 2A,1A,1E,1A,1
78s: M-1123 (11-9583/87). DM-1123 (11-9588-92). Coupled with Suite No. 3
(above). **LPs:** CAL-158. **CDs:** Pearl GEMS-0103 (3)

V. Polonaise. 78s: M-730 (17518). DM-730 (17524); Final side of post-war
issues of Brahms Symphony No. 4 (November 30, 1938).

BEETHOVEN, LUDWIG VAN
Symphony No. 3 in E♭, op. 55 "Eroica" (48:18)
BSO, conductor Serge Koussevitzky
October 29, 1945; October 30, 1945. Symphony Hall
RCA Victor, producer Macklin Marrow
Matrix: D5-RC-1227/38: 2P,1A,1,1,3A,2,1,3P,2A,1A,1,2A
78s: M-1161 (11-9796/801). DM-1161 (11-9802/07). V-8 (18-0060/65). DV-8
    (18-0066/71). **45s:** WDM-1161 (49-0462/67). **LPs:** LM-1145. CAL-404.
    VICS-1497e (U.K.). **CDs:** Pearl 9282 (2). Dante LYS-173

PROKOFIEV, SERGEI
Romeo and Juliet: **Suite No. 2, op. 64b (17:10)**
BSO, conductor Serge Koussevitzky
October 30, 1945; October 31, 1945. Symphony Hall
RCA Victor, producer Macklin Marrow
Matrix: D5-RC-1239/42: 2A,2A,1,1
78s: M-1129 (11-9608/09). DM-1129 (11-9610/11). **LPs:** LCT-1144. LVT-
    1012. AVM1-2021. **CDs:** 09026-61657-2. Biddulph WHL-045. ArkivCD
    61657

COPLAND, AARON
Appalachian Spring: **Suite (24:19)**
BSO, conductor Serge Koussevitzky
October 31, 1945. Symphony Hall
RCA Victor, producer Macklin Marrow
Matrix: D5-RC-1243/48: 1,1A,1,2A,1A,1
78s: M-1046 (11-9129/31). DM-1046 (11-9132/34). **LPs:** LCT-1134. VIC-1211
    (U.K.). AVM1-1739. **CDs:** Biddulph WHL-050. Dutton CDEA-5021

BACH, JOHANN SEBASTIAN
Sonata No. 6 in E for solo Violin, BMV 1006: Prelude (orch. Pick-
    Mangiagalli) **(3:51)**
BSO, conductor Serge Koussevitzky
October 31, 1945. Symphony Hall
RCA Victor, producer Macklin Marrow
Matrix: D5-RC-1249: 1A
78s: M-257 (8623). DM-257 (16653). Final side filler of post-war issues of
    Strauss's *Also sprach Zarathustra* (January 23, 1935). M-625 (15774). DM-
    625 (15979). Final side filler of post-war issues of Beethoven's Symphony
    No. 2 (December 3, 1938). M-1050 (11-9157). DM-1050 (11-9163). Final
    side filler of Brandenburg Concertos Nos. 3 and 4 (August 13, 14, 1945).

SIBELIUS, JEAN
Symphony No. 5 in E♭. op. 82: IV Finale: Allegro molto (8:32)
BSO, conductor Serge Koussevitzky
January 5, 1946. Symphony Hall (live)
Boston Symphony Transcription Trust, producers Jordan M. Whitelaw and
    Richard L. Kaye
CDs: BSO-CD1 (promotional). *1988 "Salute to Symphony."*

PROKOFIEV, SERGEI
Symphony No. 5 in B♭, op. 100 (40:31)
BSO, conductor Serge Koussevitzky
February 6, 1946; February 7, 1946. Symphony Hall
RCA Victor, producer Macklin Marrow
Matrix: D6-RC-5118/27: 1,2P,2P,2A,1,1,1,1,1,3A
78s: M-1095 (11-9433/37). DM-1095 (11-9438/42). **45s:** WDM-1095 (49-0184/88). **LPs:** LM-1045. LVT-1026. AVM1-2021. Franklin Mint Records Society 83/84 (2). **CDs:** 09026-61657-2. ArkivCD 61657

COPLAND, AARON
Lincoln Portrait **(13:40)**
BSO, conductor Serge Koussevitzky
Melvyn Douglas, narrator
February 7, 1946. Symphony Hall
RCA Victor, producer Macklin Marrow
Matrix: D6-RC-5128/30: 2,2,3
78s: M-1088 (11-9389/90). DM-1088 (11-9391/92). **LPs:** LCT-1152. AVM1-1739. **CDs:** Biddulph WHL-050. Y*oung's Koussevitzky discography cites a Spanish HMV 45-rpm record, but it is listed in WERM's Third Supplement under* El salón México *(December 1, 1938), which seems more appropriate for a Spanish audience. Thanks to Don Tait for raising the question.*

MOZART, WOLFGANG AMADEUS
Symphony No. 26 in E♭, K. 184 (9:35)
BSO, conductor Serge Koussevitzky
February 7, 1946. Symphony Hall
RCA Victor, producer Macklin Marrow
Matrix: D6-RC-5131/32: 1,1
78s: 11-9363. **LPs:** CAL-160. CFL-105 (6). **CDs:** LYS 142

BRITTEN, BENJAMIN
Peter Grimes: **Three Orchestral Interludes (15:32)**
BSO, conductor Serge Koussevitzky
March 2, 1946. Symphony Hall
BSO/TDK
CDs: "Tanglewood 98"

KHACHATURIAN, ARAM
Concerto for Piano and Orchestra in D♭ (35:21)
BSO, conductor Serge Koussevitzky
William Kapell, piano
April 19, 1946. Symphony Hall
RCA Victor, producers Macklin Marrow and Richard Gilbert
Matrix: D6-RC-5700/07: 1,1A,2A,2,1,1A,1,1A
78s: M-1084 (11-9364/67). DM-1084 (11-9368/71). **45s:** WDM-1084 (49-0157/60). **LPs:** LM-1006. LM-2588. AGM1-5266. **CDs:** 09026-60921-2. 09026-68993-2. 09026-68442-2 (9). Naxos 8.110673

SOUSA, JOHN PHILIP
The Stars and Stripes Forever (3:07)
BSO, conductor Serge Koussevitzky
April 19, 1946. Symphony Hall
RCA Victor, producers Macklin Marrow and Richard Gilbert
Matrix: D6-RC-5708: 2
78s: 18-0053 (12-inch red vinylite disc). **CDs:** Biddulph WHL-050

SOUSA, JOHN PHILIP
Semper Fidelis (2:20)
BSO, conductor Serge Koussevitzky
April 19, 1946. Symphony Hall
RCA Victor, producers Macklin Marrow and Richard Gilbert
Matrix: D6-RC-5709: 1
78s: 18-0053 (both 78s are 12-inch red vinylite discs). NCP-3264 *(with a banjo solo on the other side); issued to commemorate Victor's one billionth record sold.* **CDs:** Biddulph WHL-050

TCHAIKOVSKY, PETER ILYICH
Francesca da Rimini, op. 32 (25:39)
BSO, conductor Serge Koussevitzky
April 19, 1946. Symphony Hall
RCA Victor, producers Macklin Marrow and Richard Gilbert
Matrix: D6-RC-5710/15: 1A,1A1A,1,1,1
78s: M-1179 (11-9982/84). DM-1179 (11-9985/87). **LPs:** CAL-159.
CDs: Biddulph WHL-058

WAGNER, RICHARD
Parsifal: Good Friday Music (11:37)
BSO, conductor Serge Koussevitzky
April 19, 1946. Symphony Hall
RCA Victor, producers Macklin Marrow and Richard Gilbert
Matrix: D6-RC-5716/18: 2P,2A,1A
78s: M-1198 (12-0147/48). DM-1198 (12-0149/51). With Act I Prelude; April 4, 1947. **CDs:** Naxos 8.111283

STRAUSS, RICHARD
Don Juan, op. 20 (17:46)
BSO, conductor Serge Koussevitzky
April 19, 1946. Symphony Hall
RCA Victor, producers Macklin Marrow and Richard Gilbert
Matrix: D6-RC-5719/22
LPs: Neiman-Marcus First Edition DPM4-0210 (4) (RCA Special Products).
CDs: BSO-CD2 (RCA 60148-2-RC) (promotional)

BACH, JOHANN SEBASTIAN
Brandenburg Concerto No. 2 in F, BWV 1047 (12:18)
BSO, conductor Serge Koussevitzky
Roger Voisin, trumpet; Georges Laurent, flute; Richard Burgin, violin; Fernand Gillet, oboe
August 13, 1946; August 14, 1946. Theatre Concert Hall, Tanglewood
RCA Victor, producer Richard Gilbert
Matrix: D6-RC-5762/64: 3P,2A,2P
78s: M-1118 (11-9538/41). DM-1118 (11-9542/45). **LPs:** CAL-147. **CDs:** Pearl GEMS-0103 (3). M/DM-1118 also contain Brandenburg Concerto No. 5, below. *Voisin plays a late-nineteenth-century B♭ trumpet made by Ouvriers Rénnis in Paris. Nine inches long, with a wide bell, it looks like a toy bugle. (photograph in* RCA Victor Record Review, *March 1947)*

BACH, JOHANN SEBASTIAN
Brandenburg Concerto No. 5 in D, BWV 1050 (21:40)
BSO, conductor Serge Koussevitzky
Lukas Foss, piano; Georges Laurent, flute; Richard Burgin, violin
August 13, 1946; August 14, 1946. Theatre Concert Hall, Tanglewood
RCA Victor, producer Richard Gilbert
Matrix: D6-RC-5765/69: 2A,3A,2A,1,2A
78s: M-1118 (11-9538/41). DM-1118 (11-9542/45). **LPs:** CAL-147.
 CDs: Pearl GEMS-0103 (3). M/DM-1118 also contain Brandenburg Concerto No. 2, above.

BACH, JOHANN SEBASTIAN
Suite No. 4 in D, BWV 1069 (18:55)
BSO, conductor Serge Koussevitzky
August 14, 1946; August 15, 1946. Theatre Concert Hall, Tanglewood
RCA Victor, producer Richard Gilbert
Matrix: D6-RC-5770/73: 1,1,2P,3P
78s: M-1307 (12-0928/29). DM-1307 (12-0933/30). **45s:** WDM-1307 (49-0408/12). **LPs:** LM-1079. **CDs:** Pearl GEMS-0103 (3). Andante 1986 (3)

MOZART, WOLFGANG AMADEUS
Symphony No. 33 in B♭, K. 319 (20:05)
BSO, conductor Serge Koussevitzky
August 15, 1946. Theatre Concert Hall, Tanglewood
RCA Victor, producer Richard Gilbert
Matrix: D6-RC-5774/78: 1,1,2P,1,1C
78s: DM-1369 (12-1134/36). **45s:** WDM-1369 (49-1011/13). *The Victor log for this session calls the site "Opera House, Tanglewood, Mass.," but it is the Theatre Concert Hall.*

MOZART, WOLFGANG AMADEUS
String Quintet in G Minor, K. 516: Adagio ma non troppo (arr. orchestra)
(11:00)
BSO, conductor Serge Koussevitzky
August 15, 1946. Theatre Concert Hall, Tanglewood
RCA Victor, producer Richard Gilbert
Matrix: D6-RC-5779/80: one take made of each side
Unreleased. *Typed and hand-written notes in the recording log say "No parts. No wax. Lacquer only. Hold for Mr. Gilbert." This was "Electrically transferred from D6-RC-5780-1 to furnish new master" on December 13, 1946, at New York Studio No 6.*

SHOSTAKOVICH, DMITRI
Symphony No. 9 in Eb, op. 70 (24:32)
BSO, conductor Serge Koussevitzky
November 4, 1946; April 2, 1947. Symphony Hall
RCA Victor, producer Richard Gilbert
Matrix: D6-RC-6250/52 and 6254/56: 1A,3A,2A,1,1,1A
78s: M-1134 (11-9634/36). DM-1134 (11-9637/39). **LPs:** LM-2900. VCM-6174 (3). LVM2-7510 (2). PRM-234 (promotional). **CDs:** Biddulph WHL-058.
Shostakovich heard Koussevitzky's August 10, 1946, performance on the radio and wrote him that his tempo in the second movement, Moderato, was far too slow (duration 13:52). Koussevitzky and Shostakovich argued by letter as to how the music should have been written: "I cannot agree with you that I was wrong to compose it in quarter-time and not eighth" (February 11, 1947), and the composer apologized for not having included metronome markings in the score he sent Koussevitzky. The letter is in the Library of Congress, and an English translation was published by Richard Pleak in the Journal of the Dimitri Shostakovich Society, *August 1, 1989. The November 1946 recording of the symphony included the Moderato on three sides (matrices D6-RC-6251/53). After the exchange of letters, Koussevitzky re-recorded just the Moderato (duration now 7:10) on two sides; thus the gap in Matrix numbers listed here.*

RAVEL, MAURICE
***Pavane pour une infante défunte* (6:46)**
BSO, conductor Serge Koussevitzky
November 4, 1946; November 5, 1946. Symphony Hall
RCA Victor, producer Richard Gilbert
Matrix: D6-RC-6257/58: 2P,1
78s: 11-9729

WEBER, CARL MARIA VON
Oberon: Overture (8:43)
BSO, conductor Serge Koussevitzky
November 5, 1946. Symphony Hall
RCA Victor, producer Richard Gilbert
Matrix: D6-RC-6259/60: 1A,2
78s: 11-9951. **45s:** 49-0706. *Side 1, take 1 was rejected by Koussevitzky because of a cracked horn note (at 1:30). It was used because Victor lost the parts of take 2. See Young's discography for a more detailed discussion. The RCA Victor recording log does not specify which of two takes was used for the second side; timing the 45-rpm record suggests that it was the faster take 2.*

HAYDN, FRANZ JOSEPH
Symphony No. 94 in G "Surprise" (22:20)
BSO, conductor Serge Koussevitzky
November 5, 1946. Symphony Hall
RCA Victor, producer Richard Gilbert
Matrix: D6-RC-6261/66: 2P,1A,1,1A,1,2P
78s: M-1155 (11-9761/63). DM-1155 (11-9764/66). **45s:** WDM-1155 (49-0718/20). **LPs:** LM-28. LM-9034. LVT-1044. **CDs:** Andante AN-1180

HAYDN, FRANZ JOSEPH
Symphony No. 92 in G "Oxford" (25:47)
BSO, conductor Bruno Walter
January 21, 1947. Broadcast from Symphony Hall
BSO/IMG Artists
CDs: CB-100 (12)

BRAHMS, JOHANNES
Academic Festival Overture, op. 80 (9:37)
BSO, conductor Serge Koussevitzky
April 2, 1947. Symphony Hall
RCA Victor, producer Richard Gilbert
Matrix: D7-RC-7403/04: 2,2A
78s: 12-0377. **45s:** 49-0881. ERB-7021 (549-0040/39). **LPs:** LRM-7021. LM-2902. VCM-6174 (3). OPO-1002 (U.K.). **CDs:** Naxos 8.111283. United Artists UAR022 (4). *The following note appears on the labels of the 78 and the 45s: "Recording dedicated by Dr. Koussevitzky to the Bicentennial Anniversary of Princeton University." (Don Tait email, March 12, 2008)*

BEETHOVEN, LUDWIG VAN
Egmont, op. 84: Overture (8:15)
BSO, conductor Serge Koussevitzky
April 2, 1947. Symphony Hall
RCA Victor, producer Richard Gilbert
Matrix: D7-RC-7405/06: 1A,2A
78s: 12-0288. **45s:** 49-0304. ERB-7021 (549-0039/40). **LPs:** CAL-405. **LPs:** LRM-7021. LM-6001 (2). **CDs:** Dante LYS-383

WAGNER, RICHARD
Der fliegende Holländer: **Overture (10:05)**
BSO, conductor Serge Koussevitzky
April 4, 1947. Symphony Hall
RCA Victor, producer Richard Gilbert
Matrix: D7-RC-7407/08: 3B,2A
78s: 12-0958. **45s:** 49-0473. **LPs:** VICS-1497e (U.K.). **CDs:** Naxos 8.111283.
United Artists UAR022 (4)

WAGNER, RICHARD
Parsifal: **Act 1 Prelude (14:52)**
BSO, conductor Serge Koussevitzky
April 4, 1947. Symphony Hall
RCA Victor, producer Richard Gilbert
Matrix: D7-RC-7409/11: 1A,1A,1A
78s: M-1198 (12-0146/47). DM-1198 (12-0149/50). With the *Good Friday Music*; April 19, 1946. **CDs:** Naxos 8.111283

SCHUBERT, FRANZ
Symphony No. 5 in B♭ (24:34)
BSO, conductor Serge Koussevitzky
April 4, 1947. Symphony Hall
RCA Victor, producer Richard Gilbert
Matrix: D7-RC-7412/17: 1A,1,1B,1,1A,2B
78s: M-1215 (12-0273/75). DM-1215 (12-0276/78). **45s:** WDM-1215 (49-1091/93). **LPs:** CAL-106

BEETHOVEN, LUDWIG VAN
Symphony No. 9 in D Minor, op. 125 "Choral" (68:28)
BSO, conductor Serge Koussevitzky
Frances Yeend, soprano; Eunice Alberts, contralto; David Lloyd, tenor; James Pease, bass; Berkshire Music Festival Chorus, Robert Shaw, dir.
August 6, 1947; August 12, 1947; August 13, 1947. Koussevitzky Music Shed, Tanglewood
RCA Victor, producer Richard Gilbert
Matrix: D7-RC-7719/34: 1,1A,1A,1A,1,2,1,2P,2A,2A,3A,1,1,2,1,3
78s: M-1190 (12-0050/57). DM-1190 (12-0058/65). V-12 (18-0090/97). DV-12 (18-0098/105). **45s:** WDM-1190 (49-0518/25). **LPs:** LM-6001 (2). **CDs:** Dante LYS 191. *The choral portions of the Ninth Symphony were never satisfactorily recorded in monaural sound, but the diffuse acoustics of the open-air Tanglewood Music Shed ruin this entire recording.*

STRAVINSKY, IGOR
Octet for Wind Instruments (15:27)
Members of the BSO, conductor Leonard Bernstein
Georges Laurent, flute; Manuel Valerio, clarinet; Raymond Allard, Ernst Panen-
ka, bassoons; Georges Mager, Marcel Lafosse, trumpets; Jacob Raichman,
John Coffee, trombones
August 11, 1947. Theatre Concert Hall, Tanglewood
RCA Victor, producer Richard Gilbert
Matrix: D7-RC-7735/38: 1,1B,2A,1
78s: M-1197 (12-0139/40). **DM-**1197 (12-01445B/41B). **45s:** WDM-1197 (49-
0741/45). **LPs:** LM-1078. SMA-7014. **CDs:** 09026-68101-2. Andante
AND-1140. *From the Victor recording log: "The noises heard in all sides
are not system noises but mechanism noises from bassoons which could not
be eliminated."*

STRAVINSKY, IGOR
L'Histoire du soldat: **Suite** (27:02)
Members of the BSO, conductor Leonard Bernstein
Richard Burgin, violin; Victor Polatschek, clarinet; Raymond Allard, bassoon;
    Roger Voisin, trumpet; Jacob Raichman, trombone; Charles Smith, percus-
    sion; Georges Moleux, double bass
August 11, 1947. Theatre Concert Hall, Tanglewood
RCA Victor, producer Richard Gilbert
Matrix: D7-RC-7739/44: 1,1,1B,1,1,1
78s: M-1197 (12-0136/38). **DM-**1197 (12-0141A/45A,45B). **45s:** WDM-1197
    (49-0741/45). **LPs:** LM-1078. SMA-7014. **CDs:** 09026-68101-2. Andante
    AND-1140

RAVEL, MAURICE
Boléro (13:45)
BSO, conductor Serge Koussevitzky
August 13, 1947. Koussevitzky Music Shed, Tanglewood
RCA Victor, Richard Gilbert
Matrix: D7-RC-7745/48: 2A,1,2A,1
78s: M-1220 (12-0322/23). **DM-**1220 (12-0324/25). **V-**18 (18-0138/39).
    DV-18 (18-0140/41). **45s:** WDM-1220 (49-0150/51). **LPs:** LM-1012.
    CDs: Naxos 8.110154

BACH, JOHANN SEBASTIAN
Suite No. 1 in C, BWV 1066 (19:15)
BSO, conductor Serge Koussevitzky
August 14, 1947. Theatre Concert Hall, Tanglewood
RCA Victor, producer Richard Gilbert
Matrix: D7-RC-7749/54: 1C,1,2,1B,1A,1
78s: M-1307 (12-0925/27). **DM-**1307 (12-0930/34). **45s:** WDM-1307 (49-
    0408/12). **LPs:** LM-1079. **CDs:** Pearl GEMS-0103 (3)

BACH, JOHANN SEBASTIAN
Brandenburg Concerto No. 1 in F, BWV 1046 (21:12)
BSO, conductor Serge Koussevitzky
Richard Burgin, violin; John Holmes, Louis Speyer, and Joseph Lukatsky, oboes; Willem Valkenier and Walter Grant MacDonald, French horns
August 14, 1947. Theatre Concert Hall, Tanglewood
RCA Victor, producer Richard Gilbert
Matrix: D7-RC-7755/59 (one take made of each side)
Unreleased. Re-recorded August 17, 1949

BACH, JOHANN SEBASTIAN
Brandenburg Concerto No. 6 in B♭, BWV 1051 (20:27)
BSO, conductor Serge Koussevitzky
Joseph de Pasquale and Jean Cauhapé, violas
August 14, 1947. Theatre Concert Hall, Tanglewood
RCA Victor, producer Richard Gilbert
Matrix: D7-RC-7814/19: 1,2A,2P,2P,1,2A
78s: M-1211 (12-0243/45). DM-1211 (12-0246/48). **45s:** WDM-1211 (49-0780/82). **LPs:** LM-1063. **CDs:** Pearl GEMS-0103 (3). *Note the big jump in matrix numbers from those of the surrounding entries in this session. Thomas Tierney, Manager of Sony BMG Archives and Library, says this is not a unique occurrence, but that the reasons for it are lost to history.*

MOZART, WOLFGANG AMADEUS
Serenade No. 10 in B♭, K. 361, for 13 Wind Instruments: movements 1, 2, 3, 6, and 7 (30:57)
BSO, conductor Serge Koussevitzky
John Holmes, Louis Speyer, oboes; Victor Polatschek, Manuel Valerio, clarinets; Pasquale Cardillo, Rosario Mazzeo, basset horns; Raymond Allard, Ernst Panenka, bassoons; Boaz Piller, contra-bassoon; Willem Valkenier, Harold Meek, Walter Grant Macdonald, William Gebhardt, French horns
August 15, 1947. Theatre Concert Hall, Tanglewood
RCA Victor, producer Richard Gilbert
Matrix: D7-RC-7760/67: 1A,1A,2P,1,2,2,2A,1A
78s: M-1303 (12-0897/900). DM-1303 (12-0901/04). **45s:** WDM-1303 (49-0390/93). **LPs:** LM-1077

STRAUSS, RICHARD
Don Juan, op. 20 (17:58)
BSO, conductor Serge Koussevitzky
October 29, 1947. Symphony Hall
RCA Victor, producer Richard Gilbert
Matrix: D7-RC-7900/03: 1,1,1A, 1A
78s: M-1289 (12-0790/91). DM-1289 (12-1792/93). **45s:** WDM-1289 (49-0332/33). **LPs:** LM-1177. LVM2-7510 (2). **CDs:** Biddulph WHL-054

RAVEL, MAURICE
Ma Mère l'oye: Suite (16:50)
BSO, conductor Serge Koussevitzky
October 29, 1947. Symphony Hall
RCA Victor, producer Richard Gilbert
Matrix: D7-RC-7904/07: 1,2B,1,1
78s: M-1268 (12-0631/32). **DM-1268** (12-0633/34). **45s:** WDM-1268 (49-0774/75). **LPs:** LM-1012. **CDs:** Naxos 8.110154

PROKOFIEV, SERGEI
Symphony No. 1 in D, op. 25 "Classical" (11:24)
BSO, conductor Serge Koussevitzky
November 25, 1947. Carnegie Hall
RCA Victor, producer Richard Gilbert
Matrix: D7-RC-8022/24: 2P,2P,2P
78s: M-1241 (12-0420/21). DM-1241 (12-0422/23). **45s:** WDM-1241 (49-0652/53). **LPs:** LM-1215. SP-33-181 (LM-2651). BSO 0118.237. **CDs:** 09026-61657-2. Biddulph WHL-058. ArkivCD 61657

PROKOFIEV, SERGEI
Chout (The Tale of a Buffoon), **op. 21: Danse Finale (3:30)**
BSO, conductor Serge Koussevitzky
November 25, 1947. Carnegie Hall
RCA Victor, producer Richard Gilbert
Matrix: D7-RC-8025: 2A
78s: M-1241 (12-0421). DM-1241 (12-0422). **45s:** WDM-1241 (49-0652-B). **CDs:** 09026-61657-2. Biddulph WHL-058. ArkivCD 61657

MENDELSSOHN, FELIX
Symphony No. 4 in A, op. 90 "Italian" (25:10)
BSO, conductor Serge Koussevitzky
November 25, 1947. Carnegie Hall
RCA Victor, producer Richard Gilbert
Matrix: D7-RC-8026/31: 2,1A,1,1,1,1
78s: M-1259 (12-0558/60). DM-1259 (12-0561/63). **45s:** WDM-1259 (49-0654/56). **LPs:** LM-20. LM-1797

HANSON, HOWARD
Serenade for Solo Flute, Harp, and Strings, op. 35 (5:56)
Members of the BSO, conductor Serge Koussevitzky
Georges Laurent, flute; Bernard Zighera, harp
November 25, 1947. Carnegie Hall
RCA Victor, producer Richard Gilbert
Matrix: D7-RC-8032/33: 2,2
LPs: LM-2900 (released 1966). VCM-6174 (3). LVM2-7510 (2). PRM-234 (promotional). **CDs:** BSO-CD2 (RCA 60148-2-RC) (promotional)

VAUGHAN WILLIAMS, RALPH
Symphony No. 6 in E Minor: I. Allegro, II. Moderato (Rehearsal extract)
(7:13)
BSO, conductor Serge Koussevitzky
March 14, 1949. Broadcast from Symphony Hall
BSO/IMG Artists
CDs: CB-100 (12)

BERNSTEIN, LEONARD
The Age of Anxiety, **Symphony No. 2** (with original Epilogue) **(31:29)**
BSO, conductor Serge Koussevitzky
Leonard Bernstein, piano
April 9, 1949. Broadcast from Symphony Hall. *Premiered on April 8, 1949.*
BSO/IMG Artists
CDs: CB-100 (12)

TCHAIKOVSKY, PETER ILYICH
Symphony No. 4 in F Minor, op. 36 (40:17)
BSO, conductor Serge Koussevitzky
April 26, 1949. Symphony Hall
RCA Victor, producer Richard Mohr
Matrix: D9-RC-1708/1716: 2A,2,2,1,1,1,1,1B,1
78s: DM-1318 (12-0972/76). **45s:** WDM-1318 (49-0510/14). **LPs:** LM-1008.
*This was the first BSO performance recorded on magnetic tape, although it
was still done in four to five minute segments.*

IV. Finale: Allegro con fuoco (8:47). CDs: BSO-CD2 (RCA 60148-2-RC)
(promotional)

TCHAIKOVSKY, PETER ILYICH
Serenade in C for String Orchestra, op. 48: Waltz (3:32)
BSO, conductor Serge Koussevitzky
April 27, 1949. Symphony Hall
RCA Victor, producer Richard Mohr
Matrix: D9-RC-1717: 1B
78s: DM-1318 (12-0972). **45s:** WDM-1318 (49-0514). **LPs:** LM-2574. SRL-12-
11. **CDs:** 09026=63861-2 (2)

WAGNER, RICHARD
Lohengrin: **Act 1 Prelude (9:00)**
BSO, conductor Serge Koussevitzky
April 27, 1949. Symphony Hall
RCA Victor, producer Richard Mohr
Matrix: D9-RC-1718/19: 1,2A
78s: 12-1323. **45s:** 49-1378. **CDs:** Naxos 8.111283

WAGNER, RICHARD
Siegfried Idyll (17:49)
BSO, conductor Serge Koussevitzky
April 27, 1949. Symphony Hall
RCA Victor, producer Richard Mohr
Matrix: D9-RC-1720/23: 1A,1A,1,1C
45s: WDM-1571 (49-3414/15). **LPs:** LM-1177. **CDs:** Naxos 8.111283.
Koussevitzky's rehearsals were noted for their intensity, but he was relaxed and genial at recording sessions, for which he did not rehearse. "While we recorded it was a different Koussevitzky. He did not prepare for the recording. We had to play it as it was, after we had been playing it many times in concert. We would just start recording right away. The orchestra knew it, so there was no preparation." Attilio Poto, BSO second clarinet 1948-1950, in a May 16, 1998 interview, reported at http://www.classical .net/music/guide/society/krs/excerpt8.htm (March 9, 2008).

SATIE, ERIK
Gymnopédies No. 1 and 2 (orchestrated and renumbered by Debussy) (3:09/3:47)
BSO, conductor Serge Koussevitzky
April 27, 1949. Symphony Hall
RCA Victor, producer Richard Mohr
Matrix: D9-RC-1724/25: 2,1B
78s: 12-1060. **45s:** 49-0771. ERA-195 (side 2). **LPs:** CAL-376. SP-33-181 (LM-2651)

COWELL, HENRY
Hymn and Fuguing Tune No. 2 (7:17)
BSO, conductor Serge Koussevitzky
April 27, 1949. Symphony Hall. *The world premiere was on March 29, 1946.*
RCA Victor, producer Richard Mohr
Matrix: D9-RC-1726/27: 1,1
LPs: CRI-SD 248 (released 1978). **CDs:** BSO-CD2 (RCA 60148-2-RC) (promotional)

TCHAIKOVSKY, PETER ILYICH
Serenade in C for String Orchestra, op. 48 (29:48)
BSO, conductor Serge Koussevitzky
August 16, 1949. Theatre Concert Hall, Tanglewood
RCA Victor, producer Richard Mohr
Matrix: D9-RC-1870/74; 1889/90: 2,1,2D,1A,2,1,1
78s: DM-1346 (12-1070/73). **45s:** WDM-1346 (49-0804/07). **LPs:** LM-1056. LVT-1027. *The filler on sides 8 of DM-1346 and WDM-1346 is Mozart's Overture to Der Schauspieldirektor (see below).*

III: Elegie (9:18): **45s:** 49-0807

IV: Finale: *Tema Russo* (7:15): **78s:** ERA-7 (side 2). WEPR-7 (side 2)

MOZART, WOLFGANG AMADEUS
Symphony No. 36 in C, K. 425 "Linz" (23:08)
BSO, conductor Serge Koussevitzky
August 16, 1949. Theatre Concert Hall, Tanglewood
RCA Victor, producer Richard Mohr
Matrix: D9-RC-1891/96: 1,2B,1A,2A,2,2
78s: DM-1354 (12-1096/98). **45s:** WDM-1354 (49-0904/06). **LPs:** LM-1141

BACH, JOHANN SEBASTIAN
Brandenburg Concerto No. 1 in F, BWV 1046 (22:08)
BSO, conductor Serge Koussevitzky
Richard Burgin, violin; John Holmes, Louis Speyer, and Joseph Lukatsky, oboes; Willem Valkenier and Walter Grant MacDonald, French horns
August 17, 1949. Theatre Concert Hall, Tanglewood
RCA Victor, producer Richard Mohr
Matrix: D9-RC-1897/1905: 1,1,1B,1,2
78s: DM-1362 (12-1111/13). **45s:** WDM-1362 (49-0939/41). **LPs:** LM-1063.
   CDs: Pearl GEMS-0103 (3)

MOZART, WOLFGANG AMADEUS
Idomeneo, rè di Creta, **K. 366: Overture (4:26)**
BSO, conductor Serge Koussevitzky
August 17, 1949. Theatre Concert Hall, Tanglewood
RCA Victor, producer Richard Mohr
Matrix: D9-RC-1906: 1
78s: DM-1369 (12-1134). **45s:** WDM-1369 (49-1011). ERB-7021 (549-0039).
   LPs: LRM-7021. *On the initial issues of ERB-7021 and LRM-7021, RCA Victor mistakenly substituted the Overture to* Der Schauspieldirektor *(below) for that of* Idomeneo. *Side 2 has E3RL-4732-1S etched in the lead-out area. The mistake was then corrected: A later pressing, E3RL-4732-5S, reinstates* Idomeneo. *The confusion may have been abetted by both performances running exactly 4 minutes and 26 seconds.*

MOZART, WOLFGANG AMADEUS
La clemenza di Tito, **K. 621: Overture (4:18)**
BSO, conductor Serge Koussevitzky
August 17, 1949. Theatre Concert Hall, Tanglewood
RCA Victor, producer Richard Mohr
Matrix: D9-RC-1907: 2
78s: DM-1362 (12-1111). **45s:** WDM-1362 (49-0941). ERB-7021 (549-0040).
   LPs: LRM-7021

MOZART, WOLFGANG AMADEUS
Der Schauspieldirektor (The Impresario), K. 486: Overture (4:26)
BSO, conductor Serge Koussevitzky
August 17, 1949. Theatre Concert Hall, Tanglewood
RCA Victor, producer Richard Mohr
Matrix: D9-RC-1908: 2
78s: DM-1346 (12-1070-B). **45s:** WDM-1346 (49-0804). ERB-7021 (early
  pressing). **LPs:** LRM-7021 (early pressing). *See the note to* Idomeneo,
  above.

MESSIAEN, OLIVIER
Turangalila-symphonie: VI. *Jardin de sommeil d'Amour* (Rehearsal extract)
  (6:37)
BSO, conductor Leonard Bernstein
Ginette Martenot, ondes martenot; Yvonne Loriod, piano
November 28, 1949. Broadcast from Symphony Hall. *The premiere followed on
  December 2, 1949.*
BSO/IMG Artists
CDs: CB-100 (12). *Ginette Martenot was the sister of Maurice Martenot, who
  invented the electronic instrument in 1928.*

BEETHOVEN, LUDWIG VAN
Symphony No. 7 in A, op. 92 (35:42)
BSO, conductor Charles Munch
December 19, 1949. Symphony Hall
RCA, producer Richard Mohr
Matrix: D9-RC-2108/16: 1A,1,1A,1A,2,1,1A,1A,1
78s: DM-1360 (12-1123/27). **45s:** WDM-1360 (49-0951/55). **LPs:** LM-1034.
  CDs: RCA Japan BVCC-38427 (88697-04813-2). Tahra 528/529 (2)

BERLIOZ, HECTOR
Béatrice et Bénédict: Overture (7:17)
BSO, conductor Charles Munch
December 20, 1949. Symphony Hall
RCA, producer Richard Mohr
Matrix: D9-RC-2100/01: 1A,1
78s: 12-3078. **45s:** 49-3078 (two sides). ERA-68 (side 1). WDM-1700 (49-
  3768/67). **LPs:** LM-1700. **CDs:** 09026-63861-2 (2). 82876-60393-2 (10)

SCHUBERT, FRANZ
Symphony No. 2 in B♭ (25:32)
BSO, conductor Charles Munch
December 20, 1949. Symphony Hall
RCA, producer Richard Mohr
Matrix: D9-RC-2102/07: 1,1,1,1,1,1
78s: DM-1448 (12-3014/16). **45s:** WDM-1448 (49-3014/16). **LPs:** LM-41. LM-
  9032. VIC-1018 (U.K.)

BEETHOVEN, LUDWIG VAN
Gratulations-Menuet in E♭, WoO 3 (1822) (3:25)
BSO, conductor Charles Munch
December 20, 1949. Symphony Hall
RCA, producer Richard Mohr
Matrix: D9-RC-2117:1
78s: DM-1360 (12-1123-B). **45s:** WDM-1360 (49-0951). **CDs:** Tahra 528/529 (2)

BRAHMS, JOHANNES
Symphony No. 4 in E Minor, op. 98 (37:30)
BSO, conductor Charles Munch
April 10, 1950; April 11, 1950. Symphony Hall
Matrix: E0-RC-869/876: 1,2,1,1,1,?,1,1
RCA, producer Richard Mohr
78s: DM-1399 (12-1228/31). **45s:** WDM-1399 (49-1261/64). **LPs:** LM-1086. *In his Koussevitzky discography, Edward D. Young lists matrix prefixes EO- (the letter O) for recordings made in 1950; that digit represents the year, so the prefix should be E0- (the number zero). Lawrence H. Jones agrees, but points out (email September 24, 2007) that a few LP issues (LM-49, Haydn's Symphony No. 104, for example) clearly show the letter O. Jones hypothesizes that "this is simply a typesetting error by someone who was preparing the labels and did not understand the meaning of what he/she was typing and misread zero for O in whatever paperwork was presented for typesetting." From this time, RCA assigned take number one no matter how many takes of each side were recorded. These 78s were published even though three sides ran well over five minutes.*

HAYDN, FRANZ JOSEPH
Symphony No. 104 in D "London" (24:55)
BSO, conductor Charles Munch
April 10, 1950; April 11, 1950. Symphony Hall
RCA, producer Richard Mohr
Matrix: E0-RC-877/882: 1,1,1,1,1,1
78s: DM-1476 (12-3091/93). **45s:** WDM-1476 (49-3091/93). **LPs:** LVT-1044. LM-49. LM-9034. **CDs:** RCA Japan BVCC-38424 (88697-04812-2)

RAVEL, MAURICE
La Valse (10:18)
BSO, conductor Charles Munch
April 11, 1950. Symphony Hall
RCA, producer Richard Mohr
Matrix: E0-RC-883/884: 1,1
78s: 12-1207. **45s:** 49-1213. WDM-1700 (49-3768/69). ERB-7016 (549-0030/29). **LPs:** LM-1700. LRM-7016. LM-6113 (3). LM-6129 (3). PR-133 (promotional). *After the end of the 78-rpm era, matrix numbers took on new meanings, applying to issues rather than recordings. Thus we do not include matrix numbers for any recording not issued on 78s.*

PROKOFIEV, SERGEI
Peter and the Wolf, op. 67 (25:27)
BSO, conductor Serge Koussevitzky
Eleanor Roosevelt, narrator
August 11, 1950. Theatre Concert Hall, Tanglewood
RCA Victor. No producer is documented for the 1950 Tanglewood sessions.
Matrix: E0-RC-1708/13: 1,1,1,1,1,1. *Beginning with this recording, magnetic tape replaced waxes as RCA Victor's primary recording medium. From this point on, 78-rpm matrix numbers refer to studio dubbings from the tapes.*
78s: DM-1437 (12-3025/27). **45s:** WDM-1437 (49-3025/27). **LPs:** LM-45.
CDs: Naxos 8.111290. *All three issues are extremely rare: Koussevitzky had made a very popular recording with Richard Hale (April 13, 1939). Recordings issued on 78s after the LP era was under way tended to be ignored by the buying public. At the beginning of the LP era, ten-inch discs were used for shorter works, but by the time LM-45 appeared, their sales had diminished; they generally sold for only a dollar less than twelve-inch records, and the public wanted to take advantage of the LP to get as much music as possible for the cost of one disc. Finally, Mrs. Roosevelt—the widow of President Franklin D. Roosevelt—was not then the highly revered figure she has since become.*

HAYDN, FRANZ JOSEPH
Symphony No. 92 in G "Oxford" (26:37)
BSO, conductor Serge Koussevitzky
August 14, 1950. Theatre Concert Hall, Tanglewood
RCA Victor. No producer is documented for the 1950 Tanglewood sessions.
Matrix: E0-RC-1714/19: 1,1,1,1,1,1
78s: DM-1454 (12-3028/30). **45s:** WDM-1454 (49-3028/30). **LPs:** LM-1102. *I am not sure that DM-1454 was issued.*

MOZART, WOLFGANG AMADEUS
Serenade in G, K. 525 "Eine kleine Nachtmusik" (12:28)
BSO, conductor Serge Koussevitzky
August 15, 1950. Theatre Concert Hall, Tanglewood
RCA Victor. No producer is documented for the 1950 Tanglewood sessions.
Matrix: E0-RC-1722/25: 1,1,1,1. *Recorded from 10:00 AM to 11:39 AM.*
78s: DM-1451 (12-3020/21). **45s:** WDM-1451 (49-3020/21). **LPs:** LM-1102.

IV: Rondo Allegro (2:20). CDs: BSO-CD2 (RCA 60148-2-RC) (promotional)

MOZART, LEOPOLD
Cassation in G: movements 3, 4, and 7 (once known as Haydn's "Toy Symphony") **(8:00)**
BSO, conductor Serge Koussevitzky
August 15, 1950. Theatre Concert Hall, Tanglewood
RCA Victor. No producer is documented for the 1950 Tanglewood sessions.
Matrix: E0-RC-1720/21: 1,1. *Recorded from 11:47 AM to 12:42 PM.*
78s: 12-3013. **45s:** 49-3013. ERA-7. WEPR-7. **CDs:** 09026-60121-2

SIBELIUS, JEAN
Symphony No. 2 in D, op. 43 (41:34)
BSO, conductor Serge Koussevitzky
November 29, 1950. Symphony Hall
RCA, producer Richard Mohr
Matrix: E0-RC-1950/59: 1,1,1,1,1,1,1,1,1,1
45s: WDM-1602 (49-3436/40). **LPs:** LM-1172. VIC-1510. VIC-1186 (U.K.).
AGM1-5232. **CDs:** Naxos 8.111290. United Artists UAR022 (4)

GRIEG, EDVARD
Elegiac Melody, op. 34, no. 2 "The Last Spring" (5:44)
BSO, conductor Serge Koussevitzky
November 29, 1950. Symphony Hall
RCA, producer Richard Mohr
Matrix: E0-RC-1960: 1
45s: ERA-195 (side 1) released 1954. **CDs:** 09026-61826-2. Naxos 8.111290.
ArkivCD 61826

RAVEL, MAURICE
Rapsodie espagnole **(14:30)**
BSO, conductor Charles Munch
December 26, 1950. Symphony Hall
RCA, producer Richard Mohr
45s: WDM-1700 (49-3765/67). ERB-7016 (549-0029/30). **LPs:** LM-1700.
LRM-7016

HANDEL, GEORGE FRIDERIC
Water Music: Suite (arr. Hamilton Harty) **(14:25)**
BSO, conductor Charles Munch
December 26, 1950; December 27, 1950. Symphony Hall
RCA, producer Richard Mohr
45s: WDM-7009 (49-3911/13). **LPs:** LM-7009. PR-133 (promotional). **CDs:**
RCA Japan BVCC-38424 (88697-04812-2)

HAYDN, FRANZ JOSEPH
Symphony No. 103 in E♭ "Drumroll" (26:32)
BSO, conductor Charles Munch
December 26, 1950; December 27, 1950. Symphony Hall
RCA, producer Richard Mohr
45s: WDM-1621 (49-3695/96). **LPs:** LM-1200. **CDs:** RCA Japan BVCC-38424
(88697-04812-2). *The four sides of WDM-1621 average nearly seven minutes each, even though this was before RCA coined the phrase "extended-
play 45s" and switched to 549 prefixes.*

LALO, EDOUARD
Le Roi d'Ys: **Overture (9:23)**
BSO, conductor Charles Munch
December 27, 1950. Symphony Hall
RCA, producer Richard Mohr
Matrix: E0-RC-2010/11: 1A,? (78-rpm test pressing of side 1 in BSO Archives)
45s: WDM-1700 (49-3766/65). **LPs:** LM-1700

BEETHOVEN, LUDWIG VAN
Symphony No. 1 in C, op. 21 (24:49)
BSO, conductor Charles Munch
December 27, 1950. Symphony Hall
RCA, producer Richard Mohr
Matrix: E0 RC 2004/09: 1,1,1,1,1,1 (78-rpm test pressings in BSO Archives)
45s: WDM-1622 (49-3698/99). **LPs:** LM-1200. **CDs:** 09026-61399-2

BRUCH, MAX
Concerto for Violin and Orchestra No. 1 in G Minor, op. 26 (22:40)
BSO, conductor Charles Munch
Yehudi Menuhin, violin
January 18, 1951. Carnegie Hall
RCA. The producer of this session has not been identified.
45s: WDM-1547 (49-3377/79). **LPs:** LM-122. LM-1797

SAINT-SAËNS, CAMILLE
La Princesse jaune, op. 30: **Overture (6:10)**
BSO, conductor Charles Munch
January 18, 1951. Carnegie Hall
RCA. The producer of this session has not been identified.
45s: ERA-68 (side 2). WDM-1700 (49-3769-B). **LPs:** LM-1700. **CDs:** EMI 5-
    75477-2 (2)

SCHUMANN, ROBERT
Genoveva, op. 81: **Overture (8:51)**
BSO, conductor Charles Munch
January 18, 1951. Carnegie Hall
RCA. The producer of this session has not been identified.
45s: WDM-7009 (49-3912/11). **LPs:** LM-7009. PR-133 (promotional).
    CDs: 09026-60682-2

STRAVINSKY, IGOR
Le Sacre du printemps (1913-1921 version) **(31:18)**
BSO, conductor Pierre Monteux
January 28, 1951. Symphony Hall
RCA, producer Richard Mohr
45s: WDM-1548 (49-3380/83). **LPs:** LM-1149. AGM1-5239. **CDs:** 6529-2-RG.
    09026-61898-2. 09026-61893-2 (15). 82876-62314-2

SCHUMANN, ROBERT
Symphony No. 1 in B♭, op. 38 "Spring" (29:08)
BSO, conductor Charles Munch
April 25, 1951. Symphony Hall
RCA, producer Richard Mohr
45s: WDM-1608 (49-3647/50). **LPs:** LM-1190

MOZART, WOLFGANG AMADEUS
Le Nozze di Figaro, **K. 492: Overture (4:22)**
BSO, conductor Charles Munch
April 25, 1951. Symphony Hall
RCA, producer Richard Mohr
45s: WDM-7009 (49-3913). **LPs:** LM-7009

BRAHMS, JOHANNES
Concerto for Piano and Orchestra No. 2 in B♭, op. 83 (43:31)
BSO, conductor Charles Munch
Artur Rubinstein, piano
August 11, 1952. Symphony Hall
RCA, producer Richard Mohr
45s: WDM-1728 (49-3988/91). **LPs:** LM-1728. **CDs:** 09026-63022-2. **Two-track tape:** CC-6. TC-6 (monaural)

ROUSSEL, ALBERT
Bacchus et Ariane, **op. 43: Suite No. 2 (16:03)**
BSO, conductor Charles Munch
October 27, 1952; March 29, 1953. Symphony Hall
RCA, producer Richard Mohr
45s: WDM-1741 (49-4069/67). **LPs:** LM-1741. LM-6113 (3). **CDs:** 60469-2-RG. 74321-84601-2. *The reverse order of record numbers in the 45-rpm set means that this work appears on the "B" sides, starting with 49-4069, continuing on 49-4068, and finishing on 49-4067.*

HONEGGER, ARTHUR
Symphony No. 5 "Di tre re" (23:19)
BSO, conductor Charles Munch
October 27, 1952. Symphony Hall. *World premiere given on March 9, 1951.*
RCA, producer Richard Mohr
45s: WDM-1741 (49-4066/69). **LPs:** LM-1741. **CDs:** 09026-60685-2. ArkivCD 60685

RAVEL, MAURICE
Pavane pour une infante défunte **(5:19)**
BSO, conductor Charles Munch
James Stagliano, French horn
October 27, 1952. Symphony Hall
RCA, producer Richard Mohr
45s: WDM-1741 (49-4066). ERB-7016 (549-0029). **LPs:** LM-1741. LRM-7016

LISZT, FRANZ
Les Préludes (15:31)
BSO, conductor Pierre Monteux
December 8, 1952. Carnegie Hall
RCA, producer John Pfeiffer
45s: ERB-5 (549-5043/44). **LPs:** LM-1775. LM-6129 (3). OPO-1002 (U.K.).
    CDs: 09026-61890-2. 09026-61893-2 (15)

SCRIABIN, ALEXANDER
Symphony No. 4, op. 54 "Poem of Ecstasy" (19:21)
BSO, conductor Pierre Monteux
Roger Voisin, trumpet
December 8, 1952. Carnegie Hall
RCA, producer John Pfeiffer
LPs: LM-1775. **CDs:** 09026-61890-2. 09026-61893-2 (15)

BERLIOZ, HECTOR
Roméo et Juliette, op. 17 (91:20)
BSO, conductor Charles Munch
Margaret Roggero, mezzo-soprano; Leslie Chabay, tenor; Yi-Kwei Sze, bass;
    Harvard Glee Club and Radcliffe Choral Society, G. Wallace Woodward,
    dir.
February 22, 1953; February 23, 1953. Symphony Hall
RCA, producer Richard Mohr
45s: WDM-6011 (49-4138/45). **LPs:** LM-6011 (2). **CDs:** 09026-60681-2 (2).
    09026-68444-2 (8). 82876-60393-2 (10). *Although RCA had not yet an-*
    nounced "extended-play" 45s, nor adopted the 549- prefix used for them,
    this WDM set includes sides as long as 7 minutes, 55 seconds.

TCHAIKOVSKY, PETER ILYICH
Concerto for Violin and Orchestra in D, op. 35 (31:24)
BSO, conductor Charles Munch
Nathan Milstein, violin
March 29, 1953. Symphony Hall
RCA, producer Richard Mohr
LPs: LM-1760. VIC-1003 (U.K.). **CDs:** RCA Japan BVCC-37348. Naxos
    8.111259

HONEGGER, ARTHUR
Symphony No. 2 for String Orchestra (21:00)
BSO, conductor, Charles Munch
March 29, 1953. Symphony Hall
RCA, producer Richard Mohr
LPs: LM-1868. **CDs:** 09026-60685-2. ArkivCD 60685

MOZART, WOLFGANG AMADEUS
Concerto for Piano and Orchestra No. 12 in A, K. 414 (23:48)
BSO, conductor Pierre Monteux
Lili Kraus, piano
April 12, 1953. Symphony Hall
RCA, producer Richard Mohr
LPs: LM-1783. **CDs:** RCA Japan BVCC-37345. Urania SP-4228

MOZART, WOLFGANG AMADEUS
Concerto for Piano and Orchestra No. 18 in Bb, K. 456 (28:23)
BSO, conductor Pierre Monteux
Lili Kraus, piano
April 13, 1953. Symphony Hall
RCA, producer Richard Mohr
LPs: LM-1783. **CDs:** Japan BVCC-37345. Urania SP-4228

STRAUSS, RICHARD
Don Quixote, op. 35 **(41:09)**
BSO, conductor Charles Munch
Gregor Piatigorsky, cello; Joseph de Pasquale, viola; Richard Burgin, violin
August 17, 1953. Symphony Hall
RCA, producer Richard Mohr
LPs: LM-1781. **CDs:** 09026-61485-2. ArkivCD 61485. RCA Japan BVCC-
38457 (88697-05379-2). **Two-track tape:** BC-3 (monaural)

PROKOFIEV, SERGEI
The Love for Three Oranges: **Scherzo (2:12); March (1:45)**
BSO, conductor Charles Munch
November 28, 1953. Broadcast from Symphony Hall
BSO/IMG Artists
CDs: CB-100 (12)

DELIBES, LÉO
Coppélia: **Suite (25:34)**
Members of the BSO (strings: 8-6-4-4-2), conductor Pierre Monteux
Alfred Krips, violin; Manuel Valerio, clarinet
December 2, 1953; December 4, 1953. Manhattan Center, New York City
RCA, producer Richard Mohr
LPs: LM-1913. LM-6113 (3). **CDs:** 09026-61975-2. 09026-61893-2 (15). **Two-
track tape:** CC-30 (monaural)

Prelude: Mazurka (5:27). CDs: 09026-68524-2 (2). ArkivCD 68524 (2).
09026-63861-2 (2). *This excerpt represents RCA's earliest surviving stereo
recording, made with an experimental two-microphone set-up supervised by
John Pfeiffer. 09026-68524-2, produced in 1996, is called "The Age of Living Stereo: A Tribute to John Pfeiffer."*

AUBER, DANIEL FRANÇOIS
La Muette de Portici: **Overture** *(7:40)*
BSO, conductor Charles Munch
December 24, 1953. Broadcast from Symphony Hall
BSO/IMG Artists
CDs: CB-100 (12)

DELIBES, LÉO
Sylvia: **Suite (26:31)**
Members of the BSO (strings 8-6-4-4-2), conductor Pierre Monteux
Alfred Krips, violin
December 30, 1953; December 31, 1953. Symphony Hall
RCA, producer Richard Mohr
LPs: LM-1913. LM-6113 (3). Franklin Mint Record Society FM-1031/32 (2).
CDs: 09026-61975-2. 09026-61893-2 (15)). **Two-track tape:** CC-30 (monaural)

BERLIOZ, HECTOR
La Damnation de Faust, op. 24 **(121:28)**
BSO, conductor Charles Munch
Suzanne Danco, soprano (Marguerite); David Poleri, tenor (Faust); Martial
     Singher, baritone (Mephistopheles); Donald Gramm, bass (Brander); Har-
     vard Glee Club and Radcliffe Choral Society, G. Wallace Woodward, dir.
February 21, 1954; February 22, 1954. Symphony Hall.
     April 7, 1954. Manhattan Center, New York City
RCA, producers Richard Mohr and John Pfeiffer
LPs: LM-6114 (3). AVL2-0679. **CDs:** 7940-2-RG (2). 09026-68444-2 (8).
     82876-60393-2 (10)

Minuet of the Will-o'-the-Wisps **(4:58).** *Dance of the Sylphs* **(2:18).** *Rákóczy
     March* **(4:33). 45s:** ERA-250

"Dans mon coeur retentit" (Ride to the Abyss; Pandemonium, in Heaven)
     (13:42). LPs: SP-13-181

*These sessions were recorded both in monaural sound and in 3-track stereo, of
     which only the following excerpt survives:*
"Dans mon coeur retentit" (Ride to the Abyss; Pandemonium: excerpt) **(5:17)**
CDs: 09026-68524-2 (2). ArkivCD 68524 (2). *"The Age of Living Stereo: A
     Tribute to John Pfeiffer."*

BEETHOVEN, LUDWIG VAN
**Concerto for Violin and Orchestra in D, op. 61: I. Allegro ma non troppo
     (24:26)**
BSO, conductor Charles Munch
Zino Francescatti, violin
April 23, 1954. Symphony Hall (live)
BSO/TDK
CDs: "Tanglewood 98"

DEBUSSY, CLAUDE
La Mer **(22:41)**
BSO, conductor Pierre Monteux
July 19, 1954. Symphony Hall
RCA, producer John Pfeiffer
45s: ERC-1939 (549-5201/03). **LPs:** LM-1939. Quintessence PMC-7027 (fake
stereo). **CDs:** 09026-61890-2. 09026-61893-2 (15)

1. *From Dawn to Noon on the Sea* (excerpt, in stereo) **(4:22)**
CDs: 09026-68524-2 (2). ArkivCD 68524 (2). *"The Age of Living Stereo: A
Tribute to John Pfeiffer."*

MENOTTI, GIAN CARLO
Concerto for Violin and Orchestra in A Minor (27:11)
BSO, conductor Charles Munch
Tossy Spivakovsky, violin
November 8, 1954. Symphony Hall
RCA, producer Richard Mohr
LPs: LM-1868. **CDs:** RCA Japan BVCC-384679 (88697-04828-2)

BERLIOZ, HECTOR
Symphonie fantastique, op. 14 **(46:40)**
BSO, conductor Charles Munch
November 14, 1954; November 15, 1954. Symphony Hall
RCA, producers Richard Mohr and John Pfeiffer
LPs: LM-1900. VICS-1415 (U.K.), *first stereo LP issue*. AGL1-2706. AGL1-
5203. Classic Records LSC-1900. **CDs:** 6210-2-RC (2). 09026-61329-2.
09026-68444-2 (8). 09026-68979-2. 82876-60393-2 (10). **SACDs:** 82876-
67899-2. **Two-track tape:** GCS-6. *Despite a listing in Schwann catalogues,
RCA never issued an LSC-1900. Papers in the Sony BMG Archives state
"LSC was withdrawn." Manager Thomas Tierney says that always means
"withdrawn from release." Those who claim to have seen a copy probably
mistook the Classics Records LSC-1900 issue for an RCA.*

SAINT-SAËNS, CAMILLE
Concerto for Piano and Orchestra No. 4 in C Minor, op. 44 (24:49)
BSO, conductor Charles Munch
Alexander Brailowsky, piano
November 24, 1954. Symphony Hall
RCA, producer Richard Mohr
LPs: LM-1871. **CDs:** 09026-68165-2 (2). **Two-track tape:** AC-23 (monaural)

CHOPIN, FRÉDÉRIC
Concerto for Piano and Orchestra No. 2 in F Minor, op. 21 (29:10)
BSO, conductor Charles Munch
Alexander Brailowsky, piano
November 29, 1954. Symphony Hall
RCA, producer Richard Mohr
LPs: LM-1871. **CDs:** 09026-61656-2

HUMAN RIGHTS DAY CONCERT
HANDEL *Water Music*: **Suite** (arr. Hamilton Harty)
HAYDN *The Creation:* **"With Verdure Clad"** (Irmgard Seefried, soprano)
R. STRAUSS *Allerseelen. Wiegenlied. Morgen. Ständchen* (Seefried)
BERLIOZ *Symphonie fantastique*, op. 14
BSO, conductor Charles Munch
December 12 1954. United Nations General Assembly, New York City
United Nations
LPs: GRC-2577 (2). *The recording was distributed overseas.*

RESPIGHI, OTTORINO
The Pines of Rome (19:05)
BSO, conductor Guido Cantelli
December 24, 1954. Broadcast from Symphony Hall
BSO/IMG Artists
CDs: CB-100 (12)

RAVEL, MAURICE
Daphnis et Chloé (54:29)
BSO, conductor Charles Munch
New England Conservatory and Alumni Chorus, Lorna Cooke DeVaron, dir.
January 23, 1955; January 24, 1955. Symphony Hall
RCA, producer John Pfeiffer
LPs: LM/LSC-1893. Classic Records LSC-1893. Chesky RC-15. **CDs:** 60469-2-RG. 09026-61846-2. 09026-68081-2. **SACDs:** 82876-61388-2. *Early pressings of LM-1893 come in a heavy cardboard folder with a multi-page booklet containing five "Original drawings by Andy Warhol." A planned three-sided stereo-LP release (LSC-6064) was withdrawn, reinstated, and then "cancelled permanently" in 1960. LSC-1893 was issued in its place.*

Suite No. 1 (12:16). **Suite No. 2** (17:00). **LPs:** VIC/VICS-1271. VIC/VICS-1297. *The U.K. issue of VICS-1297 has the complete ballet.*
Suite No. 2. LPs: VICS-1674

TCHAIKOVSKY, PETER ILYICH
Symphony No. 6 in B Minor, op. 74 "Pathétique" (44:24)
BSO, conductor Pierre Monteux
January 26, 1955. Symphony Hall
RCA, producer John Pfeiffer
LPs: LM-1901. LM/LSC-6902 (7). VIC/VICS-1009. AGL1-1522. Time-Life Records STL-541 (4). **CDs:** 09026-61901-2 (2). 09026-61893-2 (15). **SACDs:** 82876-61397-2. **Two-track tape:** GCS-5

TCHAIKOVSKY, PETER ILYICH
Romeo and Juliet (fantasy-overture) (20:15)
BSO, conductor Igor Markevitch
March 19, 1955. Broadcast from Symphony Hall
BSO/IMG Artists
CDs: CB-100 (12)

DEBUSSY, CLAUDE
La Damoiselle élue **(19:24)**
BSO, conductor Charles Munch
Victoria de los Angeles, soprano; Carol Smith, contralto; Radcliffe Choral So-
ciety, G. Wallace Woodworth, dir.
April 11, 1955. Symphony Hall
RCA, producer Richard Mohr
LPs: LM-1907. AVM1-1412. **CDs:** 7940-2-RG. Testament SBT-3203 (3). RCA
Japan BVCC-38459 (88697-04823-2)

BERLIOZ, HECTOR
Les Nuits d'été, op. 7 **(30:06)**
BSO, conductor Charles Munch
Victoria de los Angeles, soprano
April 12, 1955; April 13, 1955. Symphony Hall
RCA, producer Richard Mohr
LPs: LM-1907. AVM1-1412. **CDs:** 09026-60681-2 (2). 09026-68444-2 (8).
82876-60393-2 (10). Testament SBT-3203 (3)

BEETHOVEN, LUDWIG VAN
Symphony No. 5 in C Minor, op. 67 (31:49)
BSO, conductor Charles Munch
May 2, 1955. Symphony Hall
RCA, producers Richard Mohr and John Pfeiffer
45s: ERB-60 (549-5178/79). **LPs:** LM-1923. VIC/VICS-1035. AGL1-1268.
CDs: 6803-2-RG. 09026-61551-2. **SACDs:** 82876-67898-2. **Two-track
tape:** ECS-7. *An RCA Victor promotional record of excerpts, SRL-12-11,
includes the start of this recording. Before it is faded out, one hears that the
first-movement repeat is taken, which does not appear on any other issue.
(Thanks to Lawrence H. Jones). One assumes it was added electronically.*

SCHUBERT, FRANZ
Symphony no. 8 in B Minor "Unfinished" (23:58)
BSO, conductor Charles Munch
May 2, 1955. Symphony Hall
RCA, producers Richard Mohr and John Pfeiffer
45s: ERB-61 (549-5180/81). **LPs:** LM-1923. VIC/VICS-1035. AGL1-1268.
CDs: 6803-2-RG. 60792-2-RV. 09026-61551-2. **SACDs:** 88697-04603-2.
Two-track tape: CCS-13

DEBUSSY, CLAUDE
Nocturnes for Orchestra: *Nuages. Fêtes. Sirènes* (22:44)
BSO, conductor Pierre Monteux
Women of the Berkshire Festival Chorus, rehearsed and prepared by Iva Dee
  Hiatt in association with Hugh Ross
August 15, 1955. Symphony Hall
RCA, producer John Pfeiffer
45s: ERC-1939 (549-5201/03). **LPs:** LM-1939. LM-2651. VIC/VICS-1027.
  Franklin Mint Record Society FM-1031/32 (2). Quintessence PMC-7027.
  CDs: 09026-61900-2. 09026-61893-2 (15). EMI/IMG Artists 5 75474 2 (2).
  ArkivCD 61900. **Two-track tape:** CCS-12

Nuages. Fêtes (13:04). **LPs:** SP-33-181 (LM-2651)

BEETHOVEN, LUDWIG VAN
Symphony No. 6 in F, op. 68 "Pastoral" (36:54)
BSO, conductor Charles Munch
August 16, 1955. Symphony Hall
RCA, producer John Pfeiffer
LPs: LM-1997. AGL1-2442 (first stereo release). **CDs:** RCA Japan BVCC-
  38427. **SACDs:** 82876-67898-2

TCHAIKOVSKY, PETER ILYICH
Symphony No. 4 in F Minor, op. 36 (42:55)
BSO, conductor Charles Munch
November 7, 1955. Symphony Hall
RCA, producer Richard Mohr
LPs: LM-1953. VIC/VICS-1100. **CDs:** RCA Japan BVCC-38451 (88697-
  04820-2)

BEETHOVEN, LUDWIG VAN
Fidelio, op. 72: Overture (6:31)
BSO, conductor Charles Munch
November 7, 1955. Symphony Hall
RCA, producer Richard Mohr
LPs: LM-2015. VICS-1471. VIC/VICS-6003 (2)

BEETHOVEN, LUDWIG VAN
Concerto for Violin and Orchestra in D, op. 61 (37:49)
BSO, conductor Charles Munch
Jascha Heifetz, violin
November 27, 1955; November 28, 1955. Symphony Hall
RCA, producer John Pfeiffer
45s: SEP-11 (549-5256/58). **LPs:** LM/LSC-1992. SLP-11 *(see note under* La
  Valse, *December 5, 1955)*. LSC-3317. VCS-7087 (2). CRL6-0720 (6).
  AGL1-5242. **CDs:** RCD1-5402. 6475. 09026-61742-2. 09026-61779-2 (5).
  09026-68980-2. **SACDs:** 82876-61391-2. **Two-track tape:** FCS-24

BRAHMS, JOHANNES
Tragic Overture, op. 81 (12:22)
BSO, conductor Charles Munch
December 5, 1955. Symphony Hall
RCA, producer Richard Mohr
LPs: LM-1959. AGL1-2702. **CDs:** 09026-60682-2. ArkivCD 60682. RCA Japan BVCC-38447 (74321-56856-2)

BRAHMS, JOHANNES
Symphony No. 2 in D, op. 73 (37:05)
BSO, conductor Charles Munch
December 5, 1955. Symphony Hall
RCA, producer Richard Mohr
LPs: LM-1959. AGL1-2702. **CDs:** 09026-60682-2. ArkivCD 60682. **Two-track tape:** FCS-14

RAVEL, MAURICE
La Valse (11:27)
BSO, conductor Charles Munch
December 5, 1955. Symphony Hall
RCA, producer Richard Mohr
45s: ERC-1984 (549-5223-B/5222-B) and (549-5227-B/5226-B). SEP-7 (549-5241-B/5245-B). **LPs:** LM/LSC-1984. SLP-7. VIC/VICS-1323. VICS-1674. "From the TV Series" (promotional). **CDs:** 09026-61956-2. **SACDs:** 82876-66374-2. **Two-track tape:** AC-21 (monaural). CCS-36. *RCA first issued ERC-1984 with record numbers 549-5222/25, but then corrected the record numbers to 549-5226/29. On the blue card in the Sony BMG Archives for 549-5226, the six is written in by hand over a printed two; both labels (459-5222 and 49-5226) are glued to that card's reverse side, with the earlier one crossed out. The same set was then issued on the RCA "spinach series" (apparently an internal company term) as SEP-7, which sold for a dollar less. To add to the confusion, the record numbers in SEP-7 are not consecutive and are out of sequence (549-5241, -5245, -5247, -5248). A final inanity is that SEP 7 and ERC 1984 both appear on the covers of some issues, as do SLP-7 and LM-1984. The Heifetz/Munch Beethoven Violin Concerto (November 27, 1955) is the only other BSO recording in the spinach series.*

CHAUSSON, ERNEST
Poème, op. 25 (15:31)
BSO, conductor Charles Munch
David Oistrakh, violin
December 14, 1955. Symphony Hall
RCA, producer John Pfeiffer
LPs: LM-1988. VIC/VICS-1058. **CDs:** 09026-60683-2. 74321-84591-2 (2). **Two-track tape:** CCS-16

SAINT-SAËNS, CAMILLE
Introduction and Rondo capriccioso in A Minor, op. 28 (8:58)
BSO, conductor Charles Munch
David Oistrakh, violin
December 14, 1955. Symphony Hall
RCA, producer John Pfeiffer
LPs: LM-1988. VIC/VICS-1058. **CDs:** 09026-60683-2. **Two-track tape:** CCS-16

RAVEL, MAURICE
Boléro (13:52)
BSO, conductor Charles Munch
January 23, 1956. Symphony Hall
RCA, producer Richard Mohr
45s: ERC-1984 (549-5225-B/5224-B) and (549-5229-B/5228-B). SEP-7 (549-5248-B/5247-B). **LPs:** LM/LSC-1984. **CDs:** 09026-61712-2. 09026-61956-2. 09026-63670-2. **SACDs:** 82876-66374-2. **Two-track tape:** CCS-21. *See note under* La Valse, *above.*

RAVEL, MAURICE
Rapsodie espagnole (14:49)
BSO, conductor Charles Munch
January 23, 1956. Symphony Hall
RCA, producer Richard Mohr
45s: ERC-1984 (549-5224-A/5225-A) and (549-5228-A/5229-A). SEP-7 (549-5247-A/5248-A). **LPs:** LM/LSC-1984. VIC/VICS-1041. **CDs:** 6522-2-RG. 09026-61712-2. 09026-61956-2. 74321-84604-2 (2). **SACDs:** 82876-66374-2. **Two-track tape:** AC-21 (monaural). CCS-36. *See* La Valse *above.*

DEBUSSY, CLAUDE
Prélude à l'après-midi d'un faune (9:00)
BSO, conductor Charles Munch
January 23, 1956; February 27, 1956. Symphony Hall
RCA, producer Richard Mohr
45s: ERC-1984 (549-5222/23) or (549-5226/27). SEP-7 (549-5245-A/5241-A). **LPs:** LM/LSC-1984. VIC/VICS-1034 (U.K.). VIC/VICS-1323. VICS-1668. **CDs:** Sony SK-685240. **Two-track tape:** CCS-21. *See* La Valse.

DEBUSSY, CLAUDE
Le Martyre de Saint Sébastien (52:59)
BSO, conductor Charles Munch
Phyllis Curtin, soprano; Catherine Akos, contralto; Florence Kopleff, contralto; Charles Munch, narrator; NECC, Lorna Cooke DeVaron, dir.
January 29, 1956; January 30, 1956. Symphony Hall
RCA, producer Richard Mo hr
LPs: LM-2030. VICS-1404. FVL3-7276 (3). **CDs:** 09026-60684-2. RCA Japan BVCC-38459 (88697-04823-2). ArkivCD 60684. *Munch gives an impassioned narration in some orchestral passages; it is absent from VICS-1404.*

STRAUSS, RICHARD
Der Rosenkavalier, op. 59: Suite *(*21:44)
BSO, conductor Pierre Monteux
February 17, 1956. Broadcast from Symphony Hall
BSO/IMG Artists
CDs: CB-100 (12)

BEETHOVEN, LUDWIG VAN
Leonore Overture No. 2, op. 72 (13:11)
BSO, conductor Charles Munch
February 26, 1956. Symphony Hall
RCA, producer Richard Mohr
LPs: LM-2015. VICS-1471

BEETHOVEN, LUDWIG VAN
Leonore Overture No. 1 in C, op. 138 (8:26)
BSO, conductor Charles Munch
February 26, 1956. Symphony Hall
RCA, producer Richard Mohr
LPs: LM-2015. VICS-1471

BEETHOVEN, LUDWIG VAN
Coriolan Overture in C Minor, op. 62 (6:10)
BSO, conductor Charles Munch
February 26, 1956; February 27, 1956. Symphony Hall
RCA, producer Richard Mohr
45s: ERA-286. **LPs:** LM-2015. LM-2071. VICS-1471. VICS-6003 (2).
    Two-track tape: BCS-48

BEETHOVEN, LUDWIG VAN
Leonore Overture No. 3, op. 72a (12:20)
BSO, conductor Charles Munch
February 27, 1956. Symphony Hall
RCA, producer Richard Mohr
LPs: LM-2015. VICS-1471. VICS-6003 (2). **CDs:** 6803-2-RG. 09026-60769-2.
    09026-61551-2. **Two-track tape:** BCS-48

TCHAIKOVSKY, PETER ILYICH
Romeo and Juliet (fantasy-overture) (17:11)
BSO, conductor Charles Munch
March 12, 1956. Symphony Hall
RCA, producer Richard Mohr
45s: ERC-2043 (549-5296/98). **LPs:** LM-2043. LM-6129 (3). VIC/VICS-1197.
    Two-track tape: BCS-22

PISTON, WALTER
Symphony No. 6 (24:04). *A BSO commission.*
BSO, conductor Charles Munch
Samuel Mayes, cello
March 12, 1956; March 14, 1956. Symphony Hall. *Premiered January 25, 1955.*
RCA, producer Richard Mohr
LPs: LM-2083. AGL1-3794. New Word NW-286. **CDs:** RCA Japan BVCC-
  384679 (88697-04828-2). *AGL1-3794 was the first stereo release, in 1981,*
  of the Piston and Martinů symphonies, 23 years after the monaural LP.

MARTINŮ, BOHUSLAV
Symphony No. 6 "Fantaisies symphoniques" (25:38). *A BSO commission.*
BSO, conductor Charles Munch
April 23, 1956. Symphony Hall. *World premiere given on January 7, 1955.*
RCA, producer Richard Mohr
LPs: LM-2083. AGL1-3794. **CDs:** EMI 5-75477-2 (2). RCA Japan BVCC-
  384679 (88697-04828-2)

TCHAIKOVSKY, PETER ILYICH
Francesca da Rimini, **op. 32 (23:07)**
BSO, conductor Charles Munch
April 23, 1956. Symphony Hall
RCA, producer Richard Mohr
45s: ERC-2043 (549-5296/98). **LPs:** LM-2043. LM-6129 (3). VIC/VICS-1197.
  Time-Life Records STL-541 (4). **Two-track tape:** DCS-51. *VICS-1197*
  lists the timing as 25:29, but it plays in 23:07.

MOZART, WOLFGANG AMADEUS
Concerto for Clarinet and Orchestra in A, K. 622 (28:34)
BSO, conductor Charles Munch
Benny Goodman, clarinet
July 9, 1956. Theatre Concert Hall, Tanglewood
RCA, producer John Peiffer
LPs: LM-2073. AGL1-5275. **CDs:** RCD1-5275. 09026-68804-2. **Two-track**
  tape: DCS-39. *Goodman recorded Mozart's Quintet for Clarinet and*
  Strings in A, K. 581, with the Boston Symphony String Quartet (Richard
  Burgin, Alfred Krips, Joseph de Pasquale, and Samuel Mayes) on July 12,
  1956. It appears with the concerto on all these issues.

BRAHMS, JOHANNES
Symphony No. 1 in C Minor, op. 68 (45:21)
BSO, conductor Charles Munch
November 19, 1956. Symphony Hall
RCA, producer Richard Mohr
LPs: LM/LSC-2097. LM/LSC-6902 (7). VIC/VICS-1062. AGL1-5201. Ara-
  besque 8056. **CDs:** 7812-2-RV. 60788-2-RV. RCA Japan BVCC-38447
  (74321-56856-2). ArkivCD 60788. **Two-track tape:** GCS-42

DEBUSSY, CLAUDE
La Mer (22:47)
BSO, conductor Charles Munch
December 9, 1956; December 10, 1956. Symphony Hall
RCA, producer Richard Mohr
LPs: LM/LSC-2111. VIC/VICS-1041. ATL1-4157. ARP1-4444. FVL3-7276
(3). **CDs:** 6719-2-RG. 09026-61387-2. 09026-61556-2. 82876-59416-2.
SACDs: 82876-61387-2. **Two-track tape:** CCS-56

IBERT, JACQUES
Escales (Palermo, Tunis-Nefta, Valencia) (15:21)
BSO, conductor Charles Munch
Ralph Gomberg, oboe
December 10, 1956. Symphony Hall
RCA, producer Richard Mohr
LPs: LM/LSC-2111. VIC/VICS-1323. ATL1-4157. ARP1-4444. **CDs:** 09026-
61500-2. **SACDs:** 82876-61387-2. **Two-track tape:** ACS-57

BERLIOZ, HECTOR
L'Enfance du Christ, op. 25 (93:29)
BSO, conductor Charles Munch
Florence Kopleff, contralto; Cesare Valleti, tenor; Gérard Souzay, baritone;
Giorgio Tozzi, bass; NECC, Lorna Cooke DeVaron, dir.
December 23, 1956; December 24, 1956. Symphony Hall
RCA, producer Richard Mohr
LPs: LM-6053 (2). VIC/VICS-6006 (2). **CDs:** 09026-61234-2 (2). 09026-
68444-2 (8). 82876-60393-2 (10). ArkivCD 61234 (2)

WALTON, WILLIAM
Concerto for Cello and Orchestra (29:21). *World premiere January 25, 1957.*
BSO, conductor Charles Munch
Gregor Piatigorsky, cello
January 28, 1957; January 30, 1957. Symphony Hall
RCA, producer Richard Mohr
LPs: LM/LSC-2109. AGL1-4086. **CDs:** 74321-29248-2. 09026-61498-2.
SACDs: 82876-66375-2

BLOCH, ERNEST
Schelomo
BSO, conductor Charles Munch
Gregor Piatigorsky, cello
January 30, 1957. Symphony Hall
RCA, producer Richard Mohr
LPs: LM/LSC-2109. AGL1-4086. **CDs:** Testament SBT-1371

PROKOFIEV, SERGEI
Romeo and Juliet, op. 64: 12 Scenes: Scene (1:40), Morning Dance (2:32), Young Juliet (4:04), Masques (2:23), Montagues and Capulets (5:27), Dance (2:03), Friar Lawrence (3:05), Death of Tybalt (4:46), Romeo and Juliet's Parting (8:49), Aubade (2:24), Romeo at Juliet's Tomb and Juliet's Death (9:00). Total: (46:21)
BSO, conductor Charles Munch
February 11, 1957; February 13, 1957. Symphony Hall
RCA, producer Richard Mohr
LPs: LM-2110. VICS-1412 (first stereo issue). **CDs:** RCA Japan BVCC-38464 (88697-04826-2)

Death of Tybalt, Montagues and Capulets, Dance, Romeo at Juliet's Tomb and Juliet's Death (21:08). **CDs:** EMI 5-75477-2 (2)

PROKOFIEV, SERGEI
Concerto for Piano and Orchestra No. 2 in G Minor, op. 16 (29:33)
BSO, conductor Charles Munch
Nicole Henriot-Schweitzer, piano
February 13, 1957. Symphony Hall
RCA, producer Richard Mohr
LPs: LM-2197. VIC/VICS-1071. **CDs:** RCA Japan BVCC-38464 (88697-04826-2

FRANCK, CÉSAR
Symphony in D Minor (36:33)
BSO, conductor Charles Munch
March 11, 1957. Symphony Hall
RCA, producer Richard Mohr
LPs: LM/LSC-2131. LM/LSC-6902 (7). VIC/VICS-1034. **CDs:** 74321-29256-2. 82876-65833-2. **Two-track tape:** ECS-58. *The U.S. issue of VICS-1034 has only the Franck Symphony. The U.K. issue of VICS-1034 also includes the January 23, 1956, recording of Debussy's* Prélude à l'après midi d'un faune. *(Lawrence H. Jones, email April 22, 2008)*

TCHAIKOVSKY, PETER ILYICH
Serenade in C for String Orchestra, op. 48 (26:42)
BSO, conductor Charles Munch
March 13, 1957. Symphony Hall
RCA, producer Richard Mohr
LPs: LM/LSC-2105. AGL1-1331. AGL1-3790. AGL1-5218. Time-Life Records STL-541 (4). **CDs:** 09026-61424-2. **Two-track tape:** CCS-66

WAGNER, RICHARD
Götterdämmerung: Rhine Journey (9:05)
BSO, conductor Charles Munch
April 1, 1957. Symphony Hall
RCA, producer Richard Mohr
LPs: LM-2119. VIC/VICS-1065. **Two-track tape:** ACS-92

WAGNER, RICHARD
Die Walküre: Magic Fire Music **(7:34)**
BSO, conductor Charles Munch
April 1, 1957. Symphony Hall
RCA, producer Richard Mohr
LPs: LM-2119. VIC/VICS-1065. **CDs:** 09026-60686-2. ArkivCD 60686. **Two-track tape:** ACS-92

WAGNER, RICHARD
Tannhäuser: **Overture and Venusberg Music** (Paris version) **(21:12)**
BSO, conductor Charles Munch
April 1, 1957. Symphony Hall
RCA, producer Richard Mohr
LPs: LM-2119. VIC/VICS-1065. **CDs:** 09026-60686-2. ArkivCD 60686. **Two-track tape:** BCS-55

ELGAR, EDWARD
Introduction and Allegro for Strings, op. 47 (14:16)
BSO, conductor Charles Munch
April 3, 1957. Symphony Hall
RCA, producer Richard Mohr
LPs: LM/LSC-2105. AGL1-3790. **CDs:** 09026-61424-2. 09026-68087-2. **Two-track tape:** BCS-139. *This piece is not listed on the front cover of LSC-2105, but it is listed on the back and on the spine.*

BARBER, SAMUEL
Adagio for Strings (from String Quartet, op. 11) **(7:45)**
BSO, conductor Charles Munch
April 3, 1957. Symphony Hall
RCA, producer Richard Mohr
LPs: LM-2105. ARL2-1421 (2). AGL1-3790. **CDs:** 09026-60833-2. 09026-61424-2. 09026-63758-2. 09026-6858-2. 09026-68832-2. **Two-track tape:** BCS-139. *This piece was omitted from the stereo LP LSC-2105.*

BARBER, SAMUEL
Medea's Meditation and Dance of Vengeance **(12:00)**
BSO, conductor Charles Munch
April 10, 1957. Symphony Hall
RCA, producer Richard Mohr
LPs: LM-2197. VICS-1391. **CDs:** 09026-61424-2. **Two-track tape:** ACS-147

BACH, JOHANN SEBASTIAN
Brandenburg Concerto No. 3 in G, BWV 1048 (13:06)
BSO, conductor Charles Munch
July 8, 1957. Theatre Concert Hall, Tanglewood
RCA, producer John Pfeiffer
LPs: LM-2182. LSC-6140 (3). **CDs:** RCA Japan BVCC-38422 (74321-56847-2 [2])

BACH, JOHANN SEBASTIAN
Brandenburg Concerto No. 1 in F, BWV 1046 (19:55)
BSO, conductor Charles Munch
Jaime Laredo, violin; James Stagliano and Harrry Shapiro, horns
July 8, 1957. Theatre Concert Hall, Tanglewood
RCA, producer John Pfeiffer
LPs: LM-2182. LSC-6140 (3). **CDs:** RCA Japan BVCC-38422 (74321-56847-2
[2])

BACH, JOHANN SEBASTIAN
Brandenburg Concerto No. 4 in G, BWV 1049 (15:47)
BSO, conductor Charles Munch
Richard Burgin, violin; Doriot Anthony Dwyer and James Pappoutsakis, flutes
July 8, 1957. Theatre Concert Hall, Tanglewood
RCA, producer John Pfeiffer
LPs: LM-2198. LSC-6140 (3). **CDs:** RCA Japan BVCC-38422 (74321-56847-2
[2])

BACH, JOHANN SEBASTIAN
Brandenburg Concerto No. 2 in F, BWV 1047 (11:50)
BSO, conductor Charles Munch
Roger Voisin, trumpet; Richard Burgin, violin; Ralph Gomberg, oboe; Doriot
Anthony Dwyer, flute
July 9, 1957. Theatre Concert Hall, Tanglewood
RCA, producer John Pfeiffer
LPs: LM-2182. LSC-6140 (3). **CDs:** RCA Japan BVCC-38422 (74321-56847-2
[2])

BACH, JOHANN SEBASTIAN
Brandenburg Concerto No. 5 in D, BWV 1050 (21:51)
BSO, conductor Charles Munch
Lukas Foss, piano, Richard Burgin, violin; Doriot Anthony Dwyer, flute
July 9, 1957. Theatre Concert Hall, Tanglewood
RCA, producer John Pfeiffer
LPs: LM-2198. LSC-6140 (3). **CDs:** RCA Japan BVCC-38422 (74321-56847-2
[2])

BACH, JOHANN SEBASTIAN
Brandenburg Concerto No. 6 in B♭, BWV 1051 (17:47)
BSO, conductor Charles Munch
July 9, 1957. Theatre Concert Hall, Tanglewood
RCA, producer John Pfeiffer
LPs: LM-2198. LSC-6140 (3). **CDs:** RCA Japan BVCC-38422 (74321-56847-2
[2])

SMITH, JOHN STAFFORD
The Star-Spangled Banner
BSO, conductor Charles Munch
October 28, 1957. Symphony Hall
RCA, producer Richard Mohr
Matrix: HO-7V 1756
78s: American Heritage Foundation AHF-1003. *The BSO and its musicians donated their services for this recording. Unlikely as it seems for 1957, this is a 7-inch, shellac 78-rpm record—a truly historical issue.*

MENDELSSOHN, FELIX
Symphony No. 5 in D, op. 107 "Reformation" (27:15)
BSO, conductor Charles Munch
October 28, 1957. Symphony Hall
RCA, producer Richard Mohr
LPs: LM/LSC-2221. LM/LSC-6902 (7). AGL1-5278. **CDs:** 6797-2-RG. 74321-84600-2 (2). **SACDs:** 82876-71616-2

DUKAS, PAUL
The Sorcerer's Apprentice **(10:29)**
BSO, conductor Charles Munch
November 4, 1957. Symphony Hall
RCA, producer Richard Mohr
LPs: LM/LSC-2292. VIC/VICS-1060. **CDs:** 09026-68978-2. 74321-84604-2 (2)

SAINT-SAËNS, CAMILLE
Le Rouet d'Omphale, op. 31 **(7:35)**
BSO, conductor Charles Munch
November 4, 1957. Symphony Hall
RCA, producer Richard Mohr
LPs: LM/LSC-2292. **CDs:** 09026-61400-2. 09026-68978-2

WAGNER, RICHARD
Tristan und Isolde: **Prelude (11:02)**
BSO, conductor Charles Munch
November 25, 1957. Symphony Hall
RCA, producer Richard Mohr
LPs: LM/LSC-2255. AGL1-1274. **CDs:** 09026-60686-2. ArkivCD 60686

WAGNER, RICHARD
Tristan und Isolde: **"Mild und leise" (Liebestod) (6:47)**
BSO, conductor Charles Munch
Eileen Farrell, soprano
November 25, 1957. Symphony Hall
RCA, producer Richard Mohr
LPs: LM/LSC-2255. AGL1-1274. Franklin Mint Record Society FM-1021/22 (2). **CDs:** 09026-60686-2. 82876-76228-2. ArkivCD 60686

WAGNER, RICHARD
Götterdämmerung: *Immolation Scene* (20:15)
BSO, conductor Charles Munch
Eileen Farrell, soprano
November 25, 1957. Symphony Hall
RCA, producer Richard Mohr
LPs: LM/LSC-2255. AGL1-1274. CDs: 09026-60686-2. ArkivCD 60686

BEETHOVEN, LUDWIG VAN
Symphony No. 3 in E♭, op. 55 "Eroica" (45:00)
BSO, conductor Charles Munch
December 2, 1957. Symphony Hall
RCA, producer Richard Mohr
LPs: LM/LSC-2233. LM/LSC-6902 (7). VICS-1626. CDs: 09026-61399-2. *The
initial pressing of the Victrola reissue (VICS-1626) was of the September
30, 1962, recording of the "Eroica" led by Erich Leinsdorf. The error was
corrected on later pressings. The Leinsdorf version splits the Funeral
March onto two sides; the Munch gets all of it on side one. (Lawrence H.
Jones, email September 26, 2007)*

DEBUSSY, CLAUDE
Images: Gigues; Ibéria; Rondes de printemps **(33:13)**
BSO, conductor Charles Munch
December 16, 1957; March 31, 1958. Symphony Hall
RCA, producer Richard Mohr
LPs: LM/LSC-2282. VICS-1391. AGL1-2122. FVL3-7276 (3). CDs: 09026-
61956-2. 74321-84591-2 (2). 82876-59416-2. SACDs: 82876-66374-2

Ibéria **(19:23)**. CDs: 09026-60684-2. 09026-61556-2

Gigues **(6:30)**. *Rondes de printemps* **(7:16)**. CDs: 09026-68081-2

RACHMANINOFF, SERGEI
Concerto for Piano and Orchestra No. 3 in D Minor, op. 30 (37:39)
BSO, conductor Charles Munch
Byron Janis, piano
December 29, 1957. Symphony Hall
RCA, producer Richard Mohr
LPs: LM/LSC-2237. VIC/VICS-1032. CDs: 60540-2-RV. 09026-55269-2.
09026-68762-2

TCHAIKOVSKY, PETER ILYICH
Symphony No. 5 in E Minor, op. 64 (43:48)
BSO, conductor Pierre Monteux
January 8, 1958. Symphony Hall
RCA, producer Richard Mohr
LPs: LM/LSC-2239. LM/LSC-6803 (6). LM/LSC-6902 (7). AGL1-1264.
CDs: 09026-61901-2 (2). 09026-61893-2 (15)

KHACHATURIAN, ARAM
Concerto for Violin and Orchestra (34:39)
BSO, conductor Pierre Monteux
Leonid Kogan, violin
January 12, 1958; January 13, 1958. Symphony Hall
RCA, producer Richard Mohr
LPs: LM-2220. VIC/VICS-1153 (first stereo edition). CDs: 09026-63708-2

SAINT-SAËNS, CAMILLE
Havanaise in E, op. 83 (8:58)
BSO, conductor Pierre Monteux.
Leonid Kogan, violin
January 12, 1958; January 13, 1958. Symphony Hall
RCA, producer Richard Mohr
LPs: LM-2220. VIC/VICS-1153 (first stereo edition). CDs: 09026-61890-2.
    09026-61893-2 (15)

MENDELSSOHN, FELIX
Symphony No. 4 in A, op. 90 "Italian" (26:33)
BSO, conductor Charles Munch
February 18, 1958. Symphony Hall
RCA, producer John Pfeiffer
LPs: LM/LSC-2221. LM/LSC-6902 (7). AGL1-5278. CDs: 6797-2-RG. 60483-
    2-RV. 09026-68090-2. 74321-84600-2 (2). SACDs: 82876-71616-2. Ar-
    kivCD 60483

RAVEL, MAURICE
Ma Mère l'oye: Suite (17:59)
BSO, conductor Charles Munch
February 19, 1958. Symphony Hall
RCA, producer Richard Mohr
LPs: LM/LSC-2292. VIC/VICS-1060. CDs: 6522-2-RG. 60692-2-RG. 09026-
    68978-2. 74321-84604-2 (2)

HANDEL, GEORGE FRIDERIC
Water Music: Suite (arr. Hamilton Harty): Overture (2:25)
BSO, conductor Charles Munch
March 8, 1958. Symphony Hall (live)
Boston Symphony Transcription Trust, producers Jordan M. Whitelaw and
    Richard L. Kaye
CDs: BSO-CD1 (promotional). *1988 "Salute to Symphony."*

ROUSSEL, ALBERT
Suite in F, op. 33 (16:10)
BSO, conductor Charles Munch
March 8, 1958. Broadcast from Symphony Hall
BSO/IMG Artists
CDs: CB-100 (12)

RAVEL, MAURICE
Concerto in G (21:05)
BSO, conductor Charles Munch
Nicole Henriot-Schweitzer, piano
March 24, 1958. Symphony Hall
RCA, producer Richard Mohr
LPs: LM/LSC-2271. VIC/VICS-1071. Classic Records LSC-2271

D' INDY, VINCENT
Symphony on French Mountain Air (25:17)
BSO, conductor Charles Munch
Nicole Henriot-Schweitzer, piano
March 24, 1958. Symphony Hall
RCA, producer Richard Mohr
LPs: LM/LSC-2271. VIC/VICS-1060. Classic Records LSC-2271. **CDs:** 6805-
    2-RG. 09026-62582-2. ArkivCD 6805

BERLIOZ, HECTOR
Harold in Italy, op. 16 (38:03)
BSO, conductor Charles Munch
William Primrose, Viola
March 31, 1958. Symphony Hall
RCA, producer Richard Mohr
LPs: LM/LSC-2228. AGL1-1526. **CDs:** 09026-62582-2. 09026-68444-2 (8).
    82876-60393-2 (10). **SACDs:** 82876-88697-2

BRAHMS, JOHANNES
Concerto for Piano and Orchestra No. 1 in D Minor, op. 15 (44:19)
BSO, conductor Charles Munch
Gary Graffman, piano
April 9, 1958. Symphony Hall
RCA, producer John Pfeiffer
LPs: LM/LSC-2274. VIC/VICS-1109. **CDs:** RCA Japan BVCC-38449 (88697-
    04819-2)

SCHUMANN, ROBERT
Concerto for Piano and Orchestra in A Minor, op. 54 (31:52)
BSO, conductor Charles Munch
Van Cliburn, piano
October 6, 1958. Symphony Hall (studio session from 12:30 to 4:30 PM, fol-
    lowed by a live performance at a BSO Pension Fund concert that evening)
RCA, producer John Pfeiffer
Unreleased. *"We edited extensively between the recording session and the per-*
    formance, and Van was teetering on the edge of approving it when the big
    [musical] love affair with Reiner was consummated, and he recorded it with
    the CSO." (Memorandum: John Pfeiffer to Michael Emmerson, January 11,
    1989). Pfeiffer writes that there was a patch session in 1959, but we can
    find no trace of one in either BSO payment sheets or RCA recording logs.

RACHMANINOFF, SERGEI
Concerto for Piano and Orchestra No. 3 in d Minor, op. 30: I. Allegro ma non tanto (16:40)
BSO, conductor Charles Munch
Van Cliburn, piano
October 6, 1958. Symphony Hall (live)
RCA, producer John Pfeiffer
Unreleased. *Cliburn's May 19, 1958, Carnegie Hall live performance of this concerto with Kirill Kondrashin had already been recorded, but RCA didn't decide to release it until April 30, 1959.*

BRAHMS, JOHANNES
Symphony No. 4 in E Minor, op. 98 (39:51)
BSO, conductor Charles Munch
October 27, 1958. Symphony Hall
RCA, producer Richard Mohr
LPs: LM/LSC-2297. LM/LSC-6411 (4). LM/LSC-6902 (7). **CDs:** 09026-61206-2. 09026-61855-2

BLACKWOOD, EASLEY
Symphony No. 1, op. 3 (31:18)
BSO, conductor Charles Munch
November 9, 1958. Symphony Hall. *World premiere given on April 18, 1958.*
RCA, producer Richard Mohr
LPs: LM/LSC-2352. **CDs:** 735131901628. Cedille CDR-90000 016

SCHUBERT, FRANZ
Symphony No. 9 in C "Great C Major" (44:33)
BSO, conductor Charles Munch
November 19, 1958. Symphony Hall
RCA, producer Richard Mohr
LPs: LM/LSC-2344. VICS-1126. AGL1-5064. **CDs:** 60792-2-RV. 09026-62678-2. **SACDs:** 88697-04603-2

BEETHOVEN, LUDWIG VAN
Symphony No. 8 in F, op. 93 (23:33)
BSO, conductor Charles Munch
November 30, 1958. Symphony Hall
RCA, producer Richard Mohr
LPs: LM/LSC-6066 (2). **CDs:** RCA Japan BVCC-38427 (88697-04813-2)

HAIEFF, ALEXEI
Symphony No. 2 (18:48)
BSO, conductor Charles Munch
November 30, 1958. Symphony Hall
RCA, producer Richard Mohr
LPs: LM/LSC-2352. Serenus SRS-12086

BERLIOZ, HECTOR
Roman Carnival Overture, op. 9 (8:01)
BSO, conductor Charles Munch
December 1, 1958. Symphony Hall
RCA, producer Richard Mohr
LPs: LM/LSC-2438. LSC-2307. LSC-6097 (2). AGL1-1277. **CDs:** 6720-2-RG.
    60478-2-RV. 09026-61400-2. 09026-61721-2. 09026-68444-2 (8). 82876-
    60393-2 (10). 74321-84587-2 (2). **SACDs:** 82876-88697-2

BERLIOZ, HECTOR
Béatrice et Bénédict: Overture (7:24)
BSO, conductor Charles Munch
December 1, 1958. Symphony Hall
RCA, producer Richard Mohr
LPs: LM/LSC-2438. AGL1-1277. **CDs:** 6805-2-RG. 09026-61400-2. 09026-
    61721-2. 09026-68444-2 (8). 82876-60393-2 (10). ArkivCD 4805. **SACDs:**
    82876-88697-2

BERLIOZ, HECTOR
Le Corsaire Overture, op. 21 (8:05)
BSO, conductor Charles Munch
December 1, 1958. Symphony Hall
RCA, producer Richard Mohr
LPs: LM/LSC-2438. AGL1-1277. **CDs:** 6720-2-RG. 60478-2-RV. 09026-
    61400-2. 09026-68444-2 (8). 82876-60393-2 (10). 74321-84587-2 (2).
    SACDs: 82876-88697-2

RAVEL, MAURICE
La Valse (11:56)
BSO, conductor Charles Munch
December 1, 1958. Symphony Hall
RCA, producer Richard Mohr
Unreleased. *This recording took place at the tail end of a four-hour recording
    session, from 1:44 PM to 1:58 PM. It is unusual to record a work in a single
    run-through (as indicated by that 14-minute time span), and this recording
    was not continued at another session, so it was not approved for issue.
    When Munch recorded* La Valse *on February 2, 1962, a total of 80 minutes
    was spent on the piece.*

BEETHOVEN, LUDWIG VAN
Symphony No. 9 in D Minor, op. 125 "Choral" (63:02)
BSO, conductor Charles Munch
Leontyne Price, soprano; Maureen Forrester, contralto: David Poleri, tenor;
    Giorgio Tozzi, bass; NECC, Lorna Cooke DeVaron, dir.
December 21, 1958; December 22, 1958. Symphony Hall
RCA, producer Richard Mohr
LPs: LM/LSC-6066 (2). VICS-1660. VICS-6003 (2). AGL1-3007. **CDs:** EMI
    5-75477-2 (2)

MAHLER, GUSTAV
Kindertotenlieder *(*24:43)
BSO, conductor Charles Munch
Maureen Forrester, contralto
December 28, 1958. Symphony Hall
RCA, producer John Pfeiffer
LPs: LM/LSC-2371. AGL1-1338. **CDs:** RCA Japan BVCC-38456 (88697-04822-2)

MAHLER, GUSTAV
Lieder eines fahrenden Gesellen *(*17:18)
BSO, conductor Charles Munch
Maureen Forrester, contralto
December 29, 1958. Symphony Hall
RCA, producer John Pfeiffer
LPs: LM/LSC-2371. AGL1-1338. **CDs:** RCA Japan BVCC-38456 (88697-04822-2)

CONCERT VIDEO (80 minutes)
BRAHMS *Tragic Overture*, op. 81 (13:16)
HINDEMITH *Noblissma Visione* (20:00)
STRAVINSKY *Pétrouchka* (34:09)
BSO, conductor Pierre Monteux
January 20, 1959. Sanders Theater (live telecast)
BSO and WGBH Educational Foundation, producer Jordan M. Whitelaw. Produced for DVD by Alan Altman
DVD: Video Artists International VAI-4316 (black and white, monaural)

STRAUSS, RICHARD
Don Quixote, op. 35 *(*39:12)
BSO, conductor Pierre Monteux
Samuel Mayes, cello; Joseph de Pasquale, viola
January 24, 1959. Broadcast from Symphony Hall
BSO/IMG Artists
CDs: CB-100 (12)

STRAVINSKY, IGOR
Pétrouchka (34:53)
BSO, conductor Pierre Monteux
January 25, 1959; January 26, 1959; January 28, 1959. Symphony Hall
RCA, producer John Pfeiffer
LPs: LM/LSC-2376. VICS-1296 (U.K.). AGL1-1272. **CDs:** 6529-2-RG. 09026-61893-2 (15). 09026-61898-2. 09026-63303-2. 82876-62314-2. **SACDs:** 82876-67897-2

TCHAIKOVSKY, PETER ILYICH
Symphony No. 4 in F Minor, op. 36 (39:40)
BSO, conductor Pierre Monteux
January 28, 1959. Symphony Hall
RCA, producer John Pfeiffer
LPs: LM/LSC-2369. AGL1-1328. AGL1-5254. **CDs:** 09026-61901-2 (2).
    09026-61893-2 (15)

CONCERT VIDEO (94 minutes)
BARBIROLLI *An Elizabethan Suite* (11:57). Arranged from works in *The Fitzwilliam Virginal Book*, a collection of early 17th-century English compositions: William Byrd's *Earl of Salisbury's Pavane*, the anonymous *The Irish Ho Hoane*, Giles Farnaby's *A Toye*, and John Bull's *The King's Hunt*.
DELIUS *A Village Romeo and Juliet:* **The Walk to the Paradise Garden (10:08)**
WALTON Partita for Orchestra (15:26)
BRAHMS Symphony No. 2 in D, op. 73 (38:50)
BSO, conductor John Barbirolli
February 3, 1959. Sanders Theater (live telecast)
BSO and WGBH Educational Foundation, producer Jordan M. Whitelaw. Produced for DVD by Alan Altman
DVD: Video Artists International VAI-4304 (black and white, monaural). *An alternative soundtrack is offered, a stereo broadcast of the same program from Symphony Hall on January 31, 1959. The sound is very much better, but the audio is no longer synchronized with the video; i.e., the Brahms finale ends 27 seconds later in Symphony Hall than in Sanders Theater.*

TCHAIKOVSKY, PETER ILYICH
Concerto for Violin and Orchestra in D, op. 35 (33:20)
BSO, conductor Charles Munch
Henryk Szeryng, violin
February 9, 1959. Symphony Hall
RCA, producer John Pfeiffer
LPs: LM/LSC-2363. VIC/VICS-1037. AVL1-0058. **CDs:** RCA Japan BVCC-38451 (88697-04820-2)

MENDELSSOHN, FELIX
Concerto for Violin and Orchestra in E Minor, op. 64 (24:01)
BSO, conductor Charles Munch
Jascha Heifetz, violin
February 23, 1959; February 25, 1959. Symphony Hall
RCA, producer John Pfeiffer
LPs: LM/LSC-2314. LSC-3304. LSC-4012. VCS-7058 (2). AGL1-5264. ARP1-4567. CRL6-0720 (6). **CDs:** 5933-2-RC. 09026-61743-2. 09026-61779-2 (5). 09026-68980-2. **SACDs:** 82876-61391-2

PROKOFIEV, SERGEI
Concerto for Violin and Orchestra No. 2 in G Minor, op. 63 (23:12)
BSO, conductor Charles Munch
Jascha Heifetz, violin
February 24, 1959; February 25, 1959. Symphony Hall
RCA, producer John Pfeiffer
LPs: LM/LSC-2314. LSC-4010. AGL1-5241. CRL6-0720 (6). **CDs:** RCD1-
7019. 09026-61744-2. 09026-61779-2 (5). **SACDs:** 82876-66372-2

SAINT-SAËNS, CAMILLE
Symphony No. 3 in C Minor, op. 78 "Organ" (34:51)
BSO, conductor Charles Munch
Berj Zamkochian, organ; Bernard Zighera and Leo Litwin, pianos
April 5, 1959; April 6, 1959. Symphony Hall
RCA, producer Richard Mohr
LPs: LM/LSC-2341. ATL1-4039. ARP1-4440. **CDs:** 5750-2-RC. 60817-2-RG.
09026-61500-2. **SACDs:** 82876-61387-2

BERLIOZ, HECTOR
Benvenuto Cellini, op. 23: Overture (10:26)
BSO, conductor Charles Munch
April 6, 1959. Symphony Hall
RCA, producer Richard Mohr
LPs: LM/LSC-2438. AGL1-1277. **CDs:** 09026-61400-2. 09026-68444-2 (8).
82876-60393-2 (10). 74321-84587-2 (2). **SACDs:** 82876-88697-2

BERLIOZ, HECTOR
Les Troyens: Royal Hunt and Storm (10:59)
BSO, conductor Charles Munch
April 6, 1959. Symphony Hall
RCA, producer Richard Mohr
LPs: LM/LSC-2438. AGL1-1277. **CDs:** 09026-61400-2. 09026-68444-2 (8).
82876-60393-2 (10). ArkivCD 53255

COPLAND, AARON
Appalachian Spring: Suite (25:21)
BSO, conductor Aaron Copland
April 13, 1959. Symphony Hall
RCA, producer Peter Dellheim
LPs: LM/LSC-2401. CRL3-3270 (3). Time-Life Records STL-570 (4). **CDs:**
6802-2-RG. 09026-60837-2. 09026-61505-2. 09026-68020-2

COPLAND, AARON
The Tender Land: Orchestral Suite (20:41)
BSO, conductor Aaron Copland
April 13, 1959. Symphony Hall
RCA, producer Peter Dellheim
LPs: LM/LSC-2401. Time-Life Records STL-570 (4). **CDs:** 6802-2-RG.
09026-61505-2. 09026-68020-2

BERLIOZ, HECTOR
Requiem, op. 5 "Grande messe des morts" (83:38)
BSO, conductor Charles Munch
Léopold Simoneau, tenor; NECC, Lorna Cooke DeVaron, dir.
April 26, 1959; April 27, 1959. Symphony Hall
RCA, producer Richard Mohr
LPs: LD/LDS-6077 (2). VICS-6043 (2). ATL2-4269 (2). ARP2-4578 (2). **CDs:**
6210-2-RC (2). 09026-68444-2 (8). 82876-60393-2 (10). **SACDs:** 82876-
66373-2 (2)

DEBUSSY, CLAUDE
Prélude à l'après-midi d'un faune (9:44)
BSO, conductor Pierre Monteux
July 19, 1959. Koussevitzky Music Shed, Tanglewood (live)
BSO/TDK
CDs: "Tanglewood 98"

SCHUMANN, ROBERT
Symphony No. 1 in B♭, op. 38 "Spring" (29:22)
BSO, conductor Charles Munch
October 5, 1959. Symphony Hall
RCA, producer Richard Mohr
LPs: LM/LSC-2474. VICS-1436. AGL1-1530. **CDs:** 60488-2-RV

SCHUMANN, ROBERT
Manfred, op. 115: Overture (11:13)
BSO, conductor Charles Munch
October 5, 1959. Symphony Hall
RCA, producer Richard Mohr
LPs: LM/LSC-2474. AGL1-1530. **CDs:** 6797-2-RG

FRANCK, CÉSAR
Le Chasseur maudit (14:19)
BSO, conductor Charles Munch
October 10, 1959. Broadcast from Symphony Hall
BSO/IMG Artists
CDs: CB-100 (12)

MENDELSSOHN, FELIX
Symphony No. 3 in A Minor, op. 56 "Scottish" (36:06)
BSO, conductor Charles Munch
December 7, 1959. Symphony Hall
RCA, producer Richard Mohr
LPs: LM/LSC-2520. **CDs:** 60483-2-RV. 74321-84600-2 (2). ArkivCD 60483

FAURÉ, GABRIEL
Pénélope: Prelude (**10:47**)
BSO, conductor Charles Munch
December 12, 1959. Broadcast from Symphony Hall
BSO/IMG Artists
CDs: CB-100 (12)

DVOŘÁK, ANTONIN
Concerto for Cello and Orchestra No. 2 in B Minor, op. 104 (42:03)
BSO, conductor Charles Munch
Gregor Piatigorsky, cello
February 22, 1960. Symphony Hall
RCA, producer Max Wilcox
LPs: LM/LSC-2490. AGL1-3878. AGL1-5265. Classic Records LSC-2490.
    CDs: 74321-21289-2. 09026-61498-2. 82876-55302-2. **SACDs:** 82876-66375-2

SCHUBERT, FRANZ
Symphony No. 2 in B♭ (27:20)
BSO, conductor Charles Munch
March 7, 1960. Symphony Hall
RCA, producer Max Wilcox
LPs: LM/LSC-2522. VICS-1436

MENDELSSOHN, FELIX
Octet in E♭, op. 20: Scherzo (4:09)
BSO, conductor Charles Munch
March 7, 1960. Symphony Hall
RCA, producer Max Wilcox
LPs: LM/LSC-2520. **CDs:** EMI 5-75477-2 (2). **SACDs:** 82876-71616-2

BEETHOVEN, LUDWIG VAN
The Creatures of Prometheus, op. 43: Overture. Act II, No. 5: Adagio. Finale
(**5:00, 7:47, 5:46**)
BSO, conductor Charles Munch
March 7, 1960. Symphony Hall
RCA, producer Max Wilcox
LPs: LM/LSC-2522. **Overture (5:00):** VICS-1471

CHOPIN, FRÉDÉRIC
Concerto for Piano and Orchestra No. 1 in E Minor, op. 11 (36:42)
BSO, conductor Charles Munch
Gary Graffman, piano
March 14, 1960. Symphony Hall
RCA, producer Max Wilcox
LPs: LM/LSC-2468. VIC/VICS-1030

MENDELSSOHN, FELIX
Capriccio brillant in B Minor, op. 22 (10:27)
BSO, conductor Charles Munch
Gary Graffman, piano
March 14, 1960. Symphony Hall
RCA, producer Max Wilcox
LPs: LM/LSC-2468. VIC/VICS-1030. **CDs:** RCA Japan BVCC-38449 (88697-04819-2)

CONCERT VIDEO (66:45)
HAYASHI *Kimi Ga Yo* (Japanese National Anthem) (1:19)
SMITH: *The Star-Spangled Banner* (1:25)
BEETHOVEN Symphony No. 3 in E♭, op. 55, "Eroica" (45:53)
RAVEL *Daphnis et Chloé:* Suite No. 2 (15:27)
BSO, conductor Charles Munch
May 4, 1960. NHK Hall, Uchisaiwai-cho Tokyo (live telecast)
NHK Classical, producer Jean-Philippe Schweitzer
DVD: NHK NSDS-9486 (black and white, stereo) Japan. *After the concert comes an eight-minute black-and-white silent newsreel film of the BSO's arrival in Japan.*

POULENC, FRANCIS
Concerto in G Minor for Organ, Strings, and Timpani (22:27)
BSO, conductor Charles Munch
Berj Zamkochian, organ; Everett Firth, timpani
October 9, 1960. Symphony Hall
RCA, producer Max Wilcox
LPs: LM/LSC-2567. AGL1-2445. **CDs:** 5750-2-RC. 60817-2-RG

BEETHOVEN, LUDWIG VAN
Concerto for Piano and Orchestra No. 1 in C, op. 15 (37:10)
BSO, conductor Charles Munch
Sviatoslav Richter, piano
November 2, 1960; November 3, 1960. Symphony Hall
RCA, producer Max Wilcox
LPs: LM/LSC-2544. VICS-1478. **CDs:** 6804-2-RG. 74321-84605-2 (2). 82876-59421-2

STRAVINSKY, IGOR
Jeu de cartes (22:04)
BSO, conductor Charles Munch
November 7, 1960. Symphony Hall
RCA, producer Max Wilcox
LPs: LM/LSC-2567. **CDs:** RCA Japan BVCC-38466 (88697-04827-2)

MILHAUD, DARIUS
Suite Provençale, op. 152b (16:57)
BSO, conductor Charles Munch
November 21, 1960. Symphony Hall
RCA, producer Max Wilcox
LPs: LD/LDS-2625. AGL1-2445. Classics Records LDS-2625. **CDs:** 09026-60685-2. ArkivCD 60685

MENDELSSOHN, FELIX
Concerto for Violin and Orchestra in E Minor, op. 64 (27:10)
BSO, conductor Charles Munch
Jaime Laredo, violin
December 24, 1960; December 26, 1960. Symphony Hall
RCA, producer Richard Mohr
LPs: VIC/VICS-1033. AVL1-0058

BACH, JOHANN SEBASTIAN
Concerto for Violin and Orchestra in A Minor, BWV 1041 (15:41)
BSO, conductor Charles Munch
Jaime Laredo, violin
December 26, 1960. Symphony Hall
RCA, producer Richard Mohr
LPs: VIC/VICS-1129. **CDs:** RCA Japan BVCC-38422 (74321-56847-2 [2])

RAVEL, MAURICE
Daphnis et Chloé (55:20)
BSO, conductor Charles Munch
NECC, Lorna Cooke DeVaron, dir.
February 26, 1961; February 27, 1961. Symphony Hall
RCA, producer Max Wilcox
LPs: LM/LSC-2568. AGL1-1270. **CDs:** 74321-84604-2 (2)

DVOŘÁK, ANTONIN
Symphony No. 8 in G, op. 88 (35:50)
BSO, conductor Charles Munch
March 13, 1961. Symphony Hall
RCA, producer Max Wilcox
LPs: LM/LSC-2629. DRL1-0051. **CDs:** 74321-21289-2. 09026-61206-2. 82876-55302-2. **SACDs:** 09026-61206-2

MILHAUD, DARIUS
La Création du Monde, op. 81 *(15:54)*
BSO, conductor Charles Munch
March 13, 1961. Symphony Hall
RCA, producer Max Wilcox
LPs: LD/LDS-2625. AGL1-2445. CRL2-3384 (2). Classics Records LDS-2625. **CDs:** 09026-60685-2. ArkivCD 60685

VERDI, GIUSEPPE
La forza del destino: **Overture** *(8:12)*
BSO, conductor Thomas Schippers
March 18, 1961. Broadcast from Symphony Hall
BSO/IMG Artists
CDs: CB-100 (12)

STRAUSS, RICHARD
Till Eulenspiegels lustige Streiche, **op. 28 (14:53)**
BSO, conductor Charles Munch
March 20, 1961. Symphony Hall
RCA, producer Max Wilcox
LPs: LM/LSC-2565. **CDs:** RCA Japan BVCC-38457 (88697-05379-2)

TCHAIKOVSKY, PETER ILYICH
Romeo and Juliet **(fantasy-overture) (19:04)**
BSO, conductor Charles Munch
April 3, 1961. Symphony Hall
RCA, producer Max Wilcox
LPs: LM/LSC-2565. AGL1-1331. AGL1-5218. **CDs:** 6527-2-RG. 09026-
61563-2. ArkivCD 6527

BERLIOZ, HECTOR
Roméo et Juliette, **op. 17 (91:35)**
BSO, conductor Charles Munch
Rosalind Elias, mezzo-soprano; Cesare Valetti, tenor; Georgio Tozzi, bass;
NECC, Lorna Cooke DeVaron, dir.
April 23, 1961; April 24, 1961. Symphony Hall
RCA, producer Richard Mohr
LPs: LD/LDS-6098 (2). VICS-6042 (2). **CDs:** 74321 34168 2 (2). 82876-
60393-2 (10).

Scène d'amour **(13:19). CDs:** 09026-68979-2. **SACDs:** 82876-67899-2

Queen Mab Scherzo **(7:46). CDs:** 09026-61400-2. 74321-84587-2 (2)

RAVEL, MAURICE
La Valse **(11:46)**
BSO, conductor Charles Munch
February 2, 1962. Broadcast from Symphony Hall
BSO/IMG Artists
CDs: CB-100 (12)

FRANCK, CÉSAR
Le Chasseur maudit *(14:04)*
BSO, conductor Charles Munch
February 26, 1962. Symphony Hall
RCA, producer Richard Mohr
LPs: LM/LSC-2647. OPO-1002 (U.K.). **CDs:** 5750-2-RC. 60817-2-RG.
09026-68978-2. 82876-65833-2

CHAUSSON, ERNEST
Symphony in B♭, op. 20 (31:38)
BSO, conductor Charles Munch
February 26, 1962. Symphony Hall
RCA, producer Richard Mohr
LPs: LM/LSC-2647. **CDs:** 09026-60683-2. 74321-84591-2 (2)

TCHAIKOVSKY, PETER ILYICH
Symphony No. 6 in B Minor, op. 74 "Pathétique" (45:19)
BSO, conductor Charles Munch
March 12, 1962. Symphony Hall
RCA, producer Richard Mohr
LPs: LM/LSC-2683. **CDs:** 6527-2-RG. 09026-61563-2. ArkivCD 6527

DEBUSSY, CLAUDE
Printemps (15:47)
BSO, conductor Charles Munch
March 13, 1962. Symphony Hall
RCA, producer Richard Mohr
LPs: LM/LSC-2668. AGL1-4084. FVL3-7276 (3). **CDs:** 6719-2-RG. 74321-
    21293-2. 74321-84591-2 (2)

DEBUSSY, CLAUDE
Prélude à l'après-midi d'un faune (9:00)
BSO, conductor Charles Munch
March 13, 1962. Symphony Hall
RCA, producer Richard Mohr
LPs: LM/LSC-2668. AGL1-4084. LSC-5017. VICS-1668. FVL3-7276 (3).
    CDs: 6719-2-RG. 09026-61556-2. 09026-63424-2. 09026-63803-2. 82876-
    59416-2

DEBUSSY, CLAUDE
Nocturnes for Orchestra: Nuages (7:21). *Fêtes* (6:38)
BSO, conductor Charles Munch
March 13, 1962. Symphony Hall
RCA, producer Richard Mohr
LPs: LM/LSC-2668. AGL1-4084. FVL3-7276 (3). **CDs:** 6719-2-RG. 60692-2-
    RG. 09026-61556-2. 74321-21293-2. 74321-84591-2 (2). 82876-59416-2

Nuages. **CDs:** 09026-63424-2. 09026-63803-2

RAVEL, MAURICE
Boléro (14:57)
BSO, conductor Charles Munch
March 26, 1962. Symphony Hall
RCA, producer Richard Mohr
LPs: LM/LSC-2664. VIC/VICS-1323. AGL1-3653. AGL1-5236. **CDs:** 6522-2-
    RG. 74321-84604-2 (2)

RAVEL, MAURICE
La Valse (11:03)
BSO, conductor Charles Munch
March 26, 1962. Symphony Hall
RCA, producer Richard Mohr
LPs: LM/LSC-2664. LSC-5002. AGL1-3653. AGL1-5236. **CDs:** 6522-2-RG.
    09026-61712-2. 74321-84604-2 (2)

RAVEL, MAURICE
Pavane pour une infante défunte (5:36)
BSO, conductor Charles Munch
James Stagliano, French horn
March 26, 1962. Symphony Hall
RCA, producer Richard Mohr
LPs: LM/LSC-2664. LSC-5005. AGL1-3653. AGL1-5236. **CDs:** 6522-2-RG.
    09026-61712-2. 74321-84604-2 (2)

DEBUSSY, CLAUDE
La Mer (24:49)
BSO, conductor Charles Munch
March 30, 1962. Broadcast from Symphony Hall
BSO/IMG Artists
CDs: CB-100 (12)

BERLIOZ, HECTOR
Symphonie fantastique, op. 14 (49:20)
BSO, conductor Charles Munch
April 9, 1962. Symphony Hall
RCA, producer Richard Mohr
LPs: LM/LSC-2608. **CDs:** 7735-2-RV. 09026-61721-2. 74321-34168-2 (2).
    82876-60393-2 (10). *This recording is 3:42 slower than the live perform-*
    ance eight days later.

CONCERT VIDEO (96 minutes)
BERLIOZ *Symphonie fantastique*, op. 14 (45:38)
DEBUSSY *La Mer* (24:30)
RAVEL *Daphnis et Chloé: Suite No. 2* (16:03)
BSO, conductor Charles Munch
April 17, 1962. Sanders Theater (live telecast)
BSO and WGBH Educational Foundation. Producer Raymond Edwards
DVD: Video Artists International VAI-4317 (black and white, monaural)

FINE, IRVING
Symphony 1962 (23:04). *Premiered on March 23, 1962.*
BSO, conductor Irving Fine
August 12, 1962. *Recorded at Symphony Hall on December 11, 1964, "from the*
    broadcast at Tanglewood, August 12, 1962."
RCA, producer Richard Mohr
LPs: LM/LSC-2829. Desto DC-7167. **CDs:** Phoenix PHCD-106

EXPERIMENTAL RECORDING SESSION
R. STRAUSS *Till Eulenspiegels lustige Streiche*, op. 28: excerpts (11:00)
PISTON Symphony No. 7: excerpts (1:15)
BEETHOVEN Symphony No. 3 in E♭, op. 55 "Eroica:" excerpts (3:30)
BSO, conductor Erich Leinsdorf
September 20, 1962. Symphony Hall
RCA, producer Richard Mohr
Unreleased. *Mohr had been dissatisfied with Symphony Hall as a recording site, so this three-hour session was called "to experiment with several seating arrangements" (Erich Leinsdorf: Cadenza). This may have been the cause of a widely told story that "all the microphones on the east coast were in use." Two panels of experts agreed upon the optimum arrangement, but Leinsdorf writes that the locations of the players shifted incrementally over the years, upsetting balances. The session has been falsely attributed to Munch, because the American Federation of Musicians contract was typed on a preprinted form that still included him as conductor. Munch was paid no wages, however; Leinsdorf's name has been typed in at the bottom of page four, and a payment has been added in the appropriate column.*

BEETHOVEN, LUDWIG VAN
Symphony No. 3 in E♭, op. 55 "Eroica" (50:15)
BSO, conductor Erich Leinsdorf
September 30, 1962. Symphony Hall
RCA, producer Richard Mohr
LPs: LM/LSC-2644. VCS-6903 (7). AGL1-1525. CDs: 7878-2-RV. 60786-2-RV. ArkivCD 60786. 09026-61713-2. *This recording was mistakenly issued on Victrola VICS-1626, supposedly the December 2, 1957, recording led by Charles Munch. The error was corrected on later pressings. The Leinsdorf splits the Funeral March onto two sides; the Munch gets all of it on side one. (Lawrence H. Jones, email September 26, 2007)*

BARTÓK, BÉLA
Concerto for Orchestra (36:39)
BSO, conductor Erich Leinsdorf
October 13, 1962; October 14, 1962. Symphony Hall
RCA, producer Richard Mohr
LPs: LM/LSC-2643. CDs: 09026-63309-2

MAHLER, GUSTAV
Symphony No. 1 in D "Titan" (53:05)
BSO, conductor Erich Leinsdorf
October 20, 1962; October 21, 1962. Symphony Hall
RCA, producer Richard Mohr
LPs: LM/LSC-2642. AGL1-2941. CDs: 09026-63469-2 (2)

MENDELSSOHN, FELIX
A Midsummer Night's Dream, op. 21 and op. 61 (48:19)
"Boston Symphony Orchestra and Chorus," conductor Erich Leinsdorf
Arlene Saunders, soprano; Helen Vanni, mezzo-soprano; Inga Swensen, narrator
November 29, 1962; November 30, 1962; January 10, 1963. Manhattan Center,
New York City
RCA, producer Richard Mohr
LPs: LM/LSC-2673. LSC/D-2673. LM/D-2673. **CDs:** 7816-2-RV. 09026-60910-2. ArkivCD 60910. *LSC/D-2673 is a limited edition, housed in a 13.5 x 17 inch hard-cover folder, which also contains reproductions of two eighteenth-century engravings of Henry Fuseli paintings based on Shakespeare's play.*

STRAVINSKY, IGOR
Le Baiser de la fée: Divertimento (24:55)
BSO, conductor Richard Burgin
December 8, 1962. Broadcast from Symphony Hall
BSO/IMG Artists
CDs: CB-100 (12)

SCHUMANN, ROBERT
Symphony No. 4 in D Minor, op. 120 (30:30)
BSO, conductor Erich Leinsdorf
January 5, 1963; January 6, 1963. Symphony Hall
RCA, producer Richard Mohr
LPs: LM/LSC-2701. **CDs:** 60488-2-RV. 09026-61855-2. 74321-21284-2

BEETHOVEN, LUDWIG VAN
Leonore Overture No. 3, op. 72a (13:25)
BSO, conductor Erich Leinsdorf
January 6, 1963. Symphony Hall
RCA, producer Richard Mohr
LPs: LM/LSC-2701. OPO-1002 (U.K.)

MOZART, WOLFGANG AMADEUS
Serenade in G, K. 525 "Eine kleine Nachtmusik" (17:49)
BSO, conductor Erich Leinsdorf
January 6, 1963. Symphony Hall
RCA, producer Richard Mohr
LPs: LM/LSC-2694. **CDs:** 9305-2-RV. 09026-60907-2. 09026-61552-2. 09026-68113-2. ArkivCD 60907

MOZART, WOLFGANG AMADEUS
Symphony No. 41 in C, K. 551 "Jupiter" (39:50)
BSO, conductor Erich Leinsdorf
January 14, 1963. Symphony Hall
RCA, producer Richard Mohr
LPs: LM/LSC-2694. **CDs:** 9305-2-RV

BERLIOZ, HECTOR
Les Troyens: *Royal Hunt and Storm* (9:45)
BSO, conductor Charles Munch
January 26, 1963. WCRB Broadcast
Boston Symphony Transcription Trust, producers Jordan M. Whitelaw and Richard L. Kaye
CDs: BSO-CD4 (promotional)

RAVEL, MAURICE
Concerto in G (21:07)
BSO, conductor Erich Leinsdorf
Lorin Hollander, piano
February 16, 1963. Symphony Hall
RCA, producer Richard Mohr
LPs: LM/LSC-2667

DELLO JOIO, NORMAN
Fantasy and Variations for Piano and Orchestra (21:24)
BSO, conductor Erich Leinsdorf
Lorin Hollander, piano
February 17, 1963. Symphony Hall
RCA, producer Richard Mohr
LPs: LM/LSC-2667

BEETHOVEN, LUDWIG VAN
Concerto for Piano and Orchestra No. 5 in E♭, op. 73 "Emperor" (37:48)
BSO, conductor Erich Leinsdorf
Artur Rubinstein, piano
March 4, 1963. Symphony Hall
RCA, producer Max Wilcox
LPs: LM/LSC-2733. VCS-6417 (4). VCS-7087 (2). CRL7-0725 (7). AGL1-4220. **CDs:** 5676-2-RC. 09026-63058-2

TCHAIKOVSKY, PETER ILYICH
Concerto for Piano and Orchestra No. 1 in B♭ Minor, op. 23 (33:31)
BSO, conductor Erich Leinsdorf
Artur Rubinstein, piano
March 5, 1963. Symphony Hall
RCA, producer Max Wilcox
LPs: LM/LSC-2681. LSC-3305. VCS-7070 (2). VCS-7086 (2). CRL7-0725 (7). AGL1-4878. AGL1-5217. **CDs:** RCD1-5363. 6259-2-RC. 09026-61262-2. 09026-63037-2. 7863562592. Philips 456 958-2 (2)

STRAUSS, RICHARD
Ein Heldenleben, op. 40 (41:26)
BSO, conductor Erich Leinsdorf
Joseph Silverstein, violin; James Stagliano, horn
RCA, producer Richard Mohr
March 9, 1963; March 10, 1963. Symphony Hall
LPs: LM/LSC-2641

PROKOFIEV, SERGEI
Symphony-Concerto in E Minor for Cello and Orchestra, op. 125 (37:10)
BSO, conductor Erich Leinsdorf
Samuel Mayes, cello
March 25, 1963. Symphony Hall
RCA, producer Richard Mohr
LPs: LM/LSC-2703. *This recording was financed by a personal friend of cellist Samuel Mayes. (Erich Leinsdorf:* Cadenza*)*

FAURÉ, GABRIEL
Elégie, op. 24 (7:15)
BSO, conductor Erich Leinsdorf
Samuel Mayes, cello
March 25, 1963. Symphony Hall
RCA, producer Richard Mohr
LPs: LM/LSC-2703

CONCERT VIDEO (89 minutes)
BRITTEN *War Requiem*, op. 66 (80:22). *American premiere.*
BSO, conductor Erich Leinsdorf
Phyllis Curtin, soprano; Nicholas Di Virgilio, tenor; Tom Krause, bass; Chorus Pro Musica, Alfred Nash Patterson, dir.; Columbus Boychoir, Donald Bryant, dir.; Daniel Pinkham, portative organ
July 23, 1963. Koussevitzky Music Shed, Tanglewood (live telecast)
BSO and WGBH Educational Foundation, producer Jordan M. Whitelaw. Produced for DVD by Allan Altman
DVD: Video Artists International VAI-4429 (black and white; stereo)

BRAHMS, JOHANNES
Symphony No. 1 in C Minor, op. 68 (42:26)
BSO, conductor Erich Leinsdorf
September 29, 1963. Symphony Hall
RCA, producer Richard Mohr
LPs: LM/LSC-2711. LSC-6186 (3)

PROKOFIEV, SERGEI
Symphony No. 5 in B♭, op. 100 (44:47)
BSO, conductor Erich Leinsdorf
October 28, 1963. Symphony Hall
RCA, producer Richard Mohr
LPs: LM/LSC-2707. **CDs:** 09026-21292-2. Testament SBT-1396

MAHLER, GUSTAV
Symphony No. 5 in C♯ Minor (64:42)
BSO, conductor Erich Leinsdorf
James Stagliano, French horn; Roger Voisin, trumpet
November 17, 1963; November 23, 1963; November 26, 1963. Symphony Hall
RCA, producer Richard Mohr
LPs: LM/LSC-7031 (2). **CDs:** 60482-2-RV. 09026-68365-2. ArkivCD 60482

BEETHOVEN, LUDWIG VAN
Symphony No. 3 in E♭, op. 55 "Eroica:" II. Funeral March (16:36)
BSO, conductor Erich Leinsdorf
November 22, 1963. Symphony Hall (live)
BSO/TDK
CDs: "Tanglewood 98" (promotional)

RIMSKY-KORSAKOV, NIKOLAI
Le Coq d'or: **Suite (23:01)**
BSO, conductor Erich Leinsdorf
November 24, 1963; April 24, 1964. Symphony Hall
RCA, producer Richard Mohr
LPs: LM/LSC-2725. AGL1-1528. *The issued version of the Suite includes King Dodon in his Palace, King Dodon in the Country, King Dodon with the Queen of Shemakha, Wedding March and Lamentable End of King Dodon.*

RIMSKY-KORSAKOV, NIKOLAI
Le Coq d'or: **"Hymn to the Sun"**
BSO, conductor Erich Leinsdorf
Anna Moffo, soprano
November 24, 1963. Symphony Hall
RCA, producer Richard Mohr
Unreleased. *This was to be included in above recording of the Suite, which then totaled 21:30. When the Suite was re-recorded in 1964, this aria was dropped and other sections added.*

VAUGHAN WILLIAMS, RALPH
Fantasia on a Theme by Thomas Tallis **(12:49)**
BSO, conductor Pierre Monteux
December 20, 1963. Broadcast from Symphony Hall
BSO/IMG Artists
CDs: CB-100 (12)

LANNER, JOSEPH
"Die Mozartisten" Waltzes, op. 196 (9:41)
BSO, conductor Erich Leinsdorf
December 31, 1963. Broadcast from Symphony Hall
Boston Symphony Transcription Trust, producers Jordan M. Whitelaw and Richard L. Kaye
CDs: BSO-CD1 (promotional). *1988 "Salute to Symphony."*

LANNER, JOSEPH
"Die Mozartisten" Waltzes, op. 196 (10:03)
BSO, conductor Erich Leinsdorf
January 3, 1964. Broadcast from Symphony Hall
BSO/IMG Artists
CDs: CB-100 (12)

MOZART, WOLFGANG AMADEUS
Requiem Mass in D Minor, K. 626 (57:30 / 88:17)
BSO, conductor Erich Leinsdorf
Sara Mae Endich, soprano; Eunice Alberts, mezzo-soprano; Nicholas Di Vir-
gilio, tenor; Mac Morgan, baritone; Berj Zamkochian, organ; Chorus Pro
Musica, Alfred Nash Patterson, dir.; Harvard Glee Club and Radcliffe Cho-
ral Society, Elliot Forbes, dir.; NECC, Lorna Cooke DeVaron, dir.
January 19, 1964. Cathedral of the Holy Cross, Boston (live)
RCA, producer Richard Mohr
LPs: LM/LSC-7030 (2). **CDs:** RCA Japan BVCC-38391/92 (88697-03206-2
[2]). *Recorded at a mass in memory of President John Fitzgerald Kennedy,*
Mozart's Requiem is incorporated into the liturgical ceremony celebrated
by Richard Cardinal Cushing. The music and the spoken sections appear on
separate LP bands and CD tracks. The BSO and its musicians donated their
services for this performance and recording. In one late issue of the LP set,
the content of side one was also pressed on side two.

BIZET, GEORGES
Symphony in C (23:42)
BSO, conductor Charles Munch
February 1, 1964. WCRB Broadcast
Boston Symphony Transcription Trust, producers Jordan M. Whitelaw and
Richard L. Kaye
CDs: BSO-CD4 (promotional). *At this performance, Munch plays no repeats in*
the symphony, not even those in the third movement, Allegro vivace (a clas-
sical Minuet form). Lawrence H. Jones brought this to my attention.

BRAHMS, JOHANNES
Concerto for Piano and Orchestra No. 1 in D Minor, op. 15 (45:51)
BSO, conductor Erich Leinsdorf
Van Cliburn, piano
March 16, 1964; March 17, 1964; March 18, 1964. Symphony Hall
RCA, producer Richard Mohr
LPs: LM/LSC-2724. **CDs:** 60357-2-RG. 09026-60357-2. ArkivCD 60357

PROKOFIEV, SERGEI
Concerto for Piano and Orchestra No. 5 in G, op. 55 (22:50)
BSO, conductor Erich Leinsdorf
Lorin Hollander, piano
March 28, 1964. Symphony Hall
RCA, producer Richard Mohr
LPs: LM/LSC-2732

BERLIOZ, HECTOR
La Damnation de Faust, op. 24: *Rákóczy March* (4:41)
BSO, conductor Erich Leinsdorf
April 8, 1964; April 13, 1964. Symphony Hall
RCA, producer Richard Mohr
LPs: LM/LSC-2757. **CDs:** 7881-2-RV

WAGNER, RICHARD
Tannhäuser: Festival March ("Entrance of the Guests") (6:40)
BSO, conductor Erich Leinsdorf
Harvard Glee Club and Radcliffe Choral Society, Elliot Forbes, dir.
April 8, 1964. Symphony Hall
RCA, producer Richard Mohr
LPs: LM/LSC-2757. **CDs:** 7881-2-RV. 09026-60847-2. 09026-61241-2

SOUSA, JOHN PHILIP
The Stars and Stripes Forever (3:12)
BSO, conductor Erich Leinsdorf
April 8, 1964. Symphony Hall
RCA, producer Richard Mohr
LPs: LM/LSC-2757. *A CD, 7881-2-RV, includes the same mix of Boston Pops and Boston Symphony marches as LM/LSC-2757, except that Leinsdorf's* The Stars and Stripes Forever *has been replaced by an Arthur Fiedler Boston Pops recording. Fiedler is a bit slower than Leinsdorf, and the BSO's piccolo solos are more vivacious than those of the Pops.*

PROKOFIEV, SERGEI
Concerto for Violin and Orchestra No. 1 in D, op. 19 (21:40)
BSO, conductor Erich Leinsdorf
Erick Friedman, violin
April 13, 1964. Symphony Hall
RCA, producer Richard Mohr
LPs: LM/LSC-2732. **CDs:** Testament SBT2-1376 (2)

TCHAIKOVSKY, PETER ILYICH
Marche slave in B♭, op. 31 (10:13)
BSO, conductor Erich Leinsdorf
April 13, 1964. Symphony Hall
RCA, producer Richard Mohr
LPs: LM/LSC-2757. **CDs:** 7881-2-RV. 60845-2-RG

BEETHOVEN, LUDWIG VAN
Concerto for Piano and Orchestra No. 4 in G, op. 58 (33:15)
BSO, conductor Erich Leinsdorf
Artur Rubinstein, piano
April 20, 1964. Symphony Hall
RCA, producer Max Wilcox
LPs: LM/LSC-2848. VCS-6417 (4). AGL1-4369. Franklin Mint Record Society FMRS-7056, 1960 (5). **CDs:** 5676-2-RC. 09026-63058-2. 09026-68083-2

BRAHMS, JOHANNES
Concerto for Piano and Orchestra No. 1 in D Minor, op. 15 (47:04)
BSO, conductor Erich Leinsdorf
Artur Rubinstein, piano
April 21, 1964; April 22, 1964; April 24, 1964. Symphony Hall
RCA, producer Max Wilcox
LPs: LM/LSC-2917. VCS-7071 (2). **CDs:** 09026-63059-2

STRAVINSKY, IGOR
The Firebird: Suite (1945) (27:01)
BSO, conductor Erich Leinsdorf
April 22, 1964; April 24, 1964. Symphony Hall
RCA, producer Richard Mohr
LPs: LM/LSC-2725. AGL1-1528. **CDs:** 60541-2-RV

BARTÓK, BÉLA
Concerto for Violin and Orchestra No. 2 (35:48)
BSO, conductor Erich Leinsdorf
Joseph Silverstein, violin
April 23, 1964; April 24, 1964. Symphony Hall
RCA, producer Richard Mohr
LPs: LM/LSC-2852

BERG, ALBAN
Wozzeck: **Act I, Scene 3; Act III, Scenes 1, 4, and 5 (18:57)**
BSO, conductor Erich Leinsdorf
Phyllis Curtin, soprano; Sacred Heart Boychoir of Roslindale, Mass. John
    Oliver, dir.
April 23, 1964. Symphony Hall
RCA, producer Richard Mohr
LPs: LM/LSC 7031 (2). *This recording joins Act III, Scene 4, after Wozzeck
drowns and continues to the end of the opera.*

SHOSTAKOVICH, DMITRI
Symphony No. 1 in F Minor, op. 10 (29:59)
BSO, conductor Erich Leinsdorf
September 26, 1964. Broadcast from Symphony Hall
BSO/IMG Artists
CDs: CB-100 (12)

VERDI, GIUSEPPE
Requiem Mass "In Memory of Manzoni" (81:27)
BSO, conductor Erich Leinsdorf
Birgit Nilsson, soprano; Lili Chookasian, mezzo-soprano; Carlos Bergonzi, te-
    nor; Ezio Flagello, bass; Chorus Pro Musica, Alfred Nash Patterson, dir.
October 5, 1964; October 6, 1964; October 7, 1964; October 19, 1964; April 5,
    1965 (patch). Symphony Hall (live)
RCA, producer Richard Mohr
LPs: LM/LSC-7040 (2). **CDs:** 09026-63747-2 (2)

SCHOENBERG, ARNOLD
Gurrelieder: Interlude (7:36); Song of the Wood Dove (10:26) (18:02)
BSO, conductor Erich Leinsdorf
Lili Chookasian, mezzo-soprano
October 19, 1964. Symphony Hall
RCA, producer Richard Mohr
LPs: LM/LSC-2785. **CDs:** 09026-63747-2 (2)

MENOTTI, GIAN CARLO
The Death of the Bishop of Brindisi (31:10)
BSO, conductor Erich Leinsdorf
George London, bass; Lili Chookasian, mezzo-soprano; NECC, Lorna Cooke
DeVaron, dir.; Members of Catholic Memorial High School and St. Jo-
seph's High School Glee Clubs, Berj Zamkochian, dir.
October 19, 1964. Symphony Hall
RCA, producer Richard Mohr
LPs: LM/LSC-2785. **CDs:** 09026-63747-2

LISZT, FRANZ
Concerto for Piano and Orchestra No. 2 in A
BSO, conductor Erich Leinsdorf
Van Cliburn, piano
November 21, 1964. Symphony Hall
RCA, producer Richard Mohr
Unreleased. *The payment sheet states that this studio recording was made from
10 AM to noon. The work was then played on the evening concert that day.*

KODÁLY, ZOLTÁN
Variations on a Hungarian Folk Song "The Peacock" (25:00)
BSO, conductor Erich Leinsdorf
November 23, 1964. Symphony Hall
RCA, producer Richard Mohr
LPs: LM/LSC-2859. **CDs:** 09026-63309-2

SCHULLER, GUNTHER
Seven Studies on Themes of Paul Klee (21:07)
BSO, conductor Erich Leinsdorf
James Pappoutsakis, flute
November 23, 1964. Symphony Hall
RCA, producer Richard Mohr
LPs: LM/LSC-2879

BRAHMS, JOHANNES
Symphony No. 2 in D, op. 73 (39:11)
BSO, conductor Erich Leinsdorf
December 14, 1964; December 16, 1964. Symphony Hall
RCA, producer Richard Mohr
LPs: LM/LSC-2809. LSC-6186 (3). **CDs:** 60129-2-RV. 09026-68082-2

FINE, IRVING
Toccata Concertante (10:28)
BSO, conductor Erich Leinsdorf
January 25, 1965. Symphony Hall
RCA, producer Richard Mohr
LPs: LM/LSC-2829. Desto DC-7167. **CDs:** Phoenix PHCD-106

FINE, IRVING
Serious Song: Lament for String Orchestra (9:56)
BSO, conductor Erich Leinsdorf
January 25, 1965; December 2, 1965; January 10, 1966. Symphony Hall
RCA, producer Richard Mohr
LPs: LM/LSC-2829. Desto DC-7167. **CDs:** Phoenix PHCD-106

BEETHOVEN, LUDWIG VAN
Concerto for Piano and Orchestra No. 3 in C Minor, op. 37 (35:23)
BSO, conductor Erich Leinsdorf
Artur Rubinstein, piano
April 5, 1965; April 6, 1965. Symphony Hall
RCA, producer Richard Mohr
LPs: LM/LSC-2947. VCS-6417 (4). **CDs:** 5675-2-RC. 09026-63057-2

STRAVINSKY, IGOR
Agon (20:36)
BSO, conductor Erich Leinsdorf
April 19, 1965. Symphony Hall
RCA, producer Richard Mohr
LPs: LM/LSC-2879

BERG, ALBAN
Le Vin (concert aria) (12:08)
BSO, conductor Erich Leinsdorf
Phyllis Curtin, soprano
April 19, 1965. Symphony Hall
RCA, producer Richard Mohr
LPs: LM/LSC-7044 (2). *Of this aria* [Der Wien] *the biographer H. F. Redlich writes: "It's a pity that Berg, whose knowledge of French seems to have been only elementary, became acquainted with Baudelaire's poems in Stefan George's translations, in which the poetical climate is radically changed. Baudelaire's elegant obscenities are often transposed to a lower key of severe solemnity, and some of the lines are deliberately rendered inaccurately. . . . In this recording Erich Leinsdorf and Phyllis Curtin have restored the original text." (Jack Diether, in the program notes to this release). Thanks to Barbara Perkel for unearthing this.*

COPLAND, AARON
Music for a Great City **(25:45)**
BSO, conductor Aaron Copland
April 10, 1965. Broadcast from Symphony Hall
BSO/IMG Artists
CDs: CB-100 (12)

MAHLER, GUSTAV
Symphony No. 6 in A Minor "Tragic" (73:45)
BSO, conductor Erich Leinsdorf
April 20, 1965; April 21, 1965. Symphony Hall
RCA, producer Richard Mohr
LPs: LM/LSC-7044 (2). **CDs:** RCA Japan BVCC-37325 (74321-91622-2)

KODÁLY, ZOLTÁN
Háry János: **Suite (20:57)**
BSO, conductor Erich Leinsdorf
Toni Koves-Steiner, cimbalom
April 22, 1965. Symphony Hall
RCA, producer Richard Mohr
LPs: LM/LSC-2859. **Intermezzo** only: U4LS-0607 (7-inch promotional LP)

STRAUSS, RICHARD
Die Ägyptische Helena, op. **75: Act II, Awakening Scene (4:52)**
BSO, conductor Erich Leinsdorf
Leontyne Price, soprano
April 22, 1965. Symphony Hall
RCA, producer Richard Mohr
LPs: LM/LSC-2849. **CDs:** 60398-2-RG. ArkivCD 60398

STRAUSS, RICHARD
Salome, op. **54:** *Dance of the Seven Veils* **(9:48)**
BSO, conductor Erich Leinsdorf
April 22, 1965. Symphony Hall
RCA, producer Richard Mohr
LPs: LM/LSC-2849

STRAVINSKY, IGOR
Concerto for Violin and Orchestra (20:54)
BSO, conductor Erich Leinsdorf
Josef Silverstein, violin
April 22, 1965; April 23, 1965. Symphony Hall
RCA, producer Richard Mohr
LPs: LM/LSC-2852

PROKOFIEV, SERGEI
Symphony No. 6 in E♭ Minor, op. 111 (42:44)
BSO, conductor Erich Leinsdorf
April 23, 1965; April 24, 1965. Symphony Hall
RCA, producer Richard Mohr
LPs: LM/LSC-2834. **CDs:** Testament SBT-1395

WAGNER, RICHARD
Lohengrin: **Preludes to Acts I and III**
BSO, conductor Erich Leinsdorf
April 24, 1965. Symphony Hall
RCA, producer Richard Mohr
LPs: LM/LSC-6710 (5). *Issued only as part of the complete* Lohengrin *(below).*

STRAUSS, RICHARD
Salome, op. 54: **Interlude and Final scene (4:09, 15:08)**
BSO, conductor Erich Leinsdorf
Leontyne Price, soprano
April 24, 1965. Symphony Hall
RCA, producer Richard Mohr
LPs: LM/LSC-2849. **CDs:** 60398-2-RG. ArkivCD 60398

FRANCK, CÉSAR
Symphonic Variations (15:57)
BSO, conductor Charles Munch
Nicole Henriot-Schweitzer, piano
August 1, 1965. WCRB Broadcast
Boston Symphony Transcription Trust, producers Jordan M. Whitelaw and
    Richard L. Kaye
CDs: BSO-CD4 (promotional)

WAGNER, RICHARD
Lohengrin (3:36:19)
BSO, conductor Erich Leinsdorf
Lucine Amara, soprano (Elsa); Sándor Kónya, tenor (Lohengrin); Rita Gorr,
    mezzo-soprano (Ortrud); Wiliam Dooley, baritone (Frederick); Jerome
    Hines, bass (King Henry); Calvin Marsh, baritone (Herald); Chorus Pro
    Musica (augmented to 180 voices), Alfred Nash Patterson, dir.
August 23, 1965; August 24, 1965; August 25, 1965; August 26, 1965; August
    27, 1965; August 28, 1965. Symphony Hall
RCA, producer Richard Mohr
LPs: LM/LSC-6710 (5). **CDs:** 74321-50164-2 (3). *The orchestra was placed on
    the main floor, the chorus up on the stage. This was the first complete re-
    cording of* Lohengrin. *It was "the most expensive five-record album ever
    produced" (Leinsdorf: Cadenza), and the biggest money-losing recording of
    all time, "a disaster for which I have readily shouldered the lion's share of
    responsibility. I was, however, most ably assisted by RCA." Leontyne Price
    was supposed to sing Elsa, but she eventually chose not to participate.*

WAGNER, RICHARD
Siegfried Idyll (18:26)
BSO, conductor Erich Leinsdorf
October 1, 1965. Broadcast from Symphony Hall
BSO/IMG Artists
CDs: CB-100 (12)

CONCERT VIDEO COLLECTION (107 minutes)
WAGNER *Götterdämmerung: Dawn and Siegfried's Rhine Journey* (11:48)
WAGNER *Siegfried Idyll* (17:45)
BEETHOVEN Symphony No. 9 in D Minor, op. 125 "Choral" (67:24)
BSO, conductor Erich Leinsdorf
Jane Marsh, soprano; Eunice Alberts, mezzo-soprano; Richard Cassilly, tenor; Thomas Paul, bass; Harvard Glee Club and Radcliffe Choral Society, Elliot Forbes, dir.; NECC, Lorna Cooke DeVaron, dir.
October 19, 1965 (Beethoven). December 14, 1965 (Wagner). Symphony Hall (live telecasts)
BSO and WGBH Educational Foundation, producer Jordan M. Whitelaw
DVD: Video Artists International VAI-4361 (black and white; monaural)

PROKOFIEV, SERGEI
Concerto for Piano and Orchestra No. 2 in G Minor, op. 16 (31:31)
BSO, conductor Erich Leinsdorf
John Browning, piano
December 1, 1965. Symphony Hall
RCA, producer Richard Mohr
LPs: LM/LSC-2897. **CDs:** Testament SBT2-1376 (2)

PROKOFIEV, SERGEI
Concerto for Piano and Orchestra No. 1 in Db, op. 10 (16:09)
BSO, conductor Erich Leinsdorf
John Browning, piano
December 1, 1965; December 2, 1965. Symphony Hall
RCA, producer Richard Mohr
LPs: LM/LSC-2897. **CDs:** Testament SBT2-1376 (2)

BRUCKNER, ANTON
Symphony No. 4 in Eb "Romantic" (60:11)
BSO, conductor Erich Leinsdorf
January 10, 1966; January 11, 1966. Symphony Hall
RCA, producer Richard Mohr
LPs: LM/LSC-2915

BRAHMS, JOHANNES
Symphony No. 3 in F, op. 90 (38:26)
BSO, conductor Erich Leinsdorf
March 7, 1966. Symphony Hall
RCA, producer Richard Mohr
LPs: LM/LSC-2936. LSC-6186 (3)

PROKOFIEV, SERGEI
Symphony No. 3 in C Minor, op. 44 (34:34)
BSO, conductor Erich Leinsdorf
April 25, 1966. Symphony Hall
RCA, producer Richard Mohr
LPs: LM/LSC-2934. **CDs:** Testament SBT-1396

BRAHMS, JOHANNES
Tragic Overture, **op. 81 (12:35)**
BSO, conductor Erich Leinsdorf
April 26, 1966. Symphony Hall
RCA, producer Richard Mohr
LPs: LM/LSC-2936

BRAHMS, JOHANNES
Symphony No. 4 in E Minor, op. 98 (39:05)
BSO, conductor Erich Leinsdorf
April 26, 1966; April 27, 1966. Symphony Hall
RCA, producer Richard Mohr
LPs: LSC-3010. LSC-6186 (3)

MOZART, WOLFGANG AMADEUS
Mass in C Minor, K. 427: "Et incarnatus est" (8:25)
BSO, conductor Erich Leinsdorf
Veronica Tyler, soprano
July 24, 1966. Koussevitzky Music Shed, Tanglewood (live)
RCA, producer Howard Scott
Unreleased. *Information about these four vocal recordings comes from BSO payment sheets and the Tanglewood concert program for July 24, 1966. The payment sheet says Symphony Hall, but these were live performances at Tanglewood. There are no recording logs in the Sony BMG Archives.*

VERDI, GIUSEPPE
Don Carlo: **"Ella giammai m'amò. . . Dormirò sol" (9:12)**
BSO, conductor Erich Leinsdorf
Simon Estes, bass
July 24, 1966. Koussevitzky Music Shed, Tanglewood (live)
RCA, producer Howard Scott
Unreleased

VERDI, GIUSEPPE
Aida: "O patria mia" (8:28)
BSO, conductor Erich Leinsdorf
Jane Marsh, soprano
July 24, 1966. Koussevitzky Music Shed, Tanglewood (live)
RCA, producer Howard Scott
Unreleased

TCHAIKOVSKY, PETER ILYICH
Eugene Onegin: **Tatiana's Letter Scene** (12:50)
BSO, conductor Erich Leinsdorf
Jane Marsh, soprano
July 24, 1966. Koussevitzky Music Shed, Tanglewood (live)
RCA, producer Howard Scott
Unreleased

JANÁČEK, LEOŠ
The Cunning Little Vixen: **Suite** (arr. Talich) (17:53)
BSO, conductor Erich Leinsdorf
September 30, 1966. Broadcast from Symphony Hall
BSO/IMG Artists
CDs: CB-100 (12)

MAHLER, GUSTAV
Symphony No. 3 in D Minor (92:18)
BSO, conductor Erich Leinsdorf
Shirley Verrett, mezzo; NECC, Lorna Cooke DeVaron, dir.; Boston Boy Choir,
   John Oliver, dir.
October 10, 1966; October 11, 1966. Symphony Hall
RCA, producer Richard Mohr
LPs: LM/LSC-7046 (2). **CDs:** 09026-63469-2 (2)

PROKOFIEV, SERGEI
Scythian Suite, op. 20 "Ala and Lolli" (19:05)
BSO, conductor Erich Leinsdorf
October 24, 1966. Symphony Hall
RCA, producer Richard Mohr
LPs: LM/LSC-2934

BEETHOVEN, LUDWIG VAN
Coriolan Overture in C Minor, op. 62 (8:38)
BSO, conductor Erich Leinsdorf
November 21, 1966. Symphony Hall
RCA, producer Richard Mohr
LPs: LM/LSC-2969. AGL1-3966

BEETHOVEN, LUDWIG VAN
Symphony No. 7 in A, op. 92 (42:58)
BSO, conductor Erich Leinsdorf
November 21, 1966. Symphony Hall
RCA, producer Richard Mohr
LPs: LM/LSC-2969. VCS-6903 (7). AGL1-3966. **CDs:** 7997-2-RV

FAURÉ, GABRIEL
Pelléas et Mélisande, **Suite from the incidental music to Maeterlinck's drama, op. 80 (17:45)**
BSO, conductor Charles Munch
December 3, 1966. Broadcast from Symphony Hall
Boston Symphony Transcription Trust, producers Jordan M. Whitelaw and
    Richard L. Kaye
CDs: BSO-CD4 (promotional)

TCHAIKOVSKY, PETER ILYICH
Concerto for Piano and Orchestra No. 1 in B♭ Minor, op. 23 (34:03)
BSO, conductor Erich Leinsdorf
Mischa Dichter, piano
December 12, 1966; December 14, 1966. Symphony Hall
RCA, producer Richard Mohr
LPs: LM/LSC-2954. **CDs:** 6526-2-RG

CONCERT VIDEO (107:46)
BERLIOZ *L'Enfance du Christ*, **op. 25 (Part I: 41:53. II and III: 51:56)**
BSO, conductor Charles Munch
Florence Kopleff, contralto; John McCollum, tenor; Theodore Uppman, bari-
    tone; Donald Gramm, bass-baritone; Donald Meaders, baritone; Harvard
    Glee Club and Radcliffe Choral Society; Elliot Forbes, dir.
December 13, 1966. Symphony Hall (live telecast)
BSO and WGBH Educational Foundation, producer Jordan M. Whitelaw. Pro-
    duced for DVD by Raymond Edwards
DVD: Video Artists International VAI-4303 (black and white; stereo)

PROKOFIEV, SERGEI
Concerto for Violin and Orchestra No. 2 in G Minor, op. 63 (25:34)
BSO, conductor Erich Leinsdorf
Itzhak Perlman, violin
December 19, 1966. Symphony Hall
RCA, producer Richard Mohr
LPs: LM/LSC-2962. AGL1-1529. **CDs:** 09026-61454-2

HAYDN, FRANZ JOSEPH
Symphony No. 93 in D (23:09)
BSO, conductor Erich Leinsdorf
December 19, 1966. Symphony Hall
RCA, producer Richard Mohr
LPs: LSC-3030

BEETHOVEN, LUDWIG VAN
Leonore Overture No. 2, op. 72 (13:54)
BSO, conductor Erich Leinsdorf
December 19, 1966; December 20, 1966; December 22, 1966. Symphony Hall
RCA, producer Richard Mohr
LPs: LM/LSC-3006

BEETHOVEN, LUDWIG VAN
Symphony No. 4 in B♭, op. 60 (34:35)
BSO, conductor Erich Leinsdorf
December 20, 1966; December 21, 1966; December 22, 1966. Symphony Hall
RCA, producer Richard Mohr
LPs: LM/LSC-3006. VCS-6903 (7). **CDs:** 7745-2-RV

SIBELIUS, JEAN
Concerto for Violin and Orchestra in D Minor, op. 47 (29:19)
BSO, conductor Erich Leinsdorf
Itzhak Perlman, violin
December 21, 1966. Symphony Hall
RCA, producer Richard Mohr
LPs: LM/LSC-2962. AGL1-1529. **CDs:** 6520-2-RG. 07863-56520-2. 09026-
    63591-2. 09026-68338-2. 82876-59419-2. ArkivCD 6520

MOZART, WOLFGANG AMADEUS
Symphony No. 40 in G Minor, K. 550: I. Molto allegro (7:00)
BSO, conductor Erich Leinsdorf
December 21, 1966. Symphony Hall
RCA, producer Richard Mohr
Unreleased

BEETHOVEN, LUDWIG VAN
Leonore Overture No. 1 in C, op. 138 : fragment (1:20)
BSO, conductor Erich Leinsdorf
December 22, 1966. Symphony Hall
RCA, producer Richard Mohr
Unreleased

CARTER, ELLIOTT
Piano Concerto (26:20). *World premiere.*
BSO, conductor Erich Leinsdorf
Jacob Lateiner, piano
January 6, 1967; January 7, 1967. Symphony Hall (live)
RCA, producer Howard Scott
LPs: LM/LSC-3001

MARTINŮ, BOHUSLAV
Double Concerto for Two String Orchestras, Piano, and Timpani (18:41)
BSO, conductor Rafael Kubelík
Charles Wilson, piano; Everett Firth, timpani
January 14, 1967. Broadcast from Symphony Hall
BSO/IMG Artists
CDs: CB-100 (12)

PROKOFIEV, SERGEI
Romeo and Juliet, op. 64: Introduction. Juliet The Young Girl. Masks. Dance of the Knights. Gavotte. Romeo. Dance of Love. Dance of the Five Couples. Duel and Death of Tybalt. Act II Finale. Interlude. At the House of Juliet. Morning Serenade. Dance of the Maidens. Act II Introduction. Juliet's Funeral. Death of the Lovers. (52:23)
BSO, conductor Erich Leinsdorf
February 13, 1967. Symphony Hall
RCA, producer Richard Mohr
LPs: LM/LSC-2994. AGL1-1273. AGL1-5267. **CDs:** Testament SBT-1394

BEETHOVEN, LUDWIG VAN
Symphony No. 2 in D, op. 36 (34:18)
BSO, conductor Erich Leinsdorf
March 6, 1967. Symphony Hall
RCA, producer Richard Mohr
LPs: LSC-3032. VCS-6903 (7). **CDs:** 60130-2-RV

COLGRASS, MICHAEL
As Quiet As (13:55)
BSO, conductor Erich Leinsdorf
April 19, 1967. Symphony Hall
RCA, producer Howard H. Scott
LPs: LM/LSC-3001

SMETANA, BEDŘICH
Má Vlast: Vltava (The Moldau) (11:24)
BSO, conductor Erich Leinsdorf
April 22, 1967. Broadcast from Symphony Hall
BSO/IMG Artists
CDs: CB-100 (12)

WAGNER, RICHARD
Der fliegende Holländer: Overture (9:56)
BSO, conductor Erich Leinsdorf
October 30, 1967. Symphony Hall
RCA, producer Richard Mohr
LPs: LM/LSC-3011

WAGNER, RICHARD
Die Meistersinger von Nürnberg: **Act I Prelude (9:43)**
BSO, conductor Erich Leinsdorf
October 30, 1967. Symphony Hall
RCA, producer Richard Mohr
LPs: LM/LSC-3011

BEETHOVEN, LUDWIG VAN
The Creatures of Prometheus, op. 43: Overture. Pastorale: Allegro. Adagio.
Finale (21:33)
BSO, conductor Erich Leinsdorf
Bernard Zighera, harp; Doriot Anthony Dwyer, flute; Sherman Walt, bassoon;
Jules Eskin, cello; Gino Cioffi, clarinet.
October 30, 1967. Symphony Hall
RCA, producer Richard Mohr
LPs: LSC-3032. **CDs:** 7878-2-RV. 60130-2-RV. 60786-2-RV. 09026-61130-2

PROKOFIEV, SERGEI
Concerto for Piano and Orchestra No. 3 in C, op. 26 (28:55)
BSO, conductor Erich Leinsdorf
John Browning, piano
November 25, 1967; November 27, 1967. Symphony Hall
RCA, producer Richard Mohr
LPs: LSC-3019. **CDs:** Testament SBT2-1376 (2)

PROKOFIEV, SERGEI
Concerto for Piano (left hand) and Orchestra No. 4 in B♭, op. 53 (22:33)
BSO, conductor Erich Leinsdorf
John Browning, piano
November 27, 1967. Symphony Hall
RCA, producer Richard Mohr
LPs: LSC-3019. **CDs:** Testament SBT2-1376 (2)

TCHAIKOVSKY, PETER ILYICH
Concerto for Violin and Orchestra in D, op. 35 (33:52)
BSO, conductor Erich Leinsdorf
Itzhak Perlman, violin
December 18, 1967; December 19, 1967. Symphony Hall
RCA, producer Richard Mohr
LPs: LSC-3014. AGL1-1266. **CDs:** 6526-2-RG. 09026-63591-2. 82876-59419-2

DVOŘÁK, ANTONIN
Romance in F Minor, op. 11 (11:55)
BSO, conductor Erich Leinsdorf
Itzhak Perlman, violin
December 18, 1967; December 19, 1967. Symphony Hall
RCA, producer Richard Mohr
LPs: LSC-3014. AGL1-1266. **CDs:** 09026-63591-2. 09026-63752-2

WAGNER, RICHARD
Tristan und Isolde: Prelude (with concert ending by Wagner) (11:42)
BSO, conductor Erich Leinsdorf
December 19, 1967. Symphony Hall
RCA, producer Richard Mohr
LPs: LM/LSC-3011

WAGNER, RICHARD
Tannhäuser: Overture (13:56)
BSO, conductor Erich Leinsdorf
December 19, 1967; December 22, 1967. Symphony Hall
RCA, producer Richard Mohr
LPs: LM/LSC-3011

DVOŘÁK, ANTONIN
Symphony No. 6 in D, op. 60 (40:45)
BSO, conductor Erich Leinsdorf
December 19, 1967; December 22, 1967. Symphony Hall
RCA, producer Richard Mohr
LPs: LSC-3017

BEETHOVEN, LUDWIG VAN
Concerto for Piano and Orchestra No. 1 in C, op. 15 (37:25)
BSO, conductor Erich Leinsdorf
Artur Rubinstein, piano
December 20, 1967; December 21, 1967. Symphony Hall
RCA, producer Max Wilcox
LPs: LSC-3013. VCS-6417 (4). **CDs:** 5674-2-RC. 09026-63057-2. 09026-
   68083-2

BEETHOVEN, LUDWIG VAN
Concerto for Piano and Orchestra No. 2 in B♭, op. 19 (29:15)
BSO, conductor Erich Leinsdorf
Artur Rubinstein, piano
December 20, 1967; December 21, 1967. Symphony Hall
RCA, producer Max Wilcox
LPs: VCS-6417 (4). ARL1-4349. **CDs:** 5675-2-RC. 09026-63059-2

MOZART, WOLFGANG AMADEUS
Symphony No. 36 in C, K. 425 "Linz" (26:48)
BSO, conductor Erich Leinsdorf
December 22, 1967. Symphony Hall
RCA, producer Richard Mohr
LPs: LSC-3097. **CDs:** 09026-60907-2. ArkivCD 60907

DVOŘÁK, ANTONIN
Slavonic Dance in E Minor, op. 72, no. 2 (5:16)
BSO, conductor Erich Leinsdorf
December 22, 1967. Symphony Hall
RCA, producer Richard Mohr
LPs: LSC-3017

DVOŘÁK, ANTONIN
Slavonic Dance in A♭, op. 72, no. 8 (6:32)
BSO, conductor Erich Leinsdorf
December 23, 1967. Symphony Hall
RCA, producer Richard Mohr
LPs: LSC-3017

BEETHOVEN, LUDWIG VAN
Symphony No. 5 in C Minor, op. 67 (31:41)
BSO, conductor Erich Leinsdorf
December 23, 1967; April 8, 1968; April 16, 1968. Symphony Hall
RCA, producer Richard Mohr
LPs: LSC-7055 (2). VCS-6903 (7). **CDs:** 7745-2-RV

MOZART, WOLFGANG AMADEUS
Don Giovanni, K. 527: **Overture** (7:13)
BSO, conductor Leopold Stokowski
January 13, 1968. Broadcast from Symphony Hall
BSO/IMG Artists
CDs: CB-100 (12)

TCHAIKOVSKY, PETER ILYICH
Hamlet (fantasy-overture) in F Minor, op. 67 (15:53)
BSO, conductor Leopold Stokowski
January 13, 1968. Broadcast from Symphony Hall
BSO/IMG Artists
CDs: CB-100 (12)

GINASTERA, ALBERTO
Concerto for Piano and Orchestra (22:28)
BSO, conductor Erich Leinsdorf
João Carlos Martins, piano
March 6, 1968. Symphony Hall
RCA, producer Richard Mohr
LPs: LSC-3029

GINASTERA, ALBERTO
Variaciones concertantes, op. 23 (21:15)
BSO, conductor Erich Leinsdorf
March 11, 1968. Symphony Hall
RCA, producer Richard Mohr
LPs: LSC-3029

PROKOFIEV, SERGEI
Symphony No. 2 in D Minor, op. 40 (31:50)
BSO, conductor Erich Leinsdorf
March 25, 1968; April 16, 1968. Symphony Hall
RCA, producer Richard Mohr
LPs: LSC-3061. **CDs:** Testament SBT-1395

HAYDN, FRANZ JOSEPH
Symphony No. 96 in D "Miracle" (23:19)
BSO, conductor Erich Leinsdorf
April 8, 1968. Symphony Hall
RCA, producer Richard Mohr
LPs: LSC-3030

MOZART, WOLFGANG AMADEUS
Symphony No. 38 in D, K. 504 "Prague": I. Allegro. II. Andante
BSO, conductor Erich Leinsdorf
April 16, 1968. Symphony Hall
RCA, producer Richard Mohr
Unreleased

PROKOFIEV, SERGEI
Lieutenant Kijé Suite, op. 60 (19:43)
BSO, conductor Erich Leinsdorf
David Clatworthy, narrator
April 22, 1968. Symphony Hall
RCA, producer Richard Mohr
LPs: LSC-3061. **CDs:** 09026-21292-2. Testament SBT-1394

BRAHMS, JOHANNES
Ein deutsches Requiem (A German Requiem), op. 45 (69:45)
BSO, conductor Erich Leinsdorf
Monserrat Caballé, soprano; Sherrill Milnes, baritone; NECC, Lorna Cooke
    DeVaron, dir.
November 25, 1968; December 16, 1968; February 17, 1969. Symphony Hall
RCA, producer Peter Dellheim
LPs: LSC-7054 (2). **CDs:** 6800-2-RG

CONCERT VIDEO (94 minutes)
R. STRAUSS *Ariadne auf Naxos* (original 1912 version) (81:07)
BSO, conductor Erich Leinsdorf
Claire Watson (Ariadne); Beverly Sills (Zerbinetta); Robert Nagy (Bacchus);
    John Reardon (Harlekin); Benita Valente (Najade); Eunice Alberts (Dry-
    ade); Carole Bogarde (Echo); Malcolm Smith (Truffaldin); John Ferrante
    (Brighella); James Billings (Scaramuccio); Andrew Raeburn (M. Jordain)
Jamuary 7, 1969. Symphony Hall (live telecast)
BSO and WGBH Educational Foundation, producer Jordan M. Whitelaw. Pro-
    duced for DVD by Allan Altman
DVD: Video Artists International VAI-4363 (color; monaural)

BEETHOVEN, LUDWIG VAN
Symphony No. 6 in F, op. 68 "Pastoral" (38:36)
BSO, conductor Erich Leinsdorf
January 13, 1969. Symphony Hall
RCA, producer Peter Dellheim
LPs: LSC-3074. VCS-6903 (7). **CDs:** 7996-2-RV. 09026-61720-2

SCHARWENKA, FRANZ XAVER
Concerto for Piano and Orchestra No. 1 in B♭ Minor, op. 32 (28:12)
BSO, conductor Erich Leinsdorf
Earl Wild, piano
January 20, 1969. Symphony Hall
RCA, producer Peter Dellheim
LPs: LSC-3080. AGL1-2876. **CDs:** Elan CD-82266

MOZART, WOLFGANG AMADEUS
Symphony No. 39 in E♭, K. 543 (28:25)
BSO, conductor Erich Leinsdorf
January 20, 1969; April 23, 1969; April 24, 1969; April 25, 1969. Symphony
    Hall
RCA, producer Peter Dellheim
LPs: LSC-3097. **CDs:** 09026-60907-2. ArkivCD 60907

BERLIOZ, HECTOR
Symphonie fantastique, op. 14 (51:19)
BSO, conductor Georges Prêtre
February 3, 1969. Symphony Hall
RCA, producer Peter Dellheim
LPs: LSC-3096. VICS-1646. **CDs:** 6720-2-RG. 60478-2-RV

BEETHOVEN, LUDWIG VAN
Symphony No. 9 in D Minor, op. 125 "Choral" (65:52)
BSO, conductor Erich Leinsdorf
Jane Marsh, soprano; Josephine Veasey, mezzo-soprano; Placido Domingo,
    tenor; Sherrill Milnes, baritone; NECC, Lorna Cooke DeVaron, dir.;
    Chorus Pro Musica, Alfred Nash Patterson, dir.
April 21, 1969; April 22, 1969. Symphony Hall
RCA, producer Peter Dellheim
LPs: LSC-7055 (2). VCS-6903 (7). **CDs:** 7880-2-RV. 09026-63682-2 (2)

SCHOENBERG, ARNOLD
A Survivor from Warsaw, op. 46 (6:30)
BSO, conductor Erich Leinsdorf
Sherrill Milnes, speaker; NECC, Lorna Cooke DeVaron, dir.
April 23, 1969. Symphony Hall
RCA, producer Peter Dellheim
LPs: LSC-7055 (2). LRL2-7531 (2). **CDs:** 09026-63682-2 (2)

BEETHOVEN, LUDWIG VAN
Symphony No. 1 in C, op. 21 (25:29)
BSO, conductor Erich Leinsdorf
April 23, 1969. Symphony Hall
RCA, producer Peter Dellheim
LPs: LSC-3098. VCS-6903 (7). **CDs:** 60128-2-RV. 09026-61720-2

BEETHOVEN, LUDWIG VAN
Symphony No. 8 in F, op. 93 (24:57)
BSO, conductor Erich Leinsdorf
April 24, 1969. Symphony Hall
RCA, producer Peter Dellheim
LPs: LSC-3098. VCS-6903 (7). **CDs:** 60128-2-RV. 74321-21279-2

PROKOFIEV, SERGEI
Concerto for Piano and Orchestra No. 5 in G, op. 55 (22:41)
BSO, conductor Erich Leinsdorf
John Browning, piano
April 25, 1969. Symphony Hall
RCA, producer Peter Dellheim
LPs: LSC-3121. **CDs:** Testament SBT2-1376 (2)

WEILL, KURT
Kleine Dreigroschenmusik **(19:42)**
Nineteen Members of the BSO, conductor Erich Leinsdorf
April 25, 1969. Symphony Hall
RCA, producer Peter Dellheim
LPs: LSC-3121

SCHUBERT, FRANZ
Symphony No. 9 in C "Great C Major" (49:11)
BSO, conductor William Steinberg
September 29, 1969. Symphony Hall
RCA, producer Peter Dellheim
LPs: LSC-3115. AGL1-3789. **CDs:** 60127-2-RV. 09026-60127-2

ORFF, CARL
Carmina Burana (62:46)
BSO, conductor Seiji Ozawa
Evelyn Mandac, soprano; Stanley Kolk, tenor; Sherrill Milnes, baritone; NECC,
    Lorna Cooke DeVaron, dir.
November 17, 1969. Symphony Hall
RCA, producer Peter Dellheim
LPs: LSC-3161. AGL1-4082. AGL1-5260. **CDs:** 6533-2-RG. 07863-56533-2.
    09026-63590-2. 82876-59417-2

STRAVINSKY, IGOR
Greeting Prelude **(0:50)**
BSO, conductor Seiji Ozawa
November 22, 1969 (live)
Boston Symphony Transcription Trust, producers Jordan M. Whitelaw and
Richard L. Kaye
CDs: BSO-CD1 (promotional). *1988 "Salute to Symphony."*

STRAVINSKY, IGOR
Pétrouchka (1947) *(32:58)*
BSO, conductor Seiji Ozawa
Michael Tilson Thomas, piano
November 24, 1969. Symphony Hall
RCA, producer Peter Dellheim
LPs: LSC-3167. VCS-7099 (2). **CDs:** 09026-63311-2

STRAVINSKY, IGOR
The Firebird: **Suite (1919) (19:30)**
BSO, conductor Seiji Ozawa
November 24, 1969. Symphony Hall
RCA, producer Peter Dellheim
LPs:. LSC-3167. VCS-7099 (2). CRL2-3384 (2). **CDs:** 09026-61557-2. 74321-
21298-2

MOZART, WOLFGANG AMADEUS
Don Giovanni, **K. 527: Overture** *(8:05)*
BSO, conductor William Steinberg
December 19, 1969. Symphony Hall (live)
Boston Symphony Transcription Trust, producers Jordan M. Whitelaw and
Richard L. Kaye
CDs: BSO-CD1 (promotional). *1988 "Salute to Symphony."*

DVOŘÁK, ANTONIN
Symphony No. 9 in E Minor, op. 95 "from the New World" (43:21)
BSO, conductor Arthur Fiedler
January 5, 1970. Symphony Hall
RCA, producer Peter Dellheim
LPs: LSC-3134. LSC-3315. AGL1-3364. AGL1-5204. **CDs:** 6530-2-RG. Ar-
kivCD 6530. *This and the* Carnival Overture *(below) were Fiedler's only
recordings with the Boston Symphony Orchestra.*

DVOŘÁK, ANTONIN
Carnival Overture, **op. 92 (9:08)**
BSO, conductor Arthur Fiedler
January 5, 1970. Symphony Hall
RCA, producer Peter Dellheim
LPs: LSC-3134. LSC-3155. LSC-3315. VICS-2024. AGL1-5204. **CDs:** 6530-2-
RG

STRAVINSKY, IGOR
Scherzo fantastique, op. 3 (11:00)
BSO, conductor William Steinberg
January 12, 1970. Symphony Hall
RCA, producer Peter Dellheim
Unreleased

STRAUSS, RICHARD
Till Eulenspiegels lustige Streiche, op. 28 (13:56)
BSO, conductor William Steinberg
January 12, 1970. Symphony Hall
RCA, producer Peter Dellheim
LPs: LSC-3155. LSC-5019. VICS-2024

SAINT-SAËNS, CAMILLE
Danse macabre, op. 40 (7:23)
BSO, conductor William Steinberg
January 12, 1970. Symphony Hall
RCA, producer Peter Dellheim
LPs: LSC-3155. LSC-3314. VICS-2024

STRAVINSKY, IGOR
Scherzo à la Russe (3:45)
BSO, conductor William Steinberg
January 12, 1970. Symphony Hall
RCA, producer Peter Dellheim
Unreleased

BRUCKNER, ANTON
Symphony No. 6 in A (53:00)
BSO, conductor William Steinberg
January 19, 1970; October 19, 1970. Symphony Hall
RCA, producer Peter Dellheim
LPs: LSC-3177

IVES, CHARLES
Three Places in New England (18:30)
BSO, conductor Michael Tilson Thomas
January 26, 1970. Symphony Hall
Deutsche Grammophon, producer Rainer Brock
LPs: 2530 048. 2721 020 (3). **CDs:** 423 243-2. 463 633-2. ArkivCD 423243.
    ArkivCD 463633. *This was the first BSO recording made for Deutsche
    Grammophon, and the first for a non-American company. Ironically, it was
    also the BSO's first recording of music by Charles Ives, the quintessentially
    American composer.*

RAVEL, MAURICE
Daphnis et Chloé: Suite No. 2 (16:16)
BSO, conductor Claudio Abbado
NECC, Lorna Cooke DeVaron, dir.
February 2, 1970. Symphony Hall
Deutsche Grammophon, producer Rainer Brock
LPs: 2530 038. 2561 012. 2563 195. 2721 020 (3). 2830 152. **CDs:** 415 370-2.
459 439-2 (2). 469 184-2 (2). ArkivCD 415370. Universal B0004487-02

DEBUSSY, CLAUDE
Nocturnes for Orchestra: *Nuages. Fêtes. Sirènes* (24:37)
BSO, conductor Claudio Abbado
NECC, Lorna Cooke DeVaron, dir.
February 2, 1970. Symphony Hall
Deutsche Grammophon, producer Rainer Brock
LPs: 2530 038. 2561 012. 2721 020 (3). 2563 193 (4). 2830 152. **CDs:** 415 370-
2. 469 130-2. Universal B0005833-02. ArkivCD 415370

RAVEL, MAURICE
Pavane pour une infante défunte (6:42)
BSO, conductor Claudio Abbado
February 2, 1970. Symphony Hall
Deutsche Grammophon, producer Rainer Brock
LPs: 2530 038. 2561 012. 2563 195. 2830 152. **CDs:** 415 370-2. Universal
B0004487-02. B00066501-02. ArkivCD 415370

TCHAIKOVSKY, PETER ILYICH
Symphony No. 1 in G Minor, op. 13 "Winter Dreams" (44:17)
BSO, conductor Michael Tilson Thomas
March 23, 1970. Symphony Hall
Deutsche Grammophon, producer Rainer Brock
LPs: 2530 078. 2563 194. **CDs:** 463 615-2

RUGGLES, CARL
Sun-treader (16:26)
BSO, conductor Michael Tilson Thomas
March 24, 1970. Symphony Hall
Deutsche Grammophon, producer Rainer Brock
LPs: 2530 048. 2721 020 (3). **CDs:** 429 860-2. 463 633-2. ArkivCD 463633

HOLST, GUSTAV
The Planets, op. 32 (45:58)
BSO, conductor William Steinberg
NECC, Lorna Cooke DeVaron, dir.
September 28, 1970; October 12, 1970. Symphony Hall
Deutsche Grammophon, producer Rainer Brock
LPs: 2530 102. 2563 193. 416 242-1. 419 475-1. **CDs:** 413 852-2 (2). 419 475-
2. 439 446-2. 463 627-2

SCHUMAN, WILLIAM
Concerto for Violin and Orchestra (31:16)
BSO, conductor Michael Tilson Thomas
Paul Zukofsky, violin
October 5, 1970. Symphony Hall
Deutsche Grammophon, producer Rainer Brock
LPs: 2530 103. **CDs:** 429 860-2

PISTON, WALTER
Symphony No. 2 (26:44)
BSO, conductor Michael Tilson Thomas
October 5, 1970. Symphony Hall
Deutsche Grammophon, producer Rainer Brock
LPs: 2530 103. **CDs:** 429 860-2. 463 633-2. ArkivCD 463633

DUKAS, PAUL
The Sorcerer's Apprentice (10:06)
BSO, conductor William Steinberg
October 26, 1970. Symphony Hall
RCA, producer Peter Dellheim
LPs: LSC-3155. LSC-3314. VICS-2024. VCS-7079 (2)

MENDELSSOHN, FELIX
Octet in E♭, op. 20: Scherzo (4:08)
BSO, conductor William Steinberg
October 26, 1970. Symphony Hall
RCA, producer Peter Dellheim
Unreleased

DEBUSSY, CLAUDE
Images: Gigues; Ibéria; Rondes de printemps (36:33)
BSO, conductor Michael Tilson Thomas
February 1, 1971; February 2, 1971. Symphony Hall
Deutsche Grammophon, producer Rainer Brock
LPs: 2530 145. 415 916-1. 419 473-1. **CDs:** 419 473-2. 463 615-2. Universal
    B0000549-02. ArkivCD 419473

DEBUSSY, CLAUDE
Prélude à l'après-midi d'un faune (9:35)
BSO, conductor Michael Tilson Thomas
Doriot Anthony Dwyer, flute
February 1, 1971; February 2, 1971. Symphony Hall
Deutsche Grammophon, producer Rainer Brock
LPs: 2530 145. 415 916-1. **CDs:** 469 130-2. Universal B0000549-02.
    B0005833-02

SCRIABIN, ALEXANDER
Symphony No. 4, op. 54 "Poem of Ecstasy" (19:30)
BSO, conductor Claudio Abbado
February 8, 1971. Symphony Hall
Deutsche Grammophon, producer Rainer Brock
LPs: 2530 137. **CDs:** 415 370-2. ArkivCD 415370

TCHAIKOVSKY, PETER ILYICH
Romeo and Juliet (fantasy-overture) (20:19)
BSO, conductor Claudio Abbado
February 8, 1971. Symphony Hall
Deutsche Grammophon, producer Rainer Brock
LPs: 2530 137. **CDs:** 427 220-2

SMETANA, BEDŘICH
Má Vlast (76:09)
BSO, conductor Rafael Kubelík
March 8, 1971; March 9, 1971; March 10, 1971. Symphony Hall
Deutsche Grammophon, producer Hans Weber
LPs: 2707 054 (2). 2720 032 (2). **CDs:** 413 251-2. 429 183-2. 459 418-2 (2). *A widely circulated story has it that, due to an engineering error, one channel of the final movement,* Blaník, *was damaged, so the other channel was electronically processed to imitate a stereo recording. This is not true of CD 413 251-2, which is faultless true stereo. The story may have originated with an earlier LP issue that suffered from an editing error.*

Vyšehrad, The Moldau, From Bohemia's Woods and Fields, Tabor (52:11).
LPs: 2535 132

Vyšehrad, The Moldau, From Bohemia's Woods and Fields (39:44). **CDs:**
427 216-2. 439 451-2

The Moldau, From Bohemia's Woods and Fields (24:27). **LPs:** 2563 195. 413
251-1. **CDs:** 413 251-2. 423 769-2. 469 623-2

The Moldau (11:58). **CDs:** 439 663-2

From Bohemia's Woods and Fields (12:33). **CDs:** 457 928-2

STRAUSS, RICHARD
Also sprach Zarathustra, op. 30 (30:05)
BSO, conductor William Steinberg
March 24, 1971. Symphony Hall
Deutsche Grammophon, producer Hans Weber
LPs: 2530 160. 2563 204. **CDs:** 463 627-2

HINDEMITH, PAUL
Symphony "Mathis der Maler" (26:10)
BSO, conductor William Steinberg
October 4, 1971; October 5, 1971. Symphony Hall
Deutsche Grammophon, producer Thomas W. Mowrey
LPs: 2530 246. CDs: 423 241-2. ArkivCD 423241

HINDEMITH, PAUL
Concert Music for Strings and Brass, op. 50 (16:36)
BSO, conductor William Steinberg
October 5, 1971. Symphony Hall
Deutsche Grammophon, producer Thomas W. Mowrey
LPs: 2530 246. CDs: 423 241-2. ArkivCD 423241

STRAVINSKY, IGOR
Le Sacre du printemps (33:43)
BSO, conductor Michael Tilson Thomas
January 24, 1972; January 25, 1972. Symphony Hall
Deutsche Grammophon, producer Thomas W. Mowrey
LPs: 2530 252. 2535 222. CDs: 435 073-2. ArkivCD 435073

STRAVINSKY, IGOR
Le Roi des étoiles (5:28)
BSO, conductor Michael Tilson Thomas
Men's Choir of the NECC, Lorna Cooke DeVaron, dir.
January 25, 1972. Symphony Hall
Deutsche Grammophon, producer Thomas W. Mowrey
LPs: 2530 252. 2535 222. CDs: 435 073-2. ArkivCD 435073

BRUCKNER, ANTON
Symphony No. 8 in C Minor (ed. Steinberg, based on Nowack, 1955) (74:42)
BSO, conductor William Steinberg
February 26, 1972. Broadcast from Symphony Hall
BSO/IMG Artists
CDs: CB-100 (12)

CONCERT VIDEO (86 minutes)
BRAHMS Symphony No. 2 in D, op.73 (40:53)
BRAHMS Symphony No. 4 in E Minor, op. 98 (41:42)
BSO, conductor Leonard Bernstein
August 22, 1972; August 25, 1972. Koussevitzky Music Shed, Tanglewood
Unitel GmbH and Amberson, producer John McClure, director Robert Englander
DVDs: Medici Arts 2072138. Bonus film: Bernstein at Tanglewood.

PROKOFIEV, SERGEI
Scythian Suite, op. 20 "Ala and Lolli" (20:36)
BSO, conductor Michael Tilson Thomas
September 22, 1972. Broadcast from Symphony Hall
BSO/IMG Artists
CDs: CB-100 (12)

VIDEO COLLECTION: "THE UNANSWERED QUESTION"

These performances were videotaped to accompany the six Charles Eliot Norton Lectures given by Leonard Bernstein at Harvard in 1973.

STRAVINSKY: *Oedipus Rex* **(53:30)**

Tatiana Troyanos, mezzo-soprano (Jocasta); René Kollo, tenor (Oedipus); Frank Hoffmeister, tenor (Shepherd); Tom Krause, bass (Creon); Ezio Flagello, bass (Tiresias); David Evitts, bass (Messenger); Michael Wager (narrator); Harvard Glee Club, F. John Adams, dir.

MOZART: Symphony No. 40 in G Minor, K. 550 (30:56)

BEETHOVEN: Symphony No. 6 in F, op. 68 "Pastoral" (45:30)

BERLIOZ: *Roméo et Juliette,* **op. 17:** *Romeo Alone; The Ball at the Capulets* **(12:43)**

WAGNER: *Tristan und Isolde: Prelude and Liebestod* **(20:21)**

DEBUSSY: *Prélude à l'après-midi d'un faune* **(11:10)**

RAVEL: *Rapsodie espagnole:* **IV.** *Feria* **(6:33)**

IVES: *The Unanswered Question* **(5:11).** *Bernstein gives a running commentary during Ives's music.*

BSO, conductor Leonard Bernstein

November 27, 1972; December 11, 1972, and December 12, 1972. WGBH Television Studio, Boston

Amberson Video, Inc., producer John McClure

VHS: Kultur 1451 (6). **DVD:** Kultur D-1570 (3). *Both sets contain the complete Norton Lectures, including other music performed by the Vienna Philharmonic. "After each lecture had been delivered, a somewhat altered version of it was re-delivered the following night in a television studio, and committed to video tape." (Leonard Bernstein:* The Unanswered Question: Six Talks at Harvard. *Harvard University Press. 1976). The music was recorded on videotape months before the lectures began on October 9, 1973. The lectures were also published in audio form on Columbia LPs, where these performances were replaced by Bernstein's Columbia recordings with the New York Philharmonic. The exception was Stravinsky's* Oedipus Rex, *which the BSO recorded for Columbia (see the next entry).*

STRAVINSKY, IGOR

Oedipus Rex **(53:30)**

BSO, conductor Leonard Bernstein

Tatiana Troyanos, mezzo-soprano (Jocasta); René Kollo, tenor (Oedipus); Frank Hoffmeister, tenor (Shepherd); Tom Krause, bass (Creon); Ezio Flagello, bass (Tiresias); David Evitts, bass (Messenger); Michael Wager (narrator); Harvard Glee Club, F. John Adams, dir.

December 15, 1972; December 16, 1972. Symphony Hall

CBS, producer John McClure

LPs: M-33999. M4X-33032 (4). **CDs:** Sony 82876-78749-2. 88697-00819-2

SCHUBERT, FRANZ
Symphony No. 8 in B Minor "Unfinished" (22:02)
BSO, conductor Eugen Jochum
January 26, 1973. Symphony Hall
Deutsche Grammophon, producer Günther Breest
LPs: 2530 357. **CDs:** 427 195-2

MOZART, WOLFGANG AMADEUS
Symphony No. 41 in C, K. 551 "Jupiter" (30:47)
BSO, conductor Eugen Jochum
January 26, 1973; January 27, 1973. Symphony Hall
Deutsche Grammophon, producer Günther Breest
LPs: 2530 357. 2543 531.

BERLIOZ, HECTOR
Symphonie fantastique, op. 14 (47:15)
BSO, conductor Seiji Ozawa
February 19, 1973; February 20, 1973. Symphony Hall
Deutsche Grammophon, producer Thomas W. Mowrey
LPs: 2530 358. **CDs:** 431 169-2. ArkivCD 431169

BERLIOZ, HECTOR
Roman Carnival Overture, op. 9
BSO, conductor Seiji Ozawa
February 20, 1973. Symphony Hall
Deutsche Grammophon, producer Thomas W. Mowrey
Unreleased

BERLIOZ, HECTOR
La Damnation de Faust, op. 24 (121:45)
BSO, conductor Seiji Ozawa
Edith Mathis, soprano (Marguerite); Stuart Burrows, tenor (Faust); Donald
    McIntyre, bass (Mephistopheles); Thomas Paul, bass (Brander); TFC, John
    Oliver, dir.; Boston Boy Choir, Theodore Marier, dir.
October 1, 1973; October 2, 1973; October 8, 1973. Symphony Hall
Deutsche Grammophon, producer Thomas W. Mowrey
LPs: 2709 048 (3). 413 197-1 (2). Musical Heritage Society 524569 (2). **CDs:**
    423 907-2 (2). 453 019-2 (2). ArkivCD 423907 (2)

BEETHOVEN, LUDWIG VAN
Concerto for Piano and Orchestra No. 5 in E♭, op. 73 "Emperor" (40:08)
BSO, conductor Seiji Ozawa
Christoph Eschenbach, piano
October 9, 1973. Symphony Hall
Deutsche Grammophon, producers Thomas W. Mowrey and Franz-Christian
    Wulff
LPs: 2530 438. *BSO payroll sheeets are signed by Mowrey.*

VAUGHAN WILLIAMS, RALPH
Symphony No. 4 in F Minor, (31:02)
BSO, conductor Colin Davis
October 26, 1973. Broadcast from Symphony Hall
BSO/IMG Artists
CDs: CB-100 (12)

BEETHOVEN, LUDWIG VAN
Symphony No. 5 in C Minor, op. 67 (36:10)
BSO, conductor Rafael Kubelík
November 26, 1973. Symphony Hall
Deutsche Grammophon, producer Hans Weber
LPs: 2530 479. 2535 407. 2740 155 (8). **CDs:** 474 463-2 (2) (Germany)

BARTÓK, BÉLA
Concerto for Orchestra (38:30)
BSO, conductor Rafael Kubelík
November 27, 1973; November 28, 1973. Symphony Hall
Deutsche Grammophon, producer Hans Weber
LPs: 2530 479. 410 993-1. **CDs:** 437 247-2. ArkivCD 437247

RAVEL, MAURICE
Boléro **(15:03)**
BSO, conductor Seiji Ozawa
March 13, 1974; April 22, 1974. Symphony Hall
Deutsche Grammophon, producer Thomas W. Mowrey
LPs: 2530 475. 2711 015 (4). 2740 120 (4). 2864 008 (4). 3584 024. 415 845-1.
    CDs: 243 739-2 (2). 415 845-2. 437 392-2 (2). 457 933-2. 474 172-2. Universal B0000736-02. B0004487-02. Decca 0003878-02

RAVEL, MAURICE
Alborada del gracioso **(7:38)**
BSO, conductor Seiji Ozawa
Sherman Walt, bassoon
March 13, 1974. Symphony Hall
Deutsche Grammophon, producer Thomas W. Mowrey
LPs: 2530 753. 2711 015 (4) 2740 120 (4). 2864 008 (4). 415 845-1. **CDs:** 243
    739-2 (2). 415 845-2. 437 392-2 (2). 457 933-2. Universal B0000736-02.
    B0004487-02

RAVEL, MAURICE
La Valse **(11:59)**
BSO, conductor Seiji Ozawa
March 13, 1974. Symphony Hall
Deutsche Grammophon, producer Thomas W. Mowrey
LPs: 2530 475. 2711 015 (4). 2740 120 (4). 2864 008 (4). 415 845-1. **CDs:** 243
    739-2 (2). 415 845-2. 437 392-2 (2). 457 933-2. 474 172-2. Universal
    B0000736-02. B0004487-02

RAVEL, MAURICE
Rapsodie espagnole (14:51)
BSO, conductor Seiji Ozawa
March 13, 1974. Symphony Hall
Deutsche Grammophon, producer Thomas W. Mowrey
LPs: 2530 475. 2711 015 (4). 2740 120 (4). 2864 008 (4). 410 844-1. **CDs:** 243
739-2 (2). 410 844-2. 437 392-2 (2). 457 933-2. 474 172-2. 469 184-2 (2).
Universal B0004487-02

HINDEMITH, PAUL
Symphony "Mathis der Maler" (29:01)
BSO, conductor Carlo Maria Giulini
March 30, 1974. Broadcast from Symphony Hall
BSO/IMG Artists
CDs: CB-100 (12)

RAVEL, MAURICE
Menuet antique (6:20)
BSO, conductor Seiji Ozawa
April 22, 1974. Symphony Hall
Deutsche Grammophon, producer Thomas W. Mowrey
LPs: 2530 752. 2711 015 (4). 2740 120 (4). 2864 008 (4). 415 845-1. **CDs:** 243
739-2 (2). 415 845-2. 437 392-2 (2)

RAVEL, MAURICE
Ma Mère l'oye (28:10)
BSO, conductor Seiji Ozawa
April 22, 1974. Symphony Hall
Deutsche Grammophon, producer Thomas W. Mowrey
LPs: 2530 752. 2711 015 (4). 2740 120 (4). 2864 008 (4). **CDs:** 243 739-2 (2).
437 392-2 (2). 474 172-2.

RAVEL, MAURICE
Le Tombeau de Couperin (17:00)
BSO, conductor Seiji Ozawa
Ralph Gomberg, oboe
October 14, 1974. Symphony Hall
Deutsche Grammophon, producer Thomas W. Mowrey
LPs: 2530 752. 2711 015 (4). 2740 120 (4). 2864 008 (4). **CDs:** 243 739-2 (2).
437 392-2 (2)

RAVEL, MAURICE
Pavane pour une infante défunte (6:14)
BSO, conductor Seiji Ozawa
October 14, 1974. Symphony Hall
Deutsche Grammophon, producer Thomas W. Mowrey
LPs: 2530 753. 2711 015 (4). 2740 120 (4). 2864 008 (4). 415 845-1. **CDs:** 243
739-2 (2). 415 845-2. 437 392-2 (2). 457 933-2. 469 184-2 (2). 474 172-2.
474 451-2

RAVEL, MAURICE
Daphnis et Chloé (51:27)
BSO, conductor Seiji Ozawa
TFC, John Oliver, dir.
October 14, 1974; October 15, 1974. Symphony Hall
Deutsche Grammophon
LPs: 2530 563. 2711 015 (4). 2740 120 (4). 2864 008 (4). Franklin Mint Record
    Society FMRS-7031/35 (5). **CDs:** 437 648-2. ArkivCD 437648

Suite No. 2 (16:16). CDs: 243 739-2 (2). 437 392-2 (2). 469-184-2 (2)

BERLIOZ, HECTOR
Les Troyens: Royal Hunt and Storm (9:50)
BSO, conductor Colin Davis
TFC, John Oliver, dir.
November 8, 1974. Broadcast from Symphony Hall
BSO/IMG Artists
CDs: CB-100 (12)

BRAHMS, JOHANNES
Academic Festival Overture, op. 80 (10:23)
BSO, conductor Klaus Tennstedt
December 14, 1974. Broadcast from Symphony Hall
BSO/IMG Artists
CDs: CB-100 (12)

SIBELIUS, JEAN
Symphony No. 5 in E♭, op. 82 (32:09)
BSO, conductor Colin Davis
January 4, 1975. Symphony Hall
Philips, producer Vittorio Negri
LPs: 6500 959. 6709 011 (5). 6998 026 (5). **CDs:** 416 600-2 (4). 446 157-2 (2).
    464 740-2. **SACD:** Pentatone PTC-5186 177

SIBELIUS, JEAN
Symphony No. 7 in C, op. 105 (21:23)
BSO, conductor Colin Davis
January 6, 1975. Symphony Hall
Philips, producer Vittorio Negri
LPs: 6500 959. 6709 011 (5). 6998 026 (5). **CDs:** 416 600-2 (4). 446 160-2 (2).
    464 740-2. **SACD:** Pentatone PTC-5186 177

MENDELSSOHN, FELIX
Symphony No. 4 in A, op. 90 "Italian" (30:20)
BSO, conductor Colin Davis
January 6, 1975. Symphony Hall
Philips, producer Vittorio Negri
LPs: 9500 068. 412 928-1. 442 302-2. **CDs:** 420 653-2. 442 302-2 (2). **SACDs:**
    Pentatone PTC-5186 102

BRAHMS, JOHANNES
Symphony No. 2 in D, op. 73 (35:39)
BSO, conductor Seiji Ozawa
April 19, 1975; April 21, 1975. Symphony Hall
Deutsche Grammophon, producer Thomas W. Mowrey
Unreleased

RAVEL, MAURICE
Une Barque sur l'océan (7:41)
BSO, conductor Seiji Ozawa
April 21, 1975. Symphony Hall
Deutsche Grammophon, producer Thomas W. Mowrey
LPs: 2530 753. 2711 015 (4). 2740 120 (4). 2864 008 (4). 415 845-1. **CDs:** 243
   739-2 (2). 415 845-2. 437 392-2 (2)

RAVEL, MAURICE
Valses nobles et sentimentales (16:46)
BSO, conductor Seiji Ozawa
April 21, 1975. Symphony Hall
Deutsche Grammophon, producer Thomas W. Mowrey
LPs: 2530 753. 2711 015 (4). 2740 120 (4). 2864 008 (4). **CDs:** 243 739-2 (2).
   437 392-2 (2). 437 648-2. 457 933-2. ArkivCD 437648

SHOSTAKOVICH, DMITRI
Concerto for Cello and Orchestra No. 2, op. 126 (33:07)
BSO, conductor Seiji Ozawa
Mstislav Rostropovich, cello
August 11, 1975. Symphony Hall
Deutsche Grammophon, producer Thomas W. Mowrey
LPs: 2530 653. CDs: 437 952-2.

GLAZUNOV, ALEXANDER
Chant du ménéstrel, op. 71 (4:13)
BSO, conductor Seiji Ozawa
Mstislav Rostropovich, cello
August 11, 1975. Symphony Hall
Deutsche Grammophon, producer Thomas W. Mowrey
LPs: 2530 653. CDs: 437 952-2. 471 620-2

BERLIOZ, HECTOR
Roméo et Juliette, op. 17 (89:22)
BSO, conductor Seiji Ozawa
Julia Hamari, mezzo-soprano; Jean Dupouy, tenor; José Van Dam, bass;
   NECC, Lorna Cooke DeVaron, dir.
October 6, 1975; October 7, 1975; October 14, 1975. Symphony Hall
Deutsche Grammophon, producer Hans-Peter Schweigmann
LPs: 2707 089 (2). **CDs:** 423 068-2 (2). Universal B0001205-02 (10). ArkivCD
   423068.

Scène d'amour (16:20). **CDs:** 431 169-2. ArkivCD 431169

RESPIGHI, OTTORINO
Ancient Airs and Dances: Set 3 (15:54)
BSO, conductor Seiji Ozawa
October 7, 1975; October 14, 1975. Symphony Hall
Deutsche Grammophon, producer Thomas W. Mowrey
LPs: 2530 891. **CDs:** 419 868-2. Decca 472 482-2

BARTÓK, BÉLA
The Miraculous Mandarin: Suite (19:33)
BSO, conductor Seiji Ozawa
November 10, 1975. Symphony Hall
Deutsche Grammophon, producer Thomas W. Mowrey
LPs: 2530 887. **CDs:** 437 247-2. ArkivCD 437247

MENDELSSOHN, FELIX
A Midsummer Night's Dream: Overture, op. 21. Scherzo, Nocturne, Wedding March, op. 61 (27:27)
BSO, conductor Colin Davis
November 29, 1975; December 1, 1975. Symphony Hall
Philips, producer Vittorio Negri
LPs: 9500 068. 412 928-1. **CDs:** 420 653-2. 442 302-2 (2)

SIBELIUS, JEAN
Symphony No. 6 in D Minor, op. 104 (24:48)
BSO, conductor Colin Davis
December 1, 1975; December 2, 1975. Symphony Hall
Philips, producer Vittorio Negri
LPs: 9500 142. 6709 011 (5). 6998 026 (5). **CDs:** 416 600-2 (4). 446 160-2 (2)

SIBELIUS, JEAN
Tapiola, op. 112 (18:02)
BSO, conductor Colin Davis
December 2, 1975. Symphony Hall
Philips, producer Vittorio Negri
LPs: 9500 143. 6709 011 (5). 6998 026 (5). Franklin Mint Record Society
FMRS-7006/10 (5). **CDs:** 416 600-2 (4). 446 160-2 (2)

GRIFFES, CHARLES TOMLINSON
The Pleasure Dome of Kubla Khan (10:32)
BSO, conductor Seiji Ozawa
January 31, 1976. Symphony Hall
New World Records, producer Andrew Raeburn
LPs: NW-273-1. **CDs:** NW 273-2. NW-80273

GRIFFES, CHARLES TOMLINSON
Three Poems of Fiona MacLeod, op. 11: "The Lament of the Proud" (4:17).
"Thy Dark Eyes to Mine" (2:57). "The Rise of Night" (4:07). (11:37)
BSO, conductor Seiji Ozawa
Phyllis Bryn-Julson, soprano
January 31, 1976. Symphony Hall
New World Records, producer Andrew Raeburn
LPs: NW-273-1. **CDs:** NW 273-2. NW-80273

ROSSINI, GIOACCHINO
Semiramide: Overture
BSO, conductor Seiji Ozawa
February 9, 1976; February 16, 1976. Symphony Hall
Deutsche Grammophon, producer Thomas W. Mowrey
Unreleased

IVES, CHARLES
Symphony No. 4 (30:55)
BSO, conductor Seiji Ozawa
Jerome Rosen, piano; TFC, John Oliver, dir.
February 9, 1976; February 16, 1976. Symphony Hall
Deutsche Grammophon, producer Thomas W. Mowrey
LPs: 2530 787. **CDs:** 423 243-2. ArkivCD 423243

IVES, CHARLES
Central Park in the Dark (7:41)
BSO, conductor Seiji Ozawa
February 16, 1976. Symphony Hall
Deutsche Grammophon, producer John McClure
LPs: 2530 787. **CDs:** 423 243-2. ArkivCD 423243

SIBELIUS, JEAN
Symphony No. 2 in D, op. 43 (45:07)
BSO, conductor Colin Davis
April 3, 1976; April 5, 1976. Symphony Hall
Philips, producer Vittorio Negri
LPs: 9500 141. 6709 011 (5). 6998 026 (5). **CDs:** 416 600-2 (4). 420 490-2. 446
157-2 (2)

SIBELIUS, JEAN
Symphony No. 1 in E Minor, op. 39 (39:28)
BSO, conductor Colin Davis
April 5, 1976; April 6, 1976. Symphony Hall
Philips, producer Vittorio Negri
LPs: 9500 140. 6709 011 (5). 6998 026 (5). **CDs:** 416 600-2 (4). 446 157-2 (2)

SIBELIUS, JEAN
Finlandia, op. 26, no. 7 (7:58)
BSO, conductor Colin Davis
April 6, 1976. Symphony Hall
Philips, producer Vittorio Negri
LPs: 9500 140. 6709 011 (5). 6998 026 (5). **CDs:** 416 600-2 (4). 420 490-2. 442 389. 446 160-2 (2)

LISZT, FRANZ
A Faust Symphony (77:01 / 81:00)
BSO, conductor Leonard Bernstein
Kenneth Riegel, tenor; TFC, John Oliver, dir.
July 26, 1976; July 27, 1976. Symphony Hall (live)
Audio recording: Deutsche Grammophon, producer Thomas W. Mowrey
Video recording: Amberson Video, Inc., producer David Griffiths
LPs: 2707 100 (2). 415 009-1. **CDs:** 431 470-2. 447 449-2. **DVD:** Euroarts 2072078. *The audio and video recordings were made simultaneously, except that the first day's audio session ran 70 minutes longer than the live performance on the video. The first movement runs about 25 seconds longer on the video recording than on the audio. The overall four-minute difference cited above also reflects the pre- and post-performance credits on the DVD, plus longer pauses between movements than on the CD.*

FALLA, MANUEL DE
The Three-Cornered Hat (39:22)
BSO, conductor Seiji Ozawa
Teresa Berganza, mezzo-soprano
October 2, 1976; October 5, 1976. Symphony Hall
Deutsche Grammophon, producer Rainer Brock
LPs: 2530 823. 410 844-1. Franklin Mint Record Society FMRS-7031/35 (5). **CDs:** 410 844-2. 429 181-2. *The Fall 1992 Opus catalogue lists 429 181-2 as including a recording of* El amor brujo *by Ozawa and the BSO, but that recording is by the London Symphony Orchestra.*

BARTÓK, BÉLA
Music for Strings, Percussion, and Celesta (31:18)
BSO, conductor Seiji Ozawa
November 13, 1976. Symphony Hall
Deutsche Grammophon, producer Rainer Brock
LPs: 2530 887. **CDs:** 402 439-2

SIBELIUS, JEAN
Symphony No. 3 in C, op. 52 (29:43)
BSO, conductor Colin Davis
November 29, 1976; December 4, 1976. Symphony Hall
Philips, producer Vittorio Negri
LPs: 9500 142. 6709 011 (5). 6998 026 (5). **CDs:** 416 600-2 (4). 446 160-2 (2)

SIBELIUS, JEAN
Symphony No. 4 in A Minor, op. 63 (37:16)
BSO, conductor Colin Davis
December 3, 1976; December 4, 1976. Symphony Hall
Philips, producer Vittorio Negri
LPs: 9500 143. 6709 011 (5). 6998 026 (5). Franklin Mint Record Society
FMRS-7006/10 (5). **CDs:** 416 600-2 (4). 446 157-2 (2)

SIBELIUS, JEAN
Lemminkäinen Suite, op. 22: No. 2 *The Swan of Tuonela* (9:22)
BSO, conductor Colin Davis
December 4, 1976. Symphony Hall
Philips, producer Vittorio Negri
LPs: 6709 011 (5). 6998 026 (5). **CDs:** 416 600-2 (4). 420 490-2. 442 389-2.
446 160-2 (2)

TCHAIKOVSKY, PETER ILYICH
Symphony No. 5 in E Minor, op. 64 (46:44)
BSO, conductor Seiji Ozawa
Charles Kavalovski, horn
February 16, 1977. Symphony Hall
Deutsche Grammophon, producer Rainer Brock
LPs: 2530 888. **CDs:** 431 603-2

VAUGHAN WILLIAMS, RALPH
The Lark Ascending
BSO, conductor Seiji Ozawa
Joseph Silverstein, violin
February 16, 1977. Symphony Hall
Deutsche Grammophon, producer Rainer Brock
Unreleased

BRAHMS, JOHANNES
Symphony No. 1 in C Minor, op. 68 (44:47)
BSO, conductor Seiji Ozawa
March 28, 1977; April 2, 1977. Symphony Hall
Deutsche Grammophon, producer Rainer Brock
LPs: 2530 889. Franklin Mint Record Society FMRS-7031/35 (5). **CDs:**
UCCG-9382 (Japan)

TAKEMITSU, TORU
Quatrain (17:02)
BSO, conductor Seiji Ozawa
Tashi (Peter Serkin, piano; Ida Kafavian, violin; Fred Sherry, cello; Richard
Stoltzman, clarinet)
March 29, 1977. Symphony Hall
Deutsche Grammophon, producer Rainer Brock
LPs: 2531 210 (rel. 1980). **CDs:** 423 253-2. 477 5381. Universal B0003974-02

RESPIGHI, OTTORINO
Ancient Airs and Dances: Set 1 (15:40)
BSO, conductor Seiji Ozawa
March 29, 1977. Symphony Hall
Deutsche Grammophon, producer Rainer Brock
LPs: 2530 891. **CDs:** 419 868-2

RIMSKY-KORSAKOV, NIKOLAI
Scheherazade, op. 35 (44:57)
BSO, conductor Seiji Ozawa
Joseph Silverstein, violin
April 2, 1977. Symphony Hall
Deutsche Grammophon, producer Rainer Brock
LPs: 2530 972. **CDs:** 696 592-2. 469 659-2.

SESSIONS, ROGER
When Lilacs Last in the Dooryard Bloom'd (42:20)
BSO, conductor Seiji Ozawa
Esther Hinds, soprano; Florence Quivar, mezzo-soprano; Dominic Cossa, baritone; TFC, John Oliver, dir.
April 23, 1977; April 25, 1977. Symphony Hall
New World Records, producer Andrew Raeburn
LPs: NW-296-1. **CDs:** NW 296-2. 80296

MARTIN, FRANK
Concerto for Seven Wind Instruments, Timpani, Percussion, and String Orchestra (20:00)
BSO, conductor Seiji Ozawa
Doriot Anthony Dwyer, flute; Ralph Gomberg, oboe; Harold Wright, clarinet; Sherman Walt, bassoon; Armando Ghitalla, trumpet; Charles Kavalovski, horn; Ronald Barron, trombone; Everett Firth, timpani
September 30, 1977. Broadcast from Symphony Hall
BSO/IMG Artists
CDs: CB-100 (12)

MAHLER, GUSTAV
Symphony No. 1 in D "Titan" (54:42 / 60:40)
BSO, conductor Seiji Ozawa
October 3, 1977. Symphony Hall
Deutsche Grammophon, producer Rainer Brock
LPs: 2530 993 (without "Blumine"). 410 845-1. **CDs:** 423 884-2. 469 660-2.
The second LP and both the CDs include the "Blumine" movement (5:58).

RESPIGHI, Ottorino
Feste romane **(24:09)**
BSO, conductor Seiji Ozawa
October 15, 1977. Symphony Hall
Deutsche Grammophon, producer Rainer Brock
LPs: 2530 890. 415 846-1. Franklin Mint Record Society FMRS-7031/35 (5).
  CDs: 415 846-2

RESPIGHI, Ottorino
The Pines of Rome **(21:54)**
BSO, conductor Seiji Ozawa
October 17, 1977. Symphony Hall
Deutsche Grammophon, producer Rainer Brock
LPs: 2530 890. 415 846-1. Franklin Mint Record Society FMRS-7031/35 (5).
  CDs: 415 846-2

RESPIGHI, Ottorino
The Fountains of Rome **(16:00)**
BSO, conductor Seiji Ozawa
October 17, 1977. Symphony Hall
Deutsche Grammophon, producer Rainer Brock
LPs: 2530 890. 415 846-1. Franklin Mint Record Society FMRS-7031/35 (5).
  CDs: 415 846-2

STRAVINSKY, Igor
Concerto for Violin and Orchestra (21:38)
BSO, conductor Seiji Ozawa
Itzhak Perlman, violin
February 6, 1978. Symphony Hall
Deutsche Grammophon, producer Rainer Brock
LPs: 2531 110. **CDs:** 413 725-2. 447 445-2

RESPIGHI, Ottorino
Ancient Airs and Dances: **Set 2 (19:51)**
BSO, conductor Seiji Ozawa
April 22, 1978. Symphony Hall
Deutsche Grammophon, producer Rainer Brock
LPs: 2530 891. **CDs:** 419 868-2

PAGANINI, Niccolò
Moto Perpetuo
BSO, conductor Seiji Ozawa
April 22, 1978. Symphony Hall
Deutsche Grammophon, producer Rainer Brock
Unreleased

WAGNER, RICHARD
Die Walküre: Act I (63:57)
BSO, conductor Seiji Ozawa
Jessye Norman, soprano (Sieglinde); Jon Vickers, tenor (Siegmund); Gwynne
   Howell, bass (Hunding)
August 12, 1978. Broadcast from Koussevitzky Music Shed, Tanglewood
WCRB Productions, Inc., producer Jordan M. Whitelaw
LPs: BSO Transcription Trust MM-79 (promotional)

MESSIAEN, OLIVIER
Trois petites liturgies de la Présence Divine (33:16)
BSO, conductor Seiji Ozawa
Yvonne Loriod, piano; Jeanne Loriod, ondes martenot; Women of the TFC,
   John Oliver, dir.
October 7, 1978. Broadcast from Symphony Hall
BSO/IMG Artists
CDs: CB-100 (12)

TCHAIKOVSKY, PETER ILYICH
Swan Lake, op. 20 (144:31)
BSO, conductor Seiji Ozawa
Joseph Silverstein, violin; Jules Eskin, cello; Bernard Zighera, harp; Armando
   Ghitalla, trumpet
November 11, 1978; November 15, 1978; November 18, 1978; November 20,
   1978. Symphony Hall
Deutsche Grammophon, producer Rainer Brock
LPs: 2709 099 (3). **CDs:** 415 367-2 (2). 453 055-2 (2)

Selections (30:46). **LPs:** 2531 351. **CDs:** 431 607-2. Universal B0001306-02.
   Entrée 477509

MOZART, WOLFGANG AMADEUS
Concerto for Bassoon and Orchestra in B♭, K. 191 (cadenza by J. Walter
   Guetter) **(19:10)**
BSO, conductor Seiji Ozawa
Sherman Walt, bassoon
November 15, 1978; November 20, 1978; December 2, 1978. Symphony Hall
Deutsche Grammophon, producer Rainer Brock
LPs: 2531 254. 419 480-1. **CDs:** 419 480-2. 437 647-2

BERG, ALBAN
Concerto for Violin and Orchestra "To the Memory of an Angel" **(26:00)**
BSO, conductor Seiji Ozawa
Itzhak Perlman, violin
November 27, 1978; November 28, 1978. Symphony Hall
Deutsche Grammophon, producer Rainer Brock
LPs: 2531 110. 413 800-1. 4137 971 (10). **CDs:** 413 725-2. 447 445-2

MOZART, WOLFGANG AMADEUS

Concerto for Clarinet and Orchestra in A, K. 622 (cadenza by Harold Wright) **(28:39)**
BSO, conductor Seiji Ozawa
Harold Wright, clarinet
November 28, 1978; December 2, 1978. Symphony Hall
Deutsche Grammophon, producer Rainer Brock
LPs: 2531 254. **CDs:** 437 647-2. Belart 450 035-2. Boston Records 1066

TAKEMITSU, TORU

A Flock Descends into the Pentagonal Garden **(13:02)**
BSO, conductor Seiji Ozawa
December 2, 1978. Symphony Hall
Deutsche Grammophon, producer Rainer Brock
LPs: 2531 210. **CDs:** 423 253-2. 477 5381. Universal B0003974-02

SCHOENBERG, ARNOLD

Gurrelieder **(107:03)**
BSO, conductor Seiji Ozawa
Jessye Norman, soprano (Tove); Tatiana Troyanos, mezzo-soprano (Wood Dove); James McCracken, tenor (Waldemar); Werner Klemperer, speaker; TFC, John Oliver, dir.
March 30, 1979; March 31, 1979; April 3, 1979 (patch). Symphony Hall (live)
Philips, producer Rainer Brock (on loan from Deutsche Grammophon)
LPs: 6769 038 (2). **CDs:** 412 511-2 (2). 464 040-2 (2). Universal B0007717-02 (2)

WU, TSU-CHIANG

Concerto for Pipa and Orchestra "Little Sisters of the Grassland" **(17:11)**
BSO, conductor Seiji Ozawa
Liu Teh-hai, pipa
March 31, 1979. Symphony Hall
Philips, producer Wilhelm Hellweg
LPs: 9500 692

LISZT, FRANZ

Concerto for Piano and Orchestra No. 1 in E♭ **(20:00)**
BSO, conductor Seiji Ozawa
Liu Shih-kun, piano
March 31, 1979. Symphony Hall
Philips, producer Wilhelm Hellweg
LPs: 9500 692

SOUSA, JOHN PHILIP

The Stars and Stripes Forever **(3:35)**
BSO, conductor Seiji Ozawa
April 3, 1979. Symphony Hall
Philips, producer Wilhelm Hellweg
LPs: 9500 692

TCHAIKOVSKY, PETER ILYICH
Concerto for Piano and Orchestra No. 1 in B♭ Minor, op. 23 (37:01)
BSO, conductor Colin Davis
Claudio Arrau, piano
April 16, 1979; April 21, 1979. Symphony Hall
Philips, producer Wilhelm Hellweg
LPs: 9500 695. **CDs:** 420 717-2. Universal B0000553-02

SIBELIUS, JEAN
Karelia Suite, op. 11 (15:35)
BSO, conductor Colin Davis
April 16, 1979; April 23, 1979. Symphony Hall
Philips, producer Wilhelm Hellweg
LPs: 9500 893. **SACDs:** Pentatone PTC-5186 164

TCHAIKOVSKY, PETER ILYICH
Romeo and Juliet (fantasy-overture) (20:48)
BSO, conductor Colin Davis
April 21, 1979; April 23, 1979. Symphony Hall
Philips, producer Wilhelm Hellweg
LPs: 9500 892. **CDs:** 411 448-2. ArkivCD 411448. **SACDs:** Pentatone PTC-5186 164

SIBELIUS, JEAN
En Saga, op. 9 (17:38)
BSO, conductor Colin Davis
April 23, 1979. Symphony Hall
Philips, producer Wilhelm Hellweg
LPs: 9500 893. **SACD:** Pentatone PTC-5186 177

BERLIOZ, HECTOR
La Damnation de Faust, op. 24: *Rákóczy March* (4:11)
BSO, conductor Seiji Ozawa
September 7, 1979. Symphony Hall (live)
Boston Symphony Transcription Trust, producers Jordan M. Whitelaw and
    Richard L. Kaye
CDs: BSO-CD1 (promotional). *1988 "Salute to Symphony."*

SMETANA, BEDŘICH
The Bartered Bride: Dance of the Comedians (3:25)
BSO, conductor Seiji Ozawa
September 8, 1979. Symphony Hall (live)
Boston Symphony Transcription Trust, producers Jordan M. Whitelaw and
    Richard L. Kaye
CDs: BSO-CD1 (promotional). *1988 "Salute to Symphony."*

RAVEL, MAURICE
Shéhérazade (16:02)
BSO, conductor Seiji Ozawa
Frederica Von Stade, mezzo-soprano
October 8, 1979. Symphony Hall
CBS, producer Paul Myers
LPs: IM-36665

HOLST, GUSTAV
The Planets, op. 32 (49:33)
BSO, conductor Seiji Ozawa
Women of the NECC, Lorna Cooke DeVaron, dir.
December 3, 1979; December 10, 1979. Symphony Hall
Philips, producer Wilhelm Hellweg
LPs: 9500 782. **CDs:** 416 456-2. 434 162-2. ArkivCD 416456

STRAVINSKY, IGOR
Le Sacre du printemps (32:24)
BSO, conductor Seiji Ozawa
December 10, 1979. Symphony Hall
Philips, producer Wilhelm Hellweg
LPs: 9500 781. 416 246-1

FAURÉ, GABRIEL
Pelléas et Mélisande, **Suite from the incidental music to Maeterlinck's drama, op. 80:** *Filieuse* (2:36); *Sicilienne* (3:38)
BSO, conductor Joseph Silverstein
February 23, 1980. Broadcast from Symphony Hall
BSO/IMG Artists
CDs: CB-100 (12)

TCHAIKOVSKY, PETER ILYICH
Overture 1812, op. 49 (16:59)
BSO, conductor Colin Davis
TFC, John Oliver, dir.
March 5, 1980. Symphony Hall
Philips, producer Wilhelm Hellweg
LPs: 9500 892. **CDs:** 411 448-2. ArkivCD 411448. **SACDs:** Pentatone PTC-5186 164

GRIEG, EDVARD
Concerto for Piano and Orchestra in A Minor, op. 16 (33:20)
BSO, conductor Colin Davis
Claudio Arrau, piano
March 8, 1980; March 10, 1980. Symphony Hall
Philips, producer Wilhelm Hellweg
LPs: 9500 891. **CDs:** 420 874-2

SIBELIUS, JEAN
Pohjola's Daughter, op. 49 (14:59)
BSO, conductor Colin Davis
March 8, 1980. Symphony Hall
Philips, producer Wilhelm Hellweg
LPs: 9500 893. **SACDs:** Pentatone PTC-5186 164

SIBELIUS, JEAN
Kuolema, op. 44, no. 1: **Valse triste (5:52)**
BSO, conductor Colin Davis
March 10, 1980. Symphony Hall
Philips, producer Wilhelm Hellweg
LPs: 9500 893. **CDs:** 420 490-2. 442 389-2. Universal B0004249-02. **SACDs:**
Pentatone PTC-5186 164

SCHUBERT, FRANZ
Symphony No. 9 in C "Great C Major" (61:23)
BSO, conductor Colin Davis
March 15, 1980; March 17, 1980. Symphony Hall
Philips, producer Wilhelm Hellweg
LPs: 9500 890. **CDs:** UCCP-3118 (Japan)

SCHUMANN, ROBERT
Concerto for Piano and Orchestra in A Minor, op. 54 (32:48)
BSO, conductor Colin Davis
Claudio Arrau, piano
March 17, 1980. Symphony Hall
Philips, producer Wilhelm Hellweg
LPs: 9500 891. **CDs:** 420 874-2

RAVEL, MAURICE
Deux mélodies hébraïques (6:17)
BSO, conductor Seiji Ozawa
Frederica Von Stade, mezzo-soprano
April 8, 1980. Symphony Hall
CBS, producer Paul Myers
LPs: IM-36665

RAVEL, MAURICE
Cinq mélodies populaires grecques: No. 1 and 2 (2:39)
BSO, conductor Seiji Ozawa
Frederica Von Stade, mezzo-soprano
April 8, 1980. Symphony Hall
CBS, producer Paul Myers
LPs: IM-36665

MENDELSSOHN, Felix
Concerto for Violin and Orchestra in E Minor, op. 64 (28:13)
BSO, conductor Seiji Ozawa
Isaac Stern, violin
September 29, 1980. Symphony Hall
CBS, producer Steven Epstein
LPs: IM-37204. **CDs:** MK-37204

BEETHOVEN, Ludwig van
Romance No. 1 in G for Violin and Orchestra, op. 40 (8:03)
BSO, conductor Seiji Ozawa
Isaac Stern, violin
September 29, 1980. Symphony Hall
CBS, producer Steven Epstein
LPs: IM-37204. **CDs:** MK-37204

BEETHOVEN, Ludwig van
Romance No. 2 in F for Violin and Orchestra, op. 50 (10:00)
BSO, conductor Seiji Ozawa
Isaac Stern, violin
September 29, 1980. Symphony Hall
CBS, producer Steven Epstein
LPs: IM-37204. **CDs:** MK-37204

MAHLER, Gustav
Symphony No. 8 in E♭, "Symphony of a Thousand" (79:24)
BSO, conductor Seiji Ozawa
Deborah Sasson, Judith Blegen, Faye Robinson, sopranos; Florence Quivar,
    mezzo-soprano; Lorna Myers, contralto; Kenneth Riegel, tenor; Benjamin
    Luxon, baritone; Gwynne Howell, bass; James David Christie, organ; TFC,
    John Oliver, dir.; Boston Boy Choir, Theodore Marier, dir.
October 13, 1980; November 4, 1980. Symphony Hall
Philips, producer Wilhelm Hellweg
LPs: 6769 069 (2). **CDs:** 410 607-2 (2). 438 874-2 (14). ArkivCD 410607 (2)

BARTÓK, Béla
Duke Bluebeard's Castle (59:44)
BSO, conductor Seiji Ozawa
Yvonne Minton, mezzo-soprano (Judith); Gwynne Howell, bass (Bluebeard)
November 8, 1980. Broadcast from Symphony Hall
BSO/IMG Artists
CDs: CB-100 (12)

BEETHOVEN, Ludwig van
Egmont, op. 84: Overture (8:34)
BSO, conductor Seiji Ozawa
January 24, 1981. Symphony Hall
Telarc, producer Robert Woods
LPs: DG 10060. **CDs:** 80060. 80240

BEETHOVEN, LUDWIG VAN
Symphony No. 5 in C Minor, op. 67 (31:10)
BSO, conductor Seiji Ozawa
January 24, 1981; January 26, 1981. Symphony Hall
Telarc, producer Robert Woods
LPs: DG-10060. **CDs:** 80060. **SACDs:** SA-60566

BEETHOVEN, LUDWIG VAN
Concerto for Piano and Orchestra No. 5 in E♭, op. 73 "Emperor" (41:05)
BSO, conductor Seiji Ozawa
Rudolf Serkin, piano
January 24, 1981; January 26, 1981. Symphony Hall
Telarc, producer Robert Woods
LPs: DG-10065. DG-10061-5 (4). **CDs:** 80065. 80061 (3). **SACDs:** SA-60566

BEETHOVEN, LUDWIG VAN
Concerto for Piano and Orchestra No. 4 in G, op. 58 (35:28)
BSO, conductor Seiji Ozawa
Rudolf Serkin, piano
October 5, 1981; October 6, 1981. Symphony Hall
Telarc, producer Robert Woods
LPs: DG-10064. DG-10061-5 (4). **CDs:** 80064. 80061 (3)

VIVALDI, ANTONIO
Concertos for Violin and Strings, op. 8, nos. 1-4, RV. 269, 315, 293, 297
    "The Four Seasons" (39:47)
BSO, conductor Seiji Ozawa
Joseph Silverstein, violin
October 10, 1981. Houghton Chapel, Wellesley College, Wellesley, Mass.
Telarc, producer Robert Woods
LPs: DG-10070. **CDs:** 80070. **SACDs:** 60700

STRAUSS, RICHARD
Also sprach Zarathustra, op. 30 (34:00)
BSO, conductor Seiji Ozawa
Joseph Silverstein, violin
December 14, 1981. Symphony Hall
Philips, producer Mike Bremner
LPs: 6514 221. **CDs:** 400 072-2. 442 645-2

STRAUSS, RICHARD
Ein Heldenleben, op. 40 (45:48)
BSO, conductor Seiji Ozawa
Joseph Silverstein, violin
December 14, 1981; December 15, 1981. Symphony Hall
Philips, producer Mike Bremner
LPs: 6514 222. **CDs:** 400 073-2. 442 645-2

SESSIONS, ROGER
Concerto for Orchestra (16:04). *A BSO commission.*
BSO, conductor Seiji Ozawa
January 30, 1982. Symphony Hall. *Premiered October 23, 1981.*
Hyperion, producer Harold Lawrence
LPs: A-66050. Musical Heritage Society MHS-4886. **CDs:** CDA-66050. Helios
CDH-55100

PANUFNIK, ANDRZEJ
Symphony No. 8 "Sinfonia Votiva" (24:09). *A BSO commission.*
BSO, conductor Seiji Ozawa
January 30, 1982. Symphony Hall. *Premiered January 28, 1982.*
Hyperion, producer Harold Lawrence
LPs: A-66050. Musical Heritage Society MHS-4886. **CDs:** CDA-66050. Helios
CDH-55100

DEBUSSY, CLAUDE
Nocturnes for Orchestra: Nuages. Fêtes. Sirènes (26:58)
BSO, conductor Colin Davis
TFC, John Oliver, dir.
March 20, 1982; March 22, 1982. Symphony Hall
Philips, producer Mike Bremner
LPs: 6514 260. **CDs:** 411 433-2

DEBUSSY, CLAUDE
La Mer (24:09)
BSO, conductor Colin Davis
March 22, 1982. Symphony Hall
Philips, producer Mike Bremner
LPs: 6514 260. **CDs:** 411 433-2

SCHUBERT, FRANZ
Rosamunde: Overture (*Die Zauberharfe*); Ballet Music No. 1: Andante;
Entr'Acte No. 3: Andantino; Ballet Music No. 2 (30:11)
BSO, conductor Colin Davis
March 22, 1982; December 18, 1982. Symphony Hall
Philips, producer Mike Bremner
LPs: 410 393-1. **CDs:** 410 393-2

DALLAPICCOLA, LUIGI
Canti di prigionia (27:04)
Members of the BSO, conductor John Oliver
Dennis Helmrich and Yehudi Wyner, pianos; TFC, John Oliver, dir.
August 30, 1982. Symphony Hall
Nonesuch
LPs: 79050-1. **CDs:** 9 79050-2. *Participating BSO musicians include Everett
Firth, timpani; Charles Smith, Arthur Press, Thomas Gauger, Frank Ep-
stein, percussion; and Ann Hobson Pilot, harp.*

BEETHOVEN, LUDWIG VAN
Fantasy for Piano, Chorus, and Orchestra in C Minor, op. 80 (20:00)
BSO, conductor Seiji Ozawa
Rudolf Serkin, piano; TFC, John Oliver, dir.
October 2, 1982. Symphony Hall
Telarc, producer Robert Woods
LPs: DG-10063. DG-10061-5 (4). **CDs:** 80063

BEETHOVEN, LUDWIG VAN
Concerto for Piano and Orchestra No. 3 in C Minor, op. 37 (36:49)
BSO, conductor Seiji Ozawa
Rudolf Serkin, piano
October 2, 1982; October 4, 1982. Symphony Hall
Telarc, producer Robert Woods
LPs: DG-10063. DG-10061-5 (4). **CDs:** 80063. 80061 (3). 80663

SCHUBERT, FRANZ
Symphony No. 8 in B Minor "Unfinished" (26:47)
BSO, conductor Colin Davis
December 18, 1982. Symphony Hall
Philips, producer Wilhelm Hellweg
LPs: 410 393-1. **CDs:** 410 393-2

KIM, EARL
Violin Concerto (22:12)
BSO, conductor Seiji Ozawa
Itzhak Perlman, violin
April 27, 1983. Symphony Hall
EMI, producer Suvi Raj Grubb
LPs: DS-38011. **CDs:** CDC7-49328 2

STARER, ROBERT
Concerto for Violin and Orchestra (21:47)
BSO, conductor Seiji Ozawa
Itzhak Perlman, violin
April 27, 1983; April 28, 1983. Symphony Hall. *Premiered October 15, 1981.*
EMI, producer Suvi Raj Grubb
LPs: DS-38011. **CDs:** CDC7-49328 2

STRAVINSKY, IGOR
The Firebird (45:45)
BSO, conductor Seiji Ozawa
April 30, 1983. Symphony Hall
EMI, producer Suvi Raj Grubb
LPs: DS-38012. **CDs:** CDC-47017. Seraphim 69131(2). ArkivCD 69131 (2)

BEETHOVEN, LUDWIG VAN
Concerto for Piano and Orchestra No. 1 in C, op. 15 (40:28)
BSO, conductor Seiji Ozawa
Rudolf Serkin, piano
October 5, 1983. Symphony Hall
Telarc, producer Robert Woods
LPs: DG-10062. DG-80061-5 (4). **CDs:** 80061 (3). 80663

DEBUSSY, CLAUDE
La Damoiselle élue (19:24)
BSO, conductor Seiji Ozawa
Frederica Von Stade, mezzo-soprano; Susanne Mentzer, reciter; TFC, John
    Oliver, dir.
October 10, 1983. Symphony Hall
CBS, producer David Mottley
LPs: IM-39098. **CDs:** MK-39098

BERLIOZ, HECTOR
Les Nuits d'été, op. 7 (32:23)
BSO, conductor Seiji Ozawa
Frederica Von Stade, mezzo-soprano
October 17, 1983. Symphony Hall
CBS, producer David Mottley
LPs: IM-39098. **CDs:** MK-39098

LIEBERSON, PETER
Piano Concerto (40:31). *A BSO commission.*
BSO, conductor Seiji Ozawa
Peter Serkin, piano
April 14, 1984. Symphony Hall. *Premiered April 21, 1983.*
New World Records, producer Elisabeth Ostrow
LPs: NW-325. **CDs:** NW-325-2. NW-80325

BEETHOVEN, LUDWIG VAN
Concerto for Piano and Orchestra No. 2 in B♭, op. 19 (30:40)
BSO, conductor Seiji Ozawa
Rudolf Serkin, piano
July 3, 1984. Symphony Hall
Telarc, producer Robert Woods
LPs: DG-10062. DG-80061-5 (4). **CDs:** 80064. 80061 (3)

WILSON, OLLY
Sinfonia (24:11). *A BSO commission.*
BSO, conductor Seiji Ozawa
October 15, 1984. Symphony Hall. *Premiered October 12, 1984.*
New World Records, producer Elisabeth Ostrow
LPs: NW-331. **CDs:** 80331-2

HARBISON, JOHN
Symphony No. 1 (23:57). *A BSO commission, premiered on March 22, 1984.*
BSO, conductor Seiji Ozawa
October 15, 1984; October 16, 1984; October 22, 1984. Symphony Hall.
New World Records, producer Elisabeth Ostrow
LPs: NW-331. **CDs:** 80331-2

SCHOENBERG, ARNOLD
Cello Concerto (after Monn: Clavicembalo Concerto in D, 1746) **(16:32)**
BSO, conductor Seiji Ozawa
Yo-Yo Ma, cello
October 22, 1984. Symphony Hall
CBS, producer James Mallinson
LPs: IM-39863. **CDs:** MK-39863

STRAUSS, RICHARD
Don Quixote, **op. 35 (45:01)**
BSO, conductor Seiji Ozawa
Yo-Yo Ma, cello; Burton Fine, viola
October 27, 1984. Symphony Hall
CBS, producer James Mallinson
LPs: IM-39863. **CDs:** MK-39863. MDK-45804. SK-94735

TCHAIKOVSKY, PETER ILYICH
Concerto for Violin and Orchestra in D, op. 35 (34:08)
BSO, conductor Seiji Ozawa
Victoria Mullova, violin
October 17, 1985. Symphony Hall
Philips, producer Wilhelm Hellweg
LPs: 416 821-1. **CDs:** 416 821-2. 464 741-2

SIBELIUS, JEAN
Concerto for Violin and Orchestra in D Minor, op. 47 (32:21)
BSO, conductor Seiji Ozawa
Victoria Mullova, violin
October 19, 1985. Symphony Hall
Philips, producer Wilhelm Hellweg
LPs: 416 821-1. **CDs:** 416 821-2. 464 741-2

BEETHOVEN, LUDWIG VAN
Egmont, **op. 84: Overture (8:43)**
BSO, conductor Seiji Ozawa
December 1, 1985. Symphony Hall (live)
Boston Symphony Transcription Trust, producers Jordan M. Whitelaw and
    Richard L. Kaye
CDs: BSO-CD1 (promotional). *1988 "Salute to Symphony."*

DVOŘÁK, Antonin
Concerto for Cello and Orchestra No. 2 in B Minor, op. 104 (38:58)
BSO, conductor Seiji Ozawa
Mstislav Rostropovich, cello
December 2, 1985. Symphony Hall
Erato, producer Michel Garcin
LPs: NUM-75282. **CDs:** ECD-862. ECD-88224. Elatus 0927467272. Warner
    Classics 447 036 (9). *Oddly, the three movements are not on consecutive*
    tracks—nor even on the same discs—in the Warner Classics 9-CD set.

TCHAIKOVSKY, Peter Ilyich
Variations on a Rococo Theme, op. 33 (17:32)
BSO, conductor Seiji Ozawa
Mstislav Rostropovich, cello
December 2, 1985. Symphony Hall
Erato, producer Michel Garcin
LPs: NUM-75282. **CDs:** ECD-862. ECD-88224. Elatus 0927467272. Warner
    Classics 49706. 447 036 (9)

CONCERT VIDEO (84:42)
BRAHMS Symphony No. 1 in C Minor, op. 68 (46:43)
R. STRAUSS *Also sprach Zarathustra*, op. 30 (37:15)
BSO, conductor Seiji Ozawa
March 1, 1986. Festival Hall, Osaka, Japan
Sony Classical, producer Takuro Uno
Laserdiscs: SLV-46378. **DVDs:** Parnassus PDVD-198

CHOPIN, Frédéric
Concerto for Piano and Orchestra No. 1 in E Minor, op. 11
BSO, conductor Seiji Ozawa
Alexis Weissenberg, piano
April 19, 1986. April 21, 1986. Symphony Hall
Deutsche Grammophon, producer Werner Mayer
Unreleased

TCHAIKOVSKY, Peter Ilyich
Symphony No. 6 in B Minor, op. 74 "Pathétique" (45:36)
BSO, conductor Seiji Ozawa
April 26, 1986. Symphony Hall
Erato, producer Yolanta Skura
LPs: NUM-75303. **CDs:** ECD-88242. 045261-2

PROKOFIEV, Sergei
Romeo and Juliet, op. 64 (144:22)
BSO, conductor Seiji Ozawa
October 18, 1986; October 20, 1986; October 21, 1986. Symphony Hall
Deutsche Grammophon, producer Wolfgang Stengel
LPs: 423 268-1 (2). **CDs:** 423 268-2 (2)

FAURÉ, GABRIEL
Pelléas et Mélisande, Suite from the incidental music to Maeterlinck's drama, op. 80 (20:40)
BSO, conductor Seiji Ozawa
Lorraine Hunt Lieberson, soprano
November 15, 1986; November 17, 1986. Symphony Hall
Deutsche Grammophon, producer Werner Mayer
LPs: 423 089-1. **CDs:** 423 089-2. 469 268-2 (2). *The third movement, Chanson de Mélisande, is played in Charles Koechlin's orchestral arrangement. The other movements are Fauré's expansions of Koechlin's orchestrations.*

FAURÉ, GABRIEL
Pavane, op. 50 (6:48)
BSO, conductor Seiji Ozawa
TFC, John Oliver, dir.
November 15, 1986. Symphony Hall
Deutsche Grammophon, producer Werner Mayer
LPs: 423 089-1. **CDs:** 423 089-2. 474 541-2. 457 196-2 (2). 469 268-2 (2). 449 846-2. Universal B0004485-02

FAURÉ, GABRIEL
Dolly, Six pieces for piano four-hands, op. 56 (orch. Henri Rabaud) (17:53)
BSO, conductor Seiji Ozawa
November 15, 1986; November 17, 1986. Symphony Hall
Deutsche Grammophon, producer Werner Mayer
LPs: 423 089-1. **CDs:** 423 089-2. 449 846-2

CHABRIER, EMMANUEL
España (6:17)
BSO, conductor Seiji Ozawa
November 15, 1986; November 17, 1986. Symphony Hall
Deutsche Grammophon, producer Werner Mayer
CDs: 423 698-2. ArkivCD 423698

FAURÉ, GABRIEL
Elégie, op. 24 (6:50)
BSO, conductor Seiji Ozawa
Jules Eskin, cello
November 17, 1986. Symphony Hall
Deutsche Grammophon, producer Werner Mayer
LPs: 423 089-1. **CDs:** 423 089-2. 469 268-2 (2)

FAURÉ, GABRIEL
Après un rêve, op. 7, no. 1; Andante (arr. Dubenskij) (3:17)
BSO, conductor Seiji Ozawa
Jules Eskin, cello
November 17, 1986. Symphony Hall
Deutsche Grammophon, producer Werner Mayer
LPs: 423 089-1. **CDs:** 423 089-2. 469 268-2 (2). Decca 00012341-2

GOUNOD, CHARLES
Faust: Ballet Music (16:55)
BSO, conductor Seiji Ozawa
November 17, 1986; November 24, 1986; November 27, 1986. Symphony Hall
Deutsche Grammophon, producers Werner Mayer and Cord Garben
CDs: 423 698-2. ArkivCD 423698

OFFENBACH, JACQUES
Gaîté Parisienne (arr. Manuel Rosenthal) (19:14)
BSO, conductor Seiji Ozawa
November 17, 1986; November 27, 1986. Symphony Hall
Deutsche Grammophon, producers Werner Mayer and Cord Garben
CDs: 423 698-2. ArkivCD 423698. *Seiji Ozawa, unaware of the many "tradi-
tional" tempo fluctuations the orchestra had become accustomed to under
Fiedler and Harry Ellis Dickson in this "Pops" repertoire, seemed puzzled
at times when the orchestra played seemingly with a mind of its own.
(Douglas Yeo, email March 23, 2008)*

MAHLER, GUSTAV
Symphony No. 2 in C Minor "Resurrection" (80:10)
BSO, conductor Seiji Ozawa
Kiri Te Kanawa, soprano; Marilyn Horne, mezzo; TFC, John Oliver, dir.
December 13, 1986; December 15, 1986. Symphony Hall
Philips, producer Wilhelm Hellweg
LPs: 420 824-1. CDs: 420 824-2 (2). 438 874-2 (14). ArkivCD 420824 (2)

LISZT, FRANZ
Concerto for Piano and Orchestra No. 2 in A (21:53)
BSO, conductor Seiji Ozawa
Krystian Zimerman, piano
April 25, 1987; April 27, 1987. Symphony Hall
Deutsche Grammophon, producer Wolfgang Stengel
CDs: 423 571-2. BMG Club D-105620

LISZT, FRANZ
Totentanz, Paraphrase on Dies Irae, for piano and orchestra (15:12)
BSO, conductor Seiji Ozawa
Krystian Zimerman, piano
April 25, 1987; April 27, 1987. Symphony Hall
Deutsche Grammophon, producer Wolfgang Stengel
CDs: 423 571-2. BMG Club D-105620

LISZT, FRANZ
Concerto for Piano and Orchestra No. 1 in E♭ (18:29)
BSO, conductor Seiji Ozawa
Krystian Zimerman, piano
April 27, 1987. Symphony Hall
Deutsche Grammophon, producer Wolfgang Stengel
CDs: 423 571-2. BMG Club D-105620

MAHLER, GUSTAV
Symphony No. 5 in C♯ Minor: Adagietto (11:29)
BSO, conductor Seiji Ozawa
August 2, 1987. Koussevitzky Music Shed, Tanglewood (live)
Boston Symphony Transcription Trust, producers Jordan M. Whitelaw and
  Richard L. Kaye
CDs: BSO-CD1 (promotional). *1988 "Salute to Symphony."*

MAHLER, GUSTAV
Symphony No. 1 in D "Titan" (53:54)
BSO, conductor Seiji Ozawa
October 5, 1987; October 6, 1987. Symphony Hall
Philips, producer Wilhelm Hellweg
CDs: 422 329-2. 438 874-2 (14)

MAHLER, GUSTAV
Symphony No. 4 in G (54:30)
BSO, conductor Seiji Ozawa
Kiri Te Kanawa, soprano
November 21, 1987; November 23, 1987; November 27, 1987. Symphony Hall
Philips, producer Wilhelm Hellweg
CDs: 422 072-2. 438 874-2 (14). ArkivCD 422072. *Deutsche Grammophon's*
  Cord Garben produced the November 27 patch session. Recording engineer
  John Newton, of Soundmirror, Inc., said (August 16, 2007) that Philips and
  Deutsche Grammophon placed their microphones in widely differing posi-
  tions; both had complete arrangements set up in Symphony Hall on that day.

POULENC, FRANCIS
Gloria in G (23:29)
BSO, conductor Seiji Ozawa
Kathleen Battle, soprano; TFC, John Oliver, dir.
November 24, 1987; November 25, 1987. Symphony Hall
Deutsche Grammophon, producer Cord Garben
CDs: 427 304-2. 445 567-2

THOMAS, AMBROISE
Mignon: **Overture (8:10)**
BSO, conductor Seiji Ozawa
November 24, 1987. Symphony Hall
Deutsche Grammophon, producer Cord Garben
CDs: 423 698-2. ArkivCD 423698

POULENC, FRANCIS
Stabat Mater (28:34)
BSO, conductor Seiji Ozawa
Kathleen Battle, soprano; TFC, John Oliver, dir.
November 25, 1987; November 27, 1987. Symphony Hall
Deutsche Grammophon, producer Cord Garben
CDs: 427 304-2

STRAVINSKY, IGOR
Symphony of Psalms (22:00). *A BSO commission.*
BSO, conductor Seiji Ozawa
TFC, John Oliver, dir.
December 5, 1987. Broadcast from Symphony Hall
BSO/IMG Artists
CDs: CB-100 (12)

STRAUSS, RICHARD
Duet-Concertino for Clarinet and Bassoon (19:47)
BSO, conductor Seiji Ozawa
Harold Wright, clarinet; Sherman Walt, bassoon
March 12, 1988. Broadcast from Symphony Hall
BSO/IMG Artists
CDs: CB-100 (12)

GUBAIDULINA, SOFIA
Offertorium (35:34)
BSO, conductor Charles Dutoit
Gidon Kremer, violin
April 4, 1988. Symphony Hall
Deutsche Grammophon, producers Thomas Frost and Wolfgang Stengel
CDs: 427 336-2. 471 625-2

STRAUSS, RICHARD
Elektra, op. 58 (102:08)
BSO, conductor Seiji Ozawa
Hildegard Behrens, soprano (Elektra); Christa Ludwig, mezzo-soprano
(Klytämnestra); Nadine Secunde, soprano (Chrysothemis); Ragnar Ulfung,
tenor (Aegisth); Jorma Hynninen, baritone (Orest); TFC, John Oliver, dir.
November 12, 1988; November 15, 1988; November 18, 1988; November 21,
1988 (patch); November 23, 1988 (patch). Symphony Hall (live)
Philips, producer Wilhelm Hellweg
CDs: 422 574-2 (2). 464 985-2 (2). Decca/London 470 583-2 (2)

MAHLER, GUSTAV
Kindertotenlieder (23:51)
BSO, conductor Seiji Ozawa
Jessye Norman, soprano
December 13, 1988. Der Alte Oper, Frankfurt am Main, Germany (live)
Philips, producer Volker Straus
CDs: 426 249-2 (2). 434 161-2. 438 874-2 (14). ArkivCD 426249 (2). *Recorded
at an 8:00 PM concert, with a patch session at 10:30 that evening.*

MAHLER, GUSTAV
Symphony No. 7 in E Minor (80:13)
BSO, conductor Seiji Ozawa
March 11, 1989; March 13, 1989. Symphony Hall
Philips, producer Wilhelm Hellweg
CDs: 426 249-2 (2). 438 874-2 (14). ArkivCD 426249

POULENC, FRANCIS
Concerto in D Minor for Two Pianos and Orchestra (20:21)
BSO, conductor Seiji Ozawa
Katia and Marielle Labèque, pianos
April 8, 1989. Symphony Hall
Philips, producer Hein Dekker
CDs: 426 284-2. ArkivCD 426284. Universal B0001221-02 (6). BMG Club D-105623

RAVEL, MAURICE
Daphnis et Chloé **(57:48)**
BSO, conductor Bernard Haitink
Doriot Anthony Dwyer, flute; TFC, John Oliver, dir.
May 1, 1989; May 2, 1989. Symphony Hall
Philips, producer Volker Straus
CDs: 426 260-2. ArkivCD 426260

MAHLER, GUSTAV
Symphony No. 9 in D (83:11)
BSO, conductor Seiji Ozawa
October 5, 1989; October 10, 1989; October 13, 1989; October 16, 1989.
   (patch). Symphony Hall (live)
Philips, producer Wilhelm Hellweg
CDs: 426 302-2 (2). 438 874-2 (14). ArkivCD 426302 (2)

BACH, JOHANN SEBASTIAN
Prelude and Fugue in E♭, BWV 552 "St. Anne" (arr. Schoenberg) **(14:46)**
BSO, conductor Seiji Ozawa
October 21, 1989. Symphony Hall
Philips, producer Wilhelm Hellweg
CDs: 432 092-2. 470 411-2. Universal B0001062-02

BACH, JOHANN SEBASTIAN
A Musical Offering, **BWV 1079. No. 8: Fuga (Ricercare a 6 Voci)** (arr. Webern) **(8:28)**
BSO, conductor Seiji Ozawa
October 21, 1989. Symphony Hall
Philips, producer Wilhelm Hellweg
CDs: 432 092-2. 470 411-2. Universal B0001062-02

BRAHMS, JOHANNES
Symphony No. 2 in D, op. 73 (47:01)
BSO, conductor Bernard Haitink
March 31, 1990; April 2, 1990; April 3, 1990. Symphony Hall
Philips, producer Volker Straus
CDs: 432 094-2. 456 030-2 (4). BMG Club D-100056. ArkivCD 432094

BRAHMS, JOHANNES
Tragic Overture, op. 81 (15:08)
BSO, conductor Bernard Haitink
April 3, 1990. Symphony Hall
Philips, producer Volker Straus
CDs: 432 094-2. 456 030-2 (4). BMG Club D-100056. ArkivCD 432094

MAHLER, GUSTAV
Symphony No. 10 in F♯ Minor: I Adagio (29:14)
BSO, conductor Seiji Ozawa
April 19, 1990; April 20, 1990; April 21, 1990; April 23, 1990 (patch). Symphony Hall (live)
Philips, producer Wilhelm Hellweg
CDs: 426 302-2 (2). 438 874-2 (14). ArkivCD 426302 (2)

BACH, JOHANN SEBASTIAN
Toccata and Fugue in D Minor, BWV 565 (arr. Stokowski) (9:06)
BSO, conductor Seiji Ozawa
April 23, 1990. Symphony Hall
Philips, producer Wilhelm Hellweg
CDs: 432 092-2. 438 887-2. 470 411-2. Universal B0001062-02. ArkivCD 438887

BACH, JOHANN SEBASTIAN
Chorale-Variations on "Vom Himmel hoch da komm' ich her," BWV 769 (arr. Stravinky) (10:43)
BSO, conductor Seiji Ozawa
TFC, John Oliver, dir.
April 24, 1990. Symphony Hall
Philips, producer Wilhelm Hellweg
CDs: 432 092-2. 470 411-2. Universal B0001062-02

BRITTEN, BENJAMIN
Peter Grimes: Four Sea Interludes (18:10)
BSO, conductor Leonard Bernstein
August 19, 1990. Koussevitzky Music Shed, Tanglewood (live)
Deutsche Grammophon/Boston Symphony Transcription Trust, producer Louise de la Fuente
CDs: 431 768-2. Universal B0002183-02 (3). BMG Club D-135095. Columbia House G2-31687. *Leonard Bernstein's last concert.*

BEETHOVEN, LUDWIG VAN
Symphony No. 7 in A, op. 92 (45:13)
BSO, conductor Leonard Bernstein
August 19, 1990. Koussevitzky Music Shed, Tanglewood (live)
Deutsche Grammophon/Boston Symphony Transcription Trust, producer Louise
   de la Fuente
CDs: 431 768-2. BMG Club D-135095. Columbia House G2-31687. *Leonard*
   Bernstein's last concert.

MAHLER, GUSTAV
Symphony No. 5 in C♯ Minor (71:32)
BSO, conductor Seiji Ozawa
September 27, 1990; September 28, 1990; October 12, 1990; October 13, 1990
   (patch); October 16, 1990 (patch). Symphony Hall (live)
Philips, producer Wilhelm Hellweg
CDs: 432 141-2. 438 874-2. ArkivCD 432141

RAVEL, MAURICE
Concerto for Piano and Orchestra in D for the Left Hand (19:22)
BSO, conductor Seiji Ozawa
Leon Fleisher, piano
October 6, 1990. Symphony Hall
Sony, producer Steven Epstein
CDs: SK-47188. Universal B0000553-02

BRITTEN, BENJAMIN
Diversions for Piano (left hand) and Orchestra, op. 21 (24:53)
BSO, conductor Seiji Ozawa
Leon Fleisher, piano
October 8, 1990. Symphony Hall
Sony, producer Steven Epstein
CDs: SK-47188. SMK-58930

BACH, JOHANN SEBASTIAN
Partita No. 2 in D minor, BWV 1004: Chaconne (arr. Saito) **(16:39)**
BSO, conductor Seiji Ozawa
October 13, 1990. Symphony Hall
Philips, producer Wilhelm Hellweg
CDs: 432 092-2. 470 411-2. Universal B0001062-02

TAKEMITSU, TORU
From me flows what you call Time, for five percussionists and orchestra. *World premiere.*
BSO, conductor Seiji Ozawa
NEXUS percussion ensemble (Bob Becker, William Cahn, Robin Engelman, Russell Hartenberger, John Wyre)
October 19, 1990. Carnegie Hall (live)
Sony BMG Masterworks.
DVD: Kultur D4179. *The payment sheet for this session states "Audio-Visual material included in a 1994 French documentary film* Music for the Movies: Toru Takemitsu. *But the BSO material was not used in that film, at least as presented on the DVD.*

TCHAIKOVSKY, PETER ILYICH
Sleeping Beauty, op. 66: Suite (20:01)
BSO, conductor Seiji Ozawa
December 8, 1990; December 15, 1990. Symphony Hall
Deutsche Grammophon, producer Christian Gansch
CDs: 435 619-2 (2). 471 744-2. Universal B0001306-02. Entrée 4775009

TCHAIKOVSKY, PETER ILYICH
The Nutcracker , op. 71 (108:19)
BSO, conductor Seiji Ozawa
December 15, 1990; December 17, 1990. Symphony Hall
Deutsche Grammophon, producer Christian Gansch
CDs: 435 619-2 (2)

Selections (23:21). CDs: Universal B0001306-02. Entrée 477509

MORET, NORBERT
En rêve (19:37)
BSO, conductor Seiji Ozawa
Anne-Sophie Mutter, violin
February 16, 1991; February 18, 1991. Symphony Hall
Deutsche Grammophon, producer Christopher Alder
CDs: 431 626-2. 445 487-2 (3). ArkivCD 431626. Universal B0004049-02.
    BMG Club D-143994

BARTÓK, BÉLA
Concerto for Violin and Orchestra No. 2 (38:35)
BSO, conductor Seiji Ozawa
Anne-Sophie Mutter, violin
February 18, 1991. Symphony Hall
Deutsche Grammophon, producer Christopher Alder
CDs: 431 626-2. 445 487-2 (3). ArkivCD 431626. Universal B0004049-02.
    BMG Club D-143994

PROKOFIEV, SERGEI
Concerto for Piano (left hand) and Orchestra No. 4 in B♭, op. 53 (23:25)
BSO, conductor Seiji Ozawa
Leon Fleisher, piano
October 15, 1991. Symphony Hall
Sony, producer Steven Epstein
CDs: SK-47188

TCHAIKOVSKY, PETER ILYICH
Pique Dame, op. 68 (156:00)
BSO, conductor Seiji Ozawa
Mirella Freni, soprano (Lisa); Vladimir Atlantov, tenor (Herman); Dmitri Hvo-
rostovsky, baritone (Prince Yeletsky); Maureen Forrester, contralto (Coun-
tess); Sergei Leiferkus, baritone (Count Tomsky); Katherine Ciesinski,
soprano (Pauline); TFC, John Oliver, dir.; American Boychoir, James Lit-
ton, dir.
October 16, 1991; October 19, 1991; October 22, 1991. Symphony Hall (live).
October 26, 1991. Carnegie Hall (live). November 11, 1991 (patch). Sym-
phony Hall
RCA, producer Jay David Saks
CDs: 09026-60992-2 (3). Highlights: 09026-61227-2. ArkivCD 61227

FRANCK, CÉSAR
Symphony in D Minor (38:59)
BSO, conductor Seiji Ozawa
November 29, 1991; November 30, 1991; December 2, 1991; December 3,
1991. Symphony Hall
Deutsche Grammophon, producer Christian Gansch
CDs: 437 827-2. ArkivCD 437827

POULENC, FRANCIS
Concert champêtre (25:07)
BSO, conductor Seiji Ozawa
Trevor Pinnock, harpsichord
November 30, 1991. Symphony Hall
Deutsche Grammophon, producer Christian Gansch
CDs: 445 567-2

POULENC, FRANCIS
Concerto in G Minor for Organ, Strings, and Timpani (22:33)
BSO, conductor Seiji Ozawa
Simon Preston, organ; Everett Firth, timpani
December 2, 1991. Symphony Hall
Deutsche Grammophon, producer Christian Gansch
CDs: 437 827-2. 445 567-2. ArkivCD 437827

MAHLER, Gustav
Symphony No. 6 in A Minor "Tragic" (82:51)
BSO, conductor Seiji Ozawa
January 30, 1992; January 31, 1992; February 4, 1992. Symphony Hall
Philips, producer Wilhelm Hellweg
CDs: 434 909-2 (3). 438 874-2 (14). ArkivCD 434909 (3)

BRITTEN, Benjamin
Variations and Fugue on a Theme of Purcell, op. 34 **"The Young Person's Guide to the Orchestra" (20:25)**
BSO, conductor Seiji Ozawa
Melissa Joan Hart, narrator
February 14, 1992. Symphony Hall
Sony, producer Tomoko Noda
CDs: SK 64079

Seiji Ozawa, narrator (in Japanese) **(19:59). CD:** Fun House FHCB-2001

PROKOFIEV, Sergei
Peter and the Wolf, op. **67 (27:55)**
BSO, conductor Seiji Ozawa
Melissa Joan Hart, narrator
February 14, 1992; February 15, 1992. Symphony Hall
Sony, producer Tomoko Noda
CDs: SK 64079.

Seiji Ozawa, narrator (in Japanese) **(28:40). CD:** Fun House FHCB-2001. *This disc was a best seller—a "chart topper"— in Japan. "We rarely heard Seiji speak Japanese; his narration is energetic and engaging, as if he was telling a child a VERY important story." (Douglas Yeo, BSO bass trombonist, email March 23, 2008)*

SAINT-SAËNS, Camille
Carnival of the Animals (verses by Ogden Nash) **(23:05)**
BSO, conductor Seiji Ozawa
Melissa Joan Hart, narrator; John Browning and Garrick Ohlsson, pianos; Jules Eskin, cello
February 15, 1992. Symphony Hall
Sony, producer Tomoko Noda
CDs: SK 64079

Seiji Ozawa, narrator (in Japanese) **(24:59). CD:** Fun House FHCB-2001

SIBELIUS, Jean
Symphony No. 2 in D, op. 43 (45:11)
BSO, conductor Vladimir Ashkenazy
March 5, 1992; March 6, 1992; March 7, 1992; March 9, 1992. Symphony Hall
Decca, producer Ray Minshull
CDs: 436 566-2. ArkivCD 436566. *This was supposed to be the start of a complete series of the Sibelius symphonies, but only this one disc was recorded.*

SIBELIUS, JEAN
Kuolema, op. 44, no. 1: **Valse triste (5:23)**
BSO, conductor Vladimir Ashkenazy
March 9, 1992. Symphony Hall
Decca, producer Ray Minshull
CDs: 436 566-2. 473 590-2 (5). Universal B0001219-02 (5). ArkivCD 436566

SIBELIUS, JEAN
Finlandia, op. 26, no. 7 **(8:16)**
BSO, conductor Vladimir Ashkenazy
March 9, 1992. Symphony Hall
Decca, producer Ray Minshull
CDs: 436 566-2. 466 687-2. ArkivCD 436566

SIBELIUS, JEAN
Romance for Strings in C, op. 43 (5:29)
BSO, conductor Vladimir Ashkenazy
March 9, 1992. Symphony Hall
Decca, producer Ray Minshull
CDs: 436 566-2. 473 590-2 (5). Universal B0001219-02 (5). ArkivCD 436566

SHOSTAKOVICH, DMITRI
Concerto for Violin and Orchestra No. 2 in C# Minor, op. 129 (32:01)
BSO, conductor Seiji Ozawa
Gidon Kremer, violin
April 16, 1992; April 17, 1992; April 18, 1992. Symphony Hall (live)
Deutsche Grammophon, producer Wolfgang Stengel
CDs: 439 890-2. Universal B0006461-02 (2).B 0002014-02 (3). Decca/London
    B0002014-02 (3). B0006769-02 (9). ArkivCD 439890

SCHUMANN, ROBERT
Concerto for Cello and Orchestra in A Minor, op. 129 (arranged by Schu-
    mann for Violin; orchestrated by Shostakovich) **(22:30)**
BSO, conductor Seiji Ozawa
Gidon Kremer, violin
April 18, 1992. Symphony Hall (live)
Deutsche Grammophon, producer Wolfgang Stengel
CDs: 439 890-2. ArkivCD 439890

BRAHMS, JOHANNES
Symphony No. 4 in E Minor, op. 98 (43:15)
BSO, conductor Bernard Haitink
April 25, 1992; April 27, 1992; May 1, 1992. Symphony Hall
Philips, producer Volker Straus
CDs: 434 991-2. 456 030-2 (4). ArkivCD 434991. Musically Speaking MS214

BRAHMS, JOHANNES
Variations on a Theme by Haydn, op. 56a (19:00)
BSO, conductor Bernard Haitink
May 1, 1992. Symphony Hall
Philips, producer Volker Straus
CDs: 434 991-2. 456 030-2 (4). ArkivCD 434991. Musically Speaking MS214

SCHUBERT, FRANZ
Symphony No. 3 in D (24:44)
BSO, conductor Bernard Haitink
May 2, 1992. Broadcast from Symphony Hall
BSO/IMG Artists
CDs: CB-100 (12)

MENDELSSOHN, FELIX
A Midsummer Night's Dream, op. 21 and op. 61 (55:38)
BSO, conductor Seiji Ozawa
Kathleen Battle, soprano; Frederica Von Stade, mezzo-soprano; Judi Dench,
    speaker; TFC, John Oliver, dir.
October 3, 1992; October 10, 1992. Symphony Hall
Deutsche Grammophon, producer Christian Gansch
CDs: 439 897-2

RACHMANINOFF, SERGEI
Concerto for Piano and Orchestra No. 3 in D Minor, op. 30 (44:24)
BSO, conductor Seiji Ozawa
Evgeni Kissin, piano
January 21, 1992; January 22, 1993; January 23, 1993; January 25, 1993. Sym-
    phony Hall (live)
RCA, producer Jay David Saks
CDs: 09026-61548-2

BRAHMS, JOHANNES
Alto Rhapsody, op. 53 (14:56)
BSO, conductor Bernard Haitink
Jard van Nes, contralto; TFC, John Oliver, dir.
March 15, 1993. Symphony Hall
Philips, producer Volker Straus
CDs: 442 120-2. 456 030-2 (4). ArkivCD 442120

BRAHMS, JOHANNES
Symphony No. 3 in F, op. 90 (38:45)
BSO, conductor Bernard Haitink
March 20, 1993; March 22, 1993. Symphony Hall
Philips, producer Volker Straus
CDs: 442 120-2. 456 030-2 (4). ArkivCD 442120

MAHLER, GUSTAV
Symphony No. 3 in D Minor (96:11)
BSO, conductor Seiji Ozawa
Jessye Norman, soprano; TFC, John Oliver, dir.; American Boychoir, James Litton, dir.
April 22, 1993; April 23, 1993; April 24, 1993; April 27, 1993. Symphony Hall
Philips, producer Wilhelm Hellweg.
CDs: 434 909-2 (3). 438 874-2 (14). ArkivCD 434 909 (3)

BERLIOZ, HECTOR
Requiem, op. 5 "Grande messe des morts" (76:03)
BSO, conductor Seiji Ozawa
Vinson Cole, tenor; TFC, John Oliver, dir.
October 21, 1993; October 22, 1993; October 23, 1993. Symphony Hall (live)
RCA, producer Jay David Saks
CDs: 09026-62544-2

COLLECTION: "DVOŘÁK IN PRAGUE: A CELEBRATION"
Timings run longer on the videos than on the CD due to applause.
***Carnival Overture*, op. 92 (9:32/9:59)**
***Humoresque in G♭*, op. 101, No. 7** (arr. Oskar Morawetz) **(3:32/4:30)**
  Itzhak Perlman, violin; Yo-Yo Ma, cello (**CDs:** SK-92828. SK-93072)
***Slavonic Dance in E Minor*, op. 72, no. 2** (arr. Oskar Morawetz) **(5:01/5:29)**
  Itzhak Perlman, violin; Yo-Yo Ma, cello (**CDs:** SK-92828)
***Slavonic Dance in C*, op. 72, no. 7 (3:33/4:11)**
***Klid (Silent Woods)*, op. 68, no. 5 (6:20/7:54)**
  Yo-Yo Ma, cello (**CDs:** SK-92828. SK-93072)
Romance in F Minor, op. 11 (11:28/12:18)
  Itzhak Perlman, violin
***Rusalka*, op. 114: "O Lovely Moon" (6:55/7:28)**
  Frederica Von Stade, mezzo-soprano
Psalm 149 for Chorus and Orchestra, op. 79 (9:00/9:39)
  Prague Philharmonic Chorus, Jaroslav Brych, dir.
Symphony No. 9 in E Minor, op. 95 "from the New World": II. Largo
(12:39). *This selection is not on the CD.*
BSO, conductor Seiji Ozawa
December 16, 1993. Smetana Hall, Prague (live)
Sony Classical, producer Thomas Frost
CDs: SK 46687. **LASER DISC:** SLV-53488. **VHS:** SHV-53488. **DVD:** Kultur 4211. *There are other works on this program that do not involve the BSO.*

HAYDN, FRANZ JOSEPH
Scena di Berenice, Hob. XXIVa:10
BSO, conductor Seiji Ozawa
Jessye Norman, soprano
February 10, 1994; February 12, 1994; February 21, 1994 (patch). Symphony
   Hall (live)
Philips
Unreleased

BRITTEN, BENJAMIN
Phaedra, op. 93
BSO, conductor Seiji Ozawa
Jessye Norman, soprano
February 10, 1994; February 12, 1994; February 21, 1994 (patch). Symphony
   Hall (live)
Philips
Unreleased

BERLIOZ, HECTOR
La Mort de Cléopâtre
BSO, conductor Seiji Ozawa
Jessye Norman, soprano
February 10, 1994; February 12, 1994; February 22, 1994 (patch). Symphony
   Hall (live)
Philips
Unreleased

MESSIAEN, OLIVIER
Oiseaux exotiques, for Piano, 11 Winds, Xylophone, Glockenspiel, and Percus-
   sion
BSO, conductor Seiji Ozawa
Mitsuko Uchida, piano
February 23, 1994. Symphony Hall
Philips
Unreleased

BARTÓK, BÉLA
Concerto for Orchestra (with the original ending) (**38:16,** including applause)
BSO, conductor Seiji Ozawa
February 24, 1994; February 25, 1994; February 26, 1994; February 28, 1994
   (patch); March 1, 1994. Symphony Hall (live)
Philips, producer Wilhelm Hellweg
CDs: 442 783-2. ArkivCD 442783. *For these performances, BSO bass trombon-*
   ist Douglas Yeo had an F bass trombone constructed which could reach the
   low B that begins the glissando at measure 90 of the fourth movement, In-
   termezzo interotto, a key point in the score; Bartók wrote it for an instru-
   ment long obsolete in the West (North: "Excursions with a Trombone"). *The*
   original ending, recorded at the patch session, was not played in concert.

BARTÓK, BÉLA
The Miraculous Mandarin (31:17)
BSO, conductor Seiji Ozawa
TFC, John Oliver, dir.
February 28, 1994. Symphony Hall
Philips, producer Wilhelm Hellweg
CDs: 442 783-2. ArkivCD 442783

FAURÉ, GABRIEL
Requiem, op. 48 (36:43)
BSO, conductor Seiji Ozawa
Barbara Bonney, soprano; Håkan Hågegard, baritone; TFC, John Oliver, dir.
March 3, 1994; March 4, 1994; March 5, 1994; April 4, 1994. Symphony Hall
RCA, producer Jay David Saks
CDs: 09026-55303-2. 09026-68659-2

BRAHMS, JOHANNES
Symphony No. 1 in C Minor, op. 68 (47:58)
BSO, conductor Bernard Haitink
April 23, 1994; April 25, 1994; April 30, 1994. Symphony Hall
Philips, producer Volker Straus
CDs: 442 799-2. 456 030-2 (4)

BRAHMS, JOHANNES
Nänie, op. 82 (12:34)
BSO, conductor Bernard Haitink
TFC, John Oliver, dir.
April 30, 1994. Symphony Hall
Philips, producer Volker Straus
CDs: 442 799-2. 456 030-2 (4)

BERNSTEIN, LEONARD
Serenade (after Plato's *Symposium*) for Violin, Harp, Percussion, and Strings (30:08)
BSO, conductor Seiji Ozawa
Itzhak Perlman, violin; Jules Eskin, cello; Ann Hobson Pilot, harp
October 1, 1994; October 3, 1994. Symphony Hall
EMI, producer John Fraser
CDs: 5-55360 2. 5-62600 2. 5-85083 2 (15). 08286 2

BARBER, SAMUEL
Concerto for Violin and Orchestra (22:22)
BSO, conductor Seiji Ozawa
Itzhak Perlman, violin
October 3, 1994; October 4, 1994. Symphony Hall
EMI, producer John Fraser
CDs: 5-55360 2. 5-62600 2. 5-85083 2 (15). 08286 2

FOSS, LUKAS
Three American Pieces (12:20)
BSO, conductor Seiji Ozawa
Itzhak Perlman, violin
October 4, 1994. Symphony Hall
EMI, producer John Fraser
CDs: 5-55360 2. 5-62600 2. 5-85083 2 (15). 08286 2

RAVEL, MAURICE
Shéhérazade (15:31)
BSO, conductor Seiji Ozawa
Sylvia McNair, soprano
April 17, 1995; April 22, 1995. Symphony Hall
Philips, producer Wilhelm Hellweg
CDs: 446 682-2

DEBUSSY, CLAUDE
La Damoiselle élue (18:19)
BSO, conductor Seiji Ozawa
Susan Graham, mezzo-soprano
April 19, 1995; April 22, 1995. Symphony Hall
Philips, producer Wilhelm Hellweg
CDs: 446 682-2

RAVEL, MAURICE
Ma Mère l'oye (28:09)
BSO, conductor Bernard Haitink
November 18, 1995. Symphony Hall
Philips, producer Volker Straus
CDs: 454 452-2

RAVEL, MAURICE
Rapsodie espagnole (15:41)
BSO, conductor Bernard Haitink
November 20, 1995. Symphony Hall
Philips, producer Volker Straus
CDs: 454 452-2

RAVEL, MAURICE
La Valse (11:57)
BSO, conductor Bernard Haitink
November 20, 1995. Symphony Hall
Philips, producer Volker Straus
CDs: 454 452-2

RAVEL, MAURICE
Menuet antique (7:05)
BSO, conductor Bernard Haitink
November 20, 1995. Symphony Hall
Philips, producer Volker Straus
CDs: 454 452-2

RAVEL, MAURICE
Le Tombeau de Couperin (18:16)
BSO, conductor Bernard Haitink
April 20, 1996. Symphony Hall
Philips, producer Volker Straus
CDs: 456 569-2. ArkivCD 456569

RAVEL, MAURICE
Boléro (15:03)
BSO, conductor Bernard Haitink
April 22, 1996. Symphony Hall
Philips, producer Volker Straus
CDs: 456 569-2. ArkivCD 456569

RAVEL, MAURICE
Une Barque sur l'océan
BSO, conductor Bernard Haitink
April 22, 1996. Symphony Hall
Philips, producer Volker Straus
Unreleased

RAVEL, MAURICE
Alborada del gracioso (7:57)
BSO, conductor Bernard Haitink
April 27, 1996. Symphony Hall
Philips, producer Volker Straus
CDs: 456 569-2. ArkivCD 456569

RAVEL, MAURICE
Valses nobles et sentimentales (17:14)
BSO, conductor Bernard Haitink
April 27, 1996. Symphony Hall
Philips, producer Volker Straus
CDs: 456 569-2. ArkivCD 45659

BRITTEN, BENJAMIN
Les Illuminations (21:10)
BSO, conductor Seiji Ozawa
Sylvia McNair, soprano
April 8, 1997; April 14, 1997. Symphony Hall
Philips, producer Volker Straus
CDs: 446 682-2

BRAHMS, JOHANNES
Concerto for Piano and Orchestra No. 2 in B♭, op. 83 (49:43)
BSO, conductor Bernard Haitink
Emanuel Ax, piano; Jules Eskin, cello
April 19, 1997; April 21, 1997. Symphony Hall
Sony, producer Grace Row
CDs: SK-63229. 88697-03510-2

RACHMANINOFF, SERGEI
Concerto for Piano and Orchestra No. 1 in F♯ Minor, op. 1 (26:32)
BSO, conductor Seiji Ozawa
Krystian Zimerman, piano
December 6, 1997; December 9, 1997. Symphony Hall
Deutsche Grammophon, producer Arend Prohmann
CDs: 459 643-2. Universal B0001858-02

WILLIAMS, JOHN
Saving Private Ryan (film score) (64:15)
Members of the BSO, conductor John Williams
Richard "Gus" Sebring, French horn; Timothy Morrison and Thomas Rolfs, trumpets
February 21, 1998; February 22, 1998; February 23, 1998. Symphony Hall
Dreamworks, producer John Williams
CDs: DRMD-50046

DUTILLEUX, HENRI
The Shadows of Time (20:55). *A BSO commission.*
BSO, conductor Seiji Ozawa
Children's voices: Joel Esher, Rachel Plotkin, Jordan Swaim
March 12, 1998; March 13, 1998. Symphony Hall (live plus patch session on both days). *Premiered October 9, 1997.*
Erato, producer Martin Sauer
CDs: 3984-22830-2. Elatus 0927-49830-2. *The Erato "single" (a 21-minute CD) was for sale at a BSO concert in the Théâtre des Champs Élysées, Paris, on March 20, 1998, only seven days after the final recording session. (Douglas Yeo, BSO bass trombonist, email, March 23, 2008)*

HOLST, GUSTAV
The Planets, op. 32: *Jupiter* (8:05)
BSO, conductor Bernard Haitink
October 22, 1998. Broadcast from Symphony Hall
BSO/IMG Artists
CDs: CB-100 (12)

WILLIAMS, JOHN
Concerto for Violin (30:08)
BSO, conductor John Williams
Gil Shaham, violin
October 18, 1999. Symphony Hall
Deutsche Grammophon, producer Christian Gansch
CDs: 471 326-2. ArkivCD 471326

WILLIAMS, JOHN
Schindler's List (film score): Main Theme (4:41). Jewish Town (Krakow Ghetto — Winter '41) (4:45). Remembrances (6:22). Total (15:48)
BSO, conductor John Williams
Itzhak Perlman, violin; Giora Feidman, clarinet
October 19, 1999. Symphony Hall
Deutsche Grammophon, producer Christian Gansch
CDs: 471 326-2. MCA MCAD-10969. ArkivCD 471326

BERLIOZ, HECTOR
Roman Carnival Overture, op. 9 (8:44)
BSO, conductor Seiji Ozawa
April 4, 2000. Broadcast from Symphony Hall
BSO/IMG Artists
CDs: CB-100 (12)

WILLIAMS, JOHN
Treesong (20:09)
BSO, conductor John Williams
Gil Shaham, violin
October 7, 2000. Symphony Hall
Deutsche Grammophon, producer Christian Gansch
CDs: 471 326-2. ArkivCD 471326

RACHMANINOFF, SERGEI
Concerto for Piano and Orchestra No. 2 in C Minor, op. 18 (35:35)
BSO, conductor Seiji Ozawa
Krystian Zimerman, piano
December 2, 2000; December 4, 2000. Symphony Hall
Deutsche Grammophon, producer Helmut Burk
CDs: 459 643-2. Universal B0001858-02

PREVIN, ANDRÉ
Concerto for Violin and Orchestra "Anne-Sophie" (39:38). *A BSO commission.*
BSO, conductor André Previn
Anne-Sophie Mutter, violin
October 26, 2002 (live); October 28, 2002 (patch). Symphony Hall. *Premiered March 14, 2002.*
Deutsche Grammophon, producer Mark Buecker
CDs: 474 500-2. Universal. B0001313-02. B0003974-02

EASTWOOD, CLINT
Mystic River (film score) orchestration by Patrick Hollenbeck.
BSO, conductor Lennie Neuhaus
TFC, John Oliver, dir.
March 31, 2003; April 1, 2003. Symphony Hall
Warner Brothers Records, producer Clint Eastwood. Score recorded and mixed
    by Shawn Murphy
CDs: 2A-485909-B. *The mix of the recorded music in the film makes it impossi-
ble to estimate the timing of the BSO's contribution.*

LIEBERSON, PETER
Neruda Songs (31:49). *World premiere of a BSO commission.*
BSO, conductor James Levine
Lorraine Hunt Lieberson, mezzo-soprano
November 25, 2005. Symphony Hall (live)
Nonesuch, producer Dirk Sobotka
CDs: 79954-2

COLLECTION: UBS PRESENTS THE BOSTON SYMPHONY ORCHESTRA
RAVEL: *Alborada del gracioso* (8:00)
    October 4, 2007; October 5, 2007; October 6, 2007. Symphony Hall (live)
RAVEL: *Pavane pour une infante défunte* (6:23)
    October 5, 2007; October 6, 2007. Symphony Hall (live)
BEETHOVEN: Coriolan Overture in C Minor, op. 62 (7:22)
    August 3, 2007. Koussevitzky Music Shed, Tanglewood (live)
SCHUMANN *Manfred*, **op. 115: Overture (12:42)**
    November 26, 2004; Novmber 30, 2004. Symphony Hall (live)
SCHULLER: *Seven Studies on Themes of Paul Klee:* **three excerpts (14:24):**
    Little Blue Devil (3:32). *The Twittering Machine* (2:29). *Arab Village*
    (8:22)
    March 29, 2007; March 30, 2007; March 31, 2007. Symphony Hall (live)
BERLIOZ: *Le Corsaire Overture*, **op. 21 (9:18)**
    September 30, 2005; October 1, 2005. Symphony Hall (live)
BSO, conductor James Levine
BSO/UBS
CDs: UBS0005 04 (promotional). *This disc was included as an insert to the
    January 2008 issue of* Boston *magazine, in a "Special Advertising Section"
    paid for by UBS, devoted to the BSO. (Marc Mandel, email May 5, 2008)*

Appendix A: Composers

AUBER, Daniel François

La Muette de Portici: Overture   Munch (December 24, 1953)

BACH, Johann Sebastian

Brandenburg Concerto No. 1   Koussevitzky (August 14, 1947)
                              Koussevitzky (August 17, 1949)
                              Munch (July 8, 1957)
Brandenburg Concerto No. 2   Koussevitzky (August 13, 1946)
                              Munch (July 9, 1957)
Brandenburg Concerto No. 3   Koussevitzky (August 14, 1945)
                              Munch (July 8, 1957)
Brandenburg Concerto No. 4   Koussevitzky (August 13, 1945)
                              Munch (July 8, 1957)
Brandenburg Concerto No. 5   Koussevitzky (August 13, 1946)
                              Munch (July 9, 1957)
Brandenburg Concerto No. 6   Koussevitzky (August 14, 1947)
                              Munch (July 9, 1957)
Violin Concerto in A Minor, BWV 1041   Munch (December 26, 1960)
Chorale-Variations "Vom Himmel hoch"   Ozawa (April 24, 1990)
Partita No. 2: Chaconne   Ozawa (October 13, 1990)
Prelude & Fugue in E♭, "St Anne"   Ozawa (October 21, 1989)
Ricercare a 6 Voci   Ozawa (October 21, 1989)
Sonata No. 6 in E: Prelude   Koussevitzky (October 31,1945)
Suite No. 1, BWV 1066   Koussevitzky (August 14, 1947)
Suite No. 2, BWV 1067   Koussevitzky (August 14, 1945)
Suite No. 3, BWV 1068   Koussevitzky (August 13, 1947)
Suite No. 4, BWV 1069   Koussevitzky (August 14, 1946)
Saint Matthew Passion   Koussevitzky (March 26, 1937)
Toccata and Fugue in D Minor, BWV 565   Ozawa (April 23, 1990)

BARBER, Samuel

Adagio for Strings	Munch (April 3, 1957)
Medea's Meditation and Dance	Munch (April 10, 1957)
Violin Concerto	Ozawa (October 3, 1994)

BARBIROLLI, John

| An Elizabethan Suite | Barbirolli (February 3, 1959) |

BARTÓK, Bela

Concerto for Orchestra	Koussevitzky (December 30, 1944)
	Leinsdorf (October 13, 1962)
	Kubelík (November 27, 1973)
	Ozawa (February 24, 1994)
Violin Concerto No. 2	Leinsdorf (April 23, 1964)
	Ozawa (February 18, 1991)
Duke Bluebeard's Castle	Ozawa (November 8, 1980)
The Miraculous Mandarin	Ozawa (February 28, 1994)
— Suite	Ozawa (November 10, 1975)
Music for Strings, Percussion and Celesta	Ozawa (November 13, 1976)

BEETHOVEN, Ludwig van

Choral Fantasy, op. 80	Ozawa (October 2, 1982)
Piano Concerto No. 1	Munch (November 2, 1960)
	Leinsdorf (December 20, 1967)
	Ozawa (October 5, 1983)
Piano Concerto No. 2	Leinsdorf (December 20, 1967)
	Ozawa (July 3, 1984)
Piano Concerto No. 3	Leinsdorf (April 5, 1965)
	Ozawa (October 2, 1982)
Piano Concerto No. 4	Leinsdorf (April 20, 1964)
	Ozawa (October 5, 1981)
Piano Concerto No. 5	Leinsdorf (March 4, 1963)
	Ozawa (October 9, 1973)
	Ozawa (January 24, 1981)
Violin Concerto	Munch (November 27, 1955)
— I. Allegro ma non troppo	Munch (April 23, 1954)
Coriolan Overture	Munch (February 26, 1956)
	Leinsdorf (November 21, 1966)
	Levine (August 3, 2007)
The Creatures of Prometheus: excerpts	Munch (March 7, 1960)
	Leinsdorf (October 30, 1967)
Egmont Overture	Koussevitzky (April 2, 1947)
	Ozawa (January 24, 1981)
	Ozawa (December 1, 1985)
Fidelio Overture	Munch (November 7, 1955)
Gratulations-Menuet in E♭	Munch (December 20, 1949)
Leonore Overture No. 1	Munch (February 26, 1956)
— fragment	Leinsdorf (December 22, 1966)

Leonore Overture No. 2	Munch (February 26, 1956)
	Leinsdorf (December 19, 1966)
Leonore Overture No. 3	Munch (February 27, 1956)
	Leinsdorf (January 6, 1963)
Mass in D, "Missa Solemnis"	Koussevitzky (April 26, 1938)
	Koussevitzky (December 2, 1938)
Romances for Violin and Orchestra	Ozawa (September 29, 1980)
Symphony No. 1	Munch (December 27, 1950)
	Leinsdorf (April 23, 1969)
Symphony No. 2	Koussevitzky (December 3, 1938)
	Leinsdorf (March 6, 1967)
"Eroica" Symphony No. 3	Koussevitzky (October 29, 1945)
	Munch (December 2, 1957)
	Munch (May 4, 1960)
	Leinsdorf (September 20, 1962)
	Leinsdorf (September 30, 1962)
— II. Funeral March	Leinsdorf (November 22, 1963)
Symphony No. 4	Leinsdorf (December 20, 1966)
Symphony No. 5	Koussevitzky (November 23, 1944)
	Munch (May 2, 1955)
	Leinsdorf (December 23, 1967)
	Kubelík (November 26, 1973)
	Ozawa (January 24, 1981)
"Pastoral" Symphony No. 6	Koussevitzky (December 18, 1928)
	Munch (August 16, 1955)
	Leinsdorf (January 13, 1969)
	Bernstein (November 27, 1972)
Symphony No. 7	Munch (December 19, 1949)
	Leinsdorf (November 21, 1966)
	Bernstein (August 19, 1990)
— IV. Finale	Muck (October 4, 1917)
Symphony No. 8	Koussevitzky (January 23, 1935)
	Koussevitzky (December 30, 1936)
	Munch (November 30, 1958)
	Leinsdorf (April 24, 1969)
"Choral" Symphony No. 9	Koussevitzky (August 6, 1947)
	Munch (December 21, 1958)
	Leinsdorf (October 19,1965)
	Leinsdorf (April 21, 1969)

BERG, Alban

Violin Concerto	Ozawa (November 27, 1978)
Le Vin	Leinsdorf (April 19, 1965)
Wozzeck: excerpts	Leinsdorf (April 23, 1964)

BERLIOZ, Hector

Béatrice et Bénédict: Overture	Munch (December 20, 1949)
	Munch (December 1, 1958)
Benvenuto Cellini: Overture	Munch (April 6, 1959)
Le Corsaire Overture	Munch (December 1, 1958)
	Levine (September 30, 2005)
La Damnation de Faust	Munch (February 21, 1954)
	Ozawa (October 1, 1973)
— Three excerpts	Koussevitzky (May 8, 1936)
— Ballet des Sylphes	Muck (October 5, 1917)
— Rákóczy March	Muck (October 3, 1917)
	Leinsdorf (April 8, 1964)
	Ozawa (September 7, 1979)
L'Enfance du Christ	Munch (December 23, 1956)
	Munch (December 13, 1966)
Harold in Italy	Koussevitzky (November 28, 1944)
	Munch (March 31, 1958)
La Mort de Cléopâtre	Ozawa (February 10, 1994)
Les Nuits d'été	Munch (April 12, 1955)
	Ozawa (October 17, 1983)
Requiem, "Grande messe des morts"	Munch (April 26, 1959)
	Ozawa (October 21, 1993)
Roman Carnival Overture	Koussevitzky (November 22, 1944)
	Munch (December 1, 1958)
	Ozawa (February 20, 1973)
	Ozawa (April 4, 2002)
Roméo et Juliette	Munch (February 22, 1953)
	Munch (April 23, 1961)
	Ozawa (October 6, 1975)
— Romeo Alone; The Ball at the Capulets	Bernstein (November 27, 1972)
Symphonie fantastique	Munch (November 14, 1954)
	Munch (December 12, 1954)
	Munch (April 9, 1962)
	Munch (April 17, 1962)
	Prêtre (February 3, 1969)
	Ozawa (February 19, 1973)
Les Troyens: Royal Hunt and Storm	Munch (April 6, 1959)
	Munch (January 26, 1963)
	Davis (November 8, 1974)

BERNSTEIN, Leonard

The Age of Anxiety, Symphony No. 2	Koussevitzky (April 9, 1949)
Serenade (after Plato's Symposium)	Ozawa (October 1, 1994)

BIZET, Georges

Carmen: Micaëla's Aria	Koussevitzky (March 20, 1940)
Symphony in C	Munch (February 1, 1964)

BLACKWOOD, Easley
Symphony No. 1   Munch (November 9, 1958)

BLOCH, Ernest
Schelomo   Munch (January 30, 1957)

BRAHMS, Johannes

Academic Festival Overture	Koussevitzky (April 2, 1947)
	Tennstedt (December 14, 1974)
Alto Rhapsody	Haitink (March 15, 1993)
Ein deutsches Requiem	Leinsdorf (November 25, 1968)
Piano Concerto No. 1	Munch (April 9, 1958)
	Leinsdorf (March 16, 1964)
	Leinsdorf (April 21, 1964)
Piano Concerto No. 2	Munch (August 11, 1952)
	Haitink (April 19, 1997)
Violin Concerto	Koussevitzky (December 21, 1937)
	Koussevitzky (April 11, 1939)
Nänie	Haitink (April 30, 1994)
Symphony No. 1	Munch (November 19, 1956)
	Leinsdorf (September 29, 1963)
	Ozawa (March 28, 1977)
	Ozawa (March 1, 1986)
	Haitink (April 23, 1994)
Symphony No. 2	Munch (December 5, 1955)
	Barbirolli (February 3, 1959)
	Leinsdorf (December 14, 1964)
	Bernstein (August 22, 1972)
	Ozawa (April 19, 1975)
	Haitink (March 31, 1990)
Symphony No. 3	Koussevitzky (January 2, 1945)
	Leinsdorf (March 7, 1966)
	Haitink (March 20, 1993)
Symphony No. 4	Koussevitzky (November 30, 1938)
	Munch (April 10, 1950)
	Munch (October 27, 1958)
	Leinsdorf (April 26, 1966)
	Bernstein (August 22, 1972)
	Haitink (April 25, 1992)
Tragic Overture	Munch (December 5, 1955)
	Monteux (Jamuary 20, 1959)
	Leinsdorf (April 26, 1966)
	Haitink (April 3, 1990)
Variations on a Theme by Haydn	Haitink (May 1, 1992)

BRITTEN, Benjamin

Diversions	Ozawa (October 8, 1990)
Les Illuminations	Ozawa (April 8, 1997)

BRITTEN, Benjamin (continued)

Peter Grimes: Three Orchestral Interludes   Koussevitzky (March 2, 1946)
— Four Sea Interludes   Bernstein (August 19, 1990)
Phaedra   Ozawa (February 10, 1994)
War Requiem   Leinsdorf (July 23, 1963)
Young Person's Guide to the Orchestra   Ozawa (February 14, 1992)

BRUCH, Max

Violin Concerto No. 1   Munch (January 18, 1951)

BRUCKNER, Anton

"Romantic" Symphony No. 4   Leinsdorf (January 10, 1966)
Symphony No. 6   Steinberg (January 19, 1970)
Symphony No. 8   Steinberg (February 26, 1972)

CARTER, Elliott

Piano Concerto   Leinsdorf (January 6, 1967)

CASADESUS, Henri Gustave

Concerto in D major (attr. K.P.E. Bach)   Koussevitzky (December 22, 1937)

CHABRIER, Emmanuel

España   Ozawa (November 15, 1986)

CHARPENTIER, Gustave

Louise: "Depuis le jour"   Koussevitzky (March 20, 1940)

CHAUSSON, Ernest

Poème   Munch (December 14, 1955)
Symphony in Bb   Munch (February 26, 1962)

CHOPIN, Frédéric

Piano Concerto No. 1   Munch (March 14, 1960)
Ozawa (April 19, 1986)
Piano Concerto No. 2   Munch (November 29, 1954)

COLGRASS, Michael

As Quiet As   Leinsdorf (April 19, 1967)

COPLAND, Aaron

Appalachian Spring: Suite   Koussevitzky (October 31, 1945)
Copland (April 13, 1959)
Lincoln Portrait   Koussevitzky (February 7, 1946)
Music for a Great City   Copland (April 10, 1965)
El salon México   Koussevitzky (December 1, 1938)
The Tender Land: Orchestral Suite   Copland (April 13, 1959)

CORELLI, Arcangelo

Suite for Strings (arr. Pinelli)   Koussevitzky (November 22, 1944)

COWELL, Henry

Hymn and Fuguing Tune No. 2   Koussevitzky (April 27, 1949)

DALLAPICCOLA, Luigi

Canti di prigionia   Oliver (August 30, 1982)

DEBUSSY, Claude

La Damoiselle élue	Munch (April 11, 1955)
	Ozawa (October 10, 1983)
	Ozawa (April 19, 1995)
Images pour orchestre	Munch (December 16, 1957)
	Tilson Thomas (February 1, 1971)
Le Martyre de St Sébastien	Munch (January 29, 1956)
La Mer	Koussevitzky (December 1, 1938)
	Monteux (July 19, 1954)
	Munch (December 9, 1956)
	Munch (March 30, 1962)
	Munch (April 17, 1962)
	Davis (March 20, 1982)
Nocturnes for Orchestra	Monteux (August 15, 1955)
	Abbado (February 2, 1970)
	Davis (March 20, 1982)
— Nuages. Fêtes	Munch (March 13, 1962)
Prélude à l'après-midi d'un faune	Koussevitzky (November 22, 1944)
	Munch (January 23, 1956)
	Monteux (July 19, 1959)
	Munch (March 13, 1962)
	Tilson Thomas (February 1, 1971)
	Bernstein (November 27, 1972)
Printemps	Munch (March 13, 1962)
"Sarabande" (orch. Ravel)	Koussevitzky (October 30, 1930)
Tarantelle Styrienne, "Danse"	Koussevitzky (October 30, 1930)

DELIBES, Léo

Coppélia: Suite	Monteux (December 2, 1953)
Sylvia: Suite	Monteux (December 30, 1953)

DELIUS, Frederick

The Walk to the Paradise Garden   Barbirolli (February 3, 1959)

DELLO JOIO, Norman

Fantasy and Variations   Leinsdorf (February 17, 1963)

DUKAS, Paul

The Sorcerer's Apprentice	Munch (November 4, 1957)
	Steinberg (October 26, 1970)

DUTILLEUX, Henri

The Shadows of Time   Ozawa (March 12, 1998)

DVOŘÁK, Antonin

Carnival Overture	Fiedler (January 5, 1970)
	Ozawa (December 16, 1993)
Cello Concerto	Munch (February 22, 1960)
	Ozawa (December 2, 1985)
Humoresque	Ozawa (December 16, 1993)
Klid (Silent Woods)	Ozawa (December 16, 1993)
Psalm 149	Ozawa (December 16, 1993)
Romance in F Minor	Leinsdorf (December 18, 1967)
	Ozawa (December 16, 1993)
Rusalka: "O Lovely Moon"	Ozawa (December 16, 1993)
Slavonic Dance in E Minor, op. 72, no. 2	Leinsdorf (December 22, 1967)
	Ozawa (December 16, 1993)
Slavonic Dance in C, op. 72, no. 7	Ozawa (December 16, 1993)
Slavonic Dance in A♭, op. 72, no. 8	Leinsdorf (December 23, 1967)
Symphony No. 6	Leinsdorf (December 19, 1967)
Symphony No. 8	Munch (March 13, 1961)
"from the New World" Symphony No. 9	Fiedler (January 5, 1970)
— II. Largo	Ozawa (December 16, 1993)

EASTWOOD, Clint
Mystic River: film score   Neuhaus (March 31, 2003)

ELGAR, Edward
Introduction and Allegro   Munch (April 3, 1957)

FALLA, Manuel de
The Three-Cornered Hat   Ozawa (October 2, 1976)

FAURÉ, Gabriel

Après un rêve	Ozawa (November 17, 1986)
Dolly Suite	Ozawa (November 15, 1986)
Elégie	Koussevitzky (December 28, 1936)
	Leinsdorf (March 25, 1963)
	Ozawa (November 17, 1986)
Pavane	Ozawa (November 15, 1986)
Pelléas et Mélisande Suite	Koussevitzky (March 18, 1940)
	Munch (December 3, 1966)
	Ozawa (November 15, 1986)
— Filieuse. Sicilienne	Silverstein (February 23, 1980)
Pénélope: Prelude	Munch (December 12, 1959)
Requiem	Ozawa (March 3, 1994)

FINE, Irving

Serious Song	Leinsdorf (January 25, 1965)
Symphony 1962	Irving Fine (August 12, 1962)
Toccata Concertante	Leinsdorf (January 25, 1965)

FOOTE, Arthur
Suite for Strings in E   Koussevitzky (March 19, 1940)

FOSS, Lukas
Three American Pieces   Ozawa (October 4, 1994)

FRANCK, César
Le Chasseur maudit   Munch (October 10, 1959)
                      Munch (February 26, 1962)
Symphonic Variations   Munch (August 1, 1965)
Symphony in D Minor   Munch (March 11, 1957)
                       Ozawa (November 29, 1991)

GINASTERA, Alberto
Piano Concerto   Leinsdorf (March 6, 1968)
Variaciones concertantes   Leinsdorf (March 11, 1968)

GLAZUNOV, Alexander
Chant du ménéstrel   Ozawa (August 11, 1975)

GLINKA, Mikhail
Russlan and Ludmilla: Overture   Koussevitzky (April 1, 1944)

GOULD, Morton
Spirituals for Orchestra   Mitropoulos (December 16, 1944)

GOUNOD, Charles
Faust: Ballet Music   Ozawa (November 17, 1986)

GRIEG, Edvard
Piano Concerto   Davis (March 8, 1980)
"The Last Spring"   Koussevitzky (March 20, 1940)
                     Koussevitzky (November 29, 1950)

GRIFFES, Charles Tomlinson
The Pleasure Dome of Kubla Khan   Ozawa (January 31, 1976)
Three Poems of Fiona MacLeod   Ozawa (January 31, 1976)

GUBAIDULINA, Sofia
Offertorium   Dutoit (April 4, 1988)

HAIEFF, Alexei
Symphony No. 2   Munch (November 30, 1958)

HANDEL, George Frideric
Concerto Grosso, op. 6/12: Larghetto   Koussevitzky (May 8, 1936)
Semele: "Oh sleep!"   Koussevitzky (November 6, 1939)
Water Music: Suite   Munch (December 26, 1950)
                      Munch (December 12, 1954)
— Overture   Munch (March 8, 1958)

HANSON, Howard

Serenade for Flute, Harp, and Strings   Koussevitzky (November 25, 1947)
Symphony No. 3   Koussevitzky (March 20, 1940)

HARBISON, John

Symphony No. 1   Ozawa (October 15, 1984)

HARRIS, Roy

"1933" Symphony No. 1   Koussevitzky (February 2, 1934)
Symphony No. 3   Koussevitzky (November 8, 1939)

HAYASHI, Hiromori

Kimi Ga Yo (Japanese national anthem)   Munch (May 4, 1960)

HAYDN, Franz Joseph

The Creation: With Verdure Clad   Munch (December 12, 1954)
Scena di Berenice   Ozawa (February 10, 1994)
"Oxford" Symphony No. 92   Bruno Walter (January 21, 1947)
Koussevitzky (August 14, 1950)
Symphony No. 93   Leinsdorf (December 19, 1966)
"Surprise" Symphony No. 94   Koussevitzky (April 22, 1929)
Koussevitzky (November 5, 1946)
"Miracle" Symphony No. 96   Leinsdorf (April 8, 1968)
Symphony No. 102   Koussevitzky (December 29, 1936)
"Drumroll" Symphony No. 103   Munch (December 26, 1950)
"London" Symphony No. 104   Munch (April 10, 1950)

HINDEMITH, Paul

Concert Music for Strings and Brass   Steinberg (October 5, 1971)
Noblissima visione   Monteux (January 20, 1959)
Symphony "Mathis der Maler"   Steinberg (October 4, 1971)
Giulini (March 30, 1974)

HOLST, Gustav

The Planets   Steinberg (September 28, 1970)
Ozawa (December 3, 1979)
— IV. Jupiter   Haitink (October 22, 1998)

HONEGGER, Arthur

Symphony No. 2   Munch (March 29, 1953)
"Di tre re" Symphony No. 5   Munch (October 27, 1952)

IBERT, Jacques

Escales   Munch (December 10, 1956)

d'INDY, Vincent

Symphony on a French Mountain Air   Munch (March 24, 1958)

IVES, Charles

Central Park in the Dark   Ozawa (February 16, 1976)
Symphony No. 4   Ozawa (February 9, 1976)
Three Places in New England   Tilson Thomas (January 26, 1970)
The Unanswered Question   Bernstein (November 27, 1972)

JANÁČEK, Leoš

The Cunning Little Vixen: Suite   Leinsdorf (September 30, 1966)

KHACHATURIAN, Aram

Piano Concerto   Koussevitzky (January 1, 1945)
                  Koussevitzky (April 19, 1946)
Violin Concerto   Monteux (January 12, 1958)

KIM, Earl

Violin Concerto   Ozawa (April 27, 1983)

KODÁLY, Zoltán

Háry János: Suite   Leinsdorf (April 22, 1965)
"Peacock" Variations   Leinsdorf (November 23, 1964)

LALO, Edouard

Le Roi d'Ys: Overture   Munch (December 27, 1950)

LANNER, Joseph

"Die Mozartisten" Waltzes   Leinsdorf (December 31, 1963)
                             Leinsdorf (January 3, 1964)

LIADOV, Anatoly

From the Apocalypse   Koussevitzky (May 1, 1943)
The Enchanted Lake   Koussevitzky (May 6, 1936)

LIEBERSON, Peter

Piano Concerto   Ozawa (April 14, 1984)
Neruda Songs   Levine (November 25, 2005)

LISZT, Franz

Piano Concerto No. 1   Ozawa (March 31, 1979)
                        Ozawa (April 27, 1987)
Piano Concerto No. 2   Leinsdorf (November 21, 1964)
                        Ozawa (April 25, 1987)
A Faust Symphony   Bernstein (July 26, 1976)
Mephisto Waltz   Koussevitzky (May 8, 1936)
Les Préludes   Monteux (December 8, 1952)
Totentanz   Ozawa (April 25, 1987)

MAHLER, Gustav

Kindertotenlieder   Munch (December 28, 1958)
                     Ozawa (December 13, 1988)
Lieder eines fahrenden Gesellen   Munch (December 29, 1958)

MAHLER, Gustav (continued)

"Titan" Symphony No. 1	Leinsdorf (October 20, 1962)
	Ozawa (October 3, 1977)
	Ozawa (October 5, 1987)
"Resurrection" Symphony No. 2	Ozawa (December 13, 1986)
Symphony No. 3	Leinsdorf (October 10, 1966)
	Ozawa (April 22, 1993)
Symphony No. 4	Ozawa (November 21, 1987)
Symphony No. 5	Leinsdorf (November 17, 1963)
	Ozawa (September 27, 1990)
— IV. Adagietto	Ozawa (August 2, 1987)
"Tragic" Symphony No. 6	Leinsdorf (April 20, 1965)
	Ozawa (January 30, 1992)
Symphony No. 7	Ozawa (March 11, 1989)
"Symphony of a Thousand" No. 8	Ozawa (October 13, 1980)
Symphony No. 9	Ozawa (October 5, 1989)
Symphony No. 10: Adagio	Ozawa (April 19, 1990)

MARTIN, Frank

Concerto for 7 Wind Instruments	Ozawa (September 30, 1977)

MARTINŮ, Bohuslav

Double Concerto	Kubelík (January 14, 1967)
"Fantaisies Symphoniques" No. 6	Munch (April 23, 1956)

McDONALD, Harl

San Juan Capistrano: 2 Evening Pictures	Koussevitzky (November 8, 1939)

MENDELSSOHN, Felix

Capriccio brillant	Munch (March 14, 1960)
Violin Concerto	Munch (February 23, 1959)
	Munch (December 24, 1960)
	Ozawa (September 29, 1980)
A Midsummer Night's Dream	Leinsdorf (November 29, 1962)
	Ozawa (October 3, 1992)
— excerpts	Davis (November 29, 1975)
Octet in E♭: Scherzo	Munch (March 7, 1960)
	Steinberg (October 26, 1970)
"Scottish" Symphony No. 3	Munch (December 7, 1959)
"Italian" Symphony No. 4	Koussevitzky (January 23, 1935)
	Koussevitzky (November 25, 1947)
	Munch (February 18, 1958)
	Davis (January 6, 1975)
"Reformation" Symphony No. 5	Munch (October 28, 1957)

MENOTTI, Gian Carlo

Violin Concerto	Munch (November 8, 1954)
The Death of the Bishop of Brindisi	Leinsdorf (October 19, 1964)

MESSIAEN, Olivier

Oiseaux exotiques	Ozawa (February 23, 1994)
3 petites liturgies de la Présence Divine	Ozawa (October 7, 1978)
Turangalila-symphonie (rehearsal)	Bernstein (November 28, 1949)

MILHAUD, Darius

La Création du Monde	Munch (March 13, 1961)
Suite Provençale	Munch (November 21, 1960)

MORET, Norbert

En rêve	Ozawa (February 16, 1991)

MOZART, Leopold

Cassation (Haydn's "Toy Symphony")	Koussevitzky (August 15, 1950)

MOZART, Wolfgang Amadeus

La clemenza di Tito: Overture	Koussevitzky (August 17, 1949)
Bassoon Concerto, K. 191	Ozawa (November 15, 1978)
Clarinet Concerto, K. 622	Munch (July 9, 1956)
	Ozawa (November 28, 1978)
Piano Concerto No. 12 in A, K. 414	Monteux (April 12, 1953)
Piano Concerto No. 18 in B♭, K. 456	Monteux (April 13, 1953)
Don Giovanni: Overture	Stokowski (January 13, 1968)
	Steinberg (December 19, 1969)
Idomeneo, rè di Creta: Overture	Koussevitzky (August 17, 1949)
Mass, K. 427: "Et incarnatus est"	Leinsdorf (July 24, 1966)
Le Nozze di Figaro: Overture	Munch (April 25, 1951)
Requiem Mass, K. 626	Leinsdorf (January 19, 1964)
Der Schauspieldirektor: Overture	Koussevitzky (August 17, 1949)
Serenade "Eine kleine Nachtmusik"	Koussevitzky (August 15, 1950)
	Leinsdorf (January 6, 1963)
Serenade No. 10 in B♭ for 13 Winds	Koussevitzky (August 15, 1947)
String Quintet, K. 516: Adagio	Koussevitzky (August 15, 1946)
Symphony No. 26	Koussevitzky (February 7, 1946)
Symphony No. 29	Koussevitzky (December 22, 1937)
Symphony No. 33	Koussevitzky (August 15, 1946)
Symphony No. 34	Koussevitzky (March 18, 1940)
"Linz" Symphony No. 36	Koussevitzky (August 16, 1949)
	Leinsdorf (December 22, 1967)
"Prague" Symphony No. 38: I and II	Leinsdorf (April 16, 1968)
Symphony No. 39	Koussevitzky (January 3, 1945)
	Leinsdorf (January 20, 1969)
Symphony No. 40 Minor	Bernstein (November 27, 1972)
— I. Molto allegro	Leinsdorf (December 21, 1966)
"Jupiter" Symphony No. 41	Leinsdorf (January 14, 1963)
	Jochum (January 26, 1973)
Die Zauberflöte: "Ach, Ich fühl's"	Koussevitzky (November 6, 1939)

MUSSORGSKY, Modest

Khovanshchina: Prelude   Koussevitzky (December 28, 1936)
Pictures at an Exhibition   Koussevitzky (October 28, 1930)

OFFENBACH, Jacques

Gaîté Parisienne   Ozawa (November 17, 1986)

ORFF, Carl

Carmina Burana   Ozawa (November 17, 1969)

PAGANINI, Niccolò

Moto Perpetuo   Ozawa (April 22, 1978)

PANUFNIK, Andrzej

"Sinfonia Votiva" Symphony No. 8   Ozawa (January 30, 1982)

PISTON, Walter

Prelude and Allegro   Koussevitzky (April 24, 1945)
Symphony No. 2   Tilson Thomas (October 5, 1970)
Symphony No. 6   Munch (March 12, 1956)
Symphony No. 7 (brief excerpt)   Leinsdorf (September 20, 1962)

POULENC, Francis

Concert champêtre   Ozawa (November 30, 1991)
Concerto for Organ, Strings, & Timpani   Munch (October 9, 1960)
Ozawa (December 2, 1991)
Two-Piano Concerto   Ozawa (April 8, 1989)
Gloria   Ozawa (November 24, 1987)
Stabat Mater   Ozawa (November 25, 1987)

PREVIN, André

Violin Concerto   André Previn (October 26, 2002)

PROKOFIEV, Sergei

Chout: Danse Finale   Koussevitzky (November 25, 1947)
Piano Concerto No. 1   Leinsdorf (December 1, 1965)
Piano Concerto No. 2   Munch (February 13, 1957)
Leinsdorf (December 1, 1965)
Piano Concerto No. 3   Leinsdorf (November 25, 1967)
Piano Concerto (left hand) No. 4   Leinsdorf (November 27, 1967)
Ozawa (October 15, 1991)
Piano Concerto No. 5   Leinsdorf (March 28, 1964)
Leinsdorf (April 25, 1969)
Violin Concerto No. 1   Leinsdorf (April 13, 1964)
Violin Concerto No. 2   Koussevitzky (December 20, 1937)
Munch (February 24, 1959)
Leinsdorf (December 19, 1966)
Lieutenant Kijé Suite   Koussevitzky (December 22, 1937)
Leinsdorf (April 22, 1968)

The Love for 3 Oranges: March; Scherzo   Koussevitzky (April 22, 1929)
       Koussevitzky (December 30, 1936)
       Munch (November 28, 1950)
     Peter and the Wolf   Koussevitzky (April 12, 1939)
       Koussevitzky (August 11, 1950)
       Ozawa (February 14, 1992)
     Romeo and Juliet   Ozawa (October 18, 1986)
     — 12 Scenes   Munch (February 11, 1957)
     — 17 Scenes   Leinsdorf (February 13, 1967)
     — Suite No. 2   Koussevitzky (October 30, 1945)
     Scythian Suite   Leinsdorf (October 24, 1966)
       Tilson Thomas (September 22, 1972)
Symphony-Concerto for Cello   Leinsdorf (March 25, 1963)
"Classical" Symphony No. 1   Koussevitzky (April 22, 1929)
       Koussevitzky (November 25, 1947)
     Symphony No. 2   Leinsdorf (March 25, 1968)
     Symphony No. 3   Leinsdorf (April 25, 1966)
     Symphony No. 5   Koussevitzky (February 6, 1946)
       Leinsdorf (October 28, 1963)
     Symphony No. 6   Leinsdorf (April 23, 1965)

RACHMANINOFF, Sergei
     Piano Concerto No. 1   Ozawa (December 6, 1997)
     Piano Concerto No. 2   Munch (October 6, 1958)
       Ozawa (December 2, 2000)
     Piano Concerto No. 3   Munch (December 29, 1957)
       Ozawa (January 21, 1992)
     The Isle of the Dead   Koussevitzky (April 23, 1945)
     Vocalise   Koussevitzky (April 24, 1945)

RAVEL, Maurice
     Alborada del gracioso   Ozawa (March 13, 1974)
       Haitink (April 27, 1996)
       Levine (October 4, 2007)
     Une Barque sur l'océan   Ozawa (April 21, 1975)
       Haitink (April 22, 1996)
     Boléro   Koussevitzky (April 14, 1930)
       Koussevitzky (August 13, 1947)
       Munch (January 23, 1956)
       Munch (March 26, 1962)
       Ozawa (March 13, 1974)
       Haitink (April 22, 1996)
     Piano Concerto in G   Munch (March 24, 1958)
       Leinsdorf (February 16, 1963)
Piano Concerto in D For the Left Hand   Ozawa (October 6, 1990)

RAVEL, Maurice (continued)

Daphnis et Chloé	Munch (January 23, 1955)
	Munch (February 26, 1961)
	Ozawa (October 14, 1974)
	Haitink (May 1, 1989)
— Suite No. 2	Koussevitzky (November 15, 1928)
	Koussevitzky (November 23, 1944)
	Munch (May 4, 1960)
	Munch (April 17, 1962)
	Abbado (February 2, 1970)
Deux mélodies hébraïques	Ozawa (April 8, 1980)
Cinq mélodies populaires grecques	Ozawa (April 8, 1980)
Menuet antique	Ozawa (April 22, 1974)
	Haitink (November 20, 1995)
Ma Mère l'oye	Ozawa (April 22, 1974)
	Haitink (November 18, 1995)
— Suite	Koussevitzky (October 27, 1930)
	Koussevitzky (October 29, 1947)
	Munch (February 19, 1958)
Pavane pour une infante défunte	Koussevitzky (November 4, 1946)
	Munch (October 27, 1952)
	Munch (March 26, 1962)
	Abbado (February 2, 1970)
	Ozawa (October 14, 1974)
	Levine (October 5, 2007)
Rapsodie espagnole	Koussevitzky (April 23, 1945)
	Munch (Decmber 26, 1950)
	Munch (January 23, 1956)
	Ozawa (March 13, 1974)
	Haitink (November 20, 1995)
— IV. Feria	Bernstein (November 27, 1972)
Shéhérazade	Ozawa (October 8, 1979)
	Ozawa (April 17, 1995)
Le Tombeau de Couperin	Ozawa (October 14, 1974)
	Haitink (April 20, 1996)
La Valse	Koussevitzky (October 29, 1930)
	Munch (April 11, 1950)
	Munch (December 5, 1955)
	Munch (December 1, 1958)
	Munch (February 2, 1962)
	Munch (March 26, 1962)
	Ozawa (March 13, 1974)
	Haitink (November 20, 1995)
Valses nobles et sentimentales	Ozawa (April 21, 1975)
	Haitink (April 27, 1996)

RESPIGHI, Ottorino

Ancient Airs and Dances: Set 1	Ozawa (March 29, 1977)
Ancient Airs and Dances: Set 2	Ozawa (April 22, 1978)
Ancient Airs and Dances: Set 3	Ozawa (October 7, 1975)
Feste romane	Ozawa (October 15, 1977)
The Fountains of Rome	Ozawa (October 17, 1977)
The Pines of Rome	Cantelli (December 24, 1954)
	Ozawa (October 17, 1977)

RIMSKY-KORSAKOV, Nikolai

Le Coq d'or: Suite	Leinsdorf (November 24, 1963)
— "Hymn to the Sun"	Leinsdorf (November 24, 1963)
Scheherazade	Ozawa (April 2, 1977)
"The Battle of Kershenetz"	Koussevitzky (November 7, 1939)

ROSSINI, Gioacchino

Semiramide: Overture	Ozawa (February 9, 1976)

ROUSSEL, Albert

Bacchus et Ariane: Suite No. 2	Munch (October 27, 1952)
Suite in F	Munch (March 8, 1958)

RUGGLES, Carl

Sun-treader	Tilson Thomas (March 24, 1970)

RUSSIAN FOLK SONGS

Dubinushka	Koussevitzky (November 7, 1939)
The Song of the Volga Boatman	Koussevitzky (December 3, 1938)

SAINT-SAËNS, Camille

Carnival of the Animals	Ozawa (February 15, 1992)
Piano Concerto No. 4	Munch (November 24, 1954)
Danse macabre	Steinberg (January 12, 1970)
Havanaise	Monteux (January 12, 1958)
Introduction and Rondo capriccioso	Munch (December 14, 1955)
La Princesse jaune: Overture	Munch (January 18, 1951)
Le Rouet d'Omphale	Munch (November 4, 1957)
"Organ" Symphony No. 3	Munch (April 5, 1959)

SATIE, Erik

Gymnopédie No. 1	Koussevitzky (April 14, 1930)
Gymnopédies No. 1 and 2	Koussevitzky (April 27, 1949)

SCHARWENKA, Franz Xaver

Piano Concerto No. 1	Leinsdorf (January 20, 1969)

SCHOENBERG, Arnold

Cello Concerto (after Monn)	Ozawa (October 22, 1984)
Gurrelieder	Ozawa (March 30, 1979)
— Song of the Wood Dove	Leinsdorf (October 19, 1964)
A Survivor from Warsaw	Leinsdorf (April 23, 1969)

SCHUBERT, Franz

Rosamunde: Excerpts	Davis (March 22, 1982)
— Ballet Music No. 2	Koussevitzky (May 8, 1936)
Symphony No. 2	Munch (December 20, 1949)
	Munch (March 7, 1960)
Symphony No. 3	Haitink (May 2, 1992)
Symphony No. 5	Koussevitzky (April 4, 1947)
"Unfinished" Symphony No. 8	Koussevitzky (May 6, 1936)
	Koussevitzky (January 3, 1945)
	Munch (May 2, 1955)
	Jochum (January 26, 1973)
	Davis (December 18, 1982)
"Great C Major" Symphony No. 9	Munch (November 19, 1958)
	Steinberg (September 29, 1969)
	Davis (March 15, 1980)

SCHULLER, Gunther

Seven Studies on Themes of Paul Klee	Leinsdorf (November 23, 1964)
— 3 excerpts	Levine (March 29, 2007)

SCHUMAN, William

Violin Concerto	Tilson Thomas (October 5, 1970)

SCHUMANN, Robert

Cello Concerto (arr. for Violin)	Ozawa (April 18, 1992)
Piano Concerto	Munch (October 6, 1958)
	Davis (March 17, 1980)
Genoveva: Overture	Munch (January 18, 1951)
Manfred: Overture	Munch (October 5, 1959)
	Levine (November 26, 2004)
"Spring" Symphony No. 1	Koussevitzky (November 6, 1939)
	Munch (April 25, 1951)
	Munch (October 5, 1959)
Symphony No. 4	Leinsdorf (January 5, 1963)

SCRIABIN, Alexander

"Poem of Ecstasy" Symphony No. 4	Monteux (December 8, 1952)
	Abbado (February 8, 1971)

SESSIONS, Roger

Concerto for Orchestra	Ozawa (January 30, 1982)
When Lilacs Last in the Dooryard Bloom'd	Ozawa (April 23, 1977)

SHOSTAKOVICH, Dmitri

Cello Concerto No. 2	Ozawa (August 11, 1975)
Violin Concerto No. 2	Ozawa (April 16, 1992)
Symphony No. 1	Leinsdorf (September 26, 1964)
Symphony No. 8: Adagio	Koussevitzky (April 25, 1945)
Symphony No. 9	Koussevitzky (November 4, 1946)

SIBELIUS, Jean

Violin Concerto	Leinsdorf (December 21, 1966)
	Ozawa (October 19, 1985)
En Saga	Davis (April 23, 1979)
Finlandia	Davis (April 6, 1976)
	Ashkenazy (March 9, 1992)
Karelia Suite	Davis (April 16, 1979)
Kuolema: Valse triste	Davis (March 10, 1980)
	Ashkenazy (March 9, 1992)
Pohjola's Daughter	Koussevitzky (May 6, 1936)
	Davis (March 8, 1980)
Romance for Strings	Ashkenazy (March 9, 1992)
The Swan of Tuonela	Davis (December 4, 1976)
Swanwhite: The Maiden with Roses	Koussevitzky (December 29, 1936)
Symphony No. 1	Davis (April 5, 1976)
Symphony No. 2	Koussevitzky (January 24, 1935)
	Koussevitzky (November 29, 1950)
	Davis (April 3, 1976)
	Ashkenazy (March 5, 1992)
Symphony No. 3	Davis (November 29, 1976)
Symphony No. 4	Davis (December 3, 1976)
Symphony No. 5	Koussevitzky (December 29, 1936)
Symphony No. 5	Davis (January 4, 1975)
— IV. Finale: Allegro molto	Koussevitzky (January 5, 1946)
Symphony No. 6	Davis (December 1, 1975)
Symphony No. 7	Davis (January 6, 1975)
Tapiola	Koussevitzky (November 7, 1939)
	Davis (December 2, 1975)

SMETANA, Bedřich

Má Vlast	Kubelík (March 8, 1971)
— The Moldau	Leinsdorf (April 22, 1967)
The Bartered Bride: Dance	Ozawa (September 8, 1979)

SMITH, John Stafford

The Star-Spangled Banner	Munch (October 28, 1957)
	Munch (May 4, 1960)

SOUSA, John Philip

Semper Fidelis	Koussevitzky (April 19, 1946)
The Stars and Stripes Forever	Koussevitzky (April 19, 1946)
	Leinsdorf (April 8, 1964)
	Ozawa (April 3, 1979)

STARER, Robert

Violin Concerto	Ozawa (April 27, 1983)

STRAUSS, Johann Jr.

Voices of Spring	Koussevitzky (December 18, 1928)
Wiener Blut	Koussevitzky (December 20, 1928)

STRAUSS, Richard

Die Ägyptische Helena: Awakening Scene	Leinsdorf (April 22, 1965)
Also sprach Zarathustra	Koussevitzky (January 22, 1935)
	Steinberg (March 24, 1971)
	Ozawa (December 14, 1981)
	Ozawa (March 1,1986)
Ariadne auf Naxos (1912)	Leinsdorf (January 7, 1969)
Don Juan	Koussevitzky (April 19, 1946)
	Koussevitzky (October 29, 1947)
Don Quixote	Munch (August 17, 1953)
	Monteux (January 24, 1959)
	Ozawa (October 27, 1984)
Duet-Concertino	Ozawa (March 12, 1988)
Elektra	Ozawa (November 12, 1988)
Ein Heldenleben	Leinsdorf (March 9, 1963)
	Ozawa (December 14, 1981)
Four Lieder	Munch (December 12, 1954)
Der Rosenkavalier: Suite	Monteux (February 17, 1956)
Salome: Dance of the Seven Veils	Leinsdorf (April 22, 1965)
— Interlude and Final scene	Leinsdorf (April 24, 1965)
Till Eulenspiegels lustige Streiche	Koussevitzky (April 24, 1945)
	Munch (March 20, 1961)
	Steinberg (January 12, 1970)
— excerpts	Leinsdorf (September 20, 1962)

STRAVINSKY, Igor

Agon	Leinsdorf (April 19, 1965)
Apollon musagète: Pas de Deux	Koussevitzky (November 14, 1928)
Le Baiser de la fée: Divertimento	Burgin (December 8, 1962)
Capriccio	Koussevitzky (March 19, 1940)
Violin Concerto	Leinsdorf (April 22, 1965)
	Ozawa (February 6, 1978)
The Firebird	Ozawa (April 30, 1983)
— Suite (1919)	Ozawa (November 24, 1969)
— Suite (1945)	Leinsdorf (April 22, 1964)
Greeting Prelude	Ozawa (November 22, 1969)
Jeu de cartes	Munch (November 7, 1960)
L'Histoire du soldat: Suite	Bernstein (August 11, 1947)
Octet for Wind Instruments	Bernstein (August 11, 1947)
Oedipus Rex	Bernstein (November 27, 1972)
	Bernstein (December 15, 1972)
Pétrouchka	Monteux (January 20,1959)
	Monteux (January 25, 1959)

Pétrouchka (1947)   Ozawa (November 24, 1969)
— Suite   Koussevitzky (November 13, 1928)
Le Roi des étoiles   Tilson Thomas (January 25, 1972)
Le Sacre du printemps   Monteux (January 28, 1951)
Tilson Thomas (January 24, 1972)
Ozawa (December 10, 1979)
Scherzo à la Russe   Steinberg (January 12, 1970)
Scherzo fantastique   Steinberg (January 12, 1970)
Symphony of Psalms   Ozawa (December 5, 1987)

TAKEMITSU, Toru
A Flock Descends the Pentagonal Garden   Ozawa (December 2, 1978)
From me flows what you call Time   Ozawa (October 19, 1990)
Quatrain   Ozawa (March 29, 1977)

TCHAIKOVSKY, Peter Ilyich
Piano Concerto No. 1   Leinsdorf (March 5, 1963)
Leinsdorf (December 12, 1966)
Davis (April 16, 1979)
Violin Concerto   Munch (March 29, 1953)
Munch (February 9, 1959)
Leinsdorf (December 18, 1967)
Ozawa (October 17, 1985)
Eugene Onegin: Tatiana's Letter Scene   Leindorf (July 24, 1966)
Francesca da Rimini   Koussevitzky (April 19, 1946)
Munch (April 23, 1956)
Hamlet   Stokowski (January 13, 1968)
Marche slave   Leinsdorf (April 13, 1964)
The Nutcracker   Ozawa (December 15, 1990)
— Waltz of the Flowers   Muck (October 4, 1917)
Overture 1812   Davis (March 5, 1980)
Pique Dame   Ozawa (October 16, 1991)
Romeo and Juliet   Koussevitzky (December 28, 1936)
Markevitch (March 19, 1955)
Munch (March 12, 1956)
Munch (April 3, 1961)
Abbado (February 8, 1971)
Davis (April 21, 1979)
Serenade in C for String Orchestra   Koussevitzky (August 16, 1949)
Munch (March 13, 1957)
— Waltz   Koussevitzky (May 8, 1936)
Koussevitzky (April 27, 1949)
Sleeping Beauty: Suite   Ozawa (December 8, 1990)
Suite No. 1: Marche Miniature   Muck (October 5, 1917)
Swan Lake   Ozawa (November 11, 1978)
"Winter Dreams" Symphony No. 1   Tilson Thomas (March 23, 1970)

TCHAIKOVSKY, Peter Ilyich (continued)

Symphony No. 4   Koussevitzky (May 4, 1936)
    Koussevitzky (April 26, 1949)
    Munch (November 7, 1955)
    Monteux (January 28, 1959)
— IV. Finale: Allegro con fuoco   Muck (October 2, 1917)
Symphony No. 5   Koussevitzky (November 22, 1944)
    Monteux (January 8, 1958)
    Ozawa (February 16, 1977)
"Pathétique" Symphony No. 6   Koussevitzky (April 14, 1930)
    Monteux (January 26, 1955)
    Munch (March 12, 1962)
    Ozawa (April 26, 1986)
Variations on a Rococo Theme   Ozawa (December 2, 1985)

THOMAS, Ambroise

Mignon: Overture   Ozawa (November 24, 1987)

THOMPSON, Randall

Testament of Freedom   Koussevitzky (April 24, 1945)

TRADITIONAL

Fair Harvard   Koussevitzky (March 23, 1937)

VAUGHAN WILLIAMS, Ralph

Fantasia on a Theme by Thomas Tallis   Monteux (December 20, 1963)
The Lark Ascending   Ozawa (February 16, 1977)
Symphony No. 4   Davis (October 26, 1973)
Symphony No. 6 (rehearsal extract)   Koussevitzky (March 14, 1949)

VERDI, Giuseppe

Aida: "O patria mia"   Leinsdorf (July 24, 1966)
Don Carlo: "Ella giammai m'amò"   Leinsdorf (July 24, 1966)
La forza del destino: Overture   Schippers (March 18, 1961)
Requiem Mass   Leinsdorf (October 5, 1964)

VIVALDI, Antonio

Concerto Grosso in D Minor, RV. 565   Koussevitzky (May 8, 1936)
"The Four Seasons"   Ozawa (October 10, 1981)

WAGNER, Richard

Siegfried Idyll   Koussevitzky (April 27, 1949)
    Leinsdorf (October 1, 1965)
    Leinsdorf (see: October 19, 1965)
Der fliegende Holländer: Overture   Koussevitzky (April 4, 1947)
    Leinsdorf (October 30, 1967)
Lohengrin   Leinsdorf (August 23, 1965)
— Preludes to Acts I and III   Leinsdorf (April 24, 1965)
— Act I Prelude   Koussevitzky (April 27, 1949)
— Act III Prelude   Muck (October 3, 1917)

Tannhäuser: Overture   Leinsdorf (December 19, 1967)
— Overture and Venusberg Music   Munch (April 1, 1957)
— "Entrance of the Guests"   Leinsdorf (April 8, 1964)
Die Meistersinger: Act I Prelude   Leinsdorf (October 30, 1967)
Die Walküre: Act I   Ozawa (August 12, 1978)
— Magic Fire Music   Munch (April 1, 1957)
Götterdämmerung: Rhine Journey   Munch (April 1, 1957)
— Dawn and Siegfried's Rhine Journey   Leinsdorf (see: October 19, 1965)
— Immolation Scene   Munch (November 25, 1957)
Tristan und Isolde: Prelude   Munch (November 25, 1957)
Leinsdorf (December 19, 1967)
— Prelude and Liebestod   Bernstein (November 27, 1972)
— "Mild und leise" (Liebestod)   Munch (November 25, 1957)
Parsifal: Act I Prelude   Koussevitzky (April 4, 1947)
— Good Friday Music   Koussevitzky (April 19, 1946)

WALTON, William
Concerto for Cello and Orchestra   Munch (January 28, 1957)
Partita for Orchestra   Barbirolli (February 3, 1959)

WEBER, Carl Maria von
Oberon: Overture   Koussevitzky (November 5, 1946)

WEILL, Kurt
Kleine Dreigroschenmusik   Leinsdorf (April 25, 1969)

WILLIAMS, John
Concerto for Violin   Williams (October 18, 1999)
Saving Private Ryan (film score)   Williams (February 21, 1998)
Schindler's List (film score)   Williams (October 19, 1999)
Treesong   Williams (October 7, 2000)

WILSON, Ollie
Sinfonia   Ozawa (October 15, 1984)

WOLF-FERRARI, Ermanno
The Secret of Suzanne: Overture   Muck (October 3, 1917)

WU, Tsu-Chiang
Concerto for Pipa and Orchestra   Ozawa (March 31, 1979)

Appendix B: Conductors

Many works in Serge Koussevitzky's repertoire were never recorded commercially, so broadcasts published on pirate recordings add significantly to his legacy. The same is true of several other conductors of the BSO—in particular, Leonard Bernstein and Klaus Tennstedt. This list includes only legitimate BSO recordings; appendix I (Pirate Recordings) has its own conductor listing.

Claudio Abbado

DEBUSSY Nocturnes for Orchestra (February 2, 1970)
RAVEL Daphnis et Chloé: Suite No. 2 (February 2, 1970)
    Pavane pour une infante défunte (February 2, 1970)
SCRIABIN Symphony No. 4 "Poem of Ecstasy" (February 8, 1971)
TCHAIKOVSKY Romeo and Juliet (February 8, 1971)

Vladimir Ashkenazy

SIBELIUS Finlandia (March 9, 1992)
    Kuolema: Valse triste (March 9, 1992)
    Romance for Strings (March 9, 1992)
    Symphony No. 2 (March 5, 1992)

John Barbirolli

BARBIROLLI An Elizabethan Suite (February 3, 1959)
BRAHMS Symphony No. 2 (February 3, 1959)
DELIUS The Walk to Paradise Garden (February 3, 1959)
WALTON Partita for Orchestra (February 3, 1959)

Leonard Bernstein

BEETHOVEN Symphony No. 6 "Pastoral" (November 27, 1972)
    Symphony No. 7 (August 19, 1990)
BERLIOZ Roméo et Juliette: Excerpts (November 27, 1972)
BRAHMS Symphonies Nos. 2 and 4 (August 22, 1972)

Leonard Bernstein (continued)

BRITTEN Peter Grimes: Four Sea Interludes (August 19, 1990)
DEBUSSY Prélude à l'après-midi d'un faune (November 27, 1972)
IVES The Unanswered Question (November 27, 1972)
LISZT A Faust Symphony (July 26, 1976)
MESSIAEN Turangalila-symphonie (rehearsal extract) (November 28, 1949)
MOZART Symphony No. 40 (November 27, 1972)
RAVEL Rapsodie espagnole: IV. Feria (November 27, 1972)
STRAVINSKY L'Histoire du soldat: Suite (August 11, 1947)
    Octet for Wind Instruments (August 11, 1947)
    Oedipus Rex (November 27, 1972), (December 15, 1972)
WAGNER Tristan und Isolde: Prelude and Liebestod (November 27, 1972)

Richard Burgin

STRAVINSKY Le Baiser de la fée: Divertimento (December 8, 1962)

Guido Cantelli

RESPIGHI The Pines of Rome (December 24, 1954)

Aaron Copland

COPLAND Appalachian Spring: Suite (April 13, 1959)
    Music for a Great City (April 10, 1965)
    The Tender Land: Orchestral Suite (April 13, 1959)

Colin Davis

BERLIOZ Les Troyens: Royal Hunt and Storm (November 8, 1974)
DEBUSSY La Mer (March 22, 1982)
    Nocturnes for Orchestra (March 20, 1982)
GRIEG Piano Concerto (March 8, 1980)
MENDELSSOHN A Midsummer Night's Dream (November 29, 1975)
    Symphony No. 4 "Italian" (January 6, 1975)
SCHUBERT Rosamunde: Overture and Ballet Music (March 22, 1982)
    Symphony No. 8 "Unfinished" (December 18, 1982)
    Symphony No. 9 "Great C Major" (March 15, 1980)
SCHUMANN Piano Concerto (March 17, 1980)
SIBELIUS En Saga (April 23, 1979)
    Finlandia (April 6, 1976)
    Karelia Suite (April 16, 1979)
    Kuolema: Valse triste (March 10, 1980)
    Lemminkäinen Suite: The Swan of Tuonela (December 4, 1976)
    Pohjola's Daughter (March 8, 1980)
    Symphony No. 1 (April 5, 1976)
    Symphony No. 2 (April 3, 1976)
    Symphony No. 3 (November 29, 1976)

SIBELIUS Symphony No. 4 (December 3, 1976)
    Symphony No. 5 (January 4, 1975)
    Symphony No. 6 (December 1, 1975)
    Symphony No. 7 (January 6, 1975)
    Tapiola (December 2, 1975)
TCHAIKOVSKY Piano Concerto No. 1 (April 16, 1979)
    Overture 1812 (March 5, 1980)
    Romeo and Juliet (April 21, 1979)
VAUGHAN WILLIAMS Symphony No. 4 (October 26, 1973)

Charles Dutoit

GUBAIDULINA Offertorium (April 4, 1988)

Arthur Fiedler

DVOŘÁK Carnival Overture (January 5, 1970)
    Symphony No. 9 "from the New World" (January 5, 1970)

Irving Fine

FINE Symphony 1962 (August 12, 1962)

Carlo Maria Giulini

HINDEMITH Mathis der Maler (March 30, 1974)

Bernard Haitink

BRAHMS Alto Rhapsody (March 15, 1993)
    Piano Concerto No. 2 (April 19, 1997)
    Nänie (April 30, 1994)
    Symphony No. 1 (April 23, 1994)
    Symphony No. 2 (March 31, 1990)
    Symphony No. 3 (March 20, 1993)
    Symphony No. 4 (April 25, 1992)
    Tragic Overture (April 3, 1990)
    Variations on a Theme by Haydn (May 1, 1992)
HOLST The Planets: Jupiter (October 22, 1998)
RAVEL Alborada del gracioso (April 27, 1996)
    Une Barque sur l'océan (April 22, 1996)
    Boléro (April 22, 1996)
    Daphnis et Chloé (May 1, 1989)
    Menuet antique (November 20, 1995)
    Ma Mère l'oye (November 18, 1995)
    Rapsodie espagnole (November 20, 1995)
    Le Tombeau de Couperin (April 20, 1996)
    La Valse (November 20, 1995)

Bernard Haitink (continued)

RAVEL Valses nobles et sentimentales (April 27, 1996)
SCHUBERT Symphony No. 3 (May 2, 1992)

Eugen Jochum

MOZART Symphony No. 41 "Jupiter" (January 26, 1973)
SCHUBERT Symphony No. 8 "Unfinished" (January 26, 1973)

Serge Koussevitzky

BACH Brandenburg Concerto No. 1 (August 14, 1947), (August 17, 1949)
   Brandenburg Concerto No. 2 (August 13, 1946)
   Brandenburg Concerto No. 3 (August 14, 1945)
   Brandenburg Concerto No. 4 (August 13, 1945)
   Brandenburg Concerto No. 5 (August 13, 1946)
   Brandenburg Concerto No. 6 (August 14, 1947)
   Saint Matthew Passion (March 26, 1937)
   Sonata No. 6 in E: Prelude (October 31, 1945)
   Suite No. 1 (August 14, 1947)
   Suite No. 2 (August 14, 1945)
   Suite No. 3 (August 13, 1945)
   Suite No. 4 (August 14, 1946)
BARTÓK Concerto for Orchestra (December 30, 1944)
BEETHOVEN Egmont Overture (April 2, 1947)
   Missa Solemnis (April 26, 1938), (December 2, 1938)
   Symphony No. 2 (December 3, 1938)
   Symphony No. 3 "Eroica" (October 29, 1945)
   Symphony No. 5 (November 23, 1944)
   Symphony No. 6 "Pastoral" (December 18, 1928)
   Symphony No. 8 (January 23, 1935), (December 30, 1936)
   Symphony No. 9 "Choral" (August 6, 1947)
BERLIOZ La Damnation de Faust: 3 excerpts (May 8, 1936)
   Harold in Italy (November 28, 1944)
   Roman Carnival Overture (November 22, 1944)
BERNSTEIN The Age of Anxiety, Symphony No. 2 (April 9, 1949)
BIZET Carmen: Micaëla's Aria (March 20, 1940)
BRAHMS Academic Festival Overture (April 2, 1947)
   Violin Concerto (December 21, 1937), (April 11, 1939)
   Symphony No. 3 (January 2, 1945)
   Symphony No. 4 (November 30, 1938)
BRITTEN Peter Grimes: excerpts (March 2, 1946)
CASADESUS Concerto in D (December 22, 1937)
CHARPENTIER: Louise: "Depuis le jour" (March 20, 1940)
COPLAND Appalachian Spring (October 31, 1945)
   Lincoln Portrait (February 7, 1946)
   El salón México (December 1, 1938)

CORELLI Suite for Strings (November 22, 1944)
COWELL Hymn and Fuguing Tune No. 2 (April 27, 1949)
DEBUSSY La Mer (December 1, 1938)
    Prélude à l'après-midi d'un faune (November 22, 1944)
    Sarabande (October 30, 1930)
    Tarantelle Styrienne, "Danse" (October 30, 1930)
FAURÉ Elégie (December 28, 1936)
    Pelléas et Mélisande (March 18, 1940)
FOOTE Suite for Strings (March 19, 1940)
GLINKA Russlan and Ludmilla: Overture (April 1, 1944)
GRIEG "The Last Spring" (March 20, 1940), (November 29, 1950)
HANDEL Concerto Grosso in B Minor, op. 6, no. 12: Larghetto (May 8, 1936)
    Semele: "Oh sleep! Why Dost Thou Leave Me?" (November 6, 1939)
HANSON Serenade for Solo Flute, Harp, and Strings (November 25, 1947)
    Symphony No. 3 (March 20, 1940)
HARRIS Symphony No. 1 "1933" (February 2, 1934)
    Symphony No. 3 (November 8, 1939)
HAYDN Symphony No. 92 "Oxford" (August 14, 1950)
    Symphony No. 94 "Surprise" (April 22, 1929), (November 5, 1946)
    Symphony No. 102 (December 29, 1936)
KHACHATURIAN Piano Concerto (January 1, 1945), (April 19, 1946)
LIADOV From the Apocalypse (May 1, 1943)
    The Enchanted Lake (May 6, 1936)
LISZT Mephisto Waltz (May 8, 1936)
McDONALD San Juan Capistrano (November 8, 1939)
MENDELSSOHN Symphony No. 4 "Italian" (January 23, 1935), (November 25, 1947)
MOZART, L. Cassation in G (Haydn's "Toy Symphony") (August 15, 1950)
MOZART La clemenza di Tito: Overture (August 17, 1949)
    Idomeneo, rè di Creta: Overture (August 17, 1949)
    Der Schauspieldirektor (The Impresario): Overture (August 17, 1949)
    Serenade in G "Eine kleine Nachtmusik" (August 15, 1950)
    Serenade for 13 Wind Instruments (August 15, 1947)
    String Quintet in G Minor (August 15, 1946)
    Symphony No. 26 (February 7, 1946)
    Symphony No. 29 (December 22, 1937)
    Symphony No. 33 (August 15, 1946)
    Symphony No. 34 (March 18, 1940)
    Symphony No. 36 "Linz" (August 16, 1949)
    Symphony No. 39 (January 3, 1945)
    Die Zauberflöte: "Ach, Ich fühl's" (November 6, 1939)
MUSSORGSKY Khovanshchina: Prelude (December 28, 1936)
    Pictures at an Exhibition (October 28, 1930)
PISTON Prelude and Allegro for Organ and Strings (April 24, 1945)
PROKOFIEV Chout (November 25, 1947)
    Violin Concerto No. 2 (December 20, 1937)

Serge Koussevitzky (continued)

PROKOFIEV Lieutenant Kijé Suite (December 22, 1937)
   The Love for Three Oranges (April 22, 1929), (December 30, 1936)
   Peter and the Wolf (April 12, 1939), (August 11, 1950)
   Romeo and Juliet: Suite No. 2 (October 30, 1945)
   Symphony No. 1 "Classical" (April 22, 1929), (November 25, 1947)
   Symphony No. 5 (February 6, 1946)
RACHMANINOFF The Isle of the Dead (April 23, 1945)
   Vocalise (April 24, 1945)
RAVEL Boléro (April 14, 1930), (August 13, 1947)
   Daphnis et Chloé: Suite No. 2 (November 15, 1928), (November 23, 1944)
   Ma Mère l'oye (Mother Goose) (October 27, 1930), (October 29, 1947)
   Pavane pour une infante défunte (November 4, 1946)
   Rapsodie espagnole (April 23, 1945)
   La Valse (October 29, 1930)
RIMSKY-KORSAKOV "The Battle of Kershenetz" (November 7, 1939)
   Dubinushka (arrangement) (November 7, 1939)
SATIE Gymnopédie No. 1 (April 14, 1930). Nos. 1 and 2 (April 27, 1949
SCHUBERT Rosamunde: Ballet Music (May 8, 1936)
   Symphony No. 5 (April 4, 1947)
   Symphony No. 8 "Unfinished" (May 6, 1936), (January 3, 1945)
SCHUMANN Symphony No. 1 "Spring" (November 6, 1939)
SHOSTAKOVICH Symphony No. 8: Adagio (April 25, 1945)
   Symphony No. 9 (November 4, 1946)
SIBELIUS Pohjola's Daughter (May 6, 1936)
   Swanwhite: The Maiden with Roses (December 29, 1936)
   Symphony No. 2 (January 24, 1935), (November 29, 1950)
   Symphony No. 5 (December 29, 1936)
   — IV. Finale: Allegro molto (January 5, 1946)
   Tapiola (November 7, 1939)
SOUSA Semper Fidelis (April 19, 1946)
   The Stars and Stripes Forever (April 19, 1946)
STRAUSS, J. Voices of Spring (December 18, 1928)
   Wiener Blut (December 20, 1928)
STRAUSS, R. Also sprach Zarathustra (January 22, 1935)
   Don Juan (April 19, 1946), (October 29, 1947)
   Till Eulenspiegel (April 24, 1945)
STRAVINSKY Apollon musagète (November 14, 1928)
   Capriccio (March 19, 1940)
   Pétrouchka: Suite (November 13, 1928)
   The Song of the Volga Boatman (arrangement) (December 3, 1938)
TCHAIKOVSKY Francesca da Rimini (April 19, 1946)
   Romeo and Juliet (December 28, 1936)
   Serenade in C for String Orchestra (August 16, 1949)
   — Waltz (May 8, 1936), (April 27, 1949)
   Symphony No. 4 (May 4, 1936), (April 26, 1949)

TCHAIKOVSKY Symphony No. 5 (November 22, 1944)
  Symphony No. 6 "Pathétique" (April 14, 1930)
THOMPSON Testament of Freedom (April 24, 1945)
TRADITIONAL Fair Harvard (March 23, 1937)
VAUGHAN WILLIAMS Symphony No. 6 (rehearsal) (March 14, 1949)
VIVALDI Concerto Grosso in D Minor, RV. 565 (May 8, 1936)
WAGNER Der fliegende Holländer: Overture (April 4, 1947)
  Lohengrin: Act 1 Prelude (April 27, 1949)
  Parsifal: Act 1 Prelude (April 4, 1947)
  Parsifal: Good Friday Music (April 19, 1946)
  Siegfried Idyll (April 27, 1949)
WEBER Oberon: Overture (November 5, 1946)

Rafael Kubelik

BARTÓK Concerto for Orchestra (November 27, 1973)
BEETHOVEN Symphony No. 5 (November 26, 1973)
MARTINŮ Double Concerto (January 14, 1967)
SMETANA Má Vlast (March 8, 1971)

Erich Leinsdorf

BARTÓK Concerto for Orchestra (October 13, 1962)
  Violin Concerto No. 2 (April 23, 1964)
BEETHOVEN Piano Concerto No. 1 (December 20, 1967)
  Piano Concerto No. 2 (December 20, 1967)
  Piano Concerto No. 3 (April 5, 1965)
  Piano Concerto No. 4 (April 20, 1964)
  Piano Concerto No. 5 "Emperor" (March 4, 1963)
  Coriolan Overture (November 21, 1966)
  The Creatures of Prometheus (October 30, 1967)
  Leonore Overture No. 1 (December 22, 1966)
  Leonore Overture No. 2 (December 19, 1966)
  Leonore Overture No. 3 (January 6, 1963)
  Symphony No. 1 (April 23, 1969)
  Symphony No. 2 (March 6, 1967)
  Symphony No. 3 "Eroica" (September 20, 30, 1962)
  — II. Funeral March (November 22, 1963)
  Symphony No. 4 (December 20, 1966)
  Symphony No. 5 (December 23, 1967)
  Symphony No. 6 "Pastoral" (January 13, 1969)
  Symphony No. 7 (November 21, 1966)
  Symphony No. 8 (April 24, 1969)
  Symphony No. 9 "Choral" (October 19, 1965), (April 21, 1969)
BERG Le Vin (April 19, 1965)
  Wozzeck: excerpts (April 23, 1964)
BERLIOZ La Damnation de Faust: Rákóczy March (April 8, 1964)

Erich Leinsdorf (continued)

BRAHMS Piano Concerto No. 1 (March 16, 1964), (April 21, 1964)
    Ein deutsches Requiem (A German Requiem) (November 25, 1968)
    Symphony No. 1 (September 29, 1963)
    Symphony No. 2 (December 14, 1964)
    Symphony No. 3 (March 7, 1966)
    Symphony No. 4 (April 26, 1966)
    Tragic Overture (April 26, 1966)
BRITTEN War Requiem (July 23, 1963)
BRUCKNER Symphony No. 4 (January 10, 1966)
CARTER Piano Concerto (January 6, 1967)
COLGRASS As Quiet As (April 19, 1967)
DELLO JOIO Fantasy and Variations (February 17, 1963)
DVOŘÁK Romance in F Minor (December 18, 1967)
    Slavonic Dance in E minor, op. 72, no. 2 (December 22, 1967)
    Slavonic Dance in A♭, op. 72, no. 8 (December 23, 1967)
    Symphony No. 6 (December 19, 1967)
FAURÉ Elégie (March 25, 1963)
FINE Serious Song: Lament for String Orchestra (January 25, 1966)
    Toccata Concertante (January 25, 1965)
GINASTERA Piano Concerto (March 6, 1968)
    Variaciones concertantes (March 11, 1968)
HAYDN Symphony No. 93 (December 19, 1966)
    Symphony No. 96 "Miracle" (April 8, 1968)
JANÁČEK The Cunning Little Vixen: Suite (September 30, 1966)
KODÁLY Háry János: Suite (April 22, 1965)
    Peacock Variations (November 23, 1964)
LANNER "Die Mozartisten" Waltzes (December 31, 1963), (January 3, 1964)
LISZT Piano Concerto No. 2 (November 21, 1964)
MAHLER Symphony No. 1 "Titan" (October 20, 1962)
    Symphony No. 3 (October 10, 1966)
    Symphony No. 5 (November 17, 1963)
    Symphony No. 6 "Tragic" (April 20, 1965)
MENDELSSOHN A Midsummer Night's Dream (November 29, 1962)
MENOTTI The Death of the Bishop of Brindisi (October 19, 1964)
MOZART Mass in C Minor, K. 427: "Et incarnatus est" (July 24, 1966)
    Requiem (January 19, 1964)
    Serenade in G, "Eine kleine Nachtmusik" (January 6, 1963)
    Symphony No. 36 "Linz" (December 22, 1967)
    Symphony No. 38 "Prague:" I and II (April 16, 1968)
    Symphony No. 39 (January 20, 1969)
    Symphony No. 40: I. Molto allegro (December 21, 1966)
    Symphony No. 41 "Jupiter" (January 14, 1963)
PISTON Symphony No. 7: excerpt (September 20, 1962)
PROKOFIEV Piano Concertos Nos. 1 and 2 (December 1, 1965)
    Piano Concerto No. 3 (November 25, 1967)

PROKOFIEV Piano Concerto (left hand) No. 4 (November 27, 1967)
Piano Concerto No. 5 (March 28, 1964), (April 25, 1969)
Violin Concerto No. 1 (April 13, 1964)
Violin Concerto No. 2 (December 19, 1966)
Lieutenant Kijé Suite (April 22, 1968)
Romeo and Juliet: excerpts (February 13, 1967)
Scythian Suite (October 24, 1966)
Symphony-Concerto for Cello and Orchestra (March 25, 1963)
Symphony No. 2 (March 25, 1968)
Symphony No. 3 (April 25, 1966)
Symphony No. 5 (October 28, 1963)
Symphony No. 6 (April 23, 1965)
RAVEL Piano Concerto in G (February 16, 1963)
RIMSKY-KORSAKOV Le Coq d'or: Suite (November 24, 1963)
Le Coq d'or: "Hymn to the Sun" (November 24, 1963)
SCHARWENKA Piano Concerto No. 1 (January 20, 1969)
SCHOENBERG A Survivor from Warsaw (April 23, 1969)
Gurrelieder: Song of the Wood Dove (October 19, 1964)
SCHULLER Seven Studies on Themes of Paul Klee (November 23, 1964)
SCHUMANN Symphony No. 4 (January 5, 1963)
SHOSTAKOVICH Symphony No. 1 (September 26, 1964)
SIBELIUS Violin Concerto (December 21, 1966)
SMETANA Má Vlast: The Moldau (April 22, 1967)
SOUSA The Stars and Stripes Forever (April 8, 1964)
STRAUSS, R. Die Ägyptische Helena: Awakening Scene (April 22, 1965)
Ariadne auf Naxos (January 7, 1969)
Ein Heldenleben (March 9, 1963)
Salome: Dance of the Seven Veils (April 22, 1965)
Salome: Interlude and Final scene (April 24, 1965)
Till Eulenspiegel: excerpt (September 20, 1962)
STRAVINSKY Agon (April 19, 1965)
Violin Concerto (April 22, 1965)
The Firebird: Suite (April 22, 1964)
TCHAIKOVSKY Piano Concerto No. 1 (March 5, 1963), (December 12, 1966)
Violin Concerto (December 18, 1967)
Eugene Onegin: Tatiana's Letter Scene (July 24, 1966)
Marche slave (April 13, 1964)
VERDI Aida: "O patria mia" (July 24, 1966)
Don Carlo: "Ella giammai m'amò . . . Dormirò sol" (July 24, 1966)
Requiem Mass (October 5, 1964)
WAGNER Der fliegende Holländer: Overture (October 30, 1967)
Götterdämmerung: Dawn and Siegfried's Rhine Journey (October 19, 1965)
Die Meistersinger: Act I Prelude (October 30, 1967)
Lohengrin (August 23, 1965)
Preludes to Acts I and III (April 24, 1965)
Siegfried Idyll (October 1, 1965), (October 19, 1965)

Erich Leinsdorf (continued)

WAGNER Tannhäuser: Overture (December 19, 1967)
  Tannhäuser: Festival March "Entrance of the Guests" (April 8, 1964)
  Tristan und Isolde: Prelude (December 19, 1967)
WEILL Kleine Dreigroschenmusik (April 25, 1969)

James Levine

BEETHOVEN Coriolan Overture (August 3, 2007)
BERLIOZ Le Corsaire Overture (September 30, 2005)
LIEBERSON Neruda Songs (November 25, 2005)
RAVEL Alborada del gracioso (October 4, 2007)
RAVEL Pavane pour une infante défunte (October 5, 2007)
SCHULLER Seven Studies on Themes of Paul Klee (March 29, 2007)
SCHUMANN Manfred Overture (November 26, 2004)

Igor Markevitch

TCHAIKOVSKY Romeo and Juliet (March 19, 1955)

Dimitri Mitropoulos

GOULD Spirituals for Orchestra (December 16, 1944)

Pierre Monteux

BRAHMS Tragic Overture (January 20, 1959)
DEBUSSY La Mer (July 19, 1954)
  Nocturnes for Orchestra (August 15, 1955)
  Prélude à l'après-midi d'un faune (July 19, 1959)
DELIBES Coppélia: Suite (December 2, 1953)
  Sylvia: Suite (December 30, 1953)
HINDEMITH Noblissima visione (January 20, 1959)
KHACHATURIAN Violin Concerto (January 12, 1958)
LISZT Les préludes (December 8, 1952)
MOZART Piano Concerto No. 12 in A, K. 414 (April 12, 1953)
  Piano Concerto No. 18 in B♭, K. 456 (April 13, 1953)
SAINT-SAËNS Havanaise (January 12, 1958)
SCRIABIN Symphony No. 4 "Poem of Ecstasy" (December 8, 1952)
STRAUSS, R. Der Rosenkavalier: Suite (February 17, 1956)
  Don Quixote (January 24, 1959)
STRAVINSKY Pétrouchka (January 20, 1959), (January 25, 1959)
  Le Sacre du printemps (January 28, 1951)
TCHAIKOVSKY Symphony No. 4 (January 28, 1959)
  Symphony No. 5 (January 8, 1958)
  Symphony No. 6 "Pathétique" (January 26, 1955)
VAUGHAN WILLIAMS Tallis Fantasia (December 20, 1963)

Karl Muck

BEETHOVEN Symphony No. 7: Finale (October 4, 1917)
BERLIOZ La Damnation de Faust: Rákóczy March (October 3, 1917)
La Damnation de Faust: Ballet des Sylphes (October 5, 1917)
TCHAIKOVSKY The Nutcracker: Waltz of the Flowers (October 4, 1917)
Suite No. 1: Marche Miniature (October 5, 1917)
Symphony No. 4: Finale (October 2, 1917)
WAGNER Lohengrin: Act 3 Prelude (October 3, 1917)
WOLF-FERRARI The Secret of Suzanne: Overture (October 3, 1917)

Charles Munch

AUBER La Muette de Portici: Overture (December 24, 1953)
BACH Brandenburg Concerto No. 1 (July 8, 1957)
Brandenburg Concerto No. 2 (July 9, 1957)
Brandenburg Concerto No. 3 (July 8, 1957)
Brandenburg Concerto No. 4 (July 8, 1957)
Brandenburg Concerto No. 5 (July 9, 1957)
Brandenburg Concerto No. 6 (July 9, 1957)
Violin Concerto in A Minor, BWV 1041 (December 26, 1960)
BARBER Adagio for Strings (April 3, 1957)
Medea's Meditation and Dance of Vengeance (April 10, 1957)
BEETHOVEN Piano Concerto No. 1 (November 2, 1960)
Violin Concerto (November 27, 1955)
— I. Allegro ma non troppo (April 23, 1954)
Coriolan Overture (February 26, 1956)
The Creatures of Prometheus (March 7, 1960)
Fidelio: Overture (November 7, 1955)
Gratulations-Menuet (December 20, 1949)
Leonore Overture No. 1 (February 26, 1956)
Leonore Overture No. 2 (February 26, 1956)
Leonore Overture No. 3 (February 27, 1956)
Symphony No. 1 (December 27, 1950)
Symphony No. 3 "Eroica" (December 2, 1957), (May 4, 1960)
Symphony No. 5 (May 2, 1955)
Symphony No. 6 "Pastoral" (August 16, 1955)
Symphony No. 7 (December 19, 1949)
Symphony No. 8 (November 30, 1958)
Symphony No. 9 "Choral" (December 21, 1958)
BERLIOZ Benvenuto Cellini: Overture (April 6, 1959)
Béatrice et Bénédict: Overture (December 20, 1949), (December 1, 1958)
Le Corsaire Overture (December 1, 1958)
La Damnation de Faust (February 21, 1954)
L'Enfance du Christ (December 23, 1956), (December 13, 1966)
Harold in Italy (March 31, 1958)
Les Nuits d'été (April 12, 1955)

Charles Munch (continued)

BERLIOZ Roman Carnival Overture (December 1, 1958)
    Roméo et Juliette (February 22, 1953), (April 23, 1961)
    Symphonie fantastique (November 14, 1954), (December 12, 1954), (April
      9, 1962), (April 17, 1962)
    Les Troyens: Royal Hunt and Storm (April 6, 1959), (January 26, 1963)
BIZET Symphony in C (February 1, 1964)
BLACKWOOD Symphony No. 1 (November 9, 1958)
BLOCH Schelomo (January 30, 1957)
BRAHMS Piano Concerto No. 1 (April 9, 1958)
    Piano Concerto No. 2 (August 11, 1952)
    Symphony No. 1 (November 19, 1956)
    Symphony No. 2 (December 5, 1955)
    Symphony No. 4 (April 10, 1950), (October 27, 1958)
    Tragic Overture (December 5, 1955)
BRUCH Violin Concerto No. 1 (January 18, 1951)
CHAUSSON Poème (December 14, 1955)
    Symphony in B♭ (February 26, 1962)
CHOPIN Piano Concerto No. 1 (March 14, 1960)
    Piano Concerto No. 2 (November 29, 1954)
DEBUSSY La Damoiselle élue (April 11, 1955)
    Images (December 16, 1957)
    Le Martyre de St. Sébastien (January 29, 1956)
    La Mer (December 9, 1956), (March 30, 1962), (April 17, 1962)
    Nocturnes for Orchestra: Nuages. Fêtes (March 13, 1962)
    Prélude à l'après-midi d'un faune (January 23, 1956), (March 13, 1962)
    Printemps (March 13, 1962)
DUKAS The Sorcerer's Apprentice (November 4, 1957)
DVOŘÁK Cello Concerto (February 22, 1960)
    Symphony No. 8 (March 13, 1961)
ELGAR Introduction and Allegro for Strings (April 3, 1957)
FAURÉ Pelléas et Mélisande Suite (December 3, 1966)
    Pénélope: Prelude (December 12, 1959)
FRANCK Le Chasseur maudit (October 10, 1959), (February 26, 1962)
    Symphonic Variations (August 1, 1965)
    Symphony in D Minor (March 11, 1957)
HAIEFF Symphony No. 2 (November 30, 1958)
HANDEL Water Music: Suite (December 26, 1950), (December 12, 1954)
    — Overture (March 8, 1958)
HAYASHI Kimi Ga Yo (Japanese national anthem) (May 4, 1960)
HAYDN The Creation: With Verdure Clad (December 12, 1954)
    Symphony No. 103 "Drumroll" (December 26, 1950)
    Symphony No. 104 "London" (April 10, 1950)
HONEGGER Symphony No. 2 (March 29, 1953)
    Symphony No. 5 "Di tre re" (October 27, 1952)

IBERT Escales (December 10, 1956)
d'INDY Symphony on French Mountain Air (March 24, 1958)
LALO Le Roi d'Ys: Overture (December 27, 1950)
MAHLER Kindertotenlieder (December 28, 1958)
  Lieder eines fahrenden Gesellen (December 29, 1958)
MARTINŮ Symphony No. 6 "Fantaisies Symphoniques" (April 23, 1956)
MENDELSSOHN Capriccio brillant (March 14, 1960)
  Violin Concerto (February 23, 1959), (December 24, 1960)
  Octet in E♭: Scherzo (March 7, 1960)
  Symphony No. 3 "Scottish" (December 7, 1959)
  Symphony No. 4 "Italian" (February 18, 1958)
  Symphony No. 5 "Reformation" (October 28, 1957)
MENOTTI Violin Concerto (November 8, 1954)
MILHAUD La Création du monde (March 13, 1961)
  Suite Provençale (November 21, 1960)
MOZART Clarinet Concerto (July 9, 1956)
  Le Nozze di Figaro: Overture (April 25, 1951)
PISTON Symphony No. 6 (March 12, 1956)
POULENC Organ Concerto (October 9, 1960)
PROKOFIEV Piano Concerto No. 2 (February 13, 1957)
  Violin Concerto No. 2 (February 24, 1959)
  The Love for Three Oranges: March, Scherzo (November 28, 1950)
  Romeo and Juliet: 12 Scenes (February 11, 1957)
RACHMANINOFF Piano Concerto No. 2 (October 6, 1958)
  Piano Concerto No. 3 (December 29, 1957)
RAVEL Boléro (January 23, 1956), (March 26, 1962)
  Concerto in G (March 24, 1958)
  Daphnis et Chloé (January 23, 1955), (February 26, 1961)
    Suite No. 2 (May 4, 1960), (April 17, 1962)
  Ma Mère l'oye: Suite (February 19, 1958)
  Pavane pour une infante défunte (October 27, 1952), (March 26, 1962)
  Rapsodie espagnole (December 26, 1950), (January 23, 1956)
  La Valse (April 11, 1950), (December 5, 1955), (December 1, 1958), (February 2, 1962), (March 26, 1962)
ROUSSEL Bacchus et Ariane: Suite No. 2 (October 27, 1952)
  Suite in F (March 8, 1958)
SAINT-SAËNS Piano Concerto No. 4 (November 24, 1954)
  Introduction and Rondo Capriccioso (December 14, 1955)
  La Princesse jaune: Overture (January 18, 1951)
  Le Rouet d'Omphale (November 4, 1957)
  Symphony No. 3 "Organ" (April 5, 1959)
SCHUBERT Symphony No. 2 (December 20, 1949), (March 7, 1960)
  Symphony No. 8 "Unfinished" (May 2, 1955)
  Symphony No. 9 "Great C Major" (November 19, 1958)
SCHUMANN Piano Concerto (October 6, 1958)
  Genoveva: Overture, (January 18, 1951)

Charles Munch (continued)

SCHUMANN Manfred: Overture (October 5, 1959)
    Symphony No. 1 "Spring" (April 25, 1951), (October 5, 1959)
SMITH The Star-Spangled Banner (October 28, 1957), (May 4, 1960)
STRAUSS, R. Four Lieder (December 12, 1954)
    Don Quixote (August 17, 1953)
    Till Eulenspiegel (March 20, 1961)
STRAVINSKY Jeu de cartes (November 7, 1960)
TCHAIKOVSKY Violin Concerto (March 29, 1953), (February 9, 1959)
    Francesca da Rimini (April 23, 1956)
    Romeo and Juliet (March 12, 1956), (April 3, 1961)
    Serenade in C for String Orchestra (March 13, 1957)
    Symphony No. 4 (November 7, 1955)
    Symphony No. 6 "Pathétique" (March 12, 1962)
WAGNER Tannhäuser: Overture and Venusberg Music (April 1, 1957)
    Die Walküre: Magic Fire Music (April 1, 1957),
    Götterdämmerung: Rhine Journey (April 1, 1957)
        Immolation Scene (November 25, 1957)
    Tristan und Isolde: Prelude and Liebestod (November 25, 1957)
WALTON Cello Concerto (January 28, 1957)

Lennie Neuhaus

EASTWOOD Mystic River (March 31, 2003)

John Oliver

DALLAPICCOLA Canti di prigionia (August 30, 1982)

Seiji Ozawa

BACH Chorale-Variations on "Vom Himmel hoch" (April 24, 1990)
    A Musical Offering: Ricercare a 6 Voci (October 21, 1989)
    Partita No. 2: Chaconne (October 13, 1990)
    Prelude and Fugue in E♭, BWV 552, "St. Anne" (October 21, 1989)
    Toccata and Fugue in D Minor, BWV 565 (April 23, 1990)
BARBER, Violin Concerto (October 3, 1994)
BARTÓK Concerto for Orchestra (February 24, 1994)
    Violin Concerto No. 2 (February 18, 1991)
    Duke Bluebeard's Castle (November 8, 1980)
    The Miraculous Mandarin (February 28, 1994)
    — Suite (November 10, 1975)
    Music for Strings, Percussion, and Celesta (November 13, 1976)
BEETHOVEN Piano Concerto No. 1 (October 5, 1983)
    Piano Concerto No. 2 (July 3, 1984)
    Piano Concerto No. 3 (October 2, 1982)
    Piano Concerto No. 4 (October 5, 1981)
    Piano Concerto No. 5 "Emperor" (October 9, 1973), (January 24, 1981)

Egmont: Overture (January 24, 1981), (December 1, 1985)
Choral Fantasy (October 2, 1982)
Two Romances for Violin and Orchestra (September 29, 1980)
Symphony No. 5 (January 24, 1981)
BERG Violin Concerto (November 27, 1978)
BERLIOZ La Damnation de Faust (October 1, 1973)
— Rákóczy March (September 7, 1979)
La Mort de Cléopâtre (February 10, 1994)
Les Nuits d'été (October 17, 1983)
Requiem (October 21, 1993)
Roman Carnival Overture (February 20, 1973), (April 4, 2002)
Roméo et Juliette (October 6, 1975)
Symphonie fantastique (February 19, 1973)
BERNSTEIN Serenade (October 1, 1994)
BRAHMS Symphony No. 1 (March 28, 1977), (March 1, 1986)
Symphony No. 2 (April 19, 1975)
BRITTEN Diversions (October 8, 1990)
Les Illuminations (April 8, 1997)
Phaedra (February 10, 1994)
"The Young Person's Guide to the Orchestra" (February 14, 1992)
CHABRIER España (November 15, 1986)
CHOPIN Piano Concerto No. 1 (April 19, 1986)
DEBUSSY La Damoiselle élue (October 10, 1983), (April 19, 1995)
DUTILLEUX The Shadows of Time (March 12, 1998)
DVOŘÁK Carnival Overture (December 16, 1993)
Cello Concerto (December 2, 1985)
Humoresque in G♭ (December 16, 1993)
Klid (Silent Woods) (December 16, 1993)
Psalm 149 (December 16, 1993)
Romance in F Minor (December 16, 1993)
Rusalka: "O Lovely Moon" (December 16, 1993)
Slavonic Dance in E Minor, op. 72, no. 2 (December 16, 1993)
Slavonic Dance in A♭, op., 72, no. 7 (December 16, 1993)
Symphony No. 9 "from the New World": II. Largo (December 16, 1993)
FALLA The Three-Cornered Hat (October 2, 1976)
FAURÉ Après un rêve (November 17, 1986)
Dolly Suite (November 15, 1986)
Elégie (November 17, 1986)
Pavane (November 15, 1986)
Pelléas et Mélisande Suite (November 15, 1986)
— Filieuse. Sicilienne (February 23, 1980)
Requiem (March 3, 1994)
FOSS Three American Pieces (October 4, 1994)
FRANCK Symphony in D Minor (November 29, 1991)
GLAZUNOV Chant du ménéstrel (August 11, 1975)
GOUNOD Faust: Ballet Music (November 17, 1986)

Seiji Ozawa (continued)

GRIFFES The Pleasure Dome of Kubla Khan (January 31, 1976)
    Three Poems of Fiona MacLeod (January 31, 1976)
HARBISON Symphony No. 1 (October 15, 1984)
HAYDN Scena di Berenice (February 10, 1994)
HOLST The Planets (December 3, 1979)
IVES Central Park in the Dark (February 16, 1976)
    Symphony No. 4 (February 9, 1976)
KIM Violin Concerto (April 27, 1983)
LIEBERSON Piano Concerto (April 14, 1984)
LISZT Piano Concerto No. 1 (March 31, 1979), (April 27, 1987)
    Piano Concerto No. 2 (April 25, 1987)
    Totentanz (April 25, 1987)
MAHLER Kindertotenlieder (December 13, 1988)
    Symphony No. 1 "Titan" (includes "Blumine") (October 3, 1977)
    Symphony No. 1 "Titan" (October 5, 1987)
    Symphony No. 2 "Resurrection" (December 13, 1986)
    Symphony No. 3 (April 22, 1993)
    Symphony No. 4 (November 21, 1987)
    Symphony No. 5 (September 27, 1990)
    — IV. Adagietto (August 2, 1987)
    Symphony No. 6 "Tragic" (January 30, 1992)
    Symphony No. 7 (March 11, 1989)
    Symphony No. 8 "Symphony of a Thousand" (October 13, 1980)
    Symphony No. 9 in D (October 5, 1989)
    Symphony No. 10: Adagio (April 19, 1990)
MARTIN Concerto for Seven Winds (September 30, 1977)
MENDELSSOHN Violin Concerto (September 29, 1980)
    A Midsummer Night's Dream (October 3, 1992)
MESSIAEN Oiseaux exotiques (February 23, 1994)
    Trois petites liturgies de la Présence Divine (October 7, 1978)
MORET En rêve (February 16, 1991)
MOZART Bassoon Concerto (November 15, 1978)
    Clarinet Concerto (November 28, 1978)
OFFENBACH Gaîté Parisienne (November 17, 1986)
ORFF Carmina Burana (November 17, 1969)
PAGANINI Moto Perpetuo (April 22, 1978)
PANUFNIK Symphony No. 8 "Sinfonia Votiva" (January 30, 1982)
POULENC Concert champêtre (November 30, 1991)
    Two-Piano Concerto (April 8, 1989)
    Organ Concerto (December 2, 1991)
    Gloria (November 24, 1987)
    Stabat Mater (November 25, 1987)
PROKOFIEV Piano Concerto No. 4 (October 15, 1991)
    Peter and the Wolf (February 14, 1992)
    Romeo and Juliet (October 18, 1986)

RACHMANINOFF Piano Concerto No. 1 (December 6, 1997)
    Piano Concerto No. 2 (December 2, 2000)
    Piano Concerto No. 3 (January 21, 1992)
RAVEL Alborada del gracioso (March 13, 1974)
    Une Barque sur l'océan (April 21, 1975)
    Boléro (March 13, 1974)
    Piano Concerto in D for the Left Hand (October 6, 1990)
    Daphnis et Chloé (October 14, 1974)
    Cinq mélodies populaires grecques (April 8, 1980)
    Deux mélodies hébraïques (April 8, 1980)
    Menuet antique (April 22, 1974)
    Ma Mère l'oye (April 22, 1974)
    Pavane pour une infante défunte (October 14, 1974)
    Rapsodie espagnole (March 13, 1974)
    Shéhérazade (October 8, 1979), (April 17, 1995)
    Le Tombeau de Couperin (October 14, 1974)
    La Valse (March 13, 1974)
    Valses nobles et sentimentales (April 21, 1975)
RESPIGHI Ancient Airs and Dances: Set 1 (March 29, 1977)
    Ancient Airs and Dances: Set 2 (April 22, 1978)
    Ancient Airs and Dances: Set 3 (October 7, 1975)
    Feste romane (October 15, 1977)
    The Fountains of Rome (October 17, 1977)
    The Pines of Rome (October 17, 1977)
RIMSKY-KORSAKOV Scheherazade (April 2, 1977)
ROSSINI Semiramide: Overture (February 9, 1976)
SAINT-SAËNS Carnival of the Animals (February 15, 1992)
SCHOENBERG Cello Concerto (after Monn) (October 22, 1984)
    Gurrelieder (March 30, 1979)
SCHUMANN Cello Concerto (arr. for Violin) (April 18, 1992)
SESSIONS Concerto for Orchestra (January 30, 1982)
    When Lilacs Last in the Dooryard Bloom'd (April 23, 1977)
SHOSTAKOVICH Cello Concerto No. 2 (August 11, 1975)
    Violin Concerto No. 2 (April 16, 1992)
SIBELIUS Violin Concerto (October 19, 1985)
SMETANA The Bartered Bride: Dance of the Comedians (September 8, 1979)
SOUSA The Stars and Stripes Forever (April 3, 1979)
STARER Violin Concerto (April 27, 1983)
STRAUSS, R. Also sprach Zarathustra (December 14, 1981), (March 1, 1986)
    Don Quixote (October 27, 1984)
    Duet-Concertino for Clarinet and Bassoon (March 12, 1988)
    Elektra (November 12, 1988)
    Ein Heldenleben (December 14, 1981)
STRAVINSKY Violin Concerto (February 6, 1978)
    The Firebird (April 30, 1983)
        Suite (November 24, 1969)

Seiji Ozawa (continued)

STRAVINSKY Greeting Prelude (November 22, 1969)
Pétrouchka (November 24, 1969)
Le Sacre du printemps (December 10, 1979)
Symphony of Psalms (December 5, 1987)
TAKEMITSU Quatrain (March 29, 1977)
A Flock Descends into the Pentagonal Garden (December 2, 1978)
From me flows what you call Time (October 19, 1990)
TCHAIKOVSKY Piano Concerto No. 1(April 16, 1979)
Violin Concerto (October 17, 1985)
The Nutcracker (December 15, 1990)
Pique Dame (October 16, 1991)
Sleeping Beauty: Suite (December 8, 1990)
Swan Lake (November 11, 1978)
Symphony No. 5 (February 16, 1977)
Symphony No. 6 "Pathétique" (April 26, 1986)
Variations on a Rococo Theme (December 2, 1985)
THOMAS Mignon: Overture (November 24, 1987)
VAUGHAN WILLIAMS The Lark Ascending (February 16, 1977)
VIVALDI "The Four Seasons" (October 10, 1981)
WAGNER Die Walküre: Act I (August 12, 1978)
WILSON Sinfonia (October 15, 1984)
WU Concerto for Pipa and Orchestra (March 31, 1979)

Georges Prêtre

BERLIOZ Symphonie fantastique (February 3, 1969)

André Previn

PREVIN Violin Concerto "Anne-Sophie" (October 26, 2002)

Thomas Schippers

VERDI La forza del destino: Overture (March 18, 1961)

Joseph Silverstein

FAURÉ Pelléas et Mélisande: Filieuse, Sicilienne (February 23, 1980)

William Steinberg

BRUCKNER Symphony No. 6 (January 19, 1970)
Symphony No. 8 (February 26, 1972)
DUKAS The Sorcerer's Apprentice (October 26, 1970)
HINDEMITH Concert Music for Strings and Brass (October 5, 1971)
Symphony "Mathis der Maler" (October 4, 1971)
HOLST The Planets (September 28, 1970)

MENDELSSOHN Octet in E♭: Scherzo (October 26, 1970)
MOZART Don Giovanni: Overture (December 19, 1969
SAINT-SAËNS Danse macabre (January 12, 1970)
SCHUBERT Symphony No. 9 "Great C Major" (September 29, 1969)
STRAUSS, R. Also sprach Zarathustra (March 24, 1971)
　　Till Eulenspiegel (January 12, 1970)
STRAVINSKY Scherzo à la Russe (January 12, 1970)
　　Scherzo fantastique (January 12, 1970)

Leopold Stokowski

MOZART Don Giovanni: Overture (January 13, 1968)
TCHAIKOVSKY Hamlet (January 13, 1968)

Klaus Tennstedt

BRAHMS Academic Festival Overture (December 14, 1974)

Michael Tilson Thomas

DEBUSSY Images (February 1, 1971)
　　Prélude à l'après-midi d'un faune (February 1, 1971)
IVES Three Places in New England (January 26, 1970)
PISTON Symphony No. 2 (October 5, 1970)
PROKOFIEV Scythian Suite (September 22, 1972)
RUGGLES Sun-treader (March 24, 1970)
SCHUMAN Violin Concerto (October 5, 1970)
STRAVINSKY Le Roi des étoiles (January 25, 1972)
　　Le Sacre du printemps (January 24, 1972)
TCHAIKOVSKY Symphony No. 1 "Winter Dreams" (March 23, 1970)

Bruno Walter

HAYDN Symphony No. 92 "Oxford" (January 21, 1947)

John Williams

WILLIAMS Violin Concerto (October 18, 1999)
　　Schindler's List (October 19, 1999)
　　Saving Private Ryan (February 21, 1998)
　　Tree Song (October 7, 2000)

Appendix C: Soloists

Catherine Akos, contralto
DEBUSSY Le Martyre de St. Sébastien (January 29, 1956)

Eunice Alberts, contralto
BEETHOVEN Symphony No. 9 (August 6, 1947), (October 19, 1965)
MOZART Requiem (January 19, 1964)
STRAUSS Ariadne auf Naxos (January 7, 1969)

Raymond Allard, bassoon
MOZART Serenade No. 10 in B♭, K. 361 (August 15, 1947)
STRAVINSKY L'Histoire du soldat: Suite (August 11, 1947)
    Octet for Wind Instruments (August 11, 1947)

Lucine Amara, soprano
WAGNER Lohengrin (August 23, 1965)

Victoria de los Angeles, soprano
BERLIOZ Les Nuits d'été (April 12, 1955)
DEBUSSY La Damoiselle élue (April 11, 1955)

Doriot Anthony, flute (see **Dwyer**)

Claudio Arrau, piano
GRIEG Piano Concerto (March 8, 1980)
SCHUMANN Piano Concerto (March 17, 1980)
TCHAIKOVSKY Piano Concerto No. 1 (April 16, 1979)

Vladimir Atlantov, tenor
TCHAIKOVSKY Pique Dame (October 16, 1991)

Emanuel Ax, piano
BRAHMS Piano Concerto No. 2 (April 19, 1997)

Ronald Barron, trombone
MARTIN Concerto for Seven Wind Instruments (September 30, 1977)

Kathleen Battle, soprano
MENDELSSOHN A Midsummer Night's Dream (October 3, 1992)
POULENC Gloria in G (November 24, 1987)
    Stabat Mater (November 25, 1987)

Jean Bedetti, cello
FAURÉ Elégie (December 28, 1936)

Hildegard Behrens, soprano
STRAUSS Elektra (November 12, 1988)

Teresa Berganza, mezzo-soprano
FALLA The Three-Cornered Hat (October 2, 1976)

Carlos Bergonzi, tenor
VERDI Requiem (October 5, 1964)

Leonard Bernstein, piano
BERNSTEIN The Age of Anxiety, Symphony No. 2 (April 9, 1949)

E. Power Biggs, organ
BEETHOVEN "Missa Solemnis" (April 26, 1938), (December 3, 1938)
PISTON Prelude and Allegro for Organ and Strings (April 24, 1945)

James Billings, baritone
STRAUSS Ariadne auf Naxos (January 7, 1969)

Judith Blegen, soprano
MAHLER Symphony No. 8 (October 13, 1980)

Carole Bogarde, soprano
STRAUSS Ariadne auf Naxos (January 7, 1969)

Barbara Bonney, soprano
FAURÉ Requiem (March 3, 1994)

Alexander Brailowsky, piano
CHOPIN Piano Concerto No. 2 (November 29, 1954)
SAINT-SAËNS Piano Concerto No. 4 (November 24, 1954)

John Browning, piano
PROKOFIEV Piano Concerto No. 1 (December 1, 1965)
    Piano Concerto No. 2 (December 1, 1965)
    Piano Concerto No. 3 (November 25, 1967)
    Piano Concerto (left hand) No. 4 (November 27, 1967)
    Piano Concerto No. 5 (April 25, 1969)
SAINT-SAËNS Carnival of the Animals (February 15, 1992)

Phyllis Bryn-Julson, soprano
GRIFFES Three Poems of Fiona MacLeod (January 31, 1976)

Richard Burgin, violin
BACH Brandenburg Concerto No. 1 (August 14, 1947), (August 17, 1949)
 Brandenburg Concerto No. 2 (August 13, 1946), (July 9, 1957)
 Brandenburg Concerto No. 4 (August 13, 1945), (July 8, 1957)
 Brandenburg Concerto No. 5 (August 13, 1946), (July 9, 1957)
STRAUSS Don Quixote (August 17, 1953)
STRAVINSKY L'Histoire du soldat: Suite (August 11, 1947)

Stuart Burrows, tenor
BERLIOZ La Damnation de Faust (October 1, 1973)

Monserrat Caballé, soprano
BRAHMS Ein deutsches Requiem (November 25, 1968)

Pasquale Cardillo, basset horn
MOZART Serenade No. 10 in B♭, K. 361 (August 15, 1947)

Richard Cassily, tenor
BEETHOVEN Symphony No. 9 (October 19, 1965)

Jean Cauhapé, viola
BACH Brandenburg Concerto No. 6 (August 14, 1947)

Leslie Chabay, tenor
BERLIOZ Roméo et Juliette (February 22, 1953)

Lili Chookasian, mezzo-soprano
SCHOENBERG Gurrelieder: Song of the Wood Dove (October 19, 1964)
VERDI Requiem (October 5, 1964)
MENOTTI The Death of the Bishop of Brindisi (October 19, 1964)

James David Christie, organ
MAHLER Symphony No. 8 (October 13, 1980)

Katherine Ciesinski, soprano
TCHAIKOVSKY Pique Dame (October 16, 1991)

Gino Cioffi, clarinet
BEETHOVEN The Creatures of Prometheus (October 30, 1967)

David Clatworthy, narrrator
PROKOFIEV Lieutenant Kijé Suite (April 22, 1968)

Van Cliburn, piano
BRAHMS Piano Concerto No. 1 (March 16, 1964)
LISZT Piano Concerto No. 2 (November 21, 1964)
RACHMANINOFF Piano Concerto No. 3 (October 6, 1958)
SCHUMANN Piano Concerto (October 6, 1958)

John Coffee, trombone
STRAVINSKY Octet for Wind Instruments (August 11, 1947)

Vinson Cole, tenor
BERLIOZ Requiem (October 21, 1993)

Norman Cordon, bass
BEETHOVEN "Missa Solemnis" (December 3, 1938)

Dominic Cossa, baritone
SESSIONS When Lilacs Last in the Dooryard Bloom'd (April 23, 1977)

Phyllis Curtin, soprano
BERG Le Vin (April 19, 1965)
   Wozzeck: excerpts (April 23, 1964)
BRITTEN War Requiem (July 23, 1963)
DEBUSSY Le Martyre de St. Sébastien (January 29, 1956)

Suzanne Danco, soprano
BERLIOZ La Damnation de Faust (February 21, 1954)

Judi Dench, speaker
MENDELSSOHN A Midsummer Night's Dream (October 3, 1992)

Mischa Dichter, piano
TCHAIKOVSKY Piano Concerto No. 1 (December 12, 1966)

Nicholas Di Virgilio, tenor
BRITTEN War Requiem (July 23, 1963)
MOZART Requiem (January 19, 1964)

Placido Domingo, tenor
BEETHOVEN Symphony No. 9 (April 21, 1969)

Wiliam Dooley, baritone
WAGNER Lohengrin (August 23, 1965)

Melvyn Douglas, narrator
COPLAND Lincoln Portrait (February 7, 1946)

Jean Dupouy, tenor
BERLIOZ Roméo et Juliette (October 6, 1975)

Doriot Anthony Dwyer, flute
BACH Brandenburg Concerto No. 2 (July 9, 1957)
   Brandenburg Concerto No. 4 (July 8, 1957)
   Brandenburg Concerto No. 5 (July 9, 1957)
BEETHOVEN The Creatures of Prometheus (October 30, 1967)
DEBUSSY Prélude à l'après-midi d'un faune (February 1, 1971)
MARTIN Concerto for Seven Wind Instruments (September 30, 1977)
RAVEL Daphnis et Chloé (May 1, 1989)

Rosalind Elias, mezzo-soprano
BERLIOZ Roméo et Juliette (April 23, 1961)

Sara Mae Endich, soprano
MOZART Requiem (January 19, 1964)

Frank Epstein, percussion
DALLAPICCOLA Canti di prigionia (August 30, 1982)

Christoph Eschenbach, piano
BEETHOVEN Piano Concerto No. 5 "Emperor" (October 9, 1973)

Jules Eskin, cello
BEETHOVEN The Creatures of Prometheus (October 30, 1967)
BERNSTEIN Serenade (October 1, 1994)
BRAHMS Piano Concerto No. 2 (April 19, 1997)
FAURÉ Après un rêve (November 17, 1986)
  Elégie (November 17, 1986)
SAINT-SAËNS Carnival of the Animals (February 15, 1992)
TCHAIKOVSKY Swan Lake (November 11, 1978)

Simon Estes, bass
VERDI Don Carlo: "Ella giammai m'amò . . . Dormirò sol" (July 24, 1966)

David Evitts, bass
STRAVINSKY Oedipus Rex (November 27, 1972), (December 15, 1972)

Keith Falkner, baritone
BACH Saint Matthew Passion (March 26, 1937)

Eileen Farrell, soprano
WAGNER Götterdammerung: Immolation Scene (November 25, 1957)
  Tristan und Isolde: Liebestod (November 25, 1957)

Giora Feidman, clarinet
WILLIAMS Schindler's List (October 19, 1999)

John Ferrante, tenor
STRAUSS Ariadne auf Naxos (January 7, 1969)

Burton Fine, viola
STRAUSS Don Quixote (October 27, 1984)

Everett Firth, timpani
DALLAPICCOLA Canti di prigionia (August 30, 1982)
MARTIN Concerto for Seven Wind Instruments (September 30, 1977)
MARTINŮ Double Concerto (January 14, 1967)
POULENC Organ Concerto (October 9, 1960), (December 2, 1991)

Ezio Flagello, bass
STRAVINSKY Oedipus Rex (November 27, 1972), (December 15, 1972)
VERDI Requiem (October 5, 1964)

Leon Fleisher, piano
BRITTEN Diversions for Piano (left hand) (October 8, 1990)
PROKOFIEV Piano Concerto No. 4 for the left hand (October 15, 1991)
RAVEL Piano Concerto in D (left hand) (October 6, 1990)

Maureen Forrester, contralto
BEETHOVEN Symphony No. 9 (December 21, 1958)
MAHLER Kindertotenlieder (December 28, 1958)
    Lieder eines fahrenden Gesellen (December 29, 1958)
TCHAIKOVSKY Pique Dame (October 16, 1991)

Lukas Foss, piano
BACH Brandenburg Concerto No. 5 (August 13, 1946), (July 9, 1957)

Zino Francescatti, violin
BEETHOVEN Violin Concerto: I. Allegro ma non troppo (April 23, 1954)

Mirella Freni, soprano
TCHAIKOVSKY Pique Dame (October 16, 1991)

John Friebe, tenor
BACH Saint Matthew Passion (March 26, 1937)

Erick Friedman, violin
PROKOFIEV Violin Concerto No. 1 (April 13, 1964)

Thomas Gauger, percussion
DALLAPICCOLA Canti di prigionia (August 30, 1982)

William Gebhardt, French horn
MOZART Serenade No. 10 in B♭, K. 361 (August 15, 1947)

Armando Ghitalla, trumpet
MARTIN Concerto for Seven Wind Instruments (September 30, 1977)
TCHAIKOVSKY Swan Lake (November 11, 1978)

Fernand Gillet, oboe
BACH Brandenburg Concerto No. 2 (August 13, 1946)

Ralph Gomberg, oboe
BACH Brandenburg Concerto No. 2 (July 9, 1957)
IBERT Escales (December 10, 1956)
MARTIN Concerto for Seven Wind Instruments (September 30, 1977)
RAVEL Le Tombeau de Couperin (October 14, 1974)

Benny Goodman, clarinet
MOZART Clarinet Concerto (July 9, 1956)

Rita Gorr, mezzo-soprano
WAGNER Lohengrin (August 23, 1965)

Gary Graffman, piano
BRAHMS Piano Concerto No. 1 (April 9, 1958)
CHOPIN Piano Concerto No. 1 (March 14, 1960)
MENDELSSOHN Capriccio brillant (March 14, 1960)

Susan Graham, mezzo
DEBUSSY La Damoiselle élue (April 19, 1995)

Donald Gramm, bass
BERLIOZ La Damnation de Faust (February 21, 1954)
BERLIOZ L'Enfance du Christ (December 13, 1966)

Håkan Hågegard, baritone
FAURÉ Requiem (March 3, 1994)

Richard Hale, narrator
PROKOFIEV Peter and the Wolf (April 12, 1939)

Julia Hamari, mezzo-soprano
BERLIOZ Roméo et Juliette (October 6, 1975)

Mack Harrell, bass
BEETHOVEN "Missa Solemnis" (April 26, 1938)

Melissa Joan Hart, narrator
BRITTEN The Young Person's Guide to the Orchestra (February 14, 1992)
PROKOFIEV Peter and the Wolf (February 14, 1992)
SAINT-SAËNS Carnival of the Animals (February 15, 1992)

Jascha Heifetz, violin
BEETHOVEN Violin Concerto (November 27, 1955)
BRAHMS Violin Concerto (December 21, 1937), (April 11, 1939)
MENDELSSOHN Violin Concerto (February 23, 1959)
PROKOFIEV Violin Concerto No. 2 (December 20, 1937), (February 24, 1959)

Dennis Helmrich, piano
DALLAPICCOLA Canti di prigionia (August 30, 1982)

Nicole Henriot-Schweitzer, piano
FRANCK Symphonic Variations (August 1, 1965)
d' INDY Symphony on French Mountain Air (March 24, 1958)
PROKOFIEV Piano Concerto No. 2 (February 13, 1957)
RAVEL Concerto in G (March 24, 1958)

Esther Hinds, soprano
SESSIONS When Lilacs Last in the Dooryard Bloom'd (April 23, 1977)

Jerome Hines, bass
WAGNER Lohengrin (August 23, 1965)

Ann Hobson, harp (see **Pilot**)

Frank Hoffmeister, tenor
STRAVINSKY Oedipus Rex (November 27, 1972), (December 15, 1972)

Lorin Hollander, piano
DELLO JOIO Fantasy and Variations (February 17, 1963)
PROKOFIEV Piano Concerto No. 5 (March 28, 1964)
RAVEL Concerto in G (February 16, 1963)

John Holmes, oboe
BACH Brandenburg Concerto No. 1 (August 14, 1947), (August 17, 1949)
MOZART Serenade No. 10 in B♭, K. 361 (August 15, 1947)

Marilyn Horne, mezzo-soprano
MAHLER Symphony No. 2 "Resurrection" (December 13, 1986)

Gwynne Howell, bass
BARTÓK Duke Bluebeard's Castle (November 8, 1980)
MAHLER Symphony No. 8 (October 13, 1980)
WAGNER Die Walküre: Act I: (August 12, 1978)

Lorraine Hunt, mezzo-soprano (see **Lieberson**)

Dmitri Hvorostovsky, baritone
TCHAIKOVSKY Pique Dame (October 16, 1991)

Jorma Hynninen, baritone
STRAUSS Elektra (November 12, 1988)

Byron Janis, piano
RACHMANINOFF Piano Concerto No. 3 (December 29, 1957)

Kiri Te Kanawa, soprano
MAHLER Symphony No. 2 (December 13, 1986)
MAHLER Symphony No. 4 (November 21, 1987)

William Kapell, piano
KHACHATURIAN Piano Concerto (January 1, 1945), (April 19, 1946)

Anna Kaskas, contralto
BEETHOVEN "Missa Solemnis" (December 3, 1938)

Charles Kavalovski, horn
MARTIN Concerto for Seven Wind Instruments (September 30, 1977)
TCHAIKOVSKY Symphony No. 5 (February 16, 1977)

Evgeni Kissin, piano
RACHMANINOFF Piano Concerto No. 3 (January 21, 1992)

Werner Klemperer, speaker
SCHOENBERG Gurrelieder (March 30, 1979)

Leonid Kogan, violin
KHACHATURIAN Violin Concerto (January 12, 1958)
SAINT-SAËNS Havanaise (January 12, 1958)

Stanley Kolk, tenor
ORFF Carmina Burana (November 17, 1969)

René Kollo, tenor
STRAVINSKY Oedipus Rex (November 27, 1972), (December 15, 1972)

Sándor Kónya, tenor
WAGNER Lohengrin (August 23, 1965)

Florence Kopleff, contralto
BERLIOZ L'Enfance du Christ (December 23, 1956), (December 13, 1966)
DEBUSSY Le Martyre de St. Sébastien (January 29, 1956)

Toni Koves-Steiner, cimbalom
KODÁLY Háry János: Suite (April 22, 1965)

Lili Kraus, piano
MOZART Piano Concerto No. 12 in A, K. 414 (April 12, 1953)
    Piano Concerto No. 18 in B♭, K. 456 (April 13, 1953)

Tom Krause, bass
BRITTEN War Requiem (July 23, 1963)
STRAVINSKY Oedipus Rex (November 27, 1972), (December 15, 1972)

Gidon Kremer, violin
GUBAIDULINA Offertorium (April 4, 1988)
SCHUMANN Cello Concerto (arr. for violin) (April 18, 1992)
SHOSTAKOVICH Violin Concerto No. 2 (April 16, 1992)

Alfred Krips, violin
DELIBES Coppélia: Suite (December 2, 1953)
    Sylvia: Suite (December 30, 1953)

Katia and Mariele Labèque, pianos
POULENC Concerto for Two Pianos (April 8, 1989)

Marcel Lafosse, trumpet
STRAVINSKY Octet for Wind Instruments (August 11, 1947)

Jaime Laredo, violin
BACH Brandenburg Concerto No. 1 (July 8, 1957)
BACH Violin Concerto in A Minor, BWV 1041 (December 26, 1960)
MENDELSSOHN Violin Concerto (December 24, 1960)

Jacob Lateiner, piano
CARTER Piano Concerto (January 6, 1967)

Georges Laurent, flute
BACH Brandenburg Concertos No. 2 and 5 (August 13, 1946)

Georges Laurent, flute (continued)
BACH Brandenburg Concerto No. 4 (August 13, 1945)
   Suite No. 2 for Flute and Strings (August 14, 1945)
HANSON Serenade for Solo Flute, Harp, and Strings (November 25, 1947)
STRAVINSKY Octet for Wind Instruments (August 11, 1947)

Fritz Lechner, bass
BACH Saint Matthew Passion (March 26, 1937)

Sergei Leiferkus, baritone
TCHAIKOVSKY Pique Dame (October 16, 1991)

Leo Litwin, piano
SAINT-SAËNS Symphony No. 3 "Organ" (April 5, 1959)

Lorraine Hunt Lieberson, mezzo-soprano
FAURÉ Pelléas et Mélisande: Suite (November 15, 1986)
LIEBERSON Neruda Songs (November 25, 2005)

Liu Shih-kun, piano
LISZT Piano Concerto No. 1 (March 31, 1979)

LiuTeh-hai, pipa
WU Concerto for Pipa and Orchestra (March 31, 1979)

David Lloyd, tenor
BEETHOVEN Symphony No. 9 (August 6, 1947)

George London, bass
MENOTTI The Death of the Bishop of Brindisi (October 19, 1964)

Jeanne Loriod, ondes martenot
MESSIAEN Trois petites liturgies de la Présence Divine (October 7, 1978)

Yvonne Loriod, piano
MESSIAEN Trois petites liturgies de la Présence Divine (October 7, 1978)
   Turangalila-symphonie (rehearsal) (November 28, 1949)

Christa Ludwig, mezzo-soprano
STRAUSS Elektra (November 12, 1988)

Joseph Lukatsky, oboe
BACH Brandenburg Concerto No. 1 (August 14, 1947), (August 17, 1949)

Benjamin Luxon, baritone
MAHLER Symphony No. 8 (October 13, 1980)

Yo-Yo Ma, cello
DVOŘÁK Humoresque in G♭, op. 101, no. 7 (December 16, 1993)
   ` Klid (Silent Woods) (December 16, 1993)
   Slavonic Dance in E Minor, op. 72, no. 2 (December 16, 1993)
SCHOENBERG Cello Concerto after Monn (October 22, 1984)
STRAUSS Don Quixote (October 27, 1984)

John McCollum, tenor
BERLIOZ L'Enfance du Christ (December 13, 1966)

James McCracken, tenor
SCHOENBERG Gurrelieder (March 30, 1979)

Walter Grant MacDonald, French horn
BACH Brandenburg Concerto No. 1 (August 14, 1947), (August 17, 1949)
MOZART Serenade No. 10 in B♭, K. 361 (August 15, 1947)

Donald McIntyre, bass
BERLIOZ La Damnation de Faust (October 1, 1973)

Sylvia McNair, soprano
BRITTEN Les Illuminations (April 8, 1997)
RAVEL Shéhérazade (April 17, 1995)

George Madsen, flute
BACH Brandenburg Concerto No. 4 (August 13, 1945)

Georges Mager, trumpet
STRAVINSKY Octet for Wind Instruments (August 11, 1947)

Evelyn Mandac, soprano
ORFF Carmina Burana (November 17, 1969)

Calvin Marsh, baritone
WAGNER Lohengrin (August 23, 1965)

Jane Marsh, soprano
BEETHOVEN Symphony No. 9 (October 19, 1965), (April 21, 1969)
TCHAIKOVSKY Eugene Onegin: Tatiana's Letter Scene (July 24, 1966)
VERDI Aida: "O patria mia" (July 24, 1966)

João Carlos Martins, piano
GINASTERA Piano Concerto (March 6, 1968)

Ginette Martenot, ondes martenot
MESSIAEN Turangalila-symphonie (rehearsal) (November 28, 1949)

Edith Mathis, soprano
BERLIOZ La Damnation de Faust (October 1, 1973)

Samuel Mayes, cello
FAURÉ Elégie (March 25, 1963)
PISTON Symphony No. 6 (March 12, 1956)
PROKOFIEV Symphony-Concerto, op. 125 (March 25, 1963)
STRAUSS Don Quixote (January 24, 1959)

Dorothy Maynor, soprano
BIZET Carmen: Micaëla's Aria (March 20, 1940)
CHARPENTIER Louise: "Depuis le jour" (March 20, 1940)
MOZART Die Zauberflöte, K. 620: "Ach, Ich fühl's" (November 6, 1939)
HANDEL Semele: "Oh sleep!" (November 6, 1939)

Rosario Mazzeo, clarinet and basset horn
COPLAND El salón México (December 1, 1938) clarinet
MOZART Serenade No. 10 in B♭, K. 361 (August 15, 1947) basset horn

Donald Meaders, baritone
BERLIOZ L'Enfance du Christ (December 13, 1966)

Harold Meek, French horn
MOZART Serenade No. 10 in B♭, K. 361 (August 15, 1947)

Kathryn Meisle, contralto
BACH Saint Matthew Passion (March 26, 1937)
BEETHOVEN "Missa Solemnis" (April 26, 1938)

Susanne Mentzer, reciter
DEBUSSY La Damoiselle élue (October 10, 1983)

Yehudi Menuhin, violin
BRUCH Violin Concerto No. 1 (January 18, 1951)

Sherrill Milnes, baritone
BEETHOVEN Symphony No. 9 (April 21, 1969)
BRAHMS Ein deutsches Requiem (November 25, 1968)
ORFF Carmina Burana (November 17, 1969)
SCHOENBERG A Survivor from Warsaw (April 23, 1969)

Nathan Milstein, violin
TCHAIKOVSKY Violin Concerto (March 29, 1953)

Yvonne Minton, mezzo-soprano
BARTÓK Duke Bluebeard's Castle (November 8, 1980)

Anna Moffo, soprano
RIMSKY-KORSAKOV "Hymn to the Sun" (November 24, 1963)

Georges Moleux, double bass
STRAVINSKY L'Histoire du soldat: Suite (August 11, 1947)

Mac Morgan, baritone
MOZART Requiem (January 19, 1964)

Timothy Morrison, trumpet
WILLIAMS Saving Private Ryan (February 21, 1998)

Victoria Mullova, violin
SIBELIUS Violin Concerto (October 19, 1985)
TCHAIKOVSKY Violin Concerto (October 17, 1985)

Charles Munch, narrator
DEBUSSY Le Martyre de St. Sébastien (January 29, 1956)

Anne-Sophie Mutter, violin
BARTÓK Violin Concerto No. 2 (February 18, 1991)
MORET En rêve (February 16, 1991)
PREVIN Violin Concerto "Anne-Sophie" (October 26, 2002)

Lorna Myers, contralto
MAHLER Symphony No. 8 (October 13, 1980)

Robert Nagy, tenor
STRAUSS Ariadne auf Naxos (January 7, 1969)

Jard van Nes, contralto
BRAHMS Alto Rhapsody (March 15, 1993)

NEXUS Percussion Ensemble
TAKEMITSU From me flows what you call Time (October 19, 1990)

Birgit Nilsson, soprano
VERDI Requiem (October 5, 1964)

Jessye Norman, soprano
BERLIOZ La Mort de Cléopâtre (February 10, 1994)
BRITTEN Phaedra (February 10, 1994)
HAYDN Scena di Berenice (February 10 1994)
MAHLER Kindertotenlieder (December 13, 1988)
    Symphony No. 3 (April 22, 1993)
SCHOENBERG Gurrelieder (March 30, 1979)
WAGNER Die Walküre: Act I (August 12, 1978)

Garrick Ohlsson, piano
SAINT-SAËNS Carnival of the Animals (February 15, 1992)

David Oistrakh, violin
CHAUSSON Poème (December 14, 1955)
SAINT-SAËNS Introduction and Rondo Capriccioso (December 14, 1955)

Seiji Ozawa, narrator (in Japanese)
BRITTEN The Young Person's Guide to the Orchestra (February 14, 1992)
PROKOFIEV Peter and the Wolf (February 14, 1992)
SAINT-SAËNS Carnival of the Animals (February 15, 1992)

Ernst Panenka, bassoon
MOZART Serenade No. 10 in B♭, K. 361 (August 15, 1947)
STRAVINSKY Octet for Wind Instruments (August 11, 1947)

James Pappoutsakis, flute
BACH Brandenburg Concerto No. 4 (July 8, 1957)
SCHULLER Seven Studies on Themes of Paul Klee (November 23, 1964)

Joseph de Pasquale, viola
  BACH Brandenburg Concerto No. 6 (August 14, 1947)
  STRAUSS Don Quixote (August 17, 1953), (January 24, 1959)

Thomas Paul, bass
  BERLIOZ La Damnation de Faust (October 1, 1973)
  BEETHOVEN Symphony No. 9 (October 19, 1965)

James Pease, bass
  BEETHOVEN Symphony No. 9 (August 6, 1947)

Itzhak Perlman, violin
  BARBER Violin Concerto (October 3, 1994)
  BERG Violin Concerto (November 27, 1978)
  BERNSTEIN Serenade (October 1, 1994)
  DVOŘÁK Humoresque in G♭, op. 101, no. 7 (December 16, 1993)
      Romance in F Minor (December 18, 1967), (December 16, 1993)
      Slavonic Dance in E Minor, op. 72, no. 2 (December 16, 1993)
  FOSS Three American Pieces (October 4, 1994)
  KIM Violin Concerto (April 27, 1983)
  PROKOFIEV Violin Concerto No. 2 (December 19, 1966)
  SIBELIUS Violin Concerto (December 21, 1966)
  STARER Violin Concerto (April 27, 1983)
  STRAUSS Don Quixote (October 27, 1984)
  STRAVINSKY Violin Concerto (February 6, 1978)
  TCHAIKOVSKY Violin Concerto (December 18, 1967)
  WILLIAMS Schindler's List (October 19, 1999)

Gregor Piatigorsky, cello
  BLOCH Schelomo (January 30, 1957)
  DVOŘÁK Cello Concerto No. 2 (February 22, 1960)
  STRAUSS Don Quixote (August 17, 1953)
  WALTON Cello Concerto (January 28, 1957)

Boaz Piller, contra-bassoon
  MOZART Serenade No. 10 in B♭, K. 361 (August 15, 1947)

Ann Hobson Pilot, harp
  BERNSTEIN Serenade (October 1, 1994)
  DALLAPICCOLA Canti di prigionia (August 30, 1982)

Daniel Pinkham, organ
  BRITTEN War Requiem (July 23, 1963)

Trevor Pinnock, harpsichord
  POULENC Concert champêtre (November 30, 1991)

Victor Polatschek, clarinet
  MOZART Serenade No. 10 in B♭, K. 361 (August 15, 1947)
  STRAVINSKY L'Histoire du soldat: Suite (August 11, 1947)

David Poleri, tenor
BEETHOVEN Symphony No. 9 (December 21, 1958)
BERLIOZ La Damnation de Faust (February 21, 1954)

Arthur Press, percussion
DALLAPICCOLA Canti di prigionia (August 30, 1982)

Simon Preston, organ
POULENC Organ Concerto (December 2, 1991)

Leontyne Price, soprano
BEETHOVEN Symphony No. 9 (December 21, 1958)
STRAUSS Die Ägyptische Helena: Awakening Scene (April 22, 1965)
Salome: Final scene (April 24, 1965)

John Priebe, tenor
BEETHOVEN "Missa Solemnis" (April 26, 1938), (December 3, 1938)

William Primrose, viola
BERLIOZ Harold in Italy, op. 16 (November 28, 1944), (March 31, 1958)

Florence Quivar, mezzo-soprano
SESSIONS When Lilacs Last in the Dooryard Bloom'd (April 23, 1977)
MAHLER Symphony No. 8 (October 13, 1980)

Andrew Raeburn, speaker
STRAUSS Ariadne auf Naxos (January 7, 1969)

Jacob Raichman, trombone
STRAVINSKY L'Histoire du soldat: Suite (August 11, 1947)
Octet for Wind Instruments (August 11, 1947)

Sviatoslav Richter, piano
BEETHOVEN Piano Concerto No. 1 (November 2, 1960)

John Reardon, baritone
STRAUSS Ariadne auf Naxos (January 7, 1969)

Kenneth Riegel, tenor
LISZT A Faust Symphony (July 26, 1976)
MAHLER Symphony No. 8 (October 13, 1980)

Faye Robinson, soprano
MAHLER Symphony No. 8 (October 13, 1980)

Margaret Roggero, mezzo-soprano
BERLIOZ Roméo et Juliette (February 22, 1953)

Thomas Rolfs, trumpet
WILLIAMS Saving Private Ryan (February 21, 1998)

Eleanor Roosevelt, narrator
PROKOFIEV Peter and the Wolf, (August 11, 1950)

Jerome Rosen, piano
   IVES Symphony No. 4 (February 9, 1976)

Mstislav Rostropovich, cello
   DVOŘÁK Cello Concerto No. 2 (December 2, 1985)
   GLAZUNOV Chant du ménéstrel (August 11, 1975)
   SHOSTAKOVICH Cello Concerto No. 2 (August 11, 1975)
   TCHAIKOVSKY Variations on a Rococo Theme (December 2, 1985)

Artur Rubinstein, piano
   BEETHOVEN Piano Concerto No. 1 (December 20, 1967
      Piano Concerto No. 2 (December 20, 1967)
      Piano Concerto No. 3 (April 5, 1965)
      Piano Concerto No. 4 (April 20, 1964)
      Piano Concerto No. 5 "Emperor" (March 4, 1963)
   BRAHMS Piano Concerto No. 1 (April 21, 1964)
      Piano Concerto No. 2 (August 11, 1952)
   TCHAIKOVSKY Piano Concerto No. 1 (March 5, 1963)

Jesús Maria Sanromá, piano
   STRAVINSKY Capriccio (March 19, 1940)

Deborah Sasson, soprano
   MAHLER Symphony No. 8 (October 13, 1980)

Arlene Saunders, soprano
   MENDELSSOHN A Midsummer Night's Dream (November 29, 1962)

Richard "Gus" Sebring, French horn
   WILLIAMS Saving Private Ryan (February 21, 1998)

Nadine Secunde, soprano
   STRAUSS Elektra (November 12, 1988)

Irmgard Seefried, soprano
   HAYDN The Creation: With Verdure Clad (December 12, 1954)
   STRAUSS Four Lieder (December 12, 1954)

Peter Serkin, piano (see also **TASHI**)
   LIEBERSON Piano Concerto (April 14, 1984)

Rudolf Serkin, piano
   BEETHOVEN Choral Fantasy (October 2, 1982)
      Piano Concerto No. 1 (October 5, 1983)
      Piano Concerto No. 2 (July 3, 1984)
      Piano Concerto No. 3 (October 2, 1982)
      Piano Concerto No. 4 (October 5, 1981)
      Piano Concerto No. 5 "Emperor" (January 24, 1981)

Gil Shaham, violin
WILLIAMS Violin Concerto (October 18, 1999)
Treesong (October 7, 2000)

Harry Shapiro, horn
BACH Brandenburg Concerto No. 1 (July 8, 1957)

Beverly Sills, soprano
STRAUSS Ariadne auf Naxos (January 7, 1969)

Joseph Silverstein, violin
BARTÓK Violin Concerto No. 2 (April 23, 1964)
RIMSKY-KORSAKOV Scheherazade (April 2, 1977)
STRAUSS Also sprach Zarathustra (December 14, 1981)
    Ein Heldenleben (March 9, 1963), (December 14, 1981)
STRAVINSKY Violin Concerto (April 22, 1965)
TCHAIKOVSKY Swan Lake (November 11, 1978)
VAUGHAN WILLIAMS The Lark Ascending (February 16, 1977)
VIVALDI "The Four Seasons" (October 10, 1981)

Léopold Simoneau, tenor
BERLIOZ Requiem (April 26, 1959)

Martial Singher, baritone
BERLIOZ La Damnation de Faust (February 21, 1954)

Carol Smith, contralto
DEBUSSY La Damoiselle élue (April 11, 1955)

Charles Smith, percussion
DALLAPICCOLA Canti di prigionia (August 30, 1982)
STRAVINSKY L'Histoire du soldat: Suite (August 11, 1947)

Malcolm Smith, bass
STRAUSS Ariadne auf Naxos (January 7, 1969)

Gérard Souzay, baritone
BERLIOZ L'Enfance du Christ (December 23, 1956)

Louis Speyer, oboe
BACH Brandenburg Concerto No. 1 (August 14, 1947), (August 17, 1949)
MOZART Serenade No. 10 in B♭, K. 361 (August 15, 1947)

Tossy Spivakovsky, violin
MENOTTI Violin Concerto in A Minor (November 8, 1954)

James Stagliano, French horn
BACH Brandenburg Concerto No. 1 (July 8, 1957)
MAHLER Symphony No. 5 (November 17, 1963)
RAVEL Pavane pour une infante défunte (October 27, 1952), (March 26, 1962)
STRAUSS Ein Heldenleben (March 9, 1963)

Isaac Stern, violin
BEETHOVEN Romances No. 1 and 2 (September 29, 1980)
MENDELSSOHN Violin Concerto (September 29, 1980)

Inga Swensen, narrator
MENDELSSOHN A Midsummer Night's Dream (November 29, 1962)

Yi-Kwei Sze, bass
BERLIOZ Roméo et Juliette (February 22, 1953)

Henryk Szeryng, violin
TCHAIKOVSKY Violin Concerto (February 9, 1959)

TASHI
TAKEMITSU Quatrain (March 29, 1977)

Michael Tilson Thomas, piano
STRAVINSKY Pétrouchka (November 24, 1969)

Giorgio Tozzi, bass
BEETHOVEN Symphony No. 9 (December 21, 1958)
BERLIOZ L'Enfance du Christ (December 23, 1956)
   Roméo et Juliette (April 23, 1961)

Tatiana Troyanos, mezzo-soprano
SCHOENBERG Gurrelieder (March 30, 1979)
STRAVINSKY Oedipus Rex (November 27, 1972), (December 15, 1972)

Veronica Tyler, soprano
MOZART Mass in C Minor, K. 427: "Et incarnatus est" (July 24, 1966)

Mitsuko Uchida, piano
MESSIAEN Oiseaux exotiques (February 23, 1994)

Ragnar Ulfung, tenor
STRAUSS Elektra (November 12, 1988)

Theodore Uppman, baritone
BERLIOZ L'Enfance du Christ (December 13, 1966)

Manuel Valerio, clarinet
DELIBES Coppélia: Suite (December 2, 1953)
MOZART Serenade No. 10 in Bb, K. 361 (August 15, 1947)
STRAVINSKY Octet for Wind Instruments (August 11, 1947)

Willem Valkenier, French horn
BACH Brandenburg Concerto No. 1 (August 14, 1947), (August 17, 1949)
MOZART Serenade No. 10 in Bb, K. 361 (August 15, 1947)

Benita Valente, soprano
STRAUSS Ariadne auf Naxos (January 7, 1969)

Cesare Valleti, tenor
BERLIOZ L'Enfance du Christ (December 23, 1956)
Roméo et Juliette (April 23, 1961)

José Van Dam, bass
BERLIOZ Roméo et Juliette (October 6, 1975)

Helen Vanni, mezzo-soprano
MENDELSSOHN A Midsummer Night's Dream (November 29, 1962)

Joesphine Veasey, mezzo-soprano
BEETHOVEN Symphony No. 9 (April 21, 1969)

Shirley Verrett, mezzo-soprano
MAHLER Symphony No. 3 (October 10, 1966)

Jon Vickers, tenor
WAGNER Die Walküre: Act I (August 12, 1978)

Roger Voisin, trumpet
BACH Brandenburg Concerto No. 2 (August 13, 1946), (July 9, 1957)
MAHLER Symphony No. 5 (November 17, 1963)
SCRIABIN Symphony No. 4 "Poem of Ecstasy" (December 8, 1952)
STRAVINSKY L'Histoire du soldat: Suite (August 11, 1947)

Frederica Von Stade, mezzo-soprano
BERLIOZ Les Nuits d'été (October 17, 1983)
DEBUSSY La Damoiselle élue (October 10, 1983)
DVOŘÁK Rusalka: "O Lovely Moon" (December 16, 1993)
MENDELSSOHN A Midsummer Night's Dream (October 3, 1992)
RAVEL Deux mélodies hébraïques (April 8, 1980)
Cinq mélodies populaires Grecques (April 8, 1980)
Shéhérazade (October 8, 1979)

Jeanette Vreeland, soprano
BACH Saint Matthew Passion (March 26, 1937)
BEETHOVEN "Missa Solemnis" (April 26, 1938), (December 3, 1938)

Michael Wager, narrator
STRAVINSKY Oedipus Rex (November 27, 1972), (December 15, 1972)

Sherman Walt, bassoon
BEETHOVEN The Creatures of Prometheus (October 30, 1967)
MARTIN Concerto for Seven Wind Instruments (September 30, 1977)
MOZART Bassoon Concerto, K. 191 (November 15, 1978)
RAVEL Alborada del gracioso (March 13, 1974)
STRAUSS Duet-Concertino for Clarinet and Bassoon (March 12, 1988)

Claire Watson, soprano
STRAUSS Ariadne auf Naxos (January 7, 1969)

Carl Weinrich, organ
BACH Saint Matthew Passion (March 26, 1937)

Alexis Weissenberg, piano
CHOPIN Piano Concerto No. 1 (April 19, 1986)

Earl Wild, piano
SCHARWENKA Piano Concerto No. 1 (January 20, 1969)

Charles Wilson, piano
MARTINŮ Double Concerto (January 14, 1967)

Ernst Victor Wolff, harpsichord
BACH Saint Matthew Passion (March 26, 1937)

Harold Wright, clarinet
MARTIN Concerto for Seven Wind Instruments (September 30, 1977)
MOZART Clarinet Concerto, K. 622 (November 28, 1978)
STRAUSS Duet-Concertino for Clarinet and Bassoon (March 12, 1988)

Yehudi Wyner, piano
DALLAPICCOLA Canti di prigionia (August 30, 1982)

Frances Yeend, soprano
BEETHOVEN Symphony No. 9 (August 6, 1947)

Berj Zamkochian, organ
MOZART Requiem (January 19, 1964)
POULENC Organ Concerto (October 9, 1960)
SAINT-SAËNS Symphony No. 3 "Organ" (April 5, 1959)

Bernard Zighera, harp and piano
BEETHOVEN The Creatures of Prometheus (October 30, 1967) harp
HANSON Serenade (November 25, 1946) harp
SAINT-SAËNS Symphony No. 3 in C Minor "Organ" (April 5, 1959) piano
TCHAIKOVSKY Swan Lake (November 11, 1978) harp

Krystian Zimerman, piano
LISZT Piano Concerto No. 1 (April 27, 1987)
    Piano Concerto No. 2 (April 25, 1987)
    Totentanz (April 25, 1987)
RACHMANINOFF Piano Concerto No. 1 (December 6, 1997)
    Piano Concerto No. 2 (December 2, 2000)

Paul Zukofsky, violin
SCHUMAN Violin Concerto (October 5, 1970)

Appendix D: Two-Track Tapes

People collect recordings for many reasons. Listening to them is, of course, the primary one, but there are many ways to listen and many things to hear. Among collectors of classical music on records, audiophiles form a highly committed sector. Many of RCA's stereo recordings of the Boston Symphony, particularly those made in Charles Munch's era, rank high among audiophile treasures. RCA "Shaded Dog" LPs from the late 1950s remain collector favorites to this day, yet two-track, 7.5-ips reel-to-reel tapes are the most valued of all. New recordings were issued on these tapes from about 1954 to 1958 and were their initial stereo releases. RCA began marketing stereo LPs in 1958, and new recordings were no longer issued on two-track tape, although the earlier ones remained in the catalogue for several years. Four-track, reel-to-reel tape became the more widely accepted format, but audiophiles were not convinced. Because the tape tracks were only half as wide and less care was taking in their production, the four-track tapes seldom achieved a comparable quality of sound (Lawrence H. Jones, email September 2007).

This appendix lists all BSO two-track, reel-to-reel tapes recorded and issued by RCA Victor. The first character of the prefix is an indication of cost: "A" indicates the lower end of the price scale, originally $6.95, and the scale runs up to "G" for the most expensive, $18.95. The few monaural-only issues were slightly less expensive than the stereos. Although there is one exception, the price varied with the length of the program, and thus the amount of tape used. The second character is a "C" for classical, and a final "S" indicates stereo. Soloists and conductors are listed; dates direct the reader to entries in the main section of this book, where greater discographic detail may be found.

BC-3 (monaural)
STRAUSS: *Don Quixote* (Piatigorsky, Munch), August 17, 1953

GCS-5
TCHAIKOVSKY Symphony No. 6 (Monteux), January 26, 1955

CC-6. TC-6 (monaural)
BRAHMS Piano Concerto No. 2 (Rubinstein, Munch), August 11, 1952. *Lawrence H. Jones reports (email, September 28, 2007) that the two incarnations use tape stock of differing thickness.*

GCS-6
BERLIOZ *Symphonie fantastique* (Munch), November 14, 1954

ECS-7
BEETHOVEN Symphony No. 5 (Munch), May 2, 1955

CCS-12
DEBUSSY Nocturnes for Orchestra (Monteux), August 15, 1955

CCS-13
SCHUBERT Symphony No. 8 "Unfinished" (Munch), May 2, 1955

FCS-14
BRAHMS Symphony No. 2 (Munch), December 5, 1955

CCS-16
CHAUSSON *Poème* (Heifetz, Munch), December 14, 1955
SAINT-SAËNS Introduction and Rondo Capriccioso (Heifetz, Munch), December 14, 1955

AC-21 (monaural). Also issued in stereo, on CCS-36.
RAVEL *La Valse* (Munch), December 5, 1955
RAVEL *Rapsodie espagnole* (Munch), January 23, 1956

CCS-21
RAVEL *Boléro* (Munch), January 23, 1956
DEBUSSY *Prélude à l'après-midi d'un faune* (Munch), January 23, 1956

BCS-22
TCHAIKOVSKY *Romeo and Juliet* (Munch), March 12, 1956

AC-23 (monaural)
SAINT-SAËNS Piano Concerto No. 4 (Brailovsky, Munch), November 24, 1954

FCS-24
BEETHOVEN Violin Concerto (Heifetz, Munch), November 27, 1955

CC-30 (monaural)
DELIBES: *Coppélia:* **Suite** (Monteux), December 2, 1953
DELIBES: *Sylvia:* **Suite** (Monteux), December 30, 1953

CCS-36 (Also: AC-21, monaural)
RAVEL *La Valse* (Munch), December 5, 1955
RAVEL *Rapsodie espagnole* (Munch), January 23, 1956

DCS-39
MOZART Clarinet Concerto (Goodman, Munch), July 9, 1956

GCS-42
BRAHMS Symphony No. 1 (Munch), November 19, 1956

BCS-48
BEETHOVEN *Leonore Overture No. 3* (Munch), February 27, 1956
BEETHOVEN *Coriolan Overture* (Munch), February 26, 1956

DCS-51
TCHAIKOVSKY *Francesca da Rimini* (Munch), April 23, 1956

BCS-55
WAGNER *Tannhäuser:* Overture and Venusberg Music (Munch),
    April 1, 1957

CCS-56
DEBUSSY *La Mer* (Munch), December 9, 1956

ACS-57
IBERT *Escales* (Munch), December 10, 1956

ECS-58
FRANCK Symphony in D Minor (Munch), March 11, 1957

CCS-66
TCHAIKOVSKY Serenade for Strings (Munch), March 13, 1957

ACS-92
WAGNER *Die Walküre: Magic Fire Music* (Munch), April 1, 1957
WAGNER *Götterdammerung: Siegfried's Rhine Journey* (Munch),
    April 1, 1957

BCS-139
BARBER Adagio for Strings (Munch), April 3, 1957
ELGAR Introduction and Allegro (Munch), April 3, 1957

ACS-147
BARBER *Medea's Meditation and Dance* (Munch), April 10, 1957

Appendix E: Video Recordings

The video entries from the main section of this discography are repeated here in their entirety, so that they may be more easily located and studied.

CONCERT VIDEO (80 minutes)
BRAHMS *Tragic Overture*, op. 81 (13:16)
HINDEMITH *Noblissma Visione* (20:00)
STRAVINSKY *Pétrouchka* (34:09)
BSO, conductor Pierre Monteux
January 20, 1959. Sanders Theater (live telecast)
BSO and WGBH Educational Foundation, producer Jordan M. Whitelaw. Produced for DVD by Alan Altman
DVD: Video Artists International VAI-4316 (black and white, monaural)

CONCERT VIDEO (94 minutes)
BARBIROLLI *An Elizabethan Suite* (11:57). Arranged from works in *The Fitzwilliam Virginal Book*, a collection of early 17th-century English compositions: William Byrd's *Earl of Salisbury's Pavane*, the anonymous *The Irish Ho Hoane*, Giles Farnaby's *A Toye*, and John Bull's *The King's Hunt*.
DELIUS *A Village Romeo and Juliet*: **The Walk to the Paradise Garden** (10:08)
WALTON Partita for Orchestra (15:26)
BRAHMS Symphony No. 2 in D, op. 73 (38:50)
BSO, conductor John Barbirolli
February 3, 1959. Sanders Theater (live telecast)
BSO and WGBH Educational Foundation, producer Jordan M. Whitelaw. Produced for DVD by Alan Altman
DVD: Video Artists International VAI-4304 (black and white, monaural). *An alternative soundtrack is offered, a stereo broadcast of the same program from Symphony Hall on January 31, 1959. The sound is very much better, but the audio is no longer synchronized with the video; e.g. the Brahms finale ends 27 seconds later in Symphony Hall than in Sanders Theater.*

219

CONCERT VIDEO (66:45)
HAYASHI *Kimi Ga Yo* (Japanese National Anthem) (1:19)
SMITH *The Star-Spangled Banner* (1:25)
BEETHOVEN Symphony No. 3 in E♭, op. 55 "Eroica" (45:53)
RAVEL *Daphnis et Chloé*: Suite No. 2 (15:27)
BSO, conductor Charles Munch
May 4, 1960. NHK Hall, Uchisaiwai-cho Tokyo (live telecast)
NHK Classical, producer Jean-Philippe Schweitzer
DVD: NHK NSDS-9486 (black and white, stereo) Japan. *After the concert comes an eight-minute black-and-white silent newsreel film of the BSO's arrival in Japan.*

CONCERT VIDEO (96 minutes)
BERLIOZ *Symphonie fantastique*, op. 14 (45:38)
DEBUSSY *La Mer* (24:30)
RAVEL *Daphnis et Chloé:* Suite No. 2 (16:03)
BSO, conductor Charles Munch
April 17, 1962. Sanders Theater (live telecast)
BSO and WGBH Educational Foundation, producer Raymond Edwards
DVD: Video Artists International VAI-4317 (black and white, monaural)

CONCERT VIDEO (89 minutes)
BRITTEN War Requiem, op. 66 (80:22). *American premiere.*
BSO, conductor Erich Leinsdorf
Phyllis Curtin, soprano; Nicholas Di Virgilio, tenor; Tom Krause, bass; Chorus Pro Musica, Alfred Nash Patterson, dir.; Columbus Boychoir, Donald Bryant, dir.; Daniel Pinkham, portative organ
July 23, 1963. Koussevitzky Music Shed, Tanglewood (live telecast)
BSO and WGBH Educational Foundation, producer Jordan M. Whitelaw. Produced for DVD by Allan Altman
DVD: Video Artists International VAI-4429 (black and white, stereo)

CONCERT VIDEO COLLECTION (107 minutes)
WAGNER *Götterdämmerung:* Dawn and Siegfried's Rhine Journey (11:48)
WAGNER *Siegfried Idyll* (17:45)
BEETHOVEN Symphony No. 9 in D Minor, op. 125 "Choral" (67:24)
BSO, conductor Erich Leinsdorf
Jane Marsh, soprano; Eunice Alberts, mezzo soprano; Richard Cassilly, tenor; Thomas Paul, bass; Harvard Glee Club and Radcliffe Choral Society, Elliot Forbes, dir.; NECC, Lorna DeVaron, dir.
October 19, 1965 (Beethoven). December 14, 1965 (Wagner). Symphony Hall (live telecasts)
BSO and WGBH Educational Foundation, producer Jordan M. Whitelaw
DVD: Video Artists International VAI-4361 (black and white, monaural)

CONCERT VIDEO (107:46)
BERLIOZ *L'Enfance du Christ*, op. 25 (Part I: 41:53. Parts II and II: 51:56)
BSO, conductor Charles Munch
Florence Kopleff, contralto; John McCollum, tenor; Theodore Uppman, baritone; Donald Gramm, bass-baritone; Donald Meaders, baritone; Harvard Glee Club and Radcliffe Choral Society, Elliot Forbes, dir.
December 13, 1966. Symphony Hall (live telecast)
BSO and WGBH Educational Foundation, producer Jordan M. Whitelaw. Produced for DVD by Raymond Edwards
DVD: Video Artists International VAI-4303 (black and white, stereo)

CONCERT VIDEO (94 minutes)
R. STRAUSS *Ariadne auf Naxos* (original 1912 version) (81:07)
BSO, conductor Erich Leinsdorf
Claire Watson (Ariadne); Beverly Sills (Zerbinetta); Robert Nagy (Bacchus); John Reardon (Harlekin); Benita Valente (Najade); Eunice Alberts (Dryade); Carole Bogarde (Echo); Malcolm Smith (Truffaldin); John Ferrante (Brighella); James Billings (Scaramuccio); Andrew Raeburn (M. Jordain)
Jamuary 7, 1969. Symphony Hall (live telecast)
BSO and WGBH Educational Foundation, producer Jordan M. Whitelaw. Produced for DVD by Allan Altman
DVD: Video Artists International VAI-4363 (color, monaural).

CONCERT VIDEO (86 minutes)
BRAHMS Symphony No. 2 in D, op.73 (40:53)
BRAHMS Symphony No. 4 in E Minor, op. 98 (41:42)
BSO, conductor Leonard Bernstein
August 22, 1972; August 25, 1972. Koussevitzky Music Shed, Tanglewood
Unitel GmbH and Amberson, producer John McClure, director Robert Englander
DVDs: Medici Arts 2072138. *Bonus film:* Bernstein at Tanglewood.

VIDEO COLLECTION: "The Unanswered Question"

These performances were videotaped to accompany the six Charles Eliot Norton Lectures given by Leonard Bernstein at Harvard in 1973.

STRAVINSKY: *Oedipus Rex* **(53:30)**

Tatiana Troyanos, mezzo-soprano (Jocasta); René Kollo, tenor (Oedipus); Frank Hoffmeister, tenor (Shepherd); Tom Krause, bass (Creon); Ezio Flagello, bass (Tiresias); David Evitts, bass (Messenger); Michael Wager (narrator); Harvard Glee Club, F. John Adams, dir.

MOZART: Symphony No. 40 in G Minor, K. 550 (30:56)

BEETHOVEN: Symphony No. 6 in F, op. 68 "Pastoral" (45:30)

BERLIOZ: *Roméo et Juliette,* **op. 17:** *Romeo Alone***;** *The Ball at the Capulets* **(12:43)**

WAGNER: *Tristan und Isolde: Prelude and Liebestod* **(20:21)**

DEBUSSY: *Prélude à l'après-midi d'un faune* **(11:10)**

RAVEL: *Rapsodie espagnole***: IV.** *Feria* **(6:33)**

IVES: *The Unanswered Question* **(5:11)** *Bernstein gives a running commentary during Ives's music.*

BSO, conducted by Leonard Bernstein

November 27, 1972, December 11, 1972 and December 12, 1972. WGBH Television Studio, Boston

Amberson Video, Inc. Producer John McClure

VHS: Kultur 1451 (6). **DVD:** Kultur D-1570 (3) *Both sets contain the complete Norton Lectures, including other music performed by the Vienna Philharmonic. "After each lecture had been delivered, a somewhat altered version of it was re-delivered the following night in a television studio, and committed to video tape." (Leonard Bernstein:* The Unanswered Question: Six Talks at Harvard. *Harvard University Press. 1976). The music was recorded on videotape months before the lectures began on October 9, 1973. The lectures were also published in audio form on Columbia LPs, where these performances were replaced by Bernstein's Columbia recordings with the New York Philharmonic. The exception is Stravinsky's* Oedipus Rex, *which the BSO recorded for Columbia (see the next entry in main section).*

LISZT, Franz

A Faust Symphony **(CD: 77:01 / DVD: 81:00)**

BSO, conductor Leonard Bernstein

Kenneth Riegel, tenor; TFC, John Oliver, dir.

July 26, 1976; July 27, 1976. Symphony Hall (live)

Audio recording: Deutsche Grammophon, producer Thomas W. Mowrey

Video recording: Amberson Video, Inc., producer David Griffiths

LP: 2707 100 (2). 415 009-1. **CD:** 431 470-2. 447 449-2. **DVD:** Euroarts 2072078. *The recordings were made simultaneously, except that the first day's audio session ran 70 minutes longer than the live performance. The first movement runs 25 seconds longer on the video recording than on the audio. The overall four-minute difference cited above also reflects the credits on the DVD, plus longer pauses between movements than on the CD.*

CONCERT VIDEO (84:42)
BRAHMS Symphony No. 1 in C Minor, op. 68 (46:43)
R. STRAUSS *Also sprach Zarathustra*, op. 30 (37:15)
BSO, conductor Seiji Ozawa
March 1, 1986. Festival Hall, Osaka, Japan (live)
Sony, producer Takuro Uno
Laserdiscs: SLV-46378. **DVDs:** Parnassus PDVD-198

TAKEMITSU, TORU
From me flows what you call Time, for five percussionists and orchestra. *World premiere.*
BSO, conductor Seiji Ozawa
NEXUS percussion ensemble (Bob Becker, William Cahn, Robin Engelman, Russell Hartenberger , John Wyre)
October 19, 1990. Carnegie Hall, New York (live)
Sony BMG Masterworks.
DVD: Kultur D4179. *The payment sheet for this session says "Audio-Visual material included in a 1994 French documentary film* Music for the Movies: Toru Takemitsu. *But the BSO material was not used in the film, at least as presented on the DVD.*

COLLECTION: "DVOŘÁK IN PRAGUE: A CELEBRATION"
Timings run longer on the videos than on the CD due to applause.
***Carnival Overture*, op. 92 (9:32/9:59)**
***Humoresque in G♭*, op. 101, No. 7** (arr. Oskar Morawetz) **(3:32/4:30)**
   Itzhak Perlman, violin; Yo-Yo Ma, cello (**CD:** SK-92828. SK-93072)
***Slavonic Dance in E Minor*, op. 72, no. 2** (arr. Oskar Morawetz) **(5:01/5:29)**
   Itzhak Perlman, violin; Yo-Yo Ma, cello (**CD:** SK-92828)
***Slavonic Dance in C*, op. 72, no. 7 (3:33/4:11)**
***Klid (Silent Woods)*, op. 68, no. 5 (6:20/7:54)**
   Yo-Yo Ma, cello (**CD:** SK-92828. SK-93072)
***Romance in F Minor*, op. 11 (11:28/12:18)**
   Itzhak Perlman, violin
***Rusalka*, op. 114: "O Lovely Moon" (6:55/7:28)**
   Frederica Von Stade, mezzo-soprano
Psalm 149 for Chorus and Orchestra, op. 79 (9:00/9:39)
   Prague Philharmonic Chorus, Jaroslav Brych, dir.
Symphony No. 9 in E Minor, op. 95 "from the New World": II. Largo (12:39). *This selection is not on the CD.*
BSO, Conductor Seiji Ozawa
December 16, 1993. Smetana Hall, Prague (live)
Sony Classical, producer Thomas Frost
CD: SK 46687. **LASER DISC:** SLV-53488. **VHS:** SHV-53488. *There are additional works on the CD and the videos which do not involve the BSO.*

Appendix F: Government Issues

During World War II, various branches of the United States government issued recordings by the Boston Symphony, for consumption by members of the armed forces or for radio broadcasts in other countries. Although the BSO was not paid directly for these recordings, their manufacture and distribution were accepted by all, initially as part of the "war effort" during World War II, and later as a contribution to America's relations with the rest of the world. These records were usually taken from radio broadcasts, but a few merely duplicated commercial releases. The government discs were never available for sale to the public and were distributed outside the United States. They were not supposed to be returned to the States; nevertheless, many were brought home, and copies exist in many libraries and archives today, as well as in private collections. Among them are many unique recordings, making them an essential part of both American and BSO history. The data presented in this appendix have been gathered from a wide range of sources; although far from complete, we hope they may add up to a critical mass for future research. Simplified titles are used for repertory works throughout this appendix, as are abbreviations when their meaning is obvious.

V-Discs

At the beginning of America's participation in World War II (1941-1946), most 78-rpm phonograph records sent to American servicemen arrived in pieces. Recognizing this, the U.S. military developed a program to record music on unbreakable materials: Vinylite, Formvar, and Alvar. Pressed by commercial record companies, they were called V-Discs, after Winston Churchill's famous "V for Victory" sign; over eight million of them were distributed. Those by the Boston Symphony Orchestra are listed here. Some were taken from the Blue Network's Saturday evening radio series "Theater of the Air." Others were taken from commercial RCA Victor records. The information is based on Richard S. Sears's *V-Discs: A History and Discography* (Greenwood Press, 1980) and on discs and concert programs held in the Boston Symphony Archives. The 12-inch

V-Discs played a few minutes longer than their commercial 78-rpm counter-parts; side 3 of the Shostakovich Ninth Symphony runs 6 minutes, 35 seconds. Listed timings may include the spoken introductions which appear on some V-Discs. Master numbers denote individual V-Disc producers; serial numbers carry coded information from the pressing company, usually RCA Victor. Each monthly (later, bi-monthly) release consisted of up to 30 records, of which one selection was often classical. Releases were assigned alphabetic designations, from A to Z, then AA to ZZ, and finally AAA through FFF.

BERLIOZ, HECTOR
La Damnation de Faust: Rákóczy March (3:51)
BSO, conductor Serge Koussevitzky
May 8, 1936. Symphony Hall
Victor Records, producer Charles O'Connell
Master VP 444. Serial D4MC 13
V-Disc 153, side A (F release). *From RCA Victor 11-9232; see main listing.*

SCHUBERT, FRANZ
Rosamunde: Ballet Music (3:52)
BSO, conductor Serge Koussevitzky
May 8, 1936. Symphony Hall
Victor Records, producer Charles O'Connell
Master VP 445. Serial D4MC 14
V-Disc 153, side B (F release). *From RCA Victor 14199; see main listing.*

COPLAND, AARON
El salón México (11:10)
BSO, conductor Serge Koussevitzky
May 8, 1936. Symphony Hall
Victor Records, producer Charles O'Connell
Master JB 372/374. Serial 028864/66
V-Discs CL-13/14. Not released. *From RCA Victor 15363/4; see main listing.*

SCHUMAN, WILLIAM
Prayer in Time of War (12:58)
BSO, conductor Serge Koussevitzky
October 6, 1944. Blue network broadcast from Symphony Hall
Master JDB 247/249. Serial D6TC 6174/76
V-Discs CL 3/4. Not released. *See Armed Forces Radio Services BSO 54, below.*

FOOTE, ARTHUR
Suite in E Major for Strings, op. 63 (13:33)
BSO, conductor Serge Koussevitzky
October 14, 1944. Blue network broadcast from Symphony Hall
Master JDB 310/312. Serial D6TC 6490/92
V-Discs CL 8/9. Not released. *See Armed Forces Radio Services BSO 49, below.*

STRAUSS, RICHARD
Salome: Dance of the Seven Veils (9:13)
BSO, conductor Fritz Reiner
December 22, 1945. ABC broadcast from Symphony Hall
Master JDB 35/36. Serial D6TC 5068/69
V-Disc 636 (GG release). Also issued on CDs: Naxos 8.111014/15 (2)

SHOSTAKOVICH, DMITRI
Symphony No. 9 (30:51)
BSO, conductor Serge Koussevitzky
August 10, 1946. ABC broadcast from Symphony Hall
Master JDB 236/240. Serial D6TC 6152/56
V-Discs 716-718 (NN release). *See note about this symphony in the entry for the RCA Victor recording (November 4, 1946).*

Armed Forces Radio Services

During and after World War II, many radio programs were rebroadcast to American servicemen in Europe and in Asia, including weekly concerts of the Boston Symphony. A letter from "Somewhere in the Philippines" captures the importance and the success of this endeavor. It was printed in the BSO program booklet for concerts of March 29 and 31, 1945, and is quoted in part:

MY DEAR DR. KOUSSEVITZKY:
. . .Tonight there were no comfortable chairs, no fine acoustics, nothing of the magnetism of a personal appearance, not even the aid which a fine amplifying system can give. A poker game, numerous incidental conversations, the noise of native children on one side and of some huge mechanical contrivance on the other, the rumble of jeeps on our corduroy roads, the enervating heat, and the sifting of dust through all, could scarcely lessen my absorption in the enjoyment of perfect music.
Here, by means of a cheap Aussie radio, here in this dirty tent, was a shining hour, a concert by the Boston Symphony. More than ten thousand miles from Boston, after more than fifteen months from home, after duty in New Guinea and the Philippines, here was something beautifully familiar.
What ever music may mean to us in Massachusetts or Rhode Island or New York, here in the tropics it is a breath of peace, a hope of home, an hour's furlough from heat and dirt. . . .
Very sincerely yours
ARTHUR B. LOGAN
Lieutenant USNR

These generally hour-long radio programs seldom contained all of the music performed at a concert. The strict one-hour limit led to several discrepancies that would not be thought acceptable today: Beethoven's Ninth was broadcast without its choral finale, and—on at least one occasion (Foote's Suite for Strings, on October 14, 1944)—tempos were radically altered. BSO concerts were not often planned with the one-hour broadcast in mind, so the fit could be awkward, some broadcasts fading out in mid-movement. Armed Forces Radio Services, established by the War Department on May 6, 1942, recorded these broadcasts on 33⅓-rpm, 16-inch glass-based (after July 1945, aluminum-based) acetate discs, also called lacquers. Copies were then pressed on vinyl by commercial record companies (usually RCA Victor) for shipment overseas. As with V-Discs, these were not distributed in the United States, and they were not supposed to be returned thereto. Nevertheless, sizable collections exist today at the Library of Congress and the New York Public Library.

These AFRS recordings encompass the majority of BSO broadcast concerts from December 26, 1942, to April 15, 1947, and possibly beyond. Broadcast announcements, usually brief, are included on the records. Many of these AFRS recordings were sources for later pirate issues, which are documented in Appendix I. This list has been prepared from several sources, primarily: (1) *Boston Symphony Orchestra Radio Broadcast and Privately Made Recordings 1935-1950* (unpublished), prepared by Edward D. Young; (2) the finder listing for The Armed Forces Radio Service Collection in the Rodgers and Hammerstein Archives of Recorded Sound at the New York Public Library; (3) data received from the Library of Congress; and (4) discs in the Boston Symphony Archives.

Each broadcast was recorded using two turntables, so there would be no break in the music, on both sides of multiple discs—for example, parts 1 and 3 on one record, parts 2 and 4 on another. The sides ran from about 5 to 15 minutes each, depending on the music, using the outer grooves of the large discs. Each broadcast was assigned a "Boston Symphony Orchestra Program number" based on the chronology of broadcasts. A few summer concerts at Tanglewood are out of sequence, at least one set is a compilation of items from earlier broadcasts, and a few are performances by other orchestras, despite the BSO series title. These broadcasts were on Saturday evenings; the notation "Premiere" means that the first performance of a work was given the day before, at the Friday concert. During the 1946–1947 season, broadcasts switched to Tuesday concerts. Beginning on November 11, 1944, Voice of America discs often duplicate those of the AFRS; but VOA discs sometimes mixed works from more than one broadcast concert, so any attempt to correlate AFRS and VOS discs would be dubious at best.

Entries in *italics* are extrapolations; that is, the concert, and these works, were broadcast on that date, but we have not been able to establish the existence of the corresponding AFRS discs. Not every broadcast is listed, only those which are likely to fit into the AFRS BSO series. ***Bold italics*** indicate that transcription discs—which may or may not be AFRS discs—of this broadcast are held in the Library of Congress. The library has a not-yet-catalogued collection of over 200,000 AFRS acetate discs (Edward D. Young), which may include the complete BSO series.

The earliest AFRS BSO program we have encountered is No. 30, the concert on January 1, 1944. This implies a previous 29 in the series; it also suggests that few copies were produced and distributed that first year. Young lists the following 26 BSO broadcasts from December 26, 1942, to December 25, 1943:

December 26, 1942. Serge Koussevitzky
PROKOFIEV Classical Symphony
BEETHOVEN Symphony No. 5

January 2, 1943. Serge Koussevitzky
RIMSKY-KORSAKOV Le Coq d'or: Introduction and Wedding March
MUSSORGSKY Khovanshchina: Prelude "Dawn on the Moskva River"
SHOSTAKOVICH Symphony No. 6

January 16, 1943. Richard Burgin
RESPIGHI Old Dances and Airs
R. STRAUSS Don Quixote (Jean Bedetti, cello; Jean Lefranc, viola)

January 23, 1943. Richard Burgin
HINDEMITH Noblissima Visione
RUSSELL BENNETT Sights and Sounds
TCHAIKOVSKY Romeo and Juliet

January 30, 1943. George Szell
SCHUBERT Symphony No. 9 in C

February 6, 1943. Serge Koussevitzky
MENDELSSOHN Symphony No. 4 "Italian"
DEBUSSY La Mer

February 20, 1943. Serge Koussevitzky
VAUGHAN WILLIAMS Fantasia on a Theme by Thomas Tallis
SCHUMANN Symphony No. 1 "Spring"

February 27, 1943. Serge Koussevitzky
Pierre DEGEYTEV Internationale (for the 25th anniversary of the Red Army)
John Stafford SMITH The Star-Spangled Banner
Edward Burlingame HILL Symphony No. 1 in B♭, op. 34
HARRIS Symphony No. 5 (Premiere)

March 6, 1943. Serge Koussevitzky
HANDEL Concerto Grosso in D Minor, op. 6, No. 10
BEETHOVEN Symphony No. 4

March 20, 1943. Richard Burgin
HAYDN Symphony No. 95
Vladimir DUKELSKY Violin Concerto in G Minor (Ruth Posselt)
Ruth Posselt appeared as violin soloist with the BSO under several conductors;
she was the wife of concertmaster/assist conductor Richard Burgin.

March 27, 1943. Serge Koussevitzky
William SCHUMAN A Free Song (Harvard/Radcliffe Choruses). Premiere
SIBELIUS Symphony No. 5

April 10, 1943. Serge Koussevitzky
BACH Two Preludes
MOZART Piano Concerto No. 9 in E♭, K. 271 (Emma Boynet)
COPLAND Lincoln Portrait (Will Geer, speaker). Incomplete

April 17, 1943. Serge Koussevitzky
BACH Brandenburg Concerto No. 3
BRAHMS Variations on a Theme by Haydn
R. STRAUSS Don Juan

April 24, 1943. Serge Koussevitzky
HANDEL Organ Concerto No. 10 in D Minor (E. Power Biggs)
SCHUBERT Symphony No. 8 "Unfinished"
WAGNER Parsifal: Prelude

May 1, 1943. Serge Koussevitzky
LIADOV From the Apocalypse
BRAHMS Symphony No. 4

October 9, 1943. Serge Koussevitzky
VIVALDI Concerto Grosso in D Minor, op. 3, No. 11
STRAVINSKY Ode (Premiere)
MUSSORGSKY/RAVEL Pictures at an Exhibition

October 16, 1943. Serge Koussevitzky
BERLIOZ Symphonie fantastique

October 23, 1943. Serge Koussevitzky
MOZART Serenade in G, K. 525 "Eine kleine Nachtmusik"
BEETHOVEN Symphony No. 6 "Pastoral"

October 30, 1943. Serge Koussevitzky
PISTON Prelude and Allegro for Organ and Strings (E. Power Biggs). Premiere
BARBER Commando March
KHACHATURIAN Piano Concerto (William Kapell)

November 6, 1943. Serge Koussevitzky
TCHAIKOVSKY Symphony No. 5

November 13, 1943. Serge Koussevitzky
William SCHUMAN Symphony No. 5 for Strings (Premiere)
SHOSTAKOVICH Symphony No. 1

November 27, 1943. Richard Burgin
BACH/SCHOENBERG Prelude and Fugue in E♭
BEETHOVEN Symphony No. 2

December 4, 1943. Richard Burgin
MAHLER Das Lied von der Erde (Jennie Tourel, mezzo; Hans J. Heinz, tenor)

December 11, 1943. Serge Koussevitzky
BRAHMS Symphony No. 2

December 18, 1943. Serge Koussevitzky
HAYDN Symphony No. 88
MOZART Symphony No. 39

December 25, 1943. Serge Koussevitzky
HANDEL Concerto Grosso, op. 6, no. 12
SIBELIUS Symphony No. 5

Armed Forces Radio Services Boston Symphony Orchestra Program No. 30
January 1, 1944. Serge Koussevitzky
C. P. E. BACH Concerto in D for Strings (arr. Maximilian Steinberg)
MARTINŮ Violin Concerto (Mischa Elman). Premiere

AFRS BSO 31? January 8, 1944. Serge Koussevitzky
MUSSORGSKY Khovanshchina: Prelude "Dawn on the Moskva River"
BEETHOVEN Symphony No. 7

AFRS BSO 32. January 15, 1944. Igor Stravinsky
STRAVINSKY Symphony in C
STRAVINSKY Four Norwegian Moods (Premiere)
STRAVINSKY Circus Polka

AFRS BSO 33. January 22, 1944. Vladimir Golschmann
BEETHOVEN Symphony No. 3 "Eroica"

AFRS BSO 34. January 29, 1944. Vladimir Golschmann
MOZART Le Nozze di Figaro: Overture
MOZART Symphony 41 "Jupiter"
MILHAUD Suite Provençal
MOZART Eine kleine Nachtmusik (incomplete). The announcer says "This
    broadcast of the Boston Symphony Orchestra is a presentation of the Armed
    Forces Radio Service" over the music of the second movement. The music
    is faded out a minute or so later, and the record comes to an end.

AFRS BSO 35. February 5, 1944. Serge Koussevitzky
BEETHOVEN Leonore Overture No. 3
BRAHMS Symphony No. 3

AFRS BSO 36. February 12, 1944. Serge Koussevitzky
SCHUBERT Symphony No. 8 "Unfinished"
COPLAND Lincoln Portrait (Will Geer, speaker)
BARBER Commando March
SOUSA The Stars and Stripes Forever

AFRS BSO 37. February 19, 1944. Serge Koussevitzky
Henri RABAUD La Procession nocturne
SCHUMANN Symphony No. 3 "Rhenish"

AFRS BSO 38? February 26, 1944. Serge Koussevitzky
Alexander GRETCHANINOFF Ecumenical Mass, op. 142 (Premiere). Maria
    Kurenko, Dorothy Cornish, Roland Hayes, Robert Hall Collins; Cecilia
    Society and Apollo Club Choruses; E. Power Biggs, organ

AFRS BSO 39. March 4, 1944. Serge Koussevitzky
MOZART Symphony No. 29
BARBER Symphony No. 2 (Premiere)

AFRS BSO 40. March 11, 1944. Serge Koussevitzky
RIMSKY-KORSAKOV Le Coq d'or: Introduction and Wedding March
DEBUSSY Nocturnes: Nuages, Fêtes
TCHAIKOVSKY Francesca da Rimini

AFRS BSO 41. March 18, 1944. Serge Koussevitzky
RIMSKY-KORSAKOV Dubinuska (arrangement of a Russian folk song)
RIMSKY-KORSAKOV Scheherazade

AFRS BSO 42? March 25, 1944. Andre Kostelanetz
KABALEVSKY Colas Breugnon: Overture
CRESTON Frontiers
GRÉTRY Zémire et Azor: "La Fauvette avec ses petits" (Lily Pons, soprano)
STRAVINSKY The Firebird Suite

AFRS BSO 43. April 1, 1944. Serge Koussevitzky
GLINKA Russlan and Ludmilla: Overture
RACHMANINOFF Symphony No. 2

AFRS BSO 44? April 8, 1944. G. Wallace Woodworth
HAYDN Symphony No. 80
PISTON Symphony No. 2

AFRS BSO 45. April 15, 1944. Serge Koussevitzky
HANDEL Concerto Grosso in G Minor, op. 3, no. 6
HARRIS Symphony No. 6 (Premiere)

AFRS BSO 46. New York Philharmonic, Artur Rodzindski, conductor.
SHOSTAKOVICH Symphony No. 8. Although part of the Boston Symphony
    Orchestra series, this is a rebroadcast (in very poor sound) of an April 2,
    1944, performance by Artur Rodzinski and the New York Philharmonic—
    the symphony's first performance in the Western hemisphere. Koussevitzky
    led the BSO in this symphony on April 22, 1944; that concert was broad-
    cast—Shostakovich heard it in Russia—but does not appear in this AFRS
    series. See April 25, 1945, in the main discography.

April 22, 1944. Boston Symphony Orchestra, Serge Koussevitzky
SHOSTAKOVICH Symphony No. 8. This is not the performance on AFRS
    BSO 46.

AFRS BSO 47. April 29, 1944. Serge Koussevitzky
VIVALDI Concerto in D Minor, op. 3, no. 10: Largo
BRAHMS Symphony No. 4

AFRS BSO 48? October 7, 1944. Serge Koussevitzky
BEETHOVEN Symphony No. 3 "Eroica"

AFRS BSO 49. October 14, 1944. Serge Koussevitzky
FOOTE Suite for Strings in E, op. 63
David DIAMOND Symphony No. 2 (Premiere)
In an attempt to fit the hour-long format of the radio broadcast, Koussevitzky
  planned to make cuts in the Saturday performance of Diamond's symphony.
  When the composer complained, the conductor decided to shorten the performance of the Foote Suite by speeding up some sections. The results were
  ludicrously fast, and the orchestra could barely keep up. The 1940 commercial recording took 15:05, this performance runs 13:33.

AFRS BSO 50. October 21, 1944. Serge Koussevitzky
CORELLI Sarabande, Gigue, and Badinerie (arr. Ettore Pinelli)
SCHOENBERG Theme and Variations for Orchestra, op. 43b (Premiere)
MOZART Piano Concerto in E♭, K. 365 (Pierre Luboshutz, Genia Nemenoff)

AFRS BSO 51. Date unknown. Serge Koussevitzky
John Stafford SMITH The Star-Spangled Banner (1:37). The National An-
  them was played and sung at the beginning of every BSO concert during
  Word War II. It probably appears on many of these AFRS records.
BACH Toccata, Adagio, and Fugue in C, BWV 564 (orch. Leo Weiner)
  (15:23)
SHOSTAKOVICH Symphony No. 8: III Scherzo (5:25)
SIBELIUS Symphony No. 5 (29:53)
These data come from listening to the discs. The announcer says this is a regular
  weekly broadcast from Symphony Hall, led by Dr. Serge Koussevitzky, but
  we can find no record of any such program, nor of his ever conducting the
  Bach/Weiner piece.

AFRS BSO 52. August 5, 1944. Serge Koussevitzky
MOZART Symphony No. 25 in G Minor, K. 183
MOZART Violin Concerto No. 4 in D, K. 218 (Ruth Posselt)

AFRS BSO 53. November 11, 1944. Serge Koussevitzky
Ernst TOCH Pinocchio, A Merry Overture
BERLIOZ Harold in Italy (William Primrose, viola)

AFRS BSO 54. November 18, 1944. Serge Koussevitzky
William SCHUMAN Prayer in Time of War
BARBER Commando March
SHOSTAKOVICH Symphony No. 6

AFRS BSO 55 is a San Francisco Symphony broadcast led by Pierre Monteux.

AFRS BSO 56. December 2, 1944. Serge Koussevitzky
MOZART Idomeneo: Overture
FRANCK Symphony in D Minor

AFRS BSO 57? December 9, 1944. Serge Koussevitzky
TCHAIKOVSKY Symphony No. 5

AFRS BSO 58? December 16, 1944. Dimitri Mitropoulos
MENDELSSOHN *Symphony No. 3 "Scottish"*
Morton GOULD *Spirituals for Orchestra*

AFRS BSO 59? December 23, 1944. Dimitri Mitropoulos
MOZART *Die Zauberflöte: Overture*
Ernst KRENEK *Variations on "I Wonder as I Wander"*
SCHUBERT *Symphony No. 2*

AFRS BSO 60. December 30, 1944. Serge Koussevitzky
MUSSORGSKY A Night on Bald Mountain (arr. Rimsky-Korsakov)
BARTÓK Concerto for Orchestra

AFRS BSO 61. January 6, 1945. Serge Koussevitzky
MOZART Divertimento in B♭ for Two Horns and Strings, K. 287
Arthur LOURIE The Feast During the Plague (Valentina Vishnevska, so-
    prano; Harvard Glee Club and Radcliffe Choral Society). Premiere

AFRS BSO 62. January 13, 1945. Serge Koussevitzky
BERLIOZ Roman Carnival Overture
SIBELIUS Symphony No. 2

AFRS BSO 63. January 20, 1945. George Szell
William Grant STILL In Memoriam: The Colored Soldiers Who Died for
    Democracy
SMETANA Má Vlast: From Bohemia's Meadows and Forests
LALO Symphonie espagnole (Ruth Posselt, violin)

AFRS BSO 64. January 27, 1945. George Szell
HAYDN Symphony No. 97
HINDEMITH Symphonic Metamorphosis on Themes by Carl Maria von
    Weber

AFRS BSO 65. February 3, 1945. Richard Burgin
BRAHMS Variations on a Theme by Haydn
CHOPIN Piano Concerto No. 2 (Witold Malcuzyński)

AFRS BSO 66. February 10, 1945. Serge Koussevitzky
TCHAIKOVSKY Symphony No. 6 "Pathétique"
RIMSKY-KORSAKOV Le Coq d'or: Introduction and Wedding March
Only the Tchaikovsky was broadcast on February 10, 1945. AFRS has added the
    Rimsky-Korsakov material, a poor-sounding dub from the March 11, 1944,
    broadcast.

AFRS BSO 67. February 17, 1945. Serge Koussevitzky
MUSSORGSKY Kovhanshchina: Prelude "Dawn on the Moskva River"
BRAHMS Symphony No. 1

AFRS BSO 68. February 24, 1945. Heitor Villa-Lobos
VILLA-LOBOS Bachianas Brasileiras No. 7: Toccata and Fugue.
VILLA-LOBOS Choros No. 12 (Premiere)

AFRS BSO 69. March 3, 1945. Serge Koussevitzky
MOZART The Impresario: Overture
Nicolai LOPATNIKOFF Concertino for Orchestra, op. 30 (Premiere)
Edward Burlingame HILL Music for English Horn and Orchestra (Louis Speyer). Premiere
MOZART Piano Concerto No. 26 "Coronation" (Robert Casadesus)

AFRS BSO 70. March 10, 1945. Serge Koussevitzky
COPLAND Quiet City (Georges Mager, trumpet; Louis Speyer, English horn)
HANSON Symphony No. 3

AFRS BSO 71. March 17, 1945. Serge Koussevitzky
GLUCK Iphigenia in Aulis: Overture
BEETHOVEN Symphony No. 7

March 31, 1945. Serge Koussevitzky
RACHMANINOFF Vocalise
RACHMANINOFF The Isle of the Dead
LIADOV The Enchanted Lake
RIMSKY-KORSAKOV Russian Easter Overture

April 7, 1945. Serge Koussevitzky
Randall THOMPSON Testament of Freedom (Harvard Glee Club)
SHOSTAKOVICH Symphony No. 8 (only the first movement was broadcast)

April 14, 1945. Serge Koussevitzky
BEETHOVEN Symphony No. 3 "Eroica"

April 21, 1945. Serge Koussevitzky
John Stafford SMITH The Star-Spangled Banner
PISTON Prelude and Allegro for Organ and Strings (E. Power Biggs)
D'INDY Symphonic Variations "Istar"
FAURÉ Pelléas et Mélisande: Suite
RAVEL Rapsodie espagnole (incomplete)

April 28, 1945. Serge Koussevitzky
BEETHOVEN Symphony No. 9 "Choral" (the finale was not broadcast)

August 4, 1945. Serge Koussevitzky
MOZART Divertimento in B♭ for strings and two horns, K. 287
BACH Piano Concerto in D Minor , BWV 1052

October 6, 1945. Serge Koussevitzky
BEETHOVEN Symphony No. 3 "Eroica"

October 13, 1945. Serge Koussevitzky
SIBELIUS The Swan of Tuonela (Louis Speyer, English horn)
SIBELIUS Symphony No. 1

AFRS BSO 78. August 11, 1945. Serge Koussevitzky
BACH Brandenburg Concerto No. 4
MOZART Sinfonia concertante in E♭, K. 364. (William Kroll, violin; Jascha Veissi, viola). Tanglewood broadcasts have been set into the AFRS BSO Series without regard to exact chronology.

AFRS BSO 79. Selections from earlier broadcasts. Serge Koussevitzky
COPLAND Quiet City (March 10, 1945)
R. STRAUSS Don Juan (April 17, 1943)
MUSSORGSKY/RAVEL Pictures at an Exhibition (October 9, 1943)

AFRS BSO 80. October 20, 1945. Serge Koussevitzky
BERLIOZ Symphonie fantastique

AFRS BSO 81. July 28, 1945. Serge Koussevitzky
BACH Suite No. 4 in D
MOZART Piano Concerto No. 23 in A, K. 488 (Alexander Brailovsky)

AFRS BSO 82. October 27, 1945. Serge Koussevitzky
RACHMANINOFF Piano Concerto No. 2 (Alexander Brailowsky)
RIMSKY-KORSAKOV Capriccio espagnol

AFRS BSO 83. November 3, 1945. Richard Burgin
Morton GOULD Spirituals for Orchestra
TCHAIKOVSKY Symphony No. 2 "Little Russian"

AFRS BSO 84. November 10, 1945. Serge Koussevitzky
MOZART Adagio and Fugue, K. 546
BRAHMS Symphony No. 2

AFRS BSO 85. November 17, 1945. Serge Koussevitzky
PROKOFIEV Classical Symphony
PROKOFIEV Symphony No. 5

AFRS BSO 86. November 24, 1945. Paul Paray
FAURÉ Pelléas et Mélisande: Suite
RAVEL La Valse
DEBUSSY Prélude à l'après-midi d'un faune
DUKAS The Sorcerer's Apprentice

AFRS BSO 87. December 1, 1945. Paul Paray
TCHAIKOVSKY Violin Concerto (Mischa Elman)
RAVEL Pavane pour une infante défunte
CHABRIER Bourrée fantasque (arr. Mottl)

AFRS BSO 88. December 8, 1945. Serge Koussevitzky
SIBELIUS Finlandia
SIBELIUS Symphony No. 2

AFRS BSO 89. December 15, 1945. Serge Koussevitzky
BEETHOVEN Coriolan Overture
BEETHOVEN Piano Concerto No. 5 "Emperor" (Alexander Borovsky)

AFRS BSO 90. December 22, 1945. Fritz Reiner
R. STRAUSS Salome: Dance of the Seven Veils
R. STRAUSS Symphonia Domestica

AFRS BSO 91? December 29, 1945. Richard Burgin
BRAHMS Academic Festival Overture
MILHAUD Saudades do Brasil
MENDELSSOHN Violin Concerto (Yehudi Menuhin)

AFRS BSO 92? January 5, 1946. Serge Koussevitzky
BACH Suite No. 2
SIBELIUS Symphony No. 5

AFRS BSO 93. January 12, 1946. Serge Koussevitzky
MOZART Symphony No. 26
BRAHMS Symphony No. 4

AFRS BSO 94. January 19, 1946. Adrian Boult
Anthony COLLINS A Threnody for a Soldier Killed in Action
BRAHMS Symphony No. 1

AFRS BSO 95? January 26, 1946. Adrian Boult
PURCELL Trumpet Tune and Air (arr. Woodgate) (Georges Mager)
VAUGHAN WILLIAMS Job: A Masque for Dancing

AFRS BSO 96? February 2, 1946. Adrian Boult
HOLST The Planets

AFRS BSO 97? February 9, 1946. Serge Koussevitzky
TCHAIKOVSKY Symphony No. 6 "Pathétique"

AFRS BSO 98? February 16, 1946. Serge Koussevitzky
BERLIOZ Roman Carnival Overture
FRANCK Symphony in D Minor

AFRS BSO 99? February 23, 1946. Igor Stravinsky
STRAVINSKY Pétrouchka: Suite
STRAVINSKY The Firebird Suite (1945)

AFRS BSO 100. March 2, 1946. Serge Koussevitzky
WAGNER Tannhäuser: Overture
WAGNER Lohengrin: Act I Prelude
WAGNER Götterdämmerung: Siegfried's Funeral Music
WAGNER Siegfried: Forest Murmurs
WAGNER Die Meistersinger: Act I Prelude

AFRS BSO 101? March 9, 1946. Serge Koussevitzky
SIBELIUS Symphony No. 6
KABALEVSKY Symphony No. 2

AFRS BSO 102? March 16, 1946. Serge Koussevitzky
BEETHOVEN Leonore Overture No. 3
BEETHOVEN Symphony No. 6 "Pastoral"

AFRS BSO 103? March 23, 1946. Leonard Bernstein
SCHUMANN Symphony No. 2

AFRS BSO 104. March 30, 1946. Serge Koussevitzky
COWELL Hymn and Fuguing Tune No. 2
BRAHMS Violin Concerto (Efrem Zimbalist)

AFRS BSO 105. April 6, 1946. Serge Koussevitzky
R. STRAUSS Don Juan
MUSSORGSKY Khovanshchina: Prelude "Dawn on the Moskva River"
TCHAIKOVSKY Romeo and Juliet

AFRS-BSO-106? April 13, 1946. Serge Koussevitzky
PISTON Prelude and Allegro for Organ and Strings (E. Power Biggs)
BRITTEN Peter Grimes: Passsacaglia and Two Sea Interludes
COPLAND Appalachian Spring

AFRS BSO-107. April 20, 1946. Serge Koussevitzky
SIBELIUS Symphony No. 7
WAGNER Parsifal: Good Friday Spell
BRAHMS Variations on a Theme by Haydn

AFRS BSO-108? April 27, 1946. Serge Koussevitzky
BEETHOVEN Symphony No. 9 "Choral" (incomplete) (Frances Yeend, Viola
*   Silva, Andrew McKinley, Robert Hall Collins; Harvard Glee Club; Rad-*
*   cliffe Choral Society)*

AFRS BSO-109. Unknown date

For the 1946–1947 season, Tuesday concerts were broadcast instead of Saturday's. Tuesday concerts were not in Boston but on tour, in nearby Cambridge or in Providence, Hartford, New London, New Haven, Pittsburgh, or Detroit.

AFRS BSO-110. October 15, 1946. Serge Koussevitzky
SHOSTAKOVICH Symphony No. 9 (28:59)
SCRIABIN Poem of Ecstasy (20:54*)***

There were 22 broadcasts from October 22, 1946, to April 8, 1947, but only 21 ARFS BSO slots are missing, so we do not attempt to match them. The Library of Congress has discs of all 22 broadcasts.

October 22, 1946. Serge Koussevitzky
RAVEL Pavane pour une infante défunte
TCHAIKOVSKY Symphony No. 4

October 29, 1946. Richard Burgin
Alexei HAIEFF Divertimento
SIBELIUS Symphony No. 1

November 12, 1946. Serge Koussevitzky
HANSON Serenade (Georges Laurent, flute; Bernard Zighera, harp)
BRAHMS Symphony No. 1

November 19, 1946. Serge Koussevitzky
DEBUSSY: Nocturnes: Nuages, Fêtes
BEETHOVEN Piano Concerto No. 4 (Myra Hess)

November 26, 1946. Richard Burgin
HAYDN Symphony No. 95
RAVEL Le Tombeau de Couperin
PROKOFIEV Chout: Suite

December 3, 1946. Serge Koussevitzky
RAVEL Pavane pour une infante défunte
RIMSKY-KORSAKOV Scheherazade

December 10, 1946. Serge Koussevitzky
MUSSORGSKY Khovanshchina: Prelude "Dawn on the Moskva River"
TCHAIKOVSKY Symphony No. 5

December 17, 1946. Richard Burgin
MENDELSSOHN Symphony No. 4 "Italian"
R. STRAUSS Tod und Verklärung

January 7, 1947. Serge Koussevitzky
BEETHOVEN Egmont: Overture
BERLIOZ Harold in Italy (Jascha Veissi, viola)

January 14, 1947. Bruno Walter
BRAHMS Tragic Overture
BRAHMS Symphony No. 2

January 21, 1947. Bruno Walter
BEETHOVEN The Creatures of Prometheus: Overture
HAYDN Symphony No. 92 "Oxford"
R. STRAUSS Don Juan

January 28, 1947. Leonard Bernstein
BEETHOVEN Leonore Overture No. 3
BEETHOVEN Symphony No. 7

February 4, 1947. Leonard Bernstein
MOZART Die Entführung aus dem Serail: Overture
SCHUBERT Symphony No. 9 "Great C Major"

February 11, 1947. Leonard Bernstein
BRAHMS Serenade No. 2
HINDEMITH Violin Concerto (Ruth Posselt)

February 18, 1947. Leonard Bernstein
MOZART Symphony No. 36 "Linz"
BARTÓK Music for Strings, Percussion, and Celesta

February 25, 1947. Serge Koussevitzky
BEETHOVEN Symphony No. 3 "Eroica"

March 4, 1947. Serge Koussevitzky
WEBER Oberon: Overture
VAUGHAN WILLIAMS Symphony No. 5

March 11, 1947. Serge Koussevitzky
SCHUBERT Symphony No. 8 "Unfinished"
Lukas FOSS The Song of Songs (Ellabelle Davis, soprano)

March 18, 1947. Bruno Walter
CORELLI Concerto Grosso in G Minor, op. 8/6 (Erwin Bodky, harpsichord)
MOZART Symphony No. 35 "Haffner"
WAGNER Siegfried Idyll

March 25, 1947. Bruno Walter
MAHLER Symphony No. 4 (Desi Halban, soprano)

April 1, 1947. Serge Koussevitzky
BRAHMS Academic Festival Overture
BRAHMS Symphony No. 4

April 8, 1947. Serge Koussevitzky
RACHMANINOFF Vocalise
RACHMANINOFF Symphony No. 3
BRAHMS Variations on a Theme by Haydn

AFRS BSO-132. April 15, 1947. Serge Koussevitzky
BACH Suite No. 3 in D, BWV 1068: Overture, Air, and Gigue (13:58)
R. STRAUSS Also sprach Zarathustra

This is the highest number we have encountered in the AFRS BSO series. Transcriptions of Boston Symphony concerts, made by radio stations as well as by government agencies, went on for years. Many of those records and tapes exist in the Library of Congress, most of them not yet catalogued.

Armed Forces Radio and Television Services

Television became part of the American scene in the late 1940s, and the Armed Forces Radio Services added television to its operations and to its name in 1954. Although magnetic tape had become the standard recording medium well before 1954, the AFRTS continued to press 16-inch, 33⅓-rpm vinyl records for radio broadcasts to American servicemen at home and abroad. Another series of BSO broadcast material began during the Korean War. The following two-record sets are held by the Library of Congress, but are not yet catalogued, so they do not appear in any publicly accessible database. Entries on an intra-library listing are fragmentary: Each bears a "Boston Symphony" number; some include repertoire and performers. None list concert or broadcast dates, which have been deduced by matching the given information with BSO performing history and newspaper broadcast announcements. Comments are added wherever a discrepancy arises among these sources. Some of the data are so fragmentary that no attempt has been made to infer dates or repertoire.

AFRTS Boston Symphony 2. October 16, 1954. Charles Munch
BEETHOVEN Symphony No. 7. This appears to be a three-record set.

AFRTS Boston Symphony 3. October 30, 1954. Richard Burgin
MUSSORGSKY/RAVEL Pictures at an Exhibition
Although not listed by the Library of Congress, this broadcast also included:
HINDEMITH Sinfonietta

Six BSO concerts were broadcast during this gap of five AFRTS numbers.

AFRTS Boston Symphony 9. January 1, 1955. Charles Munch
BRAHMS Violin Concerto (Joseph Szigeti)
Although not listed by the Library of Congress, this broadcast also included:
PFITZNER Das Christelflein: Overture

AFRTS Boston Symphony Nos. 10–22 are in the Library of Congress collection but are not otherwise identified. By 1957, BSO concerts were no longer broadcast live. The NBC radio network now aired the BSO at 8:05 PM on Monday evenings, usually presenting up to 55 minutes of music from a concert given the previous week. The daily edition of *The New York Times* lists BSO broadcasts on NBC station WRCA. We give the dates of each Friday/Saturday pair of concerts and (in parentheses) of the WRCA broadcast.

AFRTS Boston Symphony 60. February 1, 2, (4) 1957. Charles Munch
PROKOFIEV Piano Concerto No. 2 (Nicole Henriot-Schweitzer)
PROKOFIEV Romeo and Juliet: Suite. *The New York Times* (February 4) states "Works by Prokofiev," but Munch did not perform the *Romeo and Juliet* music at this time. He led a Saturday morning rehearsal at Tanglewood on July 27, 1956, and Richard Burgin led the performance that Sunday afternoon, but we can find no evidence of either being broadcast.

AFRTS Boston Symphony 61. January 25, 26, (28), 1957. Charles Munch
WALTON Cello Concerto (Gregor Piatigorsky)
BEETHOVEN Symphony No. 4: Movements 1 and 2

AFRTS Boston Symphony 62. February 15, 16, (18), 1957. Charles Munch
MOZART Die Entführung aus dem Serail: Overture.
MOZART Clarinet Concerto (Gino Cioffi)

AFRTS Boston Symphony 63. February 15, 16, (25), 1957. Charles Munch
R. STRAUSS Ein Heldenleben.
VAUGHAN WILLIAMS Fantasia on a Theme by Thomas Tallis
Munch did not perform the Vaughan Williams work with the BSO. Richard
    Burgin led the Fantasia in BSO concerts at Carnegie Hall on Wednesday,
    January 9, 1957, and at Symphony Hall on January 28 and 29, 1957.

AFRTS Boston Symphony 64. February 22, 23, (March 4), 1957. Igor Marke-
    vich
SCHUBERT Symphony No. 3
R. STRAUSS Till Eulenspiegel

AFRTS Boston Symphony 65. March 1, 2, (11), 1957. Eugene Ormandy
William SCHUMAN Credendum
HINDEMITH Symphony "Mathis der Maler"

AFRTS Boston Symphony 66. March 1, 2, (18), 1957. Eugene Ormandy
BRAHMS Symphony No. 2. This and the previous set, broadcast one week
    apart, were taken from the same concert pair.

AFRTS Boston Symphony 67. March 8, 9, (25), 1957. Charles Munch
TCHAIKOVSKY Serenade for Strings
Although not listed by the Library of Congress, this broadcast also included:
David DIAMOND Symphony No. 6

AFRTS Boston Symphony 68. March 15, 16, (April 1), 1957. Charles Munch
WAGNER Tannhäuser: Overture and Bacchanale
WAGNER Die Walküre: Magic Fire Music
WAGNER Götterdämmerung: Siegfried's Rhine Journey

AFRTS Boston Symphony 69. March 29, 30, April 2, (8), 1957. Jean Marti-
    non.
MARTINON Hymn to Life
STRAVINSKY The Firebird Suite

AFRTS Boston Symphony 70. April 4, 5, (15), 1957. Charles Munch
DUKAS La Peri
PROKOVIEV Violin Concerto No. 2 (Isaac Stern)

AFRTS Boston Symphony 71. April 18, 20, (22), 1957. Charles Munch
BACH Saint Matthew Passion (final part). Adele Addison, Florence Kopleff, John McCollum, Mack Harrell, Harvard Glee Club and Radcliffe Chorale Society, James Joyce, dir.

AFRTS Boston Symphony 72. April 12, 13, (29), 1957. Pierre Monteux
TCHAIKOVSKY Symphony No. 5

AFRTS Boston Symphony 73. April 25, 26, 27, (May 6), 1957. Charles Munch
BEETHOVEN Symphony No. 9 "Choral" (Mariquita Moll, Martha Lipton, John McCollum, Mack Harrell, Chorus Pro Musica, Alfred Nash Patterson, dir.)

AFRTS Boston Symphony Nos. 74, 75, 77, and 78 are broadcasts by the Boston Pops under Arthur Fiedler. Nos. 80–85 are also in the Library of Congress collection but are not otherwise identified.

Another series of Armed Forces Radio and Television Services recordings (numbered, with a C prefix) from the 1950s merely duplicated commercial recordings of the day, including several by the Boston Symphony. They are not listed here.

Office of War Information/Voice of America

The United States Office of War Information was created in June 1942 and immediately established its own radio network, Voice of America. A politically controversial agency, the OWI was dissolved in August 1945, after the end of World War II, but VOA still exists today. The OWI first issued recordings under its own rubric and then under VOA. During the 1960s and 1970s, the Boston Symphony Transcription Trust sent tapes of every BSO concert to VOA (Kevin P. Mostyn, November 18, 2003). We concentrate here on performances from the 1940s, before the common use of magnetic tape. During 1945 and 1946, some of these OWI/VOA recordings duplicate those of the Armed Forces Radio Services.

Office of War Information Discs

William SCHUMAN A Free Song (Secular Cantata No. 2). Premiere
TCHAIKOVSKY Romeo and Juliet
PROKOFIEV The Love for Three Oranges: Scherzo and March
BSO, conductor Serge Koussevitzky
Harvard Glee Club; Radcliffe Choral Society (in the Schuman)
March 27, 1943. Symphony Hall (live)
78-rpm OWI broadcast transcriptions: 13-2410/21 (twelve sides)

Samuel BARBER Symphony No. 2 (26:30). Premiere
BSO, conductor Serge Koussevitzky
March 4, 1944. Symphony Hall (live)
78-rpm OWI broadcast transcriptions: 13-4510/17 (eight sides)

David DIAMOND Symphony No. 2 (32:35). Premiere
BSO, conductor Serge Koussevitzky
October 14, 1944. Symphony Hall (live)
78-rpm OWI broadcast transcriptions: 13-5275/84 (ten sides)

Morton GOULD Spirituals, for string choir and orchestra (17:40)
BSO, conductor Dimitri Mitropoulos
December 16, 1944. Symphony Hall (live)
78-rpm OWI broadcast transcriptions: 13-57075/12 (six sides)

Voice of America Discs

These VOA records encompass BSO broadcast concerts from November 11, 1944, to August 7, 1949 (by 1950, the use of acetate discs for recording concerts had given way to magnetic tape). Many duplicate the corresponding AFRS recordings above, but the VOA would often combine works from other concert broadcasts to make up one hour-long set, making its contents different from those of the AFRS. The data shown here are based upon catalogues of collections in the New York Public Library and the Library of Congress, plus a few discs that we have seen and/or heard. These are 16-inch, 33⅓-rpm aluminum-based acetate discs, usually three for each one-hour broadcast. As opposed to the AFRS discs, the sides are not always arranged so that they may be played by two turntables without a break; as a result, many recordings have problematic or incomplete segues from one side to the next. In addition, some of the recordings are marked "defective." The listed timings cannot always be relied upon, as two sources often disagree; some may include an overlap from one side to the next or the reverse—music missing between sides—and some include announcements or applause. We have attempted to make reasonable judgments. Recordings on some Library of Congress sheets are assigned a number in the form of P-843-M. These were not assigned by the Library and may be some form of VOA matrix numbers.

No doubt there are many more VOA discs, corresponding to the weeks missing from this list; apparently there were far fewer copies of VOA discs than AFRS ones, as the former are seldom seen today. We have not speculated about the missing sets, but much may be implied by matching the missing dates to the AFRS list above. Musical works listed are those on known copies of these discs and do not always represent the full hour-long original BSO broadcast. Other works from a given broadcast may have been included by VOA, but the discs in question are not known to me. For example, the broadcast of December 29, 1945, included Milhaud's *Saudades do Brasil*, but the two discs in the New York Public Library's Voice of America collection do not include it; a third disc containing the Milhaud piece may have been part of the original set.

VOA BS-1. November 11, 1944. Serge Koussevitzky
Ernst TOCH Pinocchio, A Merry Overture
BERLIOZ Harold in Italy (William Primrose, viola)

VOA BS-2. November 18, 1944. Serge Koussevitzky
William SCHUMAN Prayer in Time of War
SHOSTAKOVICH Symphony No. 6

VOA BS-3. November 25, 1944. Leonard Bernstein
BEETHOVEN Egmont Overture
BRAHMS Piano Concerto No. 1 (Jesús Maria Sanroma)

VOA BS-4. December 2, 1944. Serge Koussevitzky
MOZART Idomeneo: Overture
FRANCK Symphony in D Minor

VOA BS-5. December 16, 1944. Dimitri Mitropoulos
MENDELSSOHN Symphony No. 3 "Scottish"
Morton GOULD Spirituals for Orchestra

VOA BS-6. January 6, 1945. Serge Koussevitzky
MOZART Divertimento in B♭ for Two Horns and Strings, K. 287
Arthur LOURIE The Feast During the Plague (Valentina Vishnevska, soprano; Harvard Glee Club; Radcliffe Choral Society). Premiere

VOA BS-8. January 20, 1945. George Szell
William Grant STILL In Memoriam: The Colored Soldiers Who Died for Democracy
SMETANA Má Vlast: From Bohemia's Meadows and Forests
LALO Symphonie espagnole (Ruth Posselt, violin)

VOA BS-12. February 24, 1945. Heitor Villa-Lobos
VILLA-LOBOS Bachianas Brasileiras No. 7: Toccata and Fugue
VILLA-LOBOS Choros No. 12 (Premiere)

VOA BS-13. March 3, 1945. Serge Koussevitzky
Nicolai LOPATNIKOFF Concertino for Orchestra, op. 30 (Premiere)
Edward Burlingame HILL Music for English Horn and Orchestra (Louis Speyer). Premiere
MOZART Piano Concerto No. 26 "Coronation" (Robert Casadesus)

VOA BSO-14. April 14, 1945. Serge Koussevitzky
BEETHOVEN Symphony No. 3 "Eroica"

April 21, 1945. Serge Koussevitzky
John Stafford SMITH The Star-Spangled Banner
PISTON Prelude and Allegro for Organ and Strings (E. Power Biggs, organ)
d'INDY Istar Variations
FAURÉ Pelléas et Mélisande: Suite
RAVEL Rapsodie espagnole

November 17, 1945. Serge Koussevitzky
PROKOFIEV "Classical" Symphony
PROKOFIEV Symphony No. 5

December 22, 1945. Fritz Reiner
R. STRAUSS Salome: Dance of the Seven Veils
R. STRAUSS Symphonia domestica

December 29, 1945. Richard Burgin
BRAHMS Academic Festival Overture
MENDELSSOHN Violin Concerto (Yehudi Menuhin)

January 12, 1946. Serge Koussevitzky
MOZART Symphony No. 26
BRAHMS Symphony No. 4

January 19, 1946. Adrian Boult
Anthony COLLINS A Threnody for a Soldier Killed in Action

March 16, 1946. Serge Koussevitzky
BEETHOVEN Symphony No. 6 "Pastoral"

March 23, 1946. Leonard Bernstein
SCHUMANN Symphony No. 2

March 30, 1946. Serge Koussevitzky
COWELL Hymn and Fuguing Tune No. 2
BRAHMS Violin Concerto (Efrem Zimbalist)

April 6, 1946. Serge Koussevitzky
R. STRAUSS Don Juan
MUSSORGSKY Khovanshchina: Prelude "Dawn on the Moskva River"
TCHAIKOVSKY Romeo and Juliet

April 13, 1946. Serge Koussevitzky
PISTON Prelude and Allegro for Organ and Strings (8:04) (E. Power Biggs)
BRITTEN Peter Grimes: Passsacaglia and Two Sea Interludes (15:14)
COPLAND Appalachian Spring (24:54)

April 20, 1946. Serge Koussevitzky
SIBELIUS Symphony No. 7 (19:48)
WAGNER Parsifal: Good Friday Spell (11:29)
BRAHMS Variations on a Theme by Haydn (16:54)

April 27, 1946. Serge Koussevitzky
BEETHOVEN Symphony No. 9 "Choral" (incomplete) (Frances Yeend, Viola Silva, Andrew McKinley, Robert Hall Collins; Harvard Glee Club; Radcliffe Choral Society)

VOA P-843-M. July 13, 1946. Serge Koussevitzky
BACH Brandenburg Concerto No. 3 (14:40)
MOZART Serenade No. 10, K. 361: movements I, II, III, VI, VII (29:50)

VOA P-904-M. July 20, 1946. Serge Koussevitzky
BACH Suite No. 4 in D (17:51)
MOZART Symphony No. 41 "Jupiter" (24:26)

July 27, 1946. Serge Koussevitzky
RACHMANINOFF Piano Concerto No. 2 (34:16) (Eugene List)
RAVEL Daphnis et Chloé: Suite No. 2 (19:50)

VOA P-1012-M. August 3, 1946. Serge Koussevitzky
BRAHMS Alto Rhapsody (13:00) (Carol Brice)
BRAHMS Symphony No. 2 (35:22)

VOA P-1070-M. August 10, 1946. Serge Koussevitzky
SHOSTAKOVICH Symphony No. 9 (31:20)
TCHAIKOVSKY Overture 1812 (15:10)

VOA P-1455-M. October 8, 1946. Serge Koussevitzky
BRAHMS Symphony No. 3 (33:26)
R. STRAUSS Till Eulenspiegel (13:57)

VOA P-1492-M. October 15, 1946. Serge Koussevitzky
SHOSTAKOVICH Symphony No. 9 (28:59)
SCRIABIN Poem of Ecstasy (20:54)

VOA P-1527-M. October 22, 1946. Serge Koussevitzky
RAVEL Pavane pour une infante defunte (6:31)
TCHAIKOVSKY Symphony No. 4

VOA P-1564-M. October 29, 1946. Richard Burgin
Alexei HAIEFF Divertimento (12:09)
SIBELIUS Symphony No. 1 (30:15)

VOA P-1651-M. November 12, 1946. Serge Koussevitzky
HANSON Serenade (5:54) (Georges Laurent, flute; Bernard Zighera, harp)
BRAHMS Symphony No. 1 (39:53)

VOA P-1707-M. November 19, 1946. Serge Koussevitzky
DEBUSSY: Nocturnes for Orchestra: Nuages (8:08); Fêtes (5:54)
BEETHOVEN Piano Concerto No. 4 (33:08) (Myra Hess)

VOA P-1763-M. November 26, 1946. Richard Burgin
HAYDN Symphony No. 95 (17:23)
RAVEL Le Tombeau de Couperin (13:12)
PROKOFIEV Chout: Suite No. 1 (19:20)

VOA P-1821-M. December 3, 1946. Serge Koussevitzky
RAVEL Pavane pour une infante defunte (6:10)
RIMSKY-KORSAKOV Scheherazade (40:28)

VOA P-1876-M. December 10, 1946. Serge Koussevitzky
MUSSORGSKY Khovanshchina: Prelude (6:14)
TCHAIKOVSKY Symphony No. 5

VOA P-1938-M. December 17, 1946. Serge Koussevitzky
MENDELSSOHN Symphony No. 4 "Italian" ("line breaks - can't be used")
R. STRAUSS Tod und Verklärung (23:05*)*

VOA P-2190-M. January 14, 1947. Bruno Walter
BRAHMS Tragic Overture (11:39)
BRAHMS Symphony No. 2 (36:44)

VOA P-2258-M. January 21, 1947. Bruno Walter
BEETHOVEN Prometheus Overture (4:45*)*
HAYDN Symphony No. 92 "Oxford" (25:47)
R. STRAUSS Don Juan (15:25*)*

VOA P-2294-M. January 28, 1947. Leonard Bernstein
BEETHOVEN Leonore Overture No. 3 (12:15)
BEETHOVEN Symphony No. 7 (33:05)

VOA P-2350-M. February 4, 1947. Leonard Bernstein
MOZART Die Entführung aus dem Serail: Overture (4:53)
SCHUBERT Symphony No. 9 "Great C Major" (46:00)

VOA P-2495-M. February 18, 1947. Leonard Bernstein
MOZART Symphony No. 36 "Linz" (23:19)
BARTÓK Music for Strings, Percussion, and Celesta (27:26)

VOA P-2542-M. February 25, 1947. Serge Koussevitzky
BEETHOVEN Symphony No. 3 "Eroica"

VOA P-2590-M. March 11, 1947. Serge Koussevitzky
SCHUBERT Symphony No. 8 "Unfinished"
Lukas FOSS Song of Songs (25:45) Ellabelle Davis, soprano

VOA P-2614-M. March 18, 1947. Bruno Walter
CORELLI "Christmas" Concerto (13:36)
MOZART Symphony No. 35 "Haffner" (15:55)
WAGNER Siegfried Idyll (15:36)

VOA P-2663-M. April 8, 1947. Serge Koussevitzky
RACHMANINOFF Symphony No. 3 (32:00)
BRAHMS Variations on a Theme by Haydn ("peculiar line break ruins this")

VOA P-2675-M. April 15, 1947. Serge Koussevitzky
BACH Suite No. 3 in D, BWV 1068: Overture, Air, and Gigue (13:58)
R. STRAUSS Also sprach Zarathustra

VOA P-2688-M. April 22, 1947. Serge Koussevitzky
BRAHMS A German Requiem (first five movements) **(51:20)** (Frances
    Yeend, soprano; James Pease, baritone; Harvard, Radcliffe choruses)

July 15, 1947. Serge Koussevitzky
BACH Suite No. 1 in C, BVW 1066
BACH Concerto No. 2 for 2 Harpsichords, BWV 1061 (Pierre Luboshutz and
    Genia Nemenoff, pianos)

VOA P-2968-M. July 22, 1947. Serge Koussevitzky
MOZART Serenade in B♭, K. 361: movements I, II, III, VI, VII (28:36)
MOZART Symphony No. 41 "Jupiter" ("Not usable. Defectively recorded")

July 29, 1947. Serge Koussevitzky
VIVALDI Concerto Grosso in D Minor, op. 1, no. 3
TCHAIKVSKY Piano Concerto No. 1 (Ella Goldstein)

August 5, 1947. Serge Koussevitzky
BEEETHOVEN Symphony No. 9 "Choral" (Frances Yeend, Eunice Alberts, David Lloyd, James Pease; Tanglewood Festival Chorus)

VOA P-3138-M. October 14, 1947. Richard Burgin
RAVEL Ma Mère l'oye: Suite (15:10)
BEETHOVEN Symphony No. 5 (29:01)

VOA P-3161-M. October 21, 1947. Richard Burgin
BACH Brandenburg Concerto No. 1 (18:30)
HANSON Serenade for Solo Flute, Harp, and Strings (5:40)
HINDEMITH Symphony "Mathis der Maler" (25:38)

VOA P-3180-M. October 28, 1947. Serge Koussevitzky
R. STRAUSS Don Juan (17:30)
PROKOFIEV Chout: Two movements: Slow (2:30). Dance (3:25)
SIBELIUS Symphony No. 5

VOA P-3204-M. November 4, 1947. Serge Koussevitzky
MENDELSSOHN Piano Concerto No. 1 (18:47) (Lukas Foss)
MENDELSSOHN A Midsummer Night's Dream: Scherzo (4:30)
MENDELSSOHN Symphony No. 4 "Italian" (24:10)

November 11, 1947. Serge Koussevitzky
PROKOFIEV "Classical" Symphony
BRAHMS Symphony No. 4

VOA P-3252-M. November 18, 1947. Charles Munch
FAURÉ Pelléas et Mélisande: Suite (14:58)
FRANCK Symphony in D Minor (32:50)

VOA P-3282-M. November 25, 1947. Serge Koussevitzky
BEETHOVEN Egmont: Overture
BEETHOVEN Symphony No. 3 "Eroica"

VOA P-3309-M. December 2, 1947. Serge Koussevitzky
MUSSORGSKY Khovanshchina: Prelude (6:20)
TCHAIKOVSKY Symphony No. 6 "Pathétique"

VOA P-3336-M. December 9, 1947. Serge Koussevitzky
DEBUSSY Prélude à l'après-midi d'un faune
BERLIOZ Harold in Italy. (Joseph de Pasquale, viola)

VOA P-3371-M. December 16, 1947. Eleazar De Carvalho
BERLIOZ Symphonie fantastique (52:32)

VOA P-3419-M. December 23, 1947. Serge Koussevitzky
BEETHOVEN Coriolanus: Overture (6:48)
BEETHOVEN Violin Concerto (Ginette Neveu)

VOA P-3454-M. December 30, 1947. Serge Koussevitzky
BRUCKNER Symphony No. 8 (50:40)

VOA P-3487-M. January 6, 1948. Serge Koussevitzky
TCHAIKOVSKY Symphony No. 5 (47:10)

VOA P-3523-M. January 13, 1948. Serge Koussevitzky
MOZART Divertimento n B♭, K. 287: excerpts (13:26)
TCHAIKOVKY Eugene Onegin: Letter Scene (12:30)
   (Marina Koshetz, soprano)
TCHAIKOVSKY Francesca da Rimini (22:50)

VOA P-3564-M. January 20, 1948. Leonard Bernstein
STRAVINSKY Pétrouchka: Suite (35:00) (Lukas Foss, piano)
RAVEL La Valse (12:22)

VOA P-3604-M. January 27, 1948. Leonard Bernstein
BEETHOVEN Fidelio: Overture (8:23)
BEETHOVEN Symphony No. 2 (30:38)
WEBER Der Freischütz: Overture (9:40)

VOA P-3644-M. February 3, 1948. Leonard Bernstein
David DIAMOND Symphony No. 4 (17:25)
SCHUMANN Symphony No. 2 (31:15)

VOA P-3684-M. February 10, 1948. Richard Burgin
HAYDN Symphony No. 95 (17:33)
HINDEMITH Symphonia Serena (30:13)

VOA P-3731-M. February 17, 1948. Richard Burgin
BEETHOVEN Piano Concerto No. 2 (25:20) (Bruce Simonds)
STRAVINSKY Symphony in Three Movements (21:26)

VOA P-3787-M. February 24, 1948. Serge Koussevitzky
BRAHMS Academic Festival Overture (9:30)
BRAHMS Symphony No. 2

VOA P-3828-M. March 2, 1948. Serge Koussevitzky
MOZART Symphony No. 41 "Jupiter" (25:01)
Gian Francesco MALIPIERO Symphony No. 4, "In Memoriam" (24:18)

VOA P-3870-M. March 9, 1948. Serge Koussevitzky
MOZART Eine kleine Nachtmusik (10:53)
PROKOFIEV Scythian Suite (22:04)
RAVEL Daphnis et Chloé: Suite No. 2 (14:05)

VOA P-3913-M. March 16, 1948. Serge Koussevitzky
MOZART Idomeneo: Overture (4:27)
SHOSTAKOVICH Symphony No. 5 (40:14)

VOA P-3954-M. March 23, 1948. Charles Munch
SCHUBERT Symphony No. 5 (23:52)
ROUSSEL Symphony No. 3 (27:03)

VOA P-4000-M. March 30, 1948. Charles Munch
MOZART Symphony No. 38 "Prague" (22:28)
SCHUMANN Symphony No. 4 (24:38)

VOA P-4040-M. April 6, 1948. Serge Koussevitzky
MENDELSSOHN A Midsummer Night's Dream: Overture (11:50)
BEETHOVEN Symphony No. 7 (36:11)

VOA P-4084-M. April 13, 1948. Serge Koussevitzky
PISTON Symphony No. 3 (29:54)
WAGNER Lohengrin: Act I Prelude (9:55)
WAGNER Die Meistersinger: Act I Prelude (9:37)

VOA P-4123-M. April 20, 1948. Serge Koussevitzky
BEETHOVEN Egmont: Overture (7:50)
SIBELIUS Symphony No. 2 (40:09)

VOA P-4161-M. April 27, 1948. Serge Koussevitzky
BEETHOVEN Missa Solemnis: Credo, Et Incarnatus, Crucifixus, Sanctus, Benedictus, Agnus Dei (48:15) (Eileen Farrell, soprano; Ellen Faull, contralto; David Lloyd, tenor; George London, bass-baritone; Harvard, Radcliffe Choruses)

July 20, 1948. Serge Koussevitzky
MOZART Piano Concerto No. 17 in G, K. 453 (27:40) (Lukas Foss)
MOZART Symphony No. 34 (20:48)

July 27, 1948. Serge Koussevitzky
BACH Concerto in D Minor, BWV 1063, for 3 Harpsichords: Movements 2 and 3 (11:00)
BACH Suite No. 2 in B Minor, BVW 1067 (20:19) (Georges Laurent, flute)
BACH Concerto in C Major, BWV 1064, for 3 Harpsichords (cut off before end) **(11:42)** (Lukas Foss, Bernard Zighera, and Ralph Berkowitz, pianos)

August 3, 1948. Serge Koussevitzky
PROKOFIEV Peter and the Wolf (Wesley Addy, narrator)
Johann STRAUSS Jr. Voices of Spring (6:05)
SIBELIUS Valse Triste (5:30)
RAVEL La Valse (11:35)

August 10, 1948. Serge Koussevitzky
TCHAIKOVSKY Piano Concerto No. 1 (30:55) (Seymour Lipkin)
TCHAIKOVSKY Overture 1812 (15:27)

November 22, 1948. Serge Koussevitzky
LISZT A Faust Symphony (rehearsal)

November 29, 1948. Serge Koussevitzky
C. P. E. BACH Concerto for Orchestra (rehearsal)

July 17, 1949. Serge Koussevitzky
MOZART Symphony No. 36 "Linz" (22:35)
MOZART Symphony No. 40

July 24, 1949. Serge Koussevitzky
MOZART Symphony No. 31 "Paris" (15:39)
MOZART Symphony No. 39 (23:53)

July 31, 1949. Leonard Bernstein
STRAVINSKY Scènes de Ballet (17:10)
STRAVINSKY Le Sacre du printemps (31:38)

August 7, 1949. Eleazar de Carvalho
R. STRAUSS Horn Concerto No. 2 (16:46) (James Stagliano)
R. STRAUSS Also sparch Zarathustra (incomplete)

Voice of America U. S. Composer Series

This series consists of works by American composers, taken from live performances by the New York Philharmonic, the Cleveland Orchestra, and the Boston Symphony Orchestra. The latter are listed here. These are 12-inch, 33⅓-rpm vinyl records. Note that each Voice of America USC number represents one side of an LP.

PISTON, WALTER
Viola Concerto No. 1 (20:01)
BSO, conductor Charles Munch
Joseph De Pasquale, viola
April 1, 1958. Symphony Hall (live)
Voice of America
Master No. VOA 3023
LP: USC-101

BLACKWOOD, EASLEY
Symphony No. 1, op. 3 (28:35)
BSO, conductor Richard Burgin
April 18 or 19, 1958. Symphony Hall (live)
Voice of America
Master No. VOA 3024/25
LP: USC-102/103

READ, GARDNER
Prelude and Toccata, op. 43 (6:05)
BSO, conductor Richard Burgin
October 23 or 25, 1958. Symphony Hall (live)
Master No. VOA 3039
Voice of America
LP: USC-109

RIEGGER, WALLINGFORD
Symphony No. 4 (28:29)
BSO, conductor Robert Shaw
January 9 or 10, 1959. Symphony Hall (live)
Voice of America
Master No. VOA 3038/399
LP: USC-108/109

CRESTON, PAUL
Invocation and Dance, op. 58 (11:04)
BSO, conductor Izler Solomon
April 17 or 18, 1959. Symphony Hall (live)
Voice of America
Master No. VOA 3028
LP: USC-108

LA MONTAINE, JOHN
Piano Concerto No. 1, op. 9 (25:02)
BSO, conductor Charles Munch
Jorg Bolet, piano
October 9 or 10, 1959. Symphony Hall (live)
Voice of America
Master No. VOA 3026
LP: USC-104

COPLAND, AARON
Symphony No. 1 (25:56)
BSO, conductor Aaron Copland
January 1 or 2, 1960. Symphony Hall (live)
Voice of America
Master No. VOA 3027
LP: USC-105

KIRCHNER, LEON
Toccata for Strings, Winds, and Percussion (11:22)
BSO, conductor Richard Burgin
February 5 or 6, 1960. Symphony Hall (live)
Voice of America
Master No. VOA 3024
LP: USC-102

Appendix G: BSO Pseudonyms

The entries on these lists are NOT Boston Symphony Orchestra recordings. These were orchestral recordings made in Symphony Hall (except as noted) by musicians from the Boston Symphony, contracted privately—as was permitted by their BSO contracts—and issued under pseudonyms. They are not pirate recordings (to which Appendix I is devoted), but legitimate ones for which all the musicians were paid. There are four separate groups, each using a different title: the New Orchestral Society of Boston, the Zimbler Sinfonietta, Arthur Fiedler's Sinfonietta, and the Columbia Symphony Orchestra. The Boston Pops, which once consisted of BSO musicians, needs its own discography, as it has recorded even more than the Boston Symphony. Members of the BSO have participated in innumerable other recordings, both as soloists and in ensemble; here is a peek down some of those many pathways: In 1957, Leopold Stokowski led members of the BSO (not so identified) in a Capitol recording of Harold Farberman's *Evolution*, which they had previously recorded for Boston Records under the name Boston Percussion Group. In the early 1960s, the Telemann Society Wind and Percussion Band, led by Richard Schultze, recorded Handel's *Royal Fireworks Music* for Vox; unfortunately, some BSO musicians were given period instruments but no instruction on how to play them, so the performance was—to put it kindly—not up to Boston Symphony standards.

No attempt has been made to include complete discographic details here, and none of these recordings are cross-referenced elsewhere in this book.

New Orchestral Society of Boston

Emory Cook was a leading audio engineer who pioneered high-fidelity recordings in the late 1940s and 1950s. He developed a process he called "binaural sound," using two microphones placed close together to simulate the position of a pair of ears. They were originally heard on reel-to-reel tape, but by the early 1950s he produced 33⅓-rpm vinyl records that had two tracks on each side: a left-channel and right-channel. To play them, he developed a two-headed, Yshaped arm holding two cartridges and styli the correct distance apart. I saw and heard a demonstration of this system at an audio store in New York City ca. 1951. Starting with audio test records and spectaculars with "jet engine, locomotives, Mexican firecrackers, babies, etc." (*Canfield Guide*), Cook went on to record many types of music—calypso was one of his favorites. In March 1953 he hired 40 to 80 musicians of the Boston Symphony, depending on the music, to record in Symphony Hall. A review of the first three LPs appeared in the May 4, 1953, issue of *Time* magazine. The conductor was Willis Page, a BSO double-bassist from 1940 to 1955 who was a Monteux protégé, studied with Koussevitzky, and later became conductor of the Nashville Symphony Orchestra.

Cook's initial records were binaural, with the two separated tracks, but the Livingston arm cost $165, a princely sum at that time, so few were sold. By the time of his Boston recordings, Cook was also issuing monaural LPs; conventional stereo LPs followed in the late 1950s. Each version carried the same record number; binaurals were identified by a "BN" prefix, stereos by an "sd" suffix: Brahms' First Symphony appeared as BN1060 (two 10-inch discs), 1060 (one), and 1060sd (12-inch). Cook invented a "New Microfusion Process" for making cleaner vinyl discs than other companies, and the sound of his LPs was superb, equal to or better than the finest commercial recordings of the early stereo era. Most of them also appeared briefly on the Rondo label in 1959, with the ensemble renamed "Boston Festival Orchestra." Note that two "Boston Orchestra" recordings on Rondo (music of Schubert and Kabalevsky) are not by Cook's ensemble, and that a Page-led DuBois oratorio on Cook Records has only organ accompaniment. Five-digit Cook LPs appeared about that time (again in both monaural and stereo), putting more music on each LP than did the original issues. Cook 10646 was supposed to combine the music of 1064 and 1066, and its cover lists all eight works. But the record itself did not include the Scherzo of Mendelssohn's *A Midsummer Night's Dream*; in its place (band three of the B side) was the first half of Weber's *Euryanthe* Overture, which then continued on band four, where it belonged. Later pressings (Cook did not include pressing data on his LPs) corrected the error.

In 1990, Cook donated his archive to the Smithsonian Museum, which has marketed CDs on the Cook label. They too sport the original record numbers, and their sound can be miraculous. They were individually prepared CDRs, however, and there is some evidence (from library catalogues) that not every copy of a given, numbered CD has identical contents. All but one recording may now be downloaded from www.smithsonianglobalsound.org, as either an MP3 or a FLAC file. This seems a rather amateur effort: one can hear that some tracks are dubbed from a not-always-pristine LP, and one (Debussy's *Nuages*) begins with Barber's Adagio and then includes a discussion among the engineers before switching to all of *Nuages*. The CD and the downloads of 10646 simply duplicate its first LP issue, so Mendelssohn's Scherzo is missing.

Willis Page conducts the New Orchestral Society of Boston in all these recordings. They were made in Symphony Hall, Boston. Exact dates are not
known, but the first group on this page was done in March 1953. Cook's producer Bob Bollard chose the repertoire: works that had not been adequately recorded and "were also agreeable to our conductor and sufficiently familiar to the
musicians to minimize expensive rehearsal time" (Emory Cook, in the program
notes).

BACH Brandenburg Concerto No. 3 in G, BWV 1048 **(11:05)**
No soloists are identified
LPs: Cook 1062. Rondo ST-522. **CDs:** Cook 1062

BACH (arr. Siegmund Bachrich) **Suite for Strings (12:01)**. *Arrangements of
the Praeludium, Adagio, and Gavotte from Violin Partita No. 3, BWV 1006. The
Adagio was also recorded by Arthur Fiedler's Sinfonietta (March 21, 1940).*
LPs: Cook 1062. Rondo ST-522. **CDs:** Cook 1062

BARBER Adagio for Strings (7:45)
LPs: Cook 1068. 10683. Rondo ST-502. **45:** Nixa EP-651. **CDs:** Cook 10683

BRAHMS Symphony No. 1 in C Minor, op. 68 (42:16)
LPs: Cook 1060. BN1060 (2 LPs). **CDs:** Cook 1060

DEBUSSY *Tarantelle Styrienne*, "Danse" (orch. Ravel) **(5:03)**
LPs: Cook 1068. 10683. Rondo ST-519. **CDs:** Cook 10683

HAYDN Symphony No. 100 in G, "Military" **(21:06)**
LPs: Cook 1069. 10669. Rondo ST-501. **CDs:** Cook 10659 (4)

HONEGGER *Pacific 231* **(5:53)**
LPs: Cook 1068. 10683. Rondo ST-502. **CDs:** Cook 10683

MOZART Symphony No. 40 in G Minor, K. 550 (19:55)
LPs: Cook 2065. 1065. 10657. 10659. Rondo ST-515. **CDs:** Cook 10657

STRAVINSKY Concerto in D (11:46)
LPs: Cook 1062. Rondo ST-502. **CDs:** Cook 1062

TCHAIKOVSKY Serenade in C for String Orchestra, op. 48 **(28:08)**
LPs: Cook 1169. **CDs:** Cook 1169

VILLA-LOBOS *Bachianas Brasileiras No. 5* **(11:14)**
Phyllis Curtin, soprano
LPs: Cook 1062. Rondo ST-540. **CDs:** Cook 1062

*All of the above appear in an unnumbered 1954 four-LP box set and on a four-
CD set Smithsonian/Folkways Cook 10659.*

BEETHOVEN Symphony No. 5 in C Minor, op. 67 **(28:28)**
LPs: Cook 1067. 10657. Rondo ST-509. **CDs:** Cook 10657

BIZET *Carmen:* **Introduction to Act I (2:07)**
LPs: Cook 2064. 1064. 10646. Rondo ST-510. **CDs:** Cook 10646

BRAHMS *Hungarian Dance No. 6* **(3:21)**
LPs: Cook 2066. 1066. 10646. Rondo ST-510. **CDs:** Cook 10646

DEBUSSY *Nocturnes for Orchestra: Nuages* **(8:57).** *Fêtes* **(6:03)**
LPs: Cook 1063. 10683. Rondo ST-519. **CDs:** Cook 10683

DEBUSSY *Prélude à l'après-midi d'un faune* **(9:39)**
LPs: Cook 1063. 10683. Rondo ST-519. **CDs:** Cook 10683

MENDELSSOHN *A Midsummer Night's Dream:* **Scherzo (4:30)**
LPs: Cook 2064. 1064. 10646. Rondo ST-510. **CDs:** None (explained above)

RIMSKY-KORSAKOV *Snow Maiden:* **Dance of the Buffoons (3:36)**
LPs: Cook 2066. 1066. 10646. **CDs:** Cook 10646

ROSSINI *La gazza ladra:* **Overture (8:56)**
LPs: Cook 2064. 1064. 10646. Rondo ST-510. **CDs:** Cook 10646

SAINT-SAËNS *Danse macabre* **in G Minor**, op. 40 **(6:53).**
Alfred Krips, solo violin
LPs: Cook 2066. 1066. 10646. Rondo ST-510. **CDs:** Cook 10646

J. STRAUSS *Kaiser-Waltzer* (*Emperor Waltz*), op. 437. **(7:34)**
LPs: Cook 2066. 1066. 10646. **CDs:** Cook 10646

TCHAIKOVSKY *Romeo and Juliet* **(fantasy-overture) (20:18)**
LPs: Cook 1169. **CDs:** Cook 1169

WEBER *Euryanthe:* **Overture (8:20)**
LPs: Cook 2064. 1064. 10646. Rondo ST-501. **CDs:** Cook 10646

Zimbler Sinfonietta

Josef Zimbler, a cellist in the BSO from 1933 until his death in 1959, founded the Zimbler Sinfonietta in 1945. A chamber orchestra which usually played without conductor, it was held in high esteem in the 1950s. Whereas Page's orchestra was assembled just for recordings, Zimbler's ensemble maintained an active schedule of concerts and recorded for a variety of labels. Only one of its performances has been issued on CD, probably because few were in stereo; no doubt the lack of a famous conductor contributed as well. Most of these recordings were made in Symphony Hall. Stereo numbers are set in bold type.

MUSIC OF THE BACH FAMILY (May 1956)   Boston BUA-1 (4)

Richard Burgin, conductor. Marguerite Willauer, soprano; Betty Lou Allen, mezzo-soprano; David Lloyd, tenor; McHenry Boatwright, bass; Boston University Chorus. George Zazofsky, Robert Brink, violins; Joseph de Pasquale, viola; Samuel Mayes, cello; Alfred Zighera, viola da gamba; Doriot Anthony Dwyer, Phillip Kaplan, flutes; Gino Cioffi, clarinet; Harold Meek, Harry Shapiro, horns; Max Miller, organ; Daniel Pinkham, harpsichord; Jules Wolffers, piano. *This four-LP box set was also available as four single monaural LPs. Most of the set was later issued on three stereo LPs, as noted in bold for each recording.*

Part 1:   Boston BUA-1 (4). Boston B-402

Johann BACH: *Unser Leben ist ein Schatten* (motet)   **BST-1008**
Heinrich BACH: *Ich danke dir, Gott* (cantata)   **BST-1008**
Georg Christoph BACH *Siehe, wie fein* (cantata)   **BST-1008**
Johann Christoph BACH: Prelude and Fugue for Organ.
    Es erhub sich ein Streit (cantata) (not on BUA-1 or B-402)   **BST-1008**
Johann Michael BACH: *Herr, ich warte auf dein Heil* (motet) **BST-1008**
    Chorale Prelude and Chorale Variations for Organ
Johann Nicolaus BACH: *Der Jenaische Wein und Bierrufer*   **BST-1008**

Part 2:   Boston BUA-1 (4). Boston B-403

Johann Bernhard BACH: Overture No. 4 in D for Orchestra   **BST-1006**
Johann Ludwig BACH: *Es danken dir, Gott* (motet)   **BST-1008**
    Trauer Music: *Halleluja*
W. F. BACH: Sonata in F for two Flutes   **BST-1007. BST-1403**

Part 3:   Boston BUA-1 (4). Boston B-404

W. F. BACH: Harpsichord Concerto in E♭   **BST-1007. BST-1403**
C. P. E. BACH: Trio in C. *Die Trennung* (song)
    Sinfonia in E Minor, H. 652e   **BST-1007. BST-1403**
Johann Ernst BACH: Violin Sonata in F.
    Psalm VI: *Sei mir gnädig; Meine Gebeine sind erschrokken;*
        Ach du Herr wie lange   **BST-1008**
Johann Christoph Friedrich BACH: Menuet for Piano

Part 4:   Boston BUA-1 (4). Boston B-405

Johann Christoph Friedrich BACH: *Cassandra:* **Recitative and Aria**
    Quartet in C
J. C. BACH: Vauxhall Song for Soprano and Orchestra
    Amadis de Gaule: Three instrumental pieces   **BST-1007. BST-1403**
Wilhelm Friedrich Ernst BACH: Sextet in E♭   **BST-1006**
"Das Dreyblatt" for piano six hands. *Wiegenlied einer Mutter* (song).

The following recordings are not part of the Bach Family set:

BACH Brandenburg Concerto: No. 5 in D, BWV 1050 **(24:53)**
Lukas Foss, piano and conductor;
James Pappoutsakis, flute; George Zazofsky, violin   Unicorn UNLP 1039

BACH Harpsichord Concerto No. 1 in d, BWV 1052 **(25:27)**
Lukas Foss, piano and conductor   Unicorn UNLP 1039

These two recordings of BWV 1052 are different performances.

BACH Harpsichord Concerto No. 1 in d, BWV 1052 **(24:32)**
Lukas Foss, piano   Decca 9601

BACH Harpsichord Concerto No. 5 in f, BWV 1056 **(11:18)**
Lukas Foss, piano   Decca 9601

BARTÓK Piano Concerto No. 1 (22:44)
Leonid Hambro, piano; Robert Mann, conductor   Bartok 313
This LP also contains Bartók's original Rhapsody for solo piano.

BARTÓK Divertimento for Strings (23:40). Lukas Foss, conductor
Unicorn UNLP-1037. Siena S-100 2. Turnabout TV-34154 (electronic stereo)

BOYCE Symphonies, op. 2   Decca DX 105 (DL 8513/14)
**No. 1 in B♭ (8:33); No. 2 in A (5:20); No. 3 in C (5:25);   No. 4 in F (6:00);
No. 5 in D (7:50);   No. 6 in F (8:54);   No. 7 in B♭ (9:40); No. 8 in d (10:31)**

HANDEL *Messiah* (41 numbers out of 53) **(127:30)**
Thompson Stone; conductor; Adele Addison, soprano; Lorna Sydney, con-
tralto; David Lloyd, tenor; Donald Gramm, bass; Handel and Haydn Society
of Boston Chorus. George Zazovsky, violin; Doriot Anthony Dwyer, flute;
Roger Voisin, trumpet; Earl Weidner, organ; Danuel Pinkham, harpsichord.
October 29, November 3 and 5, 1955
Unicorn UNS 1 (3). Kapp 8000; **8000-S**. Classics Record Library **SRL-4572**

HINDEMITH Theme and Variations, "The Four Temperaments" **(26:58)**
Lukas Foss, piano and conductor; Josef Zimbler, cello
Decca DL 7501 (10")

IVES *The Unanswered Question* **(5:30)**
Roger Voisin, trumpet; Lukas Foss, conductor
Unicorn UNLP-1037. Siena S 100 2. Turnabout TV-34154 electronic stereo

MILHAUD Symphony No. 4 for Strings (6:45)-
Lukas Foss, conductor
Unicorn UNLP-1037. Siena S 100 2. Turnabout TV-34154 electronic stereo

MOZART Cassation No. 1, K. 63   Decca DL-8520. DCM-3204

MOZART Clarinet Concerto in A, K. 622 (28:49)
Reginald Kell, clarinet. (Recorded in New York City, May 1950)
Decca DL-7500. DL-9732. CDs: Deutsche Grammophon 289 477 5280 (6)

MOZART Horn Concertos   Boston B-401. BST-1017. Sinequan S005X71
No. 1 in D, K. 412 (8:13);   No. 4 in E♭, K. 495 (15:16)   Boston BST-1003
No. 2 in E♭, K. 417 (13:51); No. 3 in E♭, K. 447 (14:41)   Boston BST-1002
James Stagliano, horn. (Kresge Auditorium, MIT, Cambridge, Mass.)

MOZART Serenade No. 1 in D, K.100 (23:20)   Decca DL-8520. DCM-3204

MOZART Serenade No 6 in D, K. 239, "Notturna" (11:56)   Decca DL-8522

MOZART Sinfonia Concertante in E♭, K. 364 (30:50)
Joseph Fuchs, violin; Lillian Fuchs, viola.   Decca DL 9596

SKALLKOTTAS Little Suite for Strings (7:20)
Lukas Foss, conductor
Unicorn UNLP-1037. Siena S 100 2. Turnabout TV-34154 electronic stereo

TANSMAN *Triptych for String Orchestra* (18:15)   Decca DL 9625

TELEMANN Suite for Flute and Strings in A Minor (22:10)
James Pappoutsakis, flute   Decca DL 8522

VAUGHAN WILLIAMS Concerto academico for Violin and Orchestra (15:32)
Joseph Fuchs, violin   Decca DL 9625

VIVALDI Concertos, op. 8 "The Four Seasons"
No. 1 in E, RV269, "Spring" (11:26); No. 2 in G Minor, RV315 "Summer"
(10:14); No. 3 in F, RV293, "Autumn" (11:15); No. 4 in F Minor, RV297
"Winter" (9:09)
George Zazovsky, violin   Boston B400
Recorded in both mono and stereo; the stereo may never have been issued.

VIVALDI Concertos for Bassoon and Strings.
No. 8 in F, P.318 R.485 (11:26); No. 13 in C, P.46 R.477 (10:42);
No. 14 in C Minor, P.432 R.480 (9:00); No. 17 in C, P.45 R.472 (10:24)
Sherman Walt, Bassoon   RCA Victor LM/LSC 2353

Arthur Fiedler's Sinfonietta

On October 30, 1925, Boston Symphony violist Arthur Fiedler, not yet the conductor of the Boston Pops, led an ensemble of 22 BSO players in a concert at Plymouth, Massachusetts. The group quickly gained a following, becoming known as Arthur Fiedler's Sinfonietta. Initially he struck a balance between classical and "light-classical" music, as he would later do with the Pops. Fiedler first recorded with the Pops in 1935, so when RCA Victor began recording the Sinfonietta in 1937, it carved out a new niche: early music, up to Haydn and Mozart. Hindemith's *Der Schwanendreher*, a piece based on old folk songs, was to be the only exception. Some CD releases credit Arthur Fiedler's Sinfonietta as accompanying Leontyne Price in two songs, but those 1969 recordings are by "Arthur Fiedler and his Orchestra," a New York pick-up ensemble.

All of these recordings are conducted by Arthur Fiedler; all were recorded by RCA Victor and first issued by that company. Some timings are approximations based on pre-1945 recording logs. Take numbers are marked on most log sheets; they are all first takes until January 1, 1945. Note that the Germanic Museum in Cambridge was renamed Busch-Reisinger Museum in 1950.

MOZART: Divertimento No. 15 in B♭ for Strings and Horns, K. 287 (31:00)
Arthur Fiedler's Sinfonietta
December 23, 1937. Symphony Hall. Producer Charles O'Connell
Matrix: BS-014444/45, CS-014448/49, BS-014446/47, BS-014450/52
78s: M-434 (4383/86-S, 12168). One 12" record, four 10" records (9 sides).

MOZART: Serenade No. 12 in C Minor for Wind Instruments, K. 388 (22:25)
Arthur Fiedler's Sinfonietta
December 23, 1937. Symphony Hall. Producer Charles O'Connell
Matrix: CS-014438/41; BS-014442/43
78s: M-433 (12166/67, 4382). Two 12" records; one 10" record (6 sides).
   CDs: 09026-62571-2

BACH: Brandenburg Concerto No. 2 in F (13:21)
Arthur Fiedler's Sinfonietta
Louis Speyer, oboe; James Pappoutsakis, flute; Roger Voisin, trumpet; Julius
   Theodorowicz, violin
April 12, 1939. Germanic Museum, Cambridge. Producer Charles O'Connell
Matrix: CS-035439/43
Unreleased. *A handwritten note on the recording log sheet reads: "All destroyed per coc [Charles O'Connell] 5/9/41."*

BACH: Toccata in C: Adagio (arr. A. Siloti) (3:20)
Arthur Fiedler's Sinfonietta
April 12, 1939. Germanic Museum, Cambridge. Producer Charles O'Connell
Matrix: BS-035444
Unreleased

John Christopher SMITH: Miniature Suite (trans. Harl McDonald) **(9:55)**
Arthur Fiedler's Sinfonietta
April 12, 1939. Germanic Museum, Cambridge. Producer Charles O'Connell
Matrix: BS-035445/47
78s: M-609 (4443/44)

BOYCE: The Power of Music: Overture (arr. Johann Georg Stanley) **(3:15)**
Arthur Fiedler's Sinfonietta
April 12, 1939. Germanic Museum, Cambridge. Producer Charles O'Connell
Matrix: BS-035448
78s: M-609 (4444). **CDs:** 0906-62571-2

HINDEMITH: *Der Schwanendreher* (26:07)
Arthur Fiedler's Sinfonietta. Paul Hindemith, viola
April 12, 1939. Germanic Museum, Cambridge. Producer Charles O'Connell
Matrix: CS-035449/54
78s: M-659 (15922/24). AM-659 (15925/27). DM-659 (15928/30)
    CDs: 09026-62571-2. Biddulph LAB 087

HANDEL: Organ Concerto No. 2 in B♭, op. 4, no. 2 (ed. Max Seiffert) **(9:00)**
Arthur Fiedler's Sinfonietta. E. Power Biggs, organ
April 13, 1939. Germanic Museum, Cambridge. Producer Charles O'Connell
Matrix CS-035475/76
78s: 15751

HANDEL: Organ Concerto No. 10 in D Minor, op. 7, no. 4 (15:05)
Arthur Fiedler's Sinfonietta. E. Power Biggs, organ
April 13, 1939. Germanic Museum, Cambridge. Producer Charles O'Connell
Matrix: CS-035477/78, 035484, 035479
78s: M-587 (15545/46)

HANDEL: Organ Concerto No. 11 in G Minor, op. 7, no. 5 (ca. 12:30)
Arthur Fiedler's Sinfonietta. E. Power Biggs, organ
April 13, 1939. Germanic Museum, Cambridge. Producer Charles O'Connell
Matrix: BS-035480/83
78s: 2099/2100 (10-inch records)

HANDEL: Organ Concerto No. 13 in F, "The Cuckoo and the Nightingale"
    (13:55)
Arthur Fiedler's Sinfonietta. E. Power Biggs, organ
March 17, 1940. Germanic Museum, Cambridge. Producer Charles O'Connell
Matrix: CS-048086/89
78s: M-733 (17578/79). **CDs:** 09026-62571-2

CORELLI: Violin Sonatas, op. 5: No. 3 in C (arr. Malipiero) **(10:55)**
Arthur Fiedler's Sinfonietta. E. Power Biggs, organ
March 17, 1940. Germanic Museum, Cambridge. Producer Charles O'Connell
Matrix:CS-048090/92
78s: M-924 (11-8398/99). DM-924 (11-8278/79)

CORELLI: Sonata in D for Strings and Organ (5:00)
Arthur Fiedler's Sinfonietta. E. Power Biggs, organ
March 17, 1940. Germanic Museum, Cambridge. Producer Charles O'Connell
Matrix: CS-048093
78s: M-924 (11-8399-B). DM-924 (11-8278-B)

William FELTON: Organ Concerto No. 3 in B♭ (9:55)
Arthur Fiedler's Sinfonietta. E. Power Biggs, organ
March 17, 1940. Germanic Museum, Cambridge. Producer Charles O'Connell
Matrix: BS-048094/97
78s: M-866 (2196/97). DM-866 (2198/99) 10-inch records

CORELLI: Trio Sonatas, op. 1: No. 1 in F (5:50)
Arthur Fiedler's Sinfonietta. E. Power Biggs, organ
March 17, 1940. Germanic Museum, Cambridge. Producer Charles O'Connell
Matrix: BS-048098/99
78s: 10-1105

Gaetano Maria SCHIASSI: *Christmas Symphony* (8:35)
Arthur Fiedler's Sinfonietta
Symphony Hall. March 21, 1940. Producer Charles O'Connell
Matrix: CS-047112/13
78s: 13466. 11-0025

BACH: Fantasia in C for Organ (arr. L. Bedell) **(4:50)**
Arthur Fiedler's Sinfonietta
Symphony Hall. March 21, 1940. Producer Charles O'Connell
Matrix: CS-047114
78s: 13809. **CDs:** 09026-62571-2

TELEMANN: *Don Quichotte Suite* (11:25*)**
Arthur Fiedler's Sinfonietta. Erwin Bodky, harpsichord
Symphony Hall. March 21, 1940. Producer Charles O'Connell
Matrix: CS-047131/34
78s: M-945 (11-8456/57). DM-945 (11-8458/59)

Esajas REUSNER: Suite No. 1 (arr. Johann Georg Stanley) **(9:55)**
Arthur Fiedler's Sinfonietta
Symphony Hall. March 21, 1940. Producer Charles O'Connell
Matrix: BS-047135/37
78s: M-969 (10-1094/95). DM-969 (10-1096/97)

PACHEBEL: Canon in D (3:15)
Arthur Fiedler's Sinfonietta
Symphony Hall. March 21, 1940. Producer Charles O'Connell
Matrix: BS-047138
78s: M-969 (10-1095). DM-969 (10-1096) **CDs:** 09026-62571-2.

CORELLI: Concerti Grossi, op. 6: No. 11 in B♭ (8:10)
Arthur Fiedler's Sinfonietta
Symphony Hall. March 21, 1940. Producer Charles O'Connell
Matrix: CS-047139/40
78s: 13587

BACH: Violin Sonata No. 2: Andante (arr. S. Bachrich) **(4:25)**
Arthur Fiedler's Sinfonietta
Symphony Hall. March 21, 1940. Producer Charles O'Connell
Matrix: CS-047141
78s: 13809

MOZART: Sonatas for Organ and Strings
   Sonata in C, K. 278 (3:45) *with two oboes, two trumpets, and timpani*
   Sonata in C, K. 336 (9:16) *with Biggs cadenza*
   Sonata in D, K. 144 (4:30)
   Sonata in F, K. 244 (3:42)
   Sonata in D, K. 245 (3:40)
   Sonata in G, K. 328 (4:35)
Arthur Fiedler's Sinfonietta. E. Power Biggs, organ
January 1, 1945. Symphony Hall. Producer Macklin Marrow
Matrix: D5-RC-608/613
78s: DM-1019 (11-8909/11)

MOZART: Serenade No. 12 in C Minor for Wind Instruments, K. 388
   (19:42)
Arthur Fiedler's Sinfonietta
November 22, 1954. Symphony Hall. Producer Richard Mohr
LPs: LM-1936

MOZART: Divertimento No. 15 in B♭ for Strings and Horns, K. 287 (28:12)
Arthur Fiedler's Sinfonietta
November 23, 24, 1954. Symphony Hall. Producer Richard Mohr
LPs: LM-1936

MOZART: 17 Sonatas for Organ and Strings
Arthur Fiedler's Sinfonietta. Carl Weinrich, organ
June 28, 30, 1965; July 1, 2, 1965. General Theological Seminary, New York.
   Producer Peter Dellheim
LPs: LM/LSC-7041 (2). *These "sonatas" are concerted works.*

HAYDN: Organ Concerto No. 1 in C (22:01)
Arthur Fiedler's Sinfonietta. Carl Weinrich, organ
June 28, 30, 1965; July 1, 2, 1965. General Theological Seminary, New York.
   Producer Peter Dellheim
LPs: LM/LSC-7041 (2)

HANDEL: Six Organ Concertos, op. 4
   No. 1 in G Minor (16:52)
   No. 2 in B♭ (8:55)
   No. 3 in G Minor (11:04)
   No. 4 in F (16:05)
   No. 5 in F (8:46)
   No. 6 in B♭ (8:32)
Arthur Fiedler's Sinfonietta. Carl Weinrich, organ
June 29, 30, 1966; July 1, 2, 1966. General Theological Seminary, New York.
   Producer Peter Dellheim
LPs: LSC-7047 (2)

HANDEL: Six Organ Concertos, op. 7
   No. 1 in B♭ (17:48)
   No. 2 in A (12:35)
   No. 3 in B♭ (11:54)
   No. 4 in D Minor (17:27)
   No. 5 in G Minor (12:56)
   No. 6 in B♭ (9:17)
Arthur Fiedler's Sinfonietta. Carl Weinrich, organ
June 26, 27, 28, 1967. General Theological Seminary, New York.
   Producer Peter Dellheim
LPs: LSC-7052 (2)

Columbia Symphony Orchestra

In the middle of the 20th century, Columbia and RCA Victor, the two largest American producers of classical records, maintained exclusive contracts with each major symphony orchestra and with star conductors, instrumentalists, and singers. Thus some desirable artistic matches could not take place: Artur Rubinstein never recorded with the New York Philharmonic, nor did Rudolf Serkin with the Boston Symphony (in that era). With European companies, when there was a need to cross contract lines, temporary agreements would be forged for one recording—"Madame X appears courtesy of . . . "—with some quid pro quo expected. In America, an orchestra would be privately contracted by the competing record company and be assigned a pseudonym. On RCA, "Leopold Stokowski and His Symphony Orchestra" usually meant musicians from the New York Philharmonic and/or the NBC Symphony. Across the aisle, "Columbia Symphony Orchestra" was used for a variety of such situations. It could be George Szell's Cleveland Orchestra (even though it recorded for Epic, a Columbia subsidiary), the Los Angeles musicians brought together for Bruno Walter's stereo recordings, the Vienna Symphony Orchestra, or the Boston Symphony. First-desk players often would be listed on the cover, to make sure the purchaser knew which orchestra was playing; the Boston performances were led by BSO concertmaster and associate conductor Richard Burgin.

E. Power Biggs—at that time an exclusive Columbia artist—and the new (1947/49) Aeolian-Skinner organ in Symphony Hall were a perfect fit with the BSO in these organ concertos and in Bach's music. Biggs performed the Hindemith and Poulenc Concertos with Charles Munch and the BSO on November 14, 1949, at a concert for the benefit of the Albert Schweitzer Hospital. Dr. Schweitzer had inspected the organ at the factory in July "and gave it his enthusiastic endorsement" (from the program notes to that concert).

POULENC, FRANCIS
Concerto in G Minor for Organ, Strings, and Timpani (21:21)
Columbia Symphony Orchestra, conductor Richard Burgin. E. Power Biggs,
    organ; Roman Szulc, timpani; Joseph De Pasquale, viola solo; Samuel
    Mayes, cello solo
December 1, 1949. Symphony Hall
Columbia Records. Matrix XCO-42094/98
78s: MM-951 (73137-D/73139-D). **LPs:** ML 4329

HINDEMITH, PAUL
Concerto for Organ and Chamber Orchestra, op. 46, no. 2 (14:52)
Columbia Symphony Orchestra, conductor Richard Burgin. E. Power Biggs,
    organ
March 22, 1951. Symphony Hall
Columbia Records.
LPs: ML 5199

BACH, JOHANN SEBASTIAN
Cantata No. 29: No. 1. Sinfonia (4:08)
Cantata No. 142: No. 1, Concerto; No. 8, Chorale "Alleluja" (3:56)
**Christmas Oratorio, BWV 248/6: No. 11. Chorale "Now Christ doth end in
    triumph" (3:20)**
Cantata No. 146: No. 7. Aria (Duet) "My spirit be joyful" (6:10)
Cantata No. 208: No. 9. Aria "Sheep may safely graze" (5:45)
Cantata No. 182: No. 1. Sonata (2:57)
Cantata No. 129: Chorale "Awake thou wintry earth" (2:52)
Columbia Chamber Orchestra, conductor Richard Burgin.
E. Power Biggs, organ. Roger Voisin and Jean Marcel LaFosse, solo trumpets;
    Phillip Kaplan and Lois Schaefer, solo flutes; Alfred Krips, solo violin, Sa-
    muel Mayes, solo cello
May 24, 1951. Symphony Hall
Columbia Records.
LPs: ML-4435. *Vocal parts have been rescored for solo instruments; not all
    of these recordings include strings. This album, entitled "Music of Jubi-
    lee," also contains solo organ selections, which are not listed here.*

Biggs made many more Columbia recordings in Boston, with groups labeled "New England Brass Ensemble" and "Boston Brass Ensemble," which often included players from the BSO. These were not orchestral performances by BSO musicians, nor was a stereo remake of "Music of Jubilee."

Appendix H:
Boston Symphony Chamber Players

The Boston Symphony Chamber Players consists of section leaders of the BSO. The ensemble is often augmented by other musicians from the BSO and by guest artists, as called for by the work being played. The group was founded in 1964 and has played concerts and made recordings regularly since that time. Musicians of the BSO have recorded independently, both solo and in ensemble, over an even longer span than has the orchestra itself. Douglas Yeo, BSO bass trombone and an active scholar of the orchestra's history, discovered recordings made in 1906 by an ensemble calling itself the Boston Symphony Trombone Quartet, three of whom were the BSO trombone section at the time. This appendix is devoted exclusively to the Boston Symphony Chamber Players, so it does not include recordings by any other ensembles or soloists from the orchestra.

The Boston Symphony Chamber Players recorded in a number of venues:

Symphony Hall, Boston (October 24, 1964–May 21, 1993)
Jordan Hall, New England Conservatory of Music, Boston (November 6, 1977–April 6, 1986)
Corpus Christi Rectory, Housatonic, Massachusetts (July 5– 6, 1982)
Trinity Parish Church, Lenox, Massachusetts (July 3–10, 1983)
Houghton Memorial Chapel, Wellesley College, Wellesley, Massachusetts (May 4, 1987–May 13, 1988)
Theatre Concert Hall, Tanglewood (June 26, 1981–June 28, 1991)
Seiji Ozawa Hall, Tanglewood (July 16, 1996–June 23, 1997)
St. Mark's School, Southborough, Massachusetts (May 8–13, 2006)

This appendix is complete within itself; no references are made to any other section of this book. A composer index for these recordings appears at the end of this appendix.

The members of the Boston Symphony Chamber Players are listed below, as are assisting artists from the BSO and guest artists, for whom recording session dates are listed.

Founding Members

Joseph Silverstein	Concertmaster
Clarence Knudsen	Second Violin
Burton Fine	Viola
Jules Eskin	Cello
Georges Moleux	Double Bass
Doriot Anthony Dwyer	Flute
Ralph Gomberg	Oboe
Gino Cioffi	Clarinet
Sherman Walt	Bassoon
James Stagliano	French Horn
Armando Ghitalla	Trumpet
William Gibson	Trombone

Members

Malcolm Lowe	Concertmaster
Marylou Speaker Churchill	Second Violin
Haldan Martinson	Second Violin
Steven Ansell	Viola
Jules Eskin	Cello
Henry Portnoi	Double Bass
Edwin Barker	Double Bass
Elizabeth Rowe	Flute
Alfred Genovese	Oboe
John Ferrillo	Oboe
Harold Wright	Clarinet
William R. Hudgins	Clarinet
Richard Svoboda	Bassoon
Charles Kavalovski	French Horn
James Sommerville	French Horn
Rolf Smedvig	Trumpet
Charles Schlueter	Trumpet
Ronald Barron	Trombone
Ann Hobson Pilot	Harp
Everett Firth	Percussion

Assisting BSO Members

Max Hobart	Violin
Alfred Krips	Violin
Lucia Lin	Violin
Laura Park	Violin
Cathy Basrak	Viola
Patricia McCarty	Viola
Martha Babcock	Cello
Leone Buyse	Flute
Peter Hadcock	Clarinet
Laurence Thorstenberg	English Horn
Matthew Ruggerio	Bassoon
Richard Plaster	Contrabassoon
Andre Côme	Trumpet
Timothy Morrison	Trumpet
Gordon Hallberg	Bass Trombone
Frank Epstein	Percussion
Arthur Press	Percussion
Charles Smith	Percussion
Michael Tilson Thomas	Piano

Guest Artists

David Epstein, conductor	January 31, 1970
Leon Kirchner, conductor	May 13, 1988; February 6, 1989
Yehudi Wyner, conductor	November 6, 1977
Bethany Beardsley, soprano	January 31, 1970
Frederica Von Stade, mezzo-soprano	November 9, 1979
Sanford Sylvan, baritone	November 12, 1990
Samuel Rhodes, viola	June 28, 1991
William Wrzesien, bass clarinet	February 16, 1979
Lawrence Isaacson, trombone	February 6 and 7, 1989
Claude Frank, piano	February 8, 1965–October 9, 1967
Richard Goode, piano	May 8–31, 1968
Martin Katz, piano	November 9, 1979
Gilbert Kalish, piano, celeste	April 8, 1977–June 23, 1997
Robert Levin, piano, harpsichord	September 28. October 12, 1970
Jerome Rosen, harpsichord, harmonium	April 8, 1977–February 7, 1989
Myron Romanul, cimbalom	December 9, 1974
John Gielgud, narrator	May 10, 1972
Tom Courtenay, speaker	May 10, 1972
Ron Moody, speaker	May 10, 1972

BEETHOVEN, LUDWIG VAN
Serenade in D for Flute, Violin, and Viola, op. 25 (21:18)
Dwyer, Silverstein, Fine
October 26, 1964. Symphony Hall
RCA, producer Richard Mohr
LP: LM/LSC-6167 (3)

MOZART, WOLFGANG AMADEUS
Quartet in F for Oboe and Strings, K. 370 (12:10)
Gomberg, Silverstein, Fine, Eskin
October 26, 1964. Symphony Hall
RCA, producer Richard Mohr
LP: LM/LSC-6167 (3)

MOZART, WOLFGANG AMADEUS
Quartet in D for Flute and Strings, K. 285 (12:10)
Dwyer, Silverstein, Fine, Eskin
October 27, 1964. Symphony Hall
RCA, producer Richard Mohr
LP: LM/LSC-6167 (3)

BRAHMS, JOHANNES
Quartet No. 3 in C Minor for Piano and Strings, op. 60 (36:45)
Claude Frank, piano; Silverstein, Fine, Eskin
February 8, 1965; February 9, 1965. Symphony Hall
RCA, producer Richard Mohr
LP: LM/LSC-6167 (3)

MOZART, WOLFGANG AMADEUS
Quintet in E♭ for Piano and Winds, K. 452 (25:51)
Claude Frank, piano; Gomberg, Cioffi, Walt, Stagliano
February 8, 1965; January 19, 1966; January 20, 1966. Symphony Hall
RCA, producer Richard Mohr
LP: LM/LSC-6184 (3)

COPLAND, AARON
Vitebsk, Study on a Jewish Theme, **for Violin, Cello, and Piano (12:19)**
Silverstein, Eskin; Claude Frank, piano
February 9, 1965. Symphony Hall
RCA, producer Richard Mohr
LP: LM/LSC-6167 (3)

FINE, IRVING
Fantasia for String Trio (14:21)
Silverstein, Fine, Eskin
February 9, 1965. Symphony Hall
RCA, producer Richard Mohr
LP: LM/LSC-6167 (3)

PISTON, WALTER
Divertimento (1946), for Flute, Oboe, Clarinet, Bassoon, String Quartet, and Double bass (11:23)
Dwyer, Gomberg, Cioffi, Walt, Silverstein, Krips, Fine, Eskin, Moleux
April 26, 1965. Symphony Hall
RCA, producer Richard Mohr
LP: LM/LSC-6167 (3)

CARTER, ELLIOTT
Woodwind Quintet (1948) (8:11)
Dwyer, Gomberg, Cioffi, Walt, Stagliano
April 26, 1965. Symphony Hall
RCA, producer Richard Mohr
LP: LM/LSC-6167 (3)

MOZART, WOLFGANG AMADEUS
Quartet in G Minor for Piano and Strings, K. 478 (24:52)
Claude Frank, piano; Silverstein, Fine, Eskin
January 19, 1966; January 22, 1966. Symphony Hall
RCA, producer Richard Mohr
LP: LM/LSC-6184 (3)

COLGRASS, MICHAEL
Variations for Four Drums and Viola (15:42)
Firth, Fine
April 19, 1966. Symphony Hall
RCA, producer Richard Mohr
LP: LM/LSC-6184 (3)

POULENC, FRANCIS
Sonata for Trumpet, Horn, and Trombone
Ghitalla, Stagliano, Gibson
April 20, 1966. Symphony Hall
RCA, producer Richard Mohr
Unreleased

POULENC, FRANCIS
Trio for Oboe, Bassoon, and Piano (1926) (13:07)
Gomberg, Walt; Claude Frank, piano
April 21, 1966. Symphony Hall
RCA, producer Richard Mohr
LP: LM/LSC-6184 (3)

BRAHMS, JOHANNES
Trio in E♭ for Horn, Violin, and Piano, op. 40 (30:39)
Stagliano, Silverstein; Claude Frank, piano
October 17, 1966. Symphony Hall
RCA, producer Richard Mohr
LP: LM/LSC-6184 (3)

VILLA-LOBOS, HECTOR
Bachianas brasileiras No. 6, **for Flute and Bassoon (9:44)**
Dwyer, Walt
November 14, 1966. Symphony Hall
RCA, producer Richard Mohr
LP: LM/LSC-6184 (3)

HAIEFF, ALEXEI
Three Bagatelles for Oboe and Bassoon (7:06)
Gomberg, Walt
November 14, 1966. Symphony Hall
RCA, producer Richard Mohr
LP: LM/LSC-6184 (3)

HINDEMITH, PAUL
Kleine Kammermusik, op. 24, no. 2 (13:15)
Dwyer, Gomberg, Cioffi, Walt, Stagliano
November 28, 1966. Symphony Hall
RCA, producer Richard Mohr
LP: LSC-3166

SCHUBERT, FRANZ
String Trio No. 1 in B♭ (one movement), **D. 471 (7:31)**
Silverstein, Fine, Eskin
December 22, 1966. Symphony Hall
RCA, producer Richard Mohr
LP: LM/LSC-6184 (3)

SPOHR, LUDWIG
Nonet in F, op. 31, for Wind Quintet, Violin, Viola, Cello, and Double Bass (28:23)
Dwyer, Gomberg, Cioffi, Walt, Stagliano, Silverstein, Fine, Eskin, Portnoi
February 1, 1967; February 2, 1967. Symphony Hall
RCA, producer Richard Mohr
Unreleased

MILHAUD, DARIUS
Pastorale, op. 147, for Oboe, Clarinet, and Bassoon (4:27)
Gomberg, Cioffi, Walt
February 13, 1967. Symphony Hall
RCA, producer Richard Mohr
LP: LSC-3166

COKER, WILSON
Concertino for Bassoon and String Trio (7:20)
Walt, Silverstein, Fine, Eskin
March 6, 1967. Symphony Hall
RCA, producer Richard Mohr
Unreleased

SCHUBERT, FRANZ
Piano Trio No. 1 in B♭, D. 898 (35:58)
Claude Frank, piano; Silverstein, Eskin
October 9, 1967; October 11, 1967. Symphony Hall
RCA, producer Richard Mohr
LP: LSC-3166

POULENC, FRANCIS
Sextet for Piano and Wind Quintet (1932) (18:04)
Richard Goode, piano; Dwyer, Gomberg, Cioffi, Walt, Stagliano
May 8, 1968. Symphony Hall
RCA, producer Peter Dellheim
LP: LM/LSC-6189 (3)

SCHUBERT, FRANZ
Quintet in A for Piano and Strings, D. 667 "Trout" (33:35)
Richard Goode, piano; Silverstein, Fine, Eskin, Portnoi
May 9, 1968; May 27, 1968. Symphony Hall
RCA, producer Peter Dellheim
LP: LM/LSC-6189 (3)

BARBER, SAMUEL
Summer Music, **for Wind Quintet (13:00)**
Dwyer, Gomberg, Cioffi, Walt, Stagliano
May 9, 1968. Symphony Hall
RCA, producer Peter Dellheim
Unreleased

WEBERN, ANTON
Concerto, op. 24, for Flute, Oboe, Clarinet, Horn, Trumpet, Trombone, Violin, Viola, and Piano (7:48)
Dwyer, Gomberg, Cioffi, Stagliano, Ghitalla, Gibson, Siverstein, Fine; Richard Goode, piano
May 27, 1968. Symphony Hall
RCA, producer Peter Dellheim
LP: LM/LSC-6189 (3)

DAHL, INGOLF
Duettino concertante, for Flute and Percussion (9:24)
Dwyer, Firth
May 29, 1968. Symphony Hall
RCA, producer Peter Dellheim
LP: LM/LSC-6189 (3)

BRAHMS, JOHANNES
Piano Trio No. 1 in B, op. 8 (37:14)
Richard Goode, piano; Silverstein, Eskin
May 31, 1968. Symphony Hall
RCA, producer Peter Dellheim
LP: LM/LSC-6189 (3)

MARTINŮ, BOHUSLAV
Nonet for Strings and Winds (14:52)
Silverstein, Fine, Eskin, Portnoi, Dwyer, Gomberg, Cioffi, Stagliano, Walt
May 31, 1968. Symphony Hall
RCA, producer Peter Dellheim
LP: LM/LSC-6189 (3)

DEBUSSY, CLAUDE
Sonata No. 2, for Flute, Viola, and Harp (17:10)
Dwyer, Fine, Pilot
January 26, 1970. Symphony Hall
Deutsche Grammophon, producer Thomas W. Mowrey
LP: 2530 049. 2721 020 (3). 2733 007 (3). **CD:** Universal B0005833-02.
    Eloquence 476 7703 (Australia)

LERDAHL, FRED
***Wake*, for String Trio, Harp, Percussion, and Voice (14:45)**
David Epstein, conductor; Silverstein, Fine, Eskin, Firth, Pilot, Press, Smith;
    Bethany Beardsley, soprano
January 31, 1970. Symphony Hall
Acoustic Research, in collaboration with Deutsche Grammophon, producer
    Gerald Randall
LP: 0654 083. **CD:** CRI CD-580. New World NWCR580

DEBUSSY, CLAUDE
***Syrinx*, for Flute unaccompanied (2:42)**
Dwyer
February 3, 1970. Symphony Hall
Deutsche Grammophon, producer Rainer Brock
LP: 2530 049. 2721 020 (3). 2733 007 (3). **CD:** 469 130-2. 472 404 (2).
    Eloquence 476 7703 (Australia)

DEBUSSY, CLAUDE
Sonata No. 3, for Violin and Piano (13:48)
Silverstein, Tilson Thomas
February 3, 1970. Symphony Hall
Deutsche Grammophon, producer Rainer Brock
LP: 2530 049. 2721 020 (3). 2733 007 (3). **CD:** Eloquence 476 7703 (Australia)

DEBUSSY, CLAUDE
Sonata No. 1 in D Minor, for Cello and Piano (12:19)
Eskin, Tilson Thomas
February 3, 1970. Symphony Hall
Deutsche Grammophon, producer Rainer Brock
LP: 2530 049. 2721 020 (3). 2733 007 (3). **CD:** Eloquence 476 7703 (Australia)

CARTER, ELLIOTT
Sonata for Flute, Oboe, Cello, and Harpsichord (15:49)
Dwyer, Gomberg, Eskin; Robert Levin, harpsichord
September 28, 1970. Symphony Hall
Deutsche Grammophon, producer Rainer Brock
LP: 2530 104. A September 26 session was for rehearsal only.

IVES, CHARLES
Largo for Violin, Clarinet, and Piano (5:49)
Silverstein, Wright; Robert Levin, piano
October 12, 1970. Symphony Hall
Deutsche Grammophon, producer Rainer Brock
LP: 2530 104

PORTER, QUINCY
Quintet for Oboe and Strings "Elegiac" (1966) (19:52)
Gomberg, Silverstein, Hobart, Fine, Eskin
October 12, 1970. Symphony Hall
Deutsche Grammophon, producer Rainer Brock
LP: 2530 104

DVOŘÁK, ANTONIN
String Quintet in G, op. 77 (37:59)
Silverstein, Hobart, Fine, Eskin, Portnoi
June 3, 1971; June 4, 1971; June 5, 1971. Symphony Hall
Deutsche Grammophon, producer Thomas W. Mowrey
LP: 2530 214

STRAVINSKY, IGOR
L'Histoire du soldat. Text by C. F. Ramuz; English version by Michael Flan-
ders and Kitty Black **(60:01)**
John Gielgud, narrator; Tom Courtenay (The Soldier); Ron Moody (The Devil);
Silverstein, Portnoi, Wright, Ghitalla (cornet à pistons), Gibson, Firth
May 11, 1971; May 12, 1971. Symphony Hall
Deutsche Grammophon, producer Thomas W. Mowrey
LP: 2530 609. 2535 456. 2530 489 (German issue, with Boy Gobert, Peter
Striebeck, and Kurt Meise). 2530 590 (French issue, soloists unknown)

STRAVINSKY, IGOR
Septet (11:41)
Gilbert Kalish, piano; Silverstein, Fine, Eskin, Wright, Kavalovski, Walt
December 7, 1974. Symphony Hall
Deutsche Grammophon, producer Thomas W. Mowrey
LP: 2530 551

STRAVINSKY, IGOR
Pastorale for Violin, Oboe, English Horn, Clarinet, and Bassoon
   (arr. Samuel Dushkin) **(2:57)**
Silverstein, Gomberg, Thorstenberg, Wright, Walt
December 7, 1974. Symphony Hall
Deutsche Grammophon, producer Thomas W. Mowrey
LP: 2530 551. 2545 023. **CD:** 463 667-2. 000504202 (2). 000661002 (2)

STRAVINSKY, IGOR
Octet for Wind Instruments (15:22)
Dwyer, Wright, Walt, Ruggerio, Ghitalla, Côme, Gibson, Hallberg
December 9, 1974. Symphony Hall
Deutsche Grammophon, producer Thomas W. Mowrey
LP: 2530 551. **CD:** 463 667-2

STRAVINSKY, IGOR
Ragtime for 11 Instruments (4:38)
Silverstein, Hobart, Fine, Portnoi, Dwyer, Wright, Kavalovski, Ghitalla, Gibson,
   Firth; Myron Romanul, cimbalom
December 9, 1974. Symphony Hall
Deutsche Grammophon, producer Thomas W. Mowrey
LP: 2530 551. **CD:** 463 667-2

STRAVINSKY, IGOR
Concertino for 12 Instruments (6:34)
Silverstein, Eskin, Dwyer, Gomberg, Thorstenberg, Wright, Walt, Ruggerio,
   Ghitalla, Smedvig, Gibson, Hallberg
December 9, 1974. Symphony Hall
Deutsche Grammophon, producer Thomas W. Mowrey
LP: 2530 551. **CD:** 463 667-2

STRAUSS, JOHANN JR
Wein, Weib, und Gesang, op. 333 (arr. Alban Berg) **(13:12)**
Gilbert Kalish, piano; Silverstein, Hobart, Fine, Eskin
April 8, 1977. Symphony Hall
Deutsche Grammophon, producer Rainer Brock
LP: 2530 977. 413 800-1. 413 797-1 (10). **CD:** 463 667-2. B0002051-02 (8)

STRAUSS, JOHANN JR
Kaiser-Walzer, op. 437 (arr. Arnold Schoenberg) (12:24)
Gilbert Kalish, piano; Silverstein, Hobart, Eskin, Dwyer, Wright
April 8, 1977. Symphony Hall
Deutsche Grammophon, producer Rainer Brock
LP: 2530 977. 413 797-1 (10). CD: 463 667-2

STRAUSS, JOHANN JR
Rosen aus dem Süden, op. 388 (arr. Arnold Schoenberg) (9:51)
Gilbert Kalish, piano; Jerome Rosen, harmonium; Silverstein, Hobart, Fine,
     Eskin
April 8, 1977. Symphony Hall
Deutsche Grammophon, producer Rainer Brock
LP: 2530 977. 413 797-1 (10). CD: 463 667-2

STRAUSS, JOHANN JR
Die Zigeunerbaron: Schatz-Walzer, op. 418 (arr. Anton Webern) (8.58)
Gilbert Kalish, piano; Jerome Rosen, harmonium; Silverstein, Hobart, Fine,
     Eskin
April 8, 1977. Symphony Hall
Deutsche Grammophon, producer Rainer Brock
LP: 2530 977. 413 797-1 (10). CD: 463 667-2

SCHOENBERG, ARNOLD
Chamber Symphony No. 1 in E, op. 9 (arr. Anton Webern) (21:37)
Silverstein, Dwyer, Wright, Eskin; Gilbert Kalish, piano
October 2, 1977. Symphony Hall
Deutsche Grammophon, producer Rainer Brock
LP: 2531 213

BERG, ALBAN
Chamber Concerto: Adagio (arr. Berg) (15:32)
Silverstein, Wright; Gilbert Kalish, piano
October 16, 1977. Symphony Hall
Deutsche Grammophon, producer Rainer Brock
LP: 2531 213. 413 800-1. 413 797-1 (10)

WYNER, YEHUDI
Serenade for Flute, Trumpet, Horn, Trombone, Viola, Cello, and Piano
     (14:17)
Yehudi Wyner, conductor; Dwyer, Ghitalla, Kavalovski, Barron, Fine, Eskin;
     Gilbert Kalish, piano
November 6, 1977. Jordan Hall, New England Conservatory of Music, Boston
     (live)
Composers Recordings Inc.
CD: CRI CD-701. A CRI LP contained a different performance of this piece,
     one not played by the BSCP.

DEBUSSY, CLAUDE
Prélude à l'après-midi d'un faune (transcription by Benno Sachs) **(10:50)**
Silverstein, Hobart, Fine, Eskin, Barker, Dwyer, Gomberg, Wright, Firth, antique cymbals; Frank Epstein, antique cymbals; Gilbert Kalish, piano; Jerome Rosen, harmonium
April 27, 1978. Symphony Hall
Deutsche Grammophon, producer Rainer Brock
LP: 2531 213. **CD:** Eloquence 476 7703 (Australia)

SCHOENBERG, ARNOLD
Phantasy for Violin and Piano, op. 47 (9:20)
Silverstein; Gilbert Kalish, piano
April 27, 1978. Symphony Hall
Deutsche Grammophon: Rainer Brock
LP: 2531 277

SCHOENBERG, ARNOLD
Suite for Chamber Ensemble, op. 29 (34:44)
Silverstein, Fine, Eskin, Wright, Hadcock, Wrzesien; Gilbert Kalisch, piano
February 16, 1979. Symphony Hall
Deutsche Grammophon, producer Rainer Brock
LP: 2531 277

RAVEL, MAURICE
Chansons madécasses, **for Flute, Piano, Cello, and Voice (14:52)**
Frederica Von Stade, mezzo-soprano; Martin Katz, piano; Dwyer, Eskin
November 9, 1979; November 10, 1979. Symphony Hall
CBS, producer Paul Myers
LP: M-36665

BEETHOVEN, LUDWIG VAN
Septet in E♭ for Winds and Strings, op. 20 (42:40)
Silverstein, Fine, Eskin, Barker, Wright, Walt, Kavalovski
April 14, 1980; April 15, 1980. Symphony Hall
Nonesuch, producer Judith Sherman
LP: 78015

SCHUBERT, FRANZ
Octet in F for String Quintet, Clarinet, Horn, and Bassoon, D. 803 (59:06)
Silverstein, Hobart, Fine, Eskin, Barker, Wright, Kavalovski, Walt
May 12, 1981; May 14, 1981. Symphony Hall
Nonesuch, producers Marc J. Aubort and Joanna Nickrenz
LP: 79046-1. **CD:** 79046-2

BARTÓK, BÉLA
Contrasts, for Violin, Clarinet, and Piano, Sz. 111 (17:33)
Wright, Silverstein; Gilbert Kalish, piano
June 26, 1981. Theatre Concert Hall, Tanglewood (live)
Boston Records, producer Wayne Rapier
CD: BR1066. The CD booklet claims that the performance took place in 1977, but the Boston Symphony Archives show only this 1981 performance at Tanglewood.

BRAHMS, JOHANNES
String Quintet No. 2 in G, op. 111 (30:20)
Silverstein, Hobart, Fine, McCarty, Eskin
July 5, 1982. Corpus Christi Rectory, Housatonic, Mass.
Nonesuch, producers Marc J. Aubort and Joanna Nickrenz
LP: 79068-1. CD: 79068-2

BRAHMS, JOHANNES
String Quintet No. 1 in F, op. 88 *(29:31)*
Silverstein, Hobart, Fine, McCarty, Eskin
July 6, 1982. Corpus Christi Rectory, Housatonic, Mass.
Nonesuch, producers Marc J. Aubort and Joanna Nickrenz
LP: 79068-1. CD: 79068-2

MENDELSSOHN, FELIX
Concert Piece No. 1 in F for Clarinet, Basset Horn, and Piano, op. 113 (8:35)
Wright, Walt; Gilbert Kalish, piano
April 24, 1983. Jordan Hall, New England Conservatory of Music, Boston (live)
Boston Records, producer Wayne Rapier
CD: BR1025CD

BRAHMS, JOHANNES
Trio in E♭ for Horn, Violin, and Piano, op. 40 (31:33)
Kavalovski, Silverstein; Gilbert Kalish, piano
July 3, 1983; July 4, 1983. Trinity Parish Church, Lenox, Mass.
Nonesuch, producers Marc Aubort and Joanna Nickrenz
LP: 79076-1

BRAHMS, JOHANNES
Trio in A Minor for Clarinet, Cello, and Piano, op. 114 (27:27)
Wright, Eskin; Gilbert Kalish, piano
July 3, 1983; July 4, 1983; July 5, 1983. Trinity Parish Church, Lenox, Mass.
Nonesuch, producers Marc Aubort and Joanna Nickrenz
LP: 79076-1

DVOŘÁK, ANTONIN
Sextet in A for Strings, op. 48 (32:16)
Silverstein, Hobart, Fine, McCarty, Eskin, Babcock
July 9, 1984. Trinity Parish Church, Lenox, Mass.
Nonesuch, producers Marc Aubort and Joanna Nickrenz
LP: 79128-1. **CD:** 79128-2

SMETANA, BEDŘICH
Piano Trio in G Minor, op. 15 (28:28)
Silverstein, Eskin; Gilbert Kalish, piano
July 10, 1984. Trinity Parish Church, Lenox, Mass.
Nonesuch, producers Marc Aubort and Joanna Nickrenz
LP: 79128-1. **CD:** 79128-2

MENDELSSOHN, FELIX
Concert Piece No. 2 in D Minor for Clarinet, Basset Horn, and Piano, op. 114 (9:26)
Wright, Walt; Gilbert Kalish, piano
April 6, 1986. Jordan Hall, New England Conservatory of Music, Boston (live)
Boston Records, producer Wayne Rapier
CD: BR1025CD

COPLAND, AARON
Sextet for Clarinet, Piano, and String Quartet (1937) (15:40)
Wright; Gilbert Kalish, piano; Lowe, Hobart, Fine, Eskin
May 4, 1987; May 7, 1987. Houghton Memorial Chapel, Wellesley College, Wellesley, Mass.
Elektra Nonesuch, producers Marc J. Aubert and Joanna Nickrenz
LP: 79168-1. **CD:** 79168-2

COPLAND, AARON
Quartet for Piano and Strings (20:45)
Gilbert Kalish, piano; Lowe, Fine, Eskin
May 5, 1987; May 7, 1987. Houghton Memorial Chapel, Wellesley College, Wellesley, Mass.
Elektra Nonesuch, producers Marc J. Aubert and Joanna Nickrenz
LP: 79168-1. **CD:** 79168-2

HARBISON, JOHN
Piano Quintet (22:56)
Gilbert Kalish, piano; Lowe, Lin, Fine, Eskin
May 11, 1988. Symphony Hall
Elektra Nonesuch, producers Marc Aubort and Joanna Nickrenz
CD: 79189-2

KIRCHNER, LEON
Trio for Violin, Cello, and Piano (13:50)
Gilbert Kalish, piano; Lowe, Eskin
May 11, 1988; May 12, 1988. Symphony Hall
Elektra Nonesuch, producers Marc Aubort and Joanna Nickrenz
CD: 79188-2

KIRCHNER, LEON
Music for 12 (14:36)
Leon Kirchner, conductor; Gilbert Kalish, piano and celeste; Lowe, Fine, Eskin,
  Barker, Dwyer, Genovese, Wright, Walt, Kavalovski, Schlueter, Barron
May 13, 1988. Houghton Memorial Chapel, Wellesley College, Wellesley,
  Mass.
Elektra Nonesuch, producers Marc Aubort and Joanna Nickrenz
CD: 79188-2

KIRCHNER, LEON
Concerto for Violin, Cello, Ten Winds, and Percussion (19:08)
Leon Kirchner, conductor; Lowe, Eskin, Dwyer, Genovese, Hadcock, Walt,
  Plaster, Kavalovski, Schlueter, Morrison, Barron, Isaacson, Firth, Press,
  Epstein; Jerome Rosen, harpsichord
February 6, 1989; February 7, 1989. Symphony Hall
Elektra Nonesuch, producers Marc Aubort and Joanna Nickrenz
CD: 79188-2

HARBISON, JOHN
Words from Paterson (26:55)
Sanford Sylvan, baritone; Gilbert Kalish, piano; Buyse, Genovese, Thorsten-
  berg, Fine, Eskin, Pilot
November 12, 1990. Symphony Hall
Elektra Nonesuch, producer Max Wilcox
CD: 79189-2

MOZART, WOLFGANG AMADEUS
Trio for Clarinet, Viola, and Piano in E♭, K. 498 "Kegelstatt" (20:56)
Wright; Samuel Rhodes, viola; Gilbert Kalish, piano
June 28, 1991. Theatre Concert Hall, Tanglewood (live)
Boston Records, producer Wayne Rapier
CD: BR1025CD

BRAHMS, JOHANNES
Quintet in B Minor for Clarinet and Strings, op. 115 (38:48)
Wright, Lowe, Park, Fine, Eskin
May 19, 1993, May 20, 1993. Symphony Hall
Philips, producer Ursula Singer
CD: 442 149-2

MOZART, WOLFGANG AMADEUS
Quintet in A for Clarinet and Strings, K. 581 (33:33)
Wright, Lowe, Park, Fine, Eskin
May 20, 1993; May 21, 1993. Symphony Hall
Philips, producer Ursula Singer
CD: 442 149-2

HINDEMITH, PAUL
Quartet for Clarinet, Violin, Cello, and Piano (1938)
Hudgins, Lowe, Eskin; Gilbert Kalisch, piano
July 16, 1996. Seiji Ozawa Hall, Tanglewood
Arabesque, producer Adam Abeshouse
CD: Z-6715-D

SHOSTAKOVICH, DMITRI
Quintet for Piano and Strings, op. 57
Gilbert Kalish, piano; Lowe, Churchill, Ansell, Eskin
June 23, 1997. Seiji Ozawa Hall, Tanglewood
Arabesque, producer Adam Abeshouse
CD: Z-6715-D

MOZART, WOLFGANG AMADEUS
Quintet in E♭ for Horn and Strings, K. 407 (16:29)
Sommerville, Lowe, Ansell, Basrak, Eskin
May 8, 2006. St. Mark's School, Southborough, Mass.
BSO Classics, producer Elizabeth Ostrow
Hybrid SACD: 0601

MOZART, WOLFGANG AMADEUS
Quintet in A for Clarinet and Strings, K. 581 (33:33)
Hudgins, Lowe, Martinson, Ansell, Eskin
May 9, 2006; May 11, 2006. St. Mark's School, Southborough, Mass.
BSO Classics, producer Elizabeth Ostrow
Hybrid SACD: 0601

MOZART, WOLFGANG AMADEUS
Quartet in A for Flute and Strings, K. 298 (12:05)
Rowe, Lowe, Ansell, Eskin
May 11, 2006. St. Mark's School, Southborough, Mass.
BSO Classics, producer Elizabeth Ostrow
Hybrid SACD: 0601

MOZART, WOLFGANG AMADEUS
Quartet in F for Oboe and Strings, K. 370 (14:32)
Ferrillo, Lowe, Ansell, Eskin
May 13, 2006. St. Mark's School, Southborough, Mass.
BSO Classics, producer Elizabeth Ostrow
Hybrid SACD: 0601

Composer Index for Boston Symphony Chamber Players

BARBER
Summer Music May 9, 1968

BARTÓK
Contrasts June 26, 1981

BEETHOVEN
Septet in E♭ for Winds and Strings, op. 20 April 14, 1980
Serenade in D for Flute, Violin, Viola, op. 25 October 26, 1964

BERG
Chamber Concerto: Adagio October 16, 1977

BRAHMS
Clarinet Quintet in B Minor, op. 115 May 19, 1993
Piano Quartet No. 3 in C Minor, op. 60 February 8, 1965
String Quintet No. 1 in F, op. 88 July 6, 1982
String Quintet No. 2 in G, op. 111 July 5, 1982
Clarinet Trio in A Minor, op. 114 July 3, 1983
Trio in E♭ for Horn, Violin, and Piano, op. 40 October 17, 1966; July 3, 1983
Piano Trio No. 1 in B, op. 8 May 31, 1968

CARTER
Sonata for Flute, Oboe, Cello, Harpsichord September 28, 1970
Woodwind Quintet April 26, 1965

COKER
Concertino for Bassoon and String Trio March 6, 1967

COLGRASS
Variations for Four Drums and Viola April 19, 1966

COPLAND
Quartet for Piano and Strings May 5, 1987
Sextet for Clarinet, Piano, and String Quartet May 4, 1987
Vitebsk, Study on a Jewish Theme February 9, 1965

DAHL
Duettino concertante, for Flute and Percussion May 29, 1968

DEBUSSY
Prélude à l'après-midi d'un faune April 27, 1978
Sonata No. 1 in D Minor, for Cello and Piano February 3, 1970
Sonata No. 2, for Flute, Viola, and Harp January 26, 1970
Sonata No. 3, for Violin and Piano February 3, 1970
Syrinx, for Flute unaccompanied February 3, 1970

DVOŘÁK
String Quintet in G, op. 77 June 3, 1971
String Sextet in A, op. 48 July 9, 1984

FINE
Fantasia for String Trio   February 9, 1965

HAIEFF
Three Bagatelles for Oboe and Bassoon   November 14, 1966

HARBISON
Piano Quintet   May 11, 1988
Words from Paterson   November 12, 1990

HINDEMITH
Kleine Kammermusik, op. 24, no. 2   November 28, 1966
Quartet for Clarinet, Violin, Cello, and Piano   July 16, 1996

IVES
Largo for Violin, Clarinet, and Piano   October 12, 1970

KIRCHNER
Concerto for Violin, Cello, and Ten Winds   February 6, 1989
Music for 12   May 13, 1988
Trio for Violin, Cello, and Piano   May 11, 1988

LERDAHL
Wake   January 31, 1970

MARTINŮ
Nonet for Strings and Winds   May 31, 1968

MENDELSSOHN
Concert Piece No. 1 in F, op. 113   April 24, 1983
Concert Piece No. 2 in D Minor, op. 114   April 6, 1986

MILHAUD
Pastorale, for Oboe, Clarinet, and Bassoon   February 13, 1967

MOZART
Flute Quartet in D, K. 285   October 27, 1964
Flute Quartet in A, K. 298   May 11, 2006
Oboe Quartet in F, K. 370   October 26, 1964; May 13, 2006
Piano Quartet in G Minor, K. 478   January 19, 1966
Horn Quintet in E♭, K. 407   May 8, 2006
Clarinet Quintet in A, K. 581   May 20, 1993; May 9, 2006
Piano Quintet in E♭, K. 452   February 8, 1965
Clarinet Trio in E♭, K. 498   June 28, 1991

PISTON
Divertimento for Nine Instruments   April 26, 1965

PORTER
Quintet for Oboe and Strings "Elegiac"   October 12, 1970

POULENC
Sextet for Piano and Wind Quintet	May 8, 1968
Sonata for Trumpet, Horn, and Trombone	April 20, 1966
Trio for Oboe, Bassoon, and Piano	April 21, 1966

RAVEL
Chansons madécasses	November 9, 1979

SCHOENBERG
Chamber Symphony No. 1 in E, op. 9	October 2, 1977
Phantasy for Violin and Piano, op. 47	April 27, 1978
Suite for Chamber Ensemble, op. 29	February 16, 1979

SCHUBERT
Octet in F, D. 803	May 12, 1981
Piano Quintet in A, D. 667 "Trout"	May 9, 1968
Piano Trio No. 1 in B♭, D. 898	October 9, 1967
String Trio No. 1 in B♭ (one movement), D.471	December 22, 1966

SHOSTAKOVICH
Piano Quintet, op. 57	June 23, 1997

SMETANA
Piano Trio in G Minor, op. 15	July 10, 1984

SPOHR
Nonet in F, op. 31	February 1, 1967

STRAUSS, Johann Jr
Kaiser-Walzer, op. 437	April 8, 1977
Rosen aus dem Süden, op. 388	April 8, 1977
Wein, Weib, und Gesang, op. 333	April 8, 1977
Die Zigeunerbaron: Schatz-Walzer, op. 418	April 8, 1977

STRAVINSKY
Concertino for 12 Instruments	December 9, 1974
L'Histoire du soldat	May 11, 1971
Octet for Wind Instruments	December 9, 1974
Pastorale	December 7, 1974
Ragtime for 11 Instruments	December 9, 1974
Septet	December 7, 1974

VILLA-LOBOS
Bachianas brasileiras No. 6	November 14, 1966

WEBERN
Concerto for Nine Instruments, op. 24	May 27, 1968

WYNER
Serenade for Seven Instruments	November 6, 1977

Appendix I: Pirate Recordings

It must be stated immediately that this is not a discography of BSO pirate recordings. By "pirate" we mean a recording of a live performance, which was not contracted for with the BSO, and for which the artists were neither paid nor (knowingly) contributed their services. Such a definition might include discs issued by the U.S. government during World War II and thereafter; although those records were not meant to be played in the United States, they are not pirates and are covered in Appendix F.

Whether or not the publication of a recording is illegal depends on the copyright laws of the country of publication at the time of publication. Italy generally has had shorter copyright protection than other nations, thus many pirates have been published there. Selling such discs in another country may or may not be legal, depending on local laws. Despite questions about the legality and morality of such actions, many pirate recordings exist and have become part of BSO history. To ignore them, or try to suppress information about them, is to be the proverbial ostrich with its head in the sand.

Pirate recordings usually originate from radio broadcasts, and the BSO has been broadcasting concerts on a regular basis since the mid-1930s. While some documentation exists of a majority of BSO broadcast concerts (mostly at the Library of Congress and at the Boston Symphony Orchestra Archives), we deal in this index only with recordings that have been marketed. We do not attempt to account for privately circulated tapes. All pirate LPs of which we are aware have been manufactured for sale, not just for the maker's own use. With the advent of home-made CDs, anyone with a computer can now make a copy of virtually any musical material. This appendix includes only such CD-Rs as have been offered for sale.

Much of Serge Koussevitzky's repertoire is not represented on commercial recordings, so pirate issues—notably 24 ASdisc CDs—are an important addition to his legacy. Though of generally poor sound, even for mid-1940s broadcasts, they allow us to hear his performances of both well-known works and out-of-the-way compositions. Differences between his live and recorded performances can be revealing: *The Isle of the Dead* is considerably faster in the March 31, 1945, live performance than in the studio recording made less than a month later. It was not uncommon in those days for musicians to speed up or slow down performances to meet timing limits of either 78-rpm sides or of radio broadcasts. Koussevitzky's readings of Arthur Foote's Suite for Strings are a case in point: parts of the broadcast are so fast that the orchestra can barely keep up. In addition to Koussevitzky, emphasis is given to conductors who were important to the BSO but made few commercial recordings with it, such as Leonard Bernstein, or none at all, such as Klaus Tennstedt. A few live performance recordings (notably, Bartók's Concerto for Orchestra) which first appeared as pirates later gained official status by being published in the BSO's 12-CD set, *Symphony Hall Centennial Celebration*; therefore they are covered in the main section and are not listed here.

Because its importance is repertory oriented, this list is ordered by composer and work, rather than the traditional chronological sequence. Dates listed are generally those of live radio broadcasts; exceptions are explained when known. Dates have been verified by checking the BSO's performance history. In the few cases where we cannot determine the exact day, we have listed possible alternate dates: (1/2, 3, 4/1956) or, in another case (8/14/70 or 7/24/71). Dates listed on pirate publications are notoriously unreliable; so many are wrong that we correct them without comment. A simple rule will suffice: ignore all dates listed on pirate issues. We believe that the dates listed here are correct in most cases.

Several pirate issues claiming to be BSO recordings (often with Leonard Bernstein listed as conductor) do not match any performance in BSO history. To list them with a note to that effect would be a mistake, as many discographic errors have been perpetuated for decades by listings which simply copy earlier data without examining it in proper detail. Thus we will cite only inexact examples: one Beethoven Symphony recording claims to be by Bernstein, but he never performed that symphony with the orchestra. Other attributions are so dubious—the music, conductor, and date cannot be matched to BSO performance history—that the issue is not included here.

Recordings were taken from performances given in the following venues:

Symphony Hall	Boston, Massachusetts
Sanders Theater, Harvard University	Cambridge, Massachusetts
Koussevitzky Music Shed	Tanglewood, Lenox, Massachusetts
Theatre Concert Hall	Tanglewood, Lenox, Massachusetts
Carnegie Hall	New York, New York
Hunter College Auditorium	New York, New York
Metropolitan Theater	Providence, Rhode Island
Bushnell Memorial Hall	Hartford, Connecticut
Woolsey Hall, Yale University	New Haven, Connecticut
The Syria Mosque	Pittsburgh, Pennsylvania
Masonic Temple	Detroit, Michigan
Milwaukee Auditorium	Milwaukee, Wisconsin
Great Hall of the Conservatory	Moscow, Russia
Smetana Hall	Prague, Czech Republic
Kultur und Kongresszentrum	Lucerne, Switzerland

Note that the Hunter College performances were given for radio broadcast but were not public concerts. In these listings, concerts in the Koussevitzky Music Shed are labeled simply "Tanglewood." Those in the Theatre Concert Hall are so identified.

Dates are given in the American form: Month/Day/Year. In general, the most accessible issues are listed, although that occasionally may mean a long-out-of-print Italian CD or a Japanese CD-R. A conductor listing appears at the end of this appendix. Many pirate recordings will be missing due to sheer ignorance; suggestions for additions will be welcomed, complaints about omissions will not. we cannot state too strongly, or too often, that this appendix does not pretend to be a discography.

AUBER *La Muette de Portici*: Overture
    Charles Munch (12/26/1953) Symphony Hall
    CDs: West Hill Radio Archive WHRA6015 (7)

BACH *Brandenburg Concertos*
    No. 3 in G, BWV 1048 (7/13/1946) **(14:38)**
    No. 4 in G, BWV 1049 (8/11/1945)
    Serge Koussevitzky. Theatre Concert Hall, Tanglewood
    CDs: ASdisc 572

BACH *Brandenburg Concertos*
    No. 1 in F, BWV 1046 (7/12/1974)
    No. 2 in F, BWV 1047 (7/14/1974) Ghitalla, Dwyer, Gomberg, Silverstein
    No. 3 in G, BWV 1048 (7/14/1974)
    No. 4 in G, BWV 1049 (7/12/1974) Silverstein, Dwyer, Pappoutsakis
    No. 5 in D, BWV 1050 (7/12/1974) Richter, Dwyer, Silverstein
    No. 6 in B♭, BWV 1051(7/14/1974)
    Karl Richter. Tanglewood
    CDs: Rare Moth 473/474-S (2)

BACH Suites for Orchestra
    No. 3 in D, BWV 1068 (1/5/1946) Symphony Hall
    No. 4 in D, BWV 1069 (7/8/1950) Theatre Concert Hall, Tanglewood
    Serge Koussevitzky
    CDs: ASdisc 572

BARBER Symphony No. 2, op. 19 (original version)
    Serge Koussevitzky (3/4/1944) Symphony Hall (World Premiere) **(26:50)**
    78s: Office of War Information OSA-68/75 (8 sides).
    CDs: ASdisc 563. Dis PCCD-20151

BARTÓK Music for Strings, Percussion, and Celesta
    Guido Cantelli (3/27/1954) Symphony Hall
    CDs: Pristine 081

BEETHOVEN *Ah! Perfido,* **op. 65 (12:29)**
Erich Leinsdorf. Marilyn Horne, mezzo (9/27 or 28/1968) Symphony Hall
LPs: Voce 115. **CDs:** Voce 115CD

BEETHOVEN Piano Concerto No. 1 in C, op. 15
Charles Munch. Sviatoslv Richter, piano (11/1/1960) Symphony Hall
CDs: ASdisc 335/336 (2). Dis PCCD-20029/30 (2)

BEETHOVEN Piano Concerto No. 3 in C Minor, op. 37 (35:01)
Charles Munch. Clara Haskil, piano (11/2/1956) Symphony Hall
LPs: Rococo 2104. Recital Records RR-553. **CDs:** Madrigal MADR-203.
Music & Arts 1096 (2). West Hill Radio Archive WHRA6014 (5).
Archipel ARPC-0197.

BEETHOVEN Piano Concerto No. 4 in G, op. 58
Klaus Tennstedt. Peter Serkin, piano (7/29/1977) Tanglewood **(33:55)**
CDs: A Deranged Bat Collection ADB-003 (2).
Cult of Classical Music COCOM-1012 (4)

BEETHOVEN Piano Concerto No. 5 in E♭, op. 73 "Emperor"
Charles Munch. Lelia Gousseau, piano (10/18/1957) Symphony Hall
CDs: West Hill Radio Archive WHRA6015 (7)

Charles Munch. Claudio Arrau, piano (11/30/1957) Symphony Hall
CDs: West Hill Radio Archive WHRA6014 (5)

BEETHOVEN Violin Concerto in D, op. 61
Charles Munch. Zino Francescatti, violin (4/23/1954) Symphony Hall
CDs: West Hill Radio Archive WHRA6014 (5)

Charles Munch. Jascha Heifetz, violin (11/25/1955) Symphony Hall
CDs: West Hill Radio Archive WHRA6014 (5)

Pierre Monteux. Berl Senofsky, violin (8/9/1958) Tanglewood **(33:55)**
CDs: Cembal d'amour CD-126

BEETHOVEN *Consecration of the House Overture,* **op. 124**
Charles Munch (9/30/1955) Symphony Hall
CDs: West Hill Radio Archive WHRA6014 (5)

BEETHOVEN *The Creatures of Prometheus,* **op. 43: Overture**
Bruno Walter (1/21/1947) Symphony Hall
CDs: Wing Disc WCD-58

Charles Munch (11/1/1960) Symphony Hall
CDs: ASdisc 335/336 (2). Dis PCCD-20029/30 (2)

Klaus Tennstedt (7/29/1977) Tanglewood **(5:14)**
CDs: Memories ME-1020/24 (5).
A Deranged Bat Collection ADB-003 (2).
Cult of Classical Music COCOM-1012 (4)

BEETHOVEN *Egmont*, op. 84: Overture
Serge Koussevitzky (4/20/1948) Symphony Hall **(8:00)**
CDs: ASdisc 564

BEETHOVEN *Leonore Overture No. 2*, op. 72a
Charles Munch (1/21/1956) Symphony Hall
CDs: West Hill Radio Archive WHRA6014 (5)

BEETHOVEN *Leonore Overture No. 3*, op. 72a
Serge Koussevitzky (3/16/1946) Hunter College broadcast **(13:00)**
CDs: ASdisc 564

BEETHOVEN Missa Solemnis in D, op. 123
Leonard Bernstein. Phyllis Curtin, Maureen Forrester, William Cochran,
Sherrill Milnes; TFC (7/25/1971) Tanglewood
CDs: Don Industriale DI-03 006B (2)

BEETHOVEN String Quartet No. 16 in F, op. 135: Lento assai
Charles Munch (10/26/1956) Symphony Hall
CDs: West Hill Radio Archive WHRA6014 (5)

BEETHOVEN Symphony No. 2 in D, op. 36
Charles Munch (10/17/1953) Symphony Hall
CDs: West Hill Radio Archive WHRA6015 (7)

Klaus Tennstedt (7/31/1977) Tanglewood **(32:20)**
CDs: Memories ME-1020/24 (5). "O""O""O" Classics TH-013

BEETHOVEN Symphony No. 3 in E♭, op. 55 "Eroica"
Serge Koussevitzky (10/6/1945) Symphony Hall **(47:23)**
CDs: ASdisc 561

Charles Munch (10/30/1953) Symphony Hall
CDs: West Hill Radio Archive WHRA6015 (7)

Charles Munch (9/8/1956) Moscow
CDs: Scora Classics scoracd 007

Charles Munch (11/30/1957) Symphony Hall
CDs: West Hill Radio Archive WHRA6014 (5)

William Steinberg (8/14/1970 or 7/24/1971) Tanglewood
CDs: Disco Archiva 1111

BEETHOVEN Symphony No. 3 in E♭, op. 55 "Eroica" (continued)
Klaus Tennstedt (7/30/1977) Tanglewood **(48:05)**
CDs: Rare Moth 486-S

Leonard Bernstein (8/13/1983) Tanglewood
CDs: Fachmann für Klassischer Musik Society FKM CDR-23

BEETHOVEN Symphony No. 4 in B♭, op. 60
Pierre Monteux (12/20/1963) Symphony Hall
LPs: Stradivarius STR 10001

BEETHOVEN Symphony No. 6 in F, op. 68 "Pastoral"
Charles Munch (12/8/1956) Symphony Hall
CDs: West Hill Radio Archive WHRA6014 (5)

Leonard Bernstein (12/8/1972) Symphony Hall
CDs: Don Industriale DI-03 004A

Klaus Tennstedt (7/25/1975) Tanglewood **(41:18)**
CDs: Memories ME-1020/24 (5).
A Deranged Bat Collection ADB-005.
Cult of Classical Music COCOM-1012 (4)

BEETHOVEN Symphony No. 7 in A, op. 92
Serge Koussevitzky (1/8/1944 or 3/17/1945) Hunter College broadcast
(36:45)
CDs: ASdisc 564

Leonard Bernstein (1/28/1947 Providence) **(33:05)**
CDs: Living Stage LS-1081 (2)

Charles Munch (10/15/1954) Symphony Hall
CDs: West Hill Radio Archive WHRA6014 (5)

Charles Munch (10/8/1960) Cambridge (Broadcast 4/9/1961)
CDs: "O""O""O" Classics TH-051

Leopold Stokowski (1/13/1968) Symphony Hall
CDs: Memories HR 4495/77 (3)

Klaus Tennstedt (7/29/1977) Tanglewood **(38:23)**
CDs: Memories ME-1020/24 (5). "O""O""O" Classics TH-013.
A Deranged Bat Collection ADB-003 (2).
Cult of Classical Music COCOM-1012 (4)

BEETHOVEN Symphony No. 8 in F, op. 93
Klaus Tennstedt (7/25/1975) Tanglewood **(26:13)**
CDs: Memories ME-1020/24 (5).
A Deranged Bat Collection ADB-005.
Cult of Classical Music COCOM-1012 (4)

BEETHOVEN Symphony No. 9 in D Minor, op. 125 "Choral"
Erich Leinsdorf. Beverly Sills, Florence Kopleff, John Alexzander,
Justino Diaz; TFC; Chorus Pro Musica (8/24/1969) Tanglewood
   CDs: Disco Archiva 661

Leonard Bernstein. Martina Arroyo, Lili Chookasian, Richard Lewis,
Thomas Paul; TFC; Chorus Pro Musica (4/11/1970) Symphony Hall
   CDs: Don Industriale DI-03 007A

Leonard Bernstein. Johanna Meier, Joanna Simon, Dean Wilder,
Ara Berberian; TFC (12/16/1972) Symphony Hall
   CDs: Don Industriale DI-03 005A

BERLIOZ *Les Nuits d'été*, op. 7 (28:00)
Henry Lewis. Marilyn Horne, mezzo (8/17/1969) Tanglewood
   LPs: Voce 115. **CDs:** Voce 115CD

BERLIOZ *Roméo et Juliette*, op. 17
Charles Munch. Florence Kopleff, John McCollum, Donald Gramm; TFC
(8/20/1961) Tanglewood
   CDs: "O""O""O" Classics TH-075 (2)

BERLIOZ *Symphonie fantastique*, op. 14
Serge Koussevitzky (10/16/1943) Symphony Hall **(52:05)**
   CDs: ASdisc 552

BERLIOZ *Les Troyens*: Royal Hunt and Storm
Erich Leinsdorf (8/24/1969) Tanglewood
   CDs: Disco Archiva 661

BLOCH *Baal Shem*
Charles Munch. Ruth Posselt, violin (3/21/1951) Rehearsal
   CDs: Eyewitness Records 3rd volume

BRAHMS Piano Concerto No. 1 in D Minor, op. 15
Serge Koussevitzky. Myra Hess, piano (3/4/1949) Symphony Hall
   CDs: ASdisc 567. *Bootleg recording made in the hall by a Boston
   recording studio.*

Pierre Monteux. Leon Fleisher, piano (1/29/1954) Symphony Hall
   CDs: West Hill Radio Archive WHRA6012 (2)

BRAHMS Piano Concerto No. 2 in B Flat, op. 83
Charles Munch. Claudio Arrau, piano (1/9/1953) Symphony Hall
   CDs: West Hill Radio Archive WHRA6015 (7)

Charles Munch. Sviatislav Richter, piano (11/1/1960) Symphony Hall
   CDs: ASdisc 335/36 (2). Dis PCCD-20029/30 (2)

BRAHMS Violin Concerto in D, op. 77
   Serge Koussevitzky. Efrem Zimbalist, violin (3/30/1946) Symphony Hall
      LPs: Rococo 2100. **CDs:** Eklipse EKR CD-1401. Doremi DHR 7739

   Charles Munch. Josef Szigeti, violin (12/31/1954) Symphony Hall
      CDs: Re!Discover RED-87. Madrigal MADR-201. Dis PCCD-20053

   Klaus Tennstedt. Miriam Fried, violin (12/14/1974) Symphony Hall
      CDs: Memories ME-1063/64 (2).
      A Deranged Bat Collection ABD-0001 (2).
      Cult of Classical Music COCOM-1011 (4)

BRAHMS Symphony No. 1 in C Minor, op. 68
   Serge Koussevitzky (2/17/1945) Hunter College broadcast **(41:03)**
      CDs: Music & Arts CD-1108 (2). Stradivarius STR-13614.
      Dis PCCD-20120

   Guido Cantelli (3/27/1954) Symphony Hall
      CDs: Pristine 083

   Charles Munch (11/1961)
      CDs: "O""O""O" Classics TH-067

BRAHMS Symphony No. 2 in D, op. 73
   Serge Koussevitzky (11/10/1945) Symphony Hall
      CDs: Music & Arts CD-1108 (2)

   Charles Munch (9/11/1956) Prague **(37:45)**
      CDs: Multisonic 31-0025-2. Archipel ARPCD 0202

BRAHMS Symphony No. 3 in F, op. 90
   Serge Koussevitzky (10/8/1946) Symphony Hall
      CDs: ASdisc 556. Music & Arts CD-1108 (2)

BRAHMS Symphony No. 4 in E Minor, op. 98
   Serge Koussevitzky (4/29/1944) Symphony Hall
      CDs: Music & Arts CD-1108 (2)

   Serge Koussevitzky (4/1/1947) Sanders Theater, Cambridge
      CDs: ASdisc 556

   Klaus Tennstedt (12/14/1974) Symphony Hall
      CDs: Memories ME-1063/64 (2). Rare Moth 487-S.
      A Deranged Bat Collection ADB-0001 (2).
      Cult of Classical Music COCOM-1011 (4)

BRAHMS *Variations on a Theme by Haydn*, op. 56a
   Serge Koussevitzky (4/8/1947) Symphony Hall **(20:13)**
      CDs: ASdisc 567, Dante LYS-289

Charles Munch (11/21/1953) Symphony Hall
CDs: West Hill Radio Archive WHRA6015 (7)

BUSONI *Berceuse élégiaque*
Guido Cantelli (2/6-7/1954) Symphony Hall
CDs: Pristine 086

BRUCKNER Symphony No. 4 in E♭
Klaus Tennstedt (3/11, 12, 13, or 16/1982) Symphony Hall
CDs: Rare Moth 482-S

BRUCKNER Symphony No. 8 in C Minor
Serge Koussevitzky (12/30/1947) Symphony Hall **(abridged: 50:40)**
CDs: ASdisc 560

Klaus Tennstedt (12/20/1974) Symphony Hall (1887/90 revision)
CDs: Re!Discover RED-159 (2). Navikiese NAV-4004/195 (2).
This was Tennstedt's United States debut (Leslie Gerber).

**CASELLA Concerto for Violin, Cello, Piano, and Orchestra, op. 56:
Movements 1 and 2**
Serge Koussevitzky. Alberto Poltronieri, violin; Arturo Bonucci, cello;
Alfredo Casella, piano (2/22/1936) Symphony Hall **(20:40)**
LPs: Tima Club EC-1 (2). **CDs:** ASdisc 559. *The timing is taken from
the ASdisc CD; on the LP, a long pause between movements extends
the work by about two minutes.*

COPLAND *Quiet City*
Serge Koussevitzky. George Mager, trumpet; Louis Speyer, English horn
(3/10/1945) Symphony Hall **(10:00)**
LPs: Baton 1008

CORELLI Concerto Grosso in G Minor, op. 6, no. 8 "Christmas"
Bruno Walter. Erwin Bodky, harpsichord (3/18/1947) Symphony Hall
CDs: Wing Disc WCD-57

DEBUSSY *Images pour orchestre: Ibéria*
Charles Munch (10/30/1953) Symphony Hall
CDs: West Hill Radio Archive WHRA6015 (7)

DEBUSSY *Le Martyre de St. Sébastien*: excerpts
Pierre Monteux (1/10/1958) Symphony Hall
LPs: Recital Records RR-313

DEBUSSY *La Mer*
Serge Koussevitzky (4/1/1949 or 4/2/1949) Symphony Hall
CDs: ASdisc 574

DEBUSSY *Nocturnes for Orchestra*: *Nuages*. *Fêtes*
    Serge Koussevitzky (3/11/1944) Hunter College broadcast
    CDs: ASDisc 574

DEBUSSY *Pelléas et Mélisande*: orchestral excrerpts
    Pierre Monteux (2/18/1957) Symphony Hall
    LPs: Recital Records RR-313

DEBUSSY *Prélude à l'après-midi d'un faune*
    Bernard Haitink (9/2/2001) Lucerne
    CDs: En Larmes EL-01 134

DEBUSSY *Printemps*
    Charles Munch (1/12/1962) Symphony Hall **(18:39)**
    CDs: Music & Arts CD-277

DELIUS *A Village Romeo and Juliet: The Walk to the Paradise Garden*
    John Barbirolli (10/31/1964) Symphony Hall **(9:44)**
    CDs: Music & Arts CD-251 (2)

DIAMOND Symphony No. 6
    Charles Munch (3/9/1957) Symphony Hall
    CDs: Eyewitness Records (no number)

DUKAS *The Sorcerer's Apprentice* **(10:10)**
    Charles Munch (9/9/1956) Moscow
    LPs: Melodiya M10-45697/98

DVOŘÁK Symphony No. 8 in G, op. 88
    Bernard Haitink (9/3/2001) Lucerne
    CDs: En Larmes ELS-01 135

DVOŘÁK Symphony No. 9 in E Minor, op. 95 "from the New World"
    Klaus Tennstedt (1/17/1987) Symphony Hall
    CDs: Rare Moth 484 S

ELGAR Symphony No. 2 in E♭, op. 63
    John Barbirolli (11/7/1964) Symphony Hall **(58:24)**
    CDs: Music & Arts CD-251 (2). Joy Classics JOYCD-9029/30 (2)

FAURÉ Ballade for Piano and Orchestra, op. 19 (14:39)
    Charles Munch. Nicole Henriot-Schweitzer, piano (4/2/1960)
        Symphony Hall
    LPs: Music & Arts CD-236 (2)

FAURÉ *Pelléas et Mélisande*, **op. 80: Suite (18:30)**
Charles Munch (3/7/1959) Symphony Hall
LPs: Discocorp 220. **CDs:** Music & Arts CD-236 (2)

FAURÉ Requiem, op. 48
Charles Munch. Adele Addison, Eleanor Davis, Richard Gilkey, Donald
Gramm, Harvard Glee Club and Radcliffe Choral Society (3/13/1956)
Symphony Hall
CDs: "O""O""O" Classics TH-050

FRANCK *Psyché*: **Suite**
Pierre Monteux (1/29/1954) Symphony Hall
CDs: West Hill Radio Archive WHRA6012 (2)

FRANCK Symphonic Variations (15:36)
Charles Munch. Vlado Perlemuter, piano (11/7/1961) Symphony Hall
LPs: Discocorp 221. **CDs:** Music & Arts CD-236 (2)

FRANCK Symphony in D Minor (35:15)
Charles Munch (8/5/1961) Tanglewood
CDs: Music & Arts CD-236 (2)

FRESCOBALDI (arr. GHEDINI) Four Pieces
Guido Cantelli (2/6-7/1954) Symphony Hall
CDs: Pristine 086

GLINKA *Russlan and Ludmilla:* **Overture**
Serge Koussevitzky (4/1/1944) Hunter College broadcast
LPs: Rococo 2160

HARRIS Symphony No. 6 "Gettysburg"
Serge Koussevitzky (4/15/1944) Symphony Hall   **(28:00)**
CDs: ASdisc 563. Dis PCCD-20151

HAYDN Symphony No. 85 in B♭ "La Reine"
Klaus Tennstedt (7/31/1976) Tanglewood
CDs: Cult of Classical Music COCOM-1012 (4).
A Deranged Bat Collection ADB-007

HAYDN Symphony No. 92 in G "Oxford"
John Barbirolli (11/7/1964) Symphony Hall
CDs: Joy Classics JOYCD-9029/30 (2)

HAYDN Symphony No. 94 in G "Surprise"
Pierre Monteux (9/9/1956) Moscow **(20:30)**
LPs: Melodiya M10-45699/700

HAYDN Symphony No. 100 in G "Military"
  Klaus Tennstedt (1/8/1977) Symphony Hall
    CDs: Cult of Classical Music COCOM-1011 (4).
    A Deranged Bat Collection ADB-0006 (2)

HAYDN Symphony No. 101 in D "The Clock"
  Ferenc Fricsay (11/13-17/1953) Symphony Hall
    LPs: Movimento Musica 01.048. *This LP also includes Symphony No.
    100, but Fricsay never led that work with the BSO.*

HAYDN Symphony No. 102 in B♭
  Charles Munch (9/9/1956) Moscow **(22:30)**
    LPs: Melodiya M10-45699/700

HAYDN Symphony No. 104 in D "London"
  Charles Munch (4/16/1955) Symphony Hall
    CDs: Eyewitness Records (no number)

HONEGGER *La Danse des morts*
  Charles Munch. Arnold Moss, Mariquita Moll, Betty Allen, Gerard Souzay;
    New England Conservatory Chorus (12/19/1952) Symphony Hall
    CDs: West Hill Radio Archive WHRA6015 (7)

HONEGGER Symphony No. 3 "Liturgique"
  Charles Munch (9/11/1956) Prague **(26:59)**
    CDs: Multisonic 31-0025-2. Living Stage LS-1042 (2)

IBERT Flute Concerto
  Charles Munch. Doriot Anthony Dwyer, flute (1/9/1954) Symphony Hall
    CDs: West Hill Radio Archive WHRA6015 (7)

KHRENNIKOV Symphony No. 1, op. 4
  Charles Munch (11/14/1959) Symphony Hall **(20:24)**
    LPs: Melodiya D-06095/96

LALO *Symphonie espagnole*, op. 21 (movement III omitted)
  Charles Munch. Ruth Posselt, violin (12/11/1953) Symphony Hall
    CDs: West Hill Radio Archive WHRA6015 (7)

MAHLER Symphony No. 1 in D "Titan"
  Klaus Tennstedt (7/31/1976) Tanglewood
    CDs: Cult of Classical Music COCOM-1012 (4).
    A Deranged Bat Collection ADB-007

MAHLER Symphony No. 4 in G
Bruno Walter. Desi Halban, soprano (3/25/1947) Providence
CDs: Seven Seas KICC-K30Y 305. Dante Lys 315

Klaus Tennstedt. Phyllis Bryn-Julson, soprano (1/15/1977) Symphony Hall
(57:20)
CDs: Memories ME-1031/36 (6).
A Deranged Bat Collection ADB-0002 (2)

MAHLER Symphony No. 9 in D
Leonard Bernstein (7/29/1979) Tanglewood **(85:11)**
CDs: Memories ME-1049/1950 (2). Sardana SACD-160/01 (2).
First Classics FC-109/110 (2)

MAHLER Symphony No. 10: Adagio
Charles Munch (12/5/1959) Symphony Hall
CDs: "O""O""O" Classics TH-051. *Munch also performed the Alle-gretto movement on this occasion. We don't know if it is on the CD.*

MALIPIERO Symphony No. 4 "In memoriam" (dedicated to the memory of Mme. Natalie Koussevitzky).
Serge Koussevitzky (3/2/1948) Providence **(25:00)**
LPs: Rococo 2156. **CDs:** Asdisc 559

MARTINŮ Concerto for Two Pianos and Orchestra
Charles Munch. Janine Reding and Henry Piette, pianos (11/25, 26/1960) Symphony Hall
CDs: Doremi 7816-8

MARTINŮ Violin Concerto
Serge Koussevitzky. Mischa Elman, violin (1/1/1944) Symphony Hall
CDs: Eklipse EKR CD-1404

MARTINŮ Symphony No. 6 "Fantaisies Symphoniques"
Bernard Haitink (9/3/2001) Lucerne
CDs: En Larmes ELS-01 135

MENDELSSOHN Piano Concerto No. 1 in G Minor, op. 25 (19:00)
Serge Koussevitzky. Lukas Foss, piano (11/4/1947) Symphony Hall
CDs: ASdisc 553

MENDELSSOHN Violin Concerto in E Minor, op. 64 (25:55)
Charles Munch. Mischa Elman, violin (1/27-28/1956) Symphony Hall
CDs: Wing WCD-22

MENDELSSOHN *A Midsummer Night's Dream*, op. 61: Scherzo
Serge Koussevitzky (11/4/1947) Symphony Hall **(4:35)**
CDs: ASdisc 553

MENDELSSOHN Symphony No. 4 in A, op. 90 "Italian"
Serge Koussevitzky (11/4/1947) Symphony Hall **(24:35)**
CDs: ASdisc 553

Charles Munch (11/1/1952) Symphony Hall
CDs: West Hill Radio Archive WHRA6015 (7)

MENDELSSOHN Symphony No. 5 in D, op. 107 "Reformation"
Charles Munch (4/20/1962) Symphony Hall
CDs: CinCin CCCD-1014

MOZART Piano Concerto No. 5 in D, K. 175
Adrian Boult. Malcolm Frager, piano (7/10/1966) Tanglewood
CDs: Inta'glio INCD-7211

MOZART Piano Concerto No. 20 in D Minor, K. 466 (29:19)
Charles Munch. Clara Haskil, piano (11/6/1956) Symphony Hall
LPs: Rococo 2086. **CDs:** Music & Arts CD-715. Music & Arts 1096

MOZART Violin Concerto No. 3 in G, K. 216
Charles Munch. Isaac Stern, violin (4/16/1955) Symphony Hall
CDs: Eyewitness Records (no number)

MOZART Violin Concerto No. 4 in D, K. 218
Serge Koussevitzky. Jascha Heifetz, violin (4/1/1949) Symphony Hall
CDs: Cembal d'amour CD-120

MOZART Symphony No. 29 in A, K. 201
Serge Koussevitzky (3/4/1944) Symphony Hall
CDs: ASdisc 554

Leonard Bernstein (8/15/1987) Tanglewood
CDs: Rare Moth 480/481 (2)

MOZART Symphony No. 34 in C, K. 338
Adrian Boult (7/10/1966) Tanglewood
CDs: Inta'glio INCD-7211

MOZART Symphony No. 35 in D, K. 385 "Haffner"
Bruno Walter (3/18/1947) Symphony Hall
CDs: Wing Disc WCD-58

Charles Munch (10/10/1958) Symphony Hall
CDs: "O""O""O" Classics TH-049

Klaus Tennstedt (1/15/1977) Symphony Hall **(20:54)**
   CDs: A Deranged Bat Collection ADB-0002 (2)

MOZART Symphony No. 36 in C, K. 425 "Linz"
   Serge Koussevitzky (7/17/1949) Theatre Concert Hall, Tanglewood
   (23:17)
   CDs: ASdisc 554. LYS 133

MOZART Symphony No. 39 in E Flat, K. 543
   Serge Koussevitzky (12/18/1943) Symphony Hall **(27:05)**
   CDs: ASdisc 554. LYS 133

   Charles Munch (4/9/1955) Symphony Hall
   CDs: Eyewitness Records (no number)

   Adrian Boult (7/10/1966) Tanglewood
   CDs: Inta'glio INCD-7211

MOZART Symphony No. 40 in G Minor, K. 550
   Charles Munch (7/11/1959) Tanglewood
   CDs: "O""O""O" Classics TH-049

MOZART Symphony No. 41 in C, K. 551 "Jupiter"
   Charles Munch (12/26/1952) Symphony Hall
   CDs: West Hill Radio Archive WHRA605 (7)

MUSSORGSKY *Boris Godunov:* Symphonic Synthesis (arr. Stokowski)
   Leopold Stokowski (1/13/1968) Symphony Hall
   CDs: Memories HR 4495/77 (3)

MUSSORGSKY *Khovanshchina*: Prelude (orch. Rimsky-Korsakov)
   Serge Koussevitzky (4/6/1946) Symphony Hall **(6:18)**
   CDs: Guild 2324

MUSSORGSKY *A Night on Bald Mountain* (orch. Rimsky-Korsakov)
   Serge Koussevitzky (12/30/1944) Symphony Hall **(10:59)**
   CDs: ASdisc 550. Dante LYS-113. Centurion Classics 2104. Guild 2324

MUSSORGSKY/RAVEL *Pictures at an Exhibition*
   Serge Koussevitzky (10/9/1943) Symphony Hall **(29:51)**
   CDs: Naxos 8.110105

   Guido Cantelli (2/6-7/1954) Symphony Hall
   CDs: Pristine 086

PROKOFIEV *Le Chout*, **op. 21bis: Danse**
Serge Koussevitzky (10/28/1947) Cambridge **(2:28)**
    CDs: ASdisc 570. Dante LYS-290

PROKOFIEV Violin Concerto No. 2 in G Minor, op. 63
Serge Koussevitzky. Jascha Heifetz, violin (4/1/1949) Symphony Hall
    CDs: ASdisc 568. Cembal d'amour CD-115. *Bootleg recording made*
    in the hall by a Boston recording studio.

PROKOFIEV *Scythian Suite*, **op. 20**
Serge Koussevitzky (3/9/1948) Sanders Theater, Cambridge **(22:10)**
    LPs: Discocorp SID-711 (some copies labeled IGI-711).
    CDs: ASdisc 570. Dante LYS-290

PROKOFIEV Symphony No. 1, op. 25 "Classical"
Serge Koussevitzky (11/11/1947) Woolsey Hall, New Haven **(11:30)**
    CDs: ASdisc 570. Dante LYS-290

PROKOFIEV Symphony No. 5 in B♭, op. 100
Serge Koussevitzky (11/17/1945) **(40:53)** Hunter College broadcast
    CDs: ASdisc 570. Dante LYS-290

PURCELL Suite No. 2 (arr. Barbirolli)
John Barbirolli (11/7/1964) Symphony Hall **(16:02)**
    CDs: Music & Arts CD-251 (2)

RACHMANINOFF Piano Concerto No. 3 in D Minor, op. 30
Seiji Ozawa. Alexis Weissenberg, piano (2/25/1978) Symphony Hall
    LPs: Historical Events HER-1001

RACHMANINOFF *The Isle of the Dead*, **op. 29**
Serge Koussevitzky (3/31/1945) Symphony Hall **(17:30)**
    LPs: Discocorp SID-711 (some copies labeled IGI-711).
    CDs: ASdisc 569. Dante LYS-387

RACHMANINOFF Symphony No. 2 in E Minor, op. 27
Serge Koussevitzky (4/1/1944) Hunter College broadcast
    LPs: Rococo 2160

RACHMANINOFF Symphony No. 3 in A Minor, op. 44 (32:50)
Serge Koussevitzky (4/8/1947) Hartford
    LPs: Recital Records. **CDs:** ASdisc 569. Dante LYS-387.
    Membran/Artone 222334 (4)

RACHMANINOFF Vocalise in E Minor, op. 34, no. 14
Serge Koussevitzky (3/31/1945) Symphony Hall **(8:08)**
CDs: ASdisc 569. Dante LYS-387

RAVEL *Daphnis et Chloé*
Charles Munch (7/28/1961) Tanglewood **(52:45)**
CDs: Music & Arts CD-278

RAVEL *Daphnis et Chloé*: **Suite No. 2**
Serge Koussevitzky (3/9/1948) Cambridge **(14:15)**
LPs: Discocorp SID-711 (some copies labeled IGI-711)

Charles Munch (9/8/1956) Moscow **(16:46)**
LPs: Melodiya M10-45697/98. **CDs:** Scora Classics scoracd007

RAVEL *Don Quichotte à Dulcinée*
Charles Munch. Gérard Souzay (12/19/1952 or 12/20/1952 in Symphony
Hall, 1/16/1953 in Brooklyn Academy of Music, or 1/17/1953 in Carnegie
Hall) **(6:42)**
CDs: Ponto PO-1046 (2)

RAVEL *Pavane pour une infante défunte*
Serge Koussevitzky (10/22/1946) Cambridge or (12/3/1946) Pittsburgh
CDs: ASdisc 574

RAVEL *Rapsodie espagnole*
Serge Koussevitzky (4/21/1945) Symphony Hall
CDs: ASdisc 574

RAVEL *Le Tombeau de Couperin*
Charles Munch (10/7/1953) Symphony Hall
CDs: West Hill Radio Archive WHRA6015 (7)

RESPIGHI *The Fountains of Rome*
Guido Cantelli (12/25/1954) Symphony Hall
CDs: ASdisc 507

RESPIGHI *The Pines of Rome*
Guido Cantelli (12/24 or 25/1954) Symphony Hall
CDs: ASdisc 507

RIMSKY-KORSAKOV *Russian Easter Overture*, **op. 36**
Serge Koussevitzky (3/31/1945) Symphony Hall **(14:48)**
CDs: Music & Arts CD-981

ROSSINI *Semiramide*: **Overture**
    Guido Cantelli (1/31/1953) Symphony Hall
        CDs: ASdisc 516. Memories HR-4428/29 (2)

SAINT-SAËNS Symphony No. 3 in C Minor, op. 78 "Organ"
    Charles Munch. E. Power Biggs, organ (1/1/1954) Symphony Hall
        CDs: West Hill Radio Archive WHRA6015 (7)

    Charles Munch. Berj Zamcochian, organ (3/11/1966) Symphony Hall
        CDs: CinCin CCCD-1014

SCHUBERT Mass No. 2 in G
    Charles Munch (3/17/1951) Rehearsal
        CDs: Eyewitness Records 3rd volume

SCHUBERT Symphony No. 5 in B♭
    Charles Munch (10/11/1952) Symphony Hall
        CDs: West Hill Radio Archive WHRA6015 (7)

SCHUBERT Symphony No. 8 in B Minor "Unfinished"
    Charles Munch (12/13/1952) Symphony Hall
        CDs: West Hill Radio Archive WHRA6015 (7)

SCHUBERT Symphony No. 9 in C "Great C Major"
    Leonard Bernstein (2/4/1947) Cambridge **(45:39)**
        CDs: Living Stage LS-1081 (2). *The monaural sound seems too fine to
        be a 1947 broadcast, even though the pitch drifts. The young Bernstein
        rushed most performances, which is not the case here. The Library of
        Congress lists the Voice of America recording of this broadcast per-
        formance as 46 minutes, however, so this is probably that performance.*

    Pierre Monteux (9/9/1956) Moscow **(46:48)**
        LPs: Melodiya M10-45701/02

    Klaus Tennstedt (1/8/1977) Symphony Hall **(47:09)**
        CDs: Cult of Classical Music COCOM-1011 (4).
    A Deranged Bat Collection ADB-0006 (2)

SCHUMANN *Scenes from Goethe's "Faust"*
    Erich Leinsdorf. Beverly Sills, Hermann Prey, Thomas Paul,
    Charles Bressler, Veronica Tyler, Tatilana Troyanos, Florence Kopleff,
    Batyah Godfrey; Harvard Glee Club and Radcliffe Choral Society, New
    England Conservatory Chorus, St. Gabriel's Boychoir
    (2/25/1966 or 2/26/1966) Symphony Hall **(108:16)**
        LPs: Penzance PR-7 (2). Historical Recording Enterprises HRE-261S

SCHUMANN Symphony No. 2 in C, op. 61
Leonard Bernstein (3/23/1946) Symphony Hall **(36:44)**
LPs: Melodram 206 33/30

Charles Munch (11/12/1955) Symphony Hall
CDs: West Hill Radio Archive WHRA6015 (7)

III: Adagio. Charles Munch (9/8/1956 or 9/9/1956) Moscow
(played as an encore at both concerts)
CDs: Scora Classics scoracd 007

SCHUMANN Symphony no. 4 in D Minor, op. 120
Guido Cantelli (2/6-7/1954) Symphony Hall
CDs: Pristine 086

SCRIABIN Symphony No. 4, op. 54 "Poem of Ecstasy"
Serge Koussevitzky (10/15/1946) Providence **(20:30)**
LPs: Discocorp SID-711 (some copies labeled IGI-711).
Membran/Artone 222334 (4). **CDs:** Dante LYS-113

SHOSTAKOVICH Symphony No. 5 in D Minor, op. 47
Serge Koussevitzky (3/16/1948) **(40:12)** Woolsey Hall, New Haven
CDs: ASdisc 571

Leonard Bernstein (7/22/1979) Tanglewood
CDs: Fachmann für Klassischer Musik Society FKM CDR-10

SHOSTAKOVICH Symphony No. 9 in E♭, op. 70
Serge Koussevitzky (8/10/1946) Tanglewood **(32:05)**
78s: V-Discs 716-718. **CDs:** Music & Arts CD-981. ASdisc 571. *See note about the RCA Victor recording, November 4, 1946.*

SIBELIUS *Finlandia*, **op. 26, no. 7**
Serge Koussevitzky (12/8/1945) Milwaukee **(7:03)**
CDs: ASdisc 562

SIBELIUS *The Swan of Tuonela*, **op. 22 no. 2**
Serge Koussevitzky. Louis Speyer, English horn (10/13/1945)
Symphony Hall **(8:30)**
LPs: Rococo 2103 (2). **CDs:** ASdisc 558

SIBELIUS Symphony No. 1 in E Minor, op. 39
Serge Koussevitzky (10/13/1945) Symphony Hall **(38:10)**
LPs: Rococo 2103 (2). **CDs:** ASdisc 558

SIBELIUS Symphony No. 2 in D, op. 43
John Barbirolli (10/30/1964 or 10/31/1964) Symphony Hall
CDs: Joy Classics JOYCD-9029/30 (2)

SIBELIUS Symphony No. 5 in E♭, op. 82
Serge Koussevitzky (12/25/1943 or 1/5/1946 in Symphony Hall, or
10/28/47 in Cambridge) **(30:55)**
LPs: Rococo 2103 (2). **CDs:** ASdisc 562

Leonard Bernstein (8/15/1987) Tanglewood
CDs: Rare Moth 480/481 (2)

SIBELIUS Symphony No. 6 in D Minor, op. 104
Serge Koussevitzky (3/9/1946) Symphony Hall **(24:00)**
LPs: Rococo 2103 (2). **CDs:** ASdisc 562

Thomas Beecham (1/27/1952) Symphony Hall
LPs: Sirius 5023 (3)

SIBELIUS Symphony No. 7 in C, op. 105
Serge Koussevitzky (4/20/1946) Symphony Hall **(19:48)**
LPs: Rococo RR-2103 (2)

R. STRAUSS *Also sprach Zarathustra*
Serge Koussevitzky (4/15/1947) Symphony Hall
CDs: ASdisc 573. TIOM 220980 (10)

R. STRAUSS *Don Juan*, op. 20
Serge Koussevitzky (4/6/1946) Symphony Hall
CDs: ASdisc 573. Guild GHCD-2321

Bruno Walter (1/21/1947) Symphony Hall
CDs: Wing Disc WCD-58

Charles Munch (9/9/1956) Moscow **(17:54)**
LPs: Melodiya M10-45697/98

Pierre Monteux (7/24/1959) Tanglewood **(16:03)**
CDs: Music & Arts CD-269

R. STRAUSS *Don Quixote*, op. 35
Klaus Tennstedt. Jules, Eskin, cello; Burton Fine, viola (3/6/1982)
Symphony Hall
CDs: Rare Moth 485-S

R. STRAUSS *Ein Heldenleben*, op. 40
Pierre Monteux (7/29/1962) Tanglewood **(41:51)**
CDs: Music & Arts CD-269

R. STRAUSS *Der Rosenkavalier*: **Suite**
Pierre Monteux (4/11/1953) Symphony Hall
  CDs: West Hill Radio Archive WHRA6012 (2)

R. STRAUSS *Salome: Dance of the Seven Veils*
Fritz Reiner (12/22/1945) Symphony Hall
  78s: Vdisc 636. **CDs:** Naxos 8.110114/15 (2). Dante Lys

R. STRAUSS *Till Eulenspiegel*, **op. 28**
Serge Koussevitzky (10/8/1946) Symphony Hall
  CDs: ASdisc 573

Pierre Monteux (4/9/1960) Symphony Hall **(14:04)**
  CDs: Music & Arts CD-269

STRAVINSKY *The Firebird Suite* **(1911)**
Pierre Monteux (4/11/1953) Symphony Hall
  CDs: West Hill Radio Archive WHRA6012 (2)

STRAVINSKY *Ode, elegiacal chant in three parts* (World premiere)
Serge Koussevitzky (10/9/1943) Symphony Hall
  CDs: Guild GHCD-2321

STRAVINSKY *Pétrouchka* (1911)
Pierre Monteux (4/13/1957) Symphony Hall
  LPs: Recital Records RR-312

Pierre Monteux (1/3/1958) Symphony Hall **(34:04)**
  CDs: Music & Arts CD-312

STRAVINSKY *Pulcinella*: **Suite**
Pierre Monteux (1/19/1957) Symphony Hall
  CDs: West Hill Radio Archive WHRA6012 (2)

STRAVINSKY *Le Sacre du printemps*
Pierre Monteux (4/13/1957) Symphony Hall **(32:42)**
  CDs: Music & Arts CD-312

STRAVINSKY *Symphony of Psalms*
Bernard Haitink (9/2/2001) Lucerne
  CDs: En Larmes EL-01 134

TCHAIKOVSKY Piano Concerto No. 1 in B♭ Minor, op. 23
Seiji Ozawa. Evgeni Kissin, piano (10/5/1995) Carnegie Hall
  VHS: Parnassus Custom Video PCV-32. **DVD:** PDVD-32

TCHAIKOVSKY Violin Concerto in D, op. 35
Paul Paray. Mischa Elman, violin (12/1/1945) Symphony Hall
LPs: Discocorp 453. **CDs:** Music & Arts CD-868

I: Allegro moderato (rehearsal)
Charles Munch. Michèle Auclair, violin (1/9/1951) Symphony Hall **(15:11)**
CDs: Tahra 528/19529 (2)

TCHAIKOVSKY *Francesca da Rimini*, op. 32
Serge Koussevitzky (4/6/1946) Symphony Hall **(24:49)**
CDs: ASdisc 565. Guild 2324

TCHAIKOVSKY *Overture 1812* in E♭, op. 49
Serge Koussevitzky (8/10/1946) Tanglewood
CDs: Music & Arts CD-981

TCHAIKOVSKY *Romeo and Juliet* (fantasy-overture)
Serge Koussevitzky (1950) Symphony Hall
CDs: ASdisc 551

TCHAIKOVSKY Symphony No. 4 in F Minor, op. 36
Serge Koussevitzky (10/22/1946) Cambridge
LPs: Discocorp SID-730 (2)

Serge Koussevitzky (3/11/1949) Symphony Hall **(39:46)**
CDs: ASdisc 566. Music & Arts CD-1138 (2). *Bootleg recording made*
in the hall by a Boston recording studio. The ASdisc CD includes
24 minutes of a rehearsal on 3/7/1949.

TCHAIKOVSKY Symphony No. 5 in E Minor, op. 64
Serge Koussevitzky (11/6/1943) Symphony Hall **(47:48)**
CDs: Music & Arts CD-1138 (2)

Serge Koussevitzky (12/10/1946) Detroit **(48:00)**
CDs: ASdisc 565

Guido Cantlli (1/31/1954) Symphony Hall
CDs: Pristine 085

Leonard Bernstein (7/21/1974) Tanglewood
CDs: Fachmann für Klassischer Musik Society FKM CDR-11

TCHAIKOVSKY Symphony No. 6 in B Minor, op. 74 "Pathetique"
Serge Koussevitzky (2/9/1946) Symphony Hall **(44:28)**
LPs: Discocorp SID-730 (2)
CDs: ASdisc 551. Music & Arts CD-1138 (2)

Leonard Bernstein (7/26/1986) Tanglewood
CDs: Rare Moth 480/481 (2)

Seiji Ozawa (10/5/1995) Carnegie Hall
VHS: Parnassus Custom Video PCV-32

Randall THOMPSON *The Last Words of David* (it is called *The Psalm of David* in the film).
Serge Koussevitzky (1949) Symphony Hall **(6:35)**
Film: "Tanglewood—Music School and Music Festival"

TOCH *Pinocchio, a Merry Overture*
Serge Koussevitzky (11/11/1944) Tanglewood
CDs: ASdisc 563. Dis PCCD-20151

VAUGHAN WILLIAMS Symphony No. 5 in D
Serge Koussevitzky (3/4/1947) Cambridge **(36:05)**
CDs: Guild 2324

VAUGHAN WILLIAMS Symphony No. 6 in E Minor
John Barbirolli (10/31/1964) Symphony Hall **(31:44)**
CDs: Music & Arts CD-251 (2)

VERDI Requiem Mass
Guido Cantelli. Herva Nelli, Claramae Turner, Eugene Conley,
Nicola Moscona; New England Conservatory Chorus (12/16–21/1954)
Symphony Hall
LPs: Cetra LO-503 (2). Discocorp 340 (2)

WAGNER *A Faust Overture*
Charles Munch (2/6/1954) Symphony Hall
CDs: West Hill Radio Archive WHRA6015 (7)

WAGNER *Götterdämmerung*: **Siegfried's Funeral March**
Serge Koussevitzky (3/2/1946) Symphony Hall
CDs: ASdisc 557

WAGNER *Götterdämmerung*: **Immolation Scene (19:14)**
Erich Leinsdorf. Marilyn Horne, mezzo (9/27 or 28/1968) Symphony Hall
LPs: Voce 115. **CDs:** Voce 115CD

WAGNER *Lohengrin*: **Act 1 Prelude**
Serge Koussevitzky (3/2/1946) Symphony Hall
CDs: ASdisc 557

WAGNER *Die Meistersinger von Nürnberg*: **Act I Prelude**
Serge Koussevitzky (3/2/1946) Symphony Hall
CDs: ASdisc 557

WAGNER *Die Meistersinger von Nürnberg*: **Act III excerpts**
Charles Munch (1/24/1953) Symphony Hall
CDs: West Hill Radio Archive WHRA605 (7)

WAGNER *Siegfried*: **Forest Murmurs**
Serge Koussevitzky (3/2/1946) Symphony Hall
CDs: ASdisc 557

WAGNER *Siegfried Idyll*
Bruno Walter (3/18/1947) Symphony Hall
CDs: Wing Disc WCD-58

WAGNER *Tannhäuser:* **Overture**
Serge Koussevitzky (3/2/1946) Symphony Hall
CDs: ASdisc 557

WAGNER *Tristan und Isolde: Prelude and Liebestod*
Charles Munch (10/11/1952) Symphony Hall
CDs: West Hill Radio Archive WHRA6015 (7)

WEBER *Jubilee Overture*
Erich Leinsdorf (10/22/1971) Symphony Hall
CDs: Disco Archiva 662

WEBER *Oberon*: **Overture**
Serge Koussevitzky (3/4/1947) Cambridge
CDs: Guild GHCD-2321

WEBERN Passacaglia for Large Orchestra, op. 1
Klaus Tennstedt (1/8/1977) Symphony Hall
CDs: Cult of Classical Music COCOM-1011 (4).
A Deranged Bat Collection ADB-0006 (2)

Pirate Recordings Conductor Index

John Barbirolli
DELIUS *A Village Romeo and Juliet: The Walk to the Paradise Garden*
ELGAR Symphony No. 2
HAYDN Symphony No. 92 "Oxford"
PURCELL Suite No. 2 (arr. Barbirolli)
SIBELIUS Symphony No. 2
VAUGHAN WILLIAMS Symphony No. 6

Thomas Beecham
SIBELIUS Symphony no. 6

Leonard Bernstein
BEETHOVEN Missa Solemnis. Symphonies: Nos. 3, 6, 7, and 9
MAHLER Symphony No. 9
MOZART Symphony No. 29
SCHUBERT Symphony No. 9 "Great C Major"
SCHUMANN Symphony No. 2
SHOSTAKOVICH Symphony No. 5
SIBELIUS Symphony No. 5
TCHAIKOVSKY Symphonies Nos. 5 and 6

Adrian Boult
MOZART Piano Concerto No. 5. Symphonies No. 34 and 39

Guido Cantelli
BARTÓK Music for Strings, Percussion, and Celesta
BRAHMS Symphony No. 1
BUSONI *Berceuse élégiaque*
FRESCOBALDI/GHEDINI Four Pieces
MUSSORGSKY/RAVEL *Pictures at an Exhibition*
RESPIGHI *The Fountains of Rome. The Pines of Rome*
ROSSINI *Semiramide:* Overture
SCHUMANN Symphony No. 4
TCHAIKOVSKY Symphony No. 5
VERDI Requiem Mass

Ferenc Fricsay
HAYDN Symphony No. 101 "The Clock"

Bernard Haitink
DEBUSSY *Prélude à l'après-midi d'un faune*
DVOŘÁK Symphony No. 8
MARTINŮ Symphony No. 6 "Fantaisies Symphoniques"
STRAVINSKY *Symphony of Psalms*

Serge Koussevitzky
BACH *Brandenburg Concertos Nos. 3 and 4.* Suites for Orchestra Nos. 3 and 4
BARBER Symphony No. 2
BEETHOVEN *Egmont:* Overture. *Leonore Overture No. 3.*
  Symphonies Nos. 3 and 7
BERLIOZ *Symphonie fantastique*
BRAHMS Piano Concerto No. 1. Violin Concerto.
  Symphonies Nos. 1, 2, 3, and 4. *Variations on a Theme by Haydn*
BRUCKNER Symphony No. 8
CASELLA Concerto for Violin, Cello, Piano, and Orchestra
COPLAND *Quiet City*
DEBUSSY *La Mer. Nocturnes for Orchestra: Nuages, Fêtes*
GLINKA *Russlan and Ludmilla:* Overture
HARRIS Symphony No. 6 "Gettysburg"
MALIPIERO Symphony No. 4 "In Memoriam"
MARTINŮ Violin Concerto
MENDELSSOHN Piano Concerto No. 1. Symphony No. 4 "Italian."
  A Midsummer Night's Dream: Scherzo
MOZART Violin Concerto No. 4. Symphonies Nos. 29, 36, and 39
MUSSORGSKY *Khovanshchina:* Prelude. *A Night on Bald Mountain.*
MUSSORGSKY/RAVEL *Pictures at an Exhibition*
PROKOFIEV *Le Chout:* Danse. Violin Concerto No. 2. *Scythian Suite.*
  Classical Symphony. Symphony No. 5
RACHMANINOFF *The Isle of the Dead.* Symphonies Nos. 2 and 3. Vocalise
RAVEL *Daphnis et Chloé:* Suite No. 2. *Pavane pour une enfant défunte.*
  Rapsodie espagnole
RIMSKY-KORSAKOV *Russian Easter Overture*
SCRIABIN Symphony No. 4 "Poem of Ecstasy"
SHOSTAKOVICH Symphonies Nos. 5 and 9
SIBELIUS *Finlandia. The Swan of Tuonela.* Symphonies Nos. 1, 5, 6, and 7
R. STRAUSS *Also sprach Zarathustra. Don Juan. Till Eulenspiegel*
STRAVINSKY *Ode*
TCHAIKOVSKY *Francesca da Rimini. Overture 1812. Romeo and Juliet.*
  Symphonies Nos. 4, 5, and 6
THOMPSON *The Last Words of David (The Song of David)*
TOCH *Pinocchio, a Merry Overture*
VAUGHAN WILLIAMS Symphony No. 5
WAGNER *Götterdämmerung:* Siegfried's Funeral March.
  Lohengrin: Act 1 Prelude. *Die Meistersinger:* Act I Prelude.
  Siegfried: Forest Murmurs. *Tannhäuser:* Overture
WEBER *Oberon:* Overture

Erich Leinsdorf
BEETHOVEN *Ah! Perfido*. Symphony No. 9
BERLIOZ *Les Troyens*: Royal Hunt and Storm
SCHUMANN *Scenes from Goethe's "Faust"*
WAGNER *Gotterdammerung*: Immolation Scene
WEBER *Jubilee Overture*

Henry Lewis
BERLIOZ *Les Nuits d'été*

Pierre Monteux
BEETHOVEN Violin Concerto. Symphony No. 4
BRAHMS Piano Concerto No. 1
DEBUSSY *Le martyre de Saint Sebastien. Pelléas et Mélisande* (excerpts)
FRANCK Psyché: Suite
HAYDN Symphony No. 94 "Surprise"
SCHUBERT Symphony No. 9
R. STRAUSS *Don Juan. Ein Heldenleben. Der Rosenkavalier. Till Eulenspiegel*
STRAVINSKY *Firebird Suite. Pétrouchka. Pulcinella. Le Sacre du printemps*

Charles Munch
AUBER *La Muette de Portici:* Overture
BEETHOVEN Piano Concertos 1, 3, 5. Violin Concerto. *Consecration of the House. Prometheus. Leonore No. 2.* Quartet No. 16. Symphonies 2, 3, 6, 7
BERLIOZ *Roméo et Juliette*
BLOCH Baal Shem
BRAHMS Concerto No. 2. Violin Concerto. Symphonies 1, 2. *Haydn Variations*
DEBUSSY *Ibéria. Printemps*
DIAMOND Symphony No. 6
DUKAS *The Sorcerer's Apprentice*
FAURÉ *Ballade. Pelléas et Mélisande.* Requiem
FRANCK Symphonic Variations. Symphony in D Minor
HAYDN Symphonies Nos. 102 and 104
HONEGGER *La Danse des morts.* Symphony No. 3 "Liturgic"
IBERT Flute Concerto
KHRENNIKOV Symphony No. 1
LALO *Symphonie espagnole*
MAHLER Symphony No. 10: Adagio
MARTINŮ Concerto for Two Pianos and Orchestra
MENDELSSOHN Violin Concerto. Symphonies Nos. 4 and 5
MOZART Concerto No. 20. Violin Concerto No. 3. Symphonies 35, 39, 40, 41
RAVEL *Daphnis et Chloé. Don Quichotte à Dulcinée. Le Tombeau de Couperin*
SAINT-SAËNS Symphony No. 3
SCHUBERT Mass No. 2. Symphonies Nos. 5 and 8
SCHUMANN Symphony No. 2
R. STRAUSS *Don Juan*
TCHAIKOVSKY Violin Concerto: I Allegro moderato
WAGNER *A Faust Overture. Die Meistersinger. Tristan und Isolde*

Seiji Ozawa
RACHMANINOFF Piano Concerto No. 3
TCHAIKOVSKY Piano Concerto No. 1. Symphony No. 6 "Pathetique"

Paul Paray
TCHAIKOVSKY Violin Concerto

Fritz Reiner
R. STRAUSS: *Salome: Dance of the Seven Veils*

Karl Richter
BACH *Brandenburg Concertos*

William Steinberg
BEETHOVEN Symphony No. 3 "Eroica"

Leopold Stokowski
BEETHOVEN Symphony No. 7
MUSSORGSKY *Boris Godunov*: Symphonic Synthesis

Klaus Tennstedt
BEETHOVEN Piano Concerto No. 4. *The Creatures of Prometheus*: Overture
BEETHOVEN Symphonies Nos. 2, 3, 6, 7, and 8
BRAHMS Violin Concerto. Symphony No. 4
BRUCKNER Symphonies No. 4 and 8
DVOŘÁK Symphony No. 9 "from the New World"
HAYDN Symphony No. 85 "La Reine." Symphony No. 100 "Military"
MAHLER Symphonies Nos. 1 and 4
MOZART Symphony No. 35 "Haffner"
SCHUBERT Symphony No. 9 "Great C Major"
R. STRAUSS *Don Quixote*
WEBERN Passacaglia

Bruno Walter
BEETHOVEN *The Creatures of Prometheus*: Overture
CORELLI Concerto Grosso in G Minor, op. 6, no. 8 "Christmas Concerto"
MAHLER Symphony No. 4
MOZART Symphony No. 35 "Haffner"
R. STRAUSS *Don Juan*
WAGNER *Siegfried Idyll*

Bibliography

Canfield, David E. *Canfield Guide to Classical Recordings*. 5th ed. Ellettsville, Ind.: Ars Antiqua, 2000.

Clough, Francis F., and G. J. Cuming. *The World's Encyclopaedia of Recorded Music* (with three supplements). Westport, Conn.: Greenwood Press, 1970.

Darrell, R. D., comp. *The Gramophone Shop Encyclopedia of Recorded Music*. New York: The Gramophone Shop, 1936.

Fagan, Ted. "Pre-LP Recordings of RCA at 33 1/3 rpm. through 1931 to 1934." Parts 1, 2. *ARSC Journal* 13, no. 1 (1981): 25-68; 15, no. 1 (1983): 20-42.

Hitchcock, H. Wiley, and Stanley Sadie, eds. *The New Grove Dictionary of American Music*. London: Macmillan & Co., 1986.

Holoman, D. Kern. *Writing about Music: A Style Sheet from the Editors of 19th-Century Music*. Berkeley and Los Angeles: University of California Press, 1988.

Leinsdorf, Erich. *Cadenza. A Musical Career*. Boston: Houghton Mifflin Company, 1976.

MacKenzie, Harry. *The Directory of the Armed Forces Radio Service Series*. Westport, Conn.: Greenwood Press, 1999.

Moore, Robin. *Fiedler: The Colorful Mr. Pops—The Man and His Music*. Boston: Little, Brown and Company, 1968.

The New York Times (1917-2008).

North, James H. *New York Philharmonic: The Authorized Recordings 1917-2005. A Discography*. Lanham, Md.: Scarecrow Press, 2006.

———. "The Boston Symphony Orchestra Preserves Its History: The BSO Archives and BSO Classics Compact Discs." *Fanfare* 18, no. 3 (January/February 1995): 34-40.

———. "Excursions with a Trombone." *Fanfare* 14, no. 5 (May/June 1991): 56-60.

Reid, Robert H., ed. *The Gramophone Shop Encyclopedia of Recorded Music*. 3rd ed. New York: Crown Publishers, 1948.

Sadie, Stanley, ed. *The New Grove Dictionary of Music and Musicians*. London: Macmillan & Co., 1980.

————. *The New Grove Dictionary of Music and Musicians*, 2nd ed. London: Macmillan & Co., 2001.

Sears, Richard S. *V-Discs: A History and Discography.* Westport, Conn.: Greenwood Press, 1980.

Smith, Moses. *Koussevitzky.* New York: Allen, Towne, and Heath, Inc., 1947.

Young, Edward D. "Serge Koussevitzky: A Complete Discography, Part I." *ARSC Journal* 21, no. 1 (1990): 45-129.

————."Serge Koussevitzky: A Complete Discography, Part II." *ARSC Journal* 21, no. 2 (1990): 241-265.

————. "Boston Symphony Orchestra Radio Broadcast and Privately Made Recordings 1935–1950." Unpublished. 1989 (in the Boston Symphony Orchestra Archives).

————. "Listings of Recordings Needed from the Library of Congress for Boston Symphony Transcription Tape-Recording Work." Unpublished. 1989 (in the Boston Symphony Orchestra Archives).

Record and CD Catalogues

Bielefelder Katalog Klassik (1963-2005).

Classical Recordaid (1954).

Gramophone Classical Catalogue (1965-1996).

RCA Victor Record Catalog (1940-1941, 1948).

Schwann Long Playing Record Catalogue; also *Schwann-1 Record & Tape Guide, Schwann-2 Record & Tape Guide, The New Schwann, Schwann Compact Disc Catalogue, Opus, Schwann Opus* (1949-2001).

Schwann Artist Issue (1965-2001).

Web Sites

www.arkivmusic.com (2003-2008).

www.classicalreference.com (2006-2007).

www.koussevitzky.com (February 6, 2008).

www.muziekweb.nl (2008)

www.towerrecords.com (1998-2006).

www.yeodoug.com (February 9, 2008).

About the Author

The son of a pianist and an engineer, **James H. North** has led a life enriched by music and mathematics. A graduate of Williams College, with a double major in physics and music, he was for thirty-five years a member of the Mathematical Sciences Department at IBM's Thomas J. Watson Research Laboratory. His work in the 1950s has been called a foundation stone of artificial intelligence, and his development of automated problem-solving algorithms enabled the physical design of computer logic chips. Since 1988 he has been a freelance journalist and music critic, writing for such publications as *Fanfare* and *Classic Record Collector*. He has written program notes for LPs and CDs on the Past Masters, Koch, Music & Arts, and Teldec labels and has published major studies on composers Donald Erb and Joanna Bruzdowicz, pianist Youri Egorov, and record producer/executive Goddard Lieberson. In the introduction to the author's monograph on the relationship between Willem Mengelberg and Gustav Mahler, English editor Tully Potter cited North as "a leading American critic." Mr. North's publications include *New York Philharmonic: The Authorized Recordings 1905-2005: A Discography*, as well as discographies in four of the New York Philharmonic's multi-CD historical sets: *The Mahler Broadcasts*, *An American Celebration*, *Bernstein Live*, and *Kurt Masur at the New York Philharmonic*.